McDonald INSTITUTE MONOGRAPHS

Towards reflexive method in archaeology:
the example at Çatalhöyük

By Members of the Çatalhöyük teams

Edited by
Ian Hodder

BRITISH INSTITUTE OF ARCHAEOLOGY AT ANKARA

BIAA Monograph No. 28

This volume is dedicated to the memory of Maria Mangafa.

Published by:

McDonald Institute for Archaeological Research
University of Cambridge
Downing Street
Cambridge
CB2 3ER
(0)(1223) 339336

Distributed by Oxbow Books, Park End Place, Oxford, OX1 1HN.
  Tel: (0)(1865) 241249; Fax: (0)(1865) 794449

ISBN: 1-902937-02-3
ISSN: 1363-1349

Edited for the Institute by Chris Scarre (*Series Editor*) and Dora A. Kemp (*Production Editor*).

Film produced by Gary Reynolds Typesetting, 13 Sturton Street, Cambridge, CB1 2QG.
Printed and bound by Short Run Press, Bittern Rd, Sowton Industrial Estate, Exeter, EX2 7LW.

Cover illustration: *Investigating different modes of representation: Mark Knight and Nessa Leibhammer engaged in recording the same bins in 'scientific' and 'artistic' modes.*

CONTENTS

Introduction

Part A   *The Integration of Methods*

Part B   *The Dispersion of 'Site' and the Problem of Representation*

Part C   *Presenting the Sites*

CONTRIBUTORS

MELTEM AĞCABAY	Department of Archaeometry, University of Çukurova
PETER ANDREWS	Natural History Museum, London
BANU AYDINOĞLU	Istanbul
AYFER BARTU	Department of Anthropology, Koç University, Istanbul
ADNAN BAYSAL	University College London
ÅSA BERGGREN	Lund, Sweden
PETER BOYER	Çatalhöyük Research Project, Cambridge
BAŞAK BOZ	British Institute of Archaeology at Ankara
JENNY BREDENBERG	Çatalhöyük Research Project, Cambridge
DOROTHÉE BRILL	Hochschule für Gestaltung, Karlsruhe
TOM CAWDRON	Department of Archaeology, University of Cambridge
CRAIG CESSFORD	Cambridge Archaeological Unit
JAMES CONOLLY	Institute of Archaeology, University College London
ANWEN COOPER	Royal Commission of Historic and Ancient Monuments
MARTIN EMELE	Hochschule für Gestaltung, Karlsruhe
BEGUMŞEN ERGENEKON	Middle East Technical University, Ankara
AYLAN ERKAL	Middle East Technical University, Ankara
SHAHINA FARID	Çatalhöyük Research Project, Cambridge
CAROLYN HAMILTON	University of Witwatersrand, Johannesburg
NAOMI HAMILTON	Department of Archaeology, University of Edinburgh
CHRISTINE HASTORF	Department of Anthropology, University of California, Berkeley
LUCY HAWKES	Department of Archaeology, Cambridge
IAN HODDER	Department of Cultural and Social Anthropology, Stanford University
MARK KNIGHT	Cambridge Archaeological Unit
MINE KÜÇÜK	Science Museum of Minnesota
JONATHAN LAST	Hertfordshire Archaeological Trust
SU LEAVER	Çatalhöyük Research Project, Cambridge
NESSA LEIBHAMMER	University of Witwatersrand, Johannesburg
LOUISE MARTIN	Institute of Archaeology, University College London
FRANK MATERO	Graduate School of Fine Arts, University of Pennsylvania
WENDY MATTHEWS	British Institute of Archaeology at Ankara
WILLIAM MIDDLETON	Laboratory for Archaeological Chemistry, University of Wisconsin-Madison
THEYA MOLLESON	Natural History Museum, London
JULIE NEAR	Department of Anthropology, University of California, Berkeley
ARLENE ROSEN	Institute of Archaeology, University College London
NERISSA RUSSELL	Department of Anthropology, Cornell University
ORRIN SHANE	Department of Anthropology & Museum Studies, University of Minnesota
DAVID SHANKLAND	Department of Anthropology, University of Wales, Lampeter
MIRJANA STEVANOVIC	Department of Anthropology, University of California, Berkeley
JOHN-GORDON SWOGGER	Çatalhöyük Research Project, Cambridge
RUTH I. TRINGHAM	Department of Anthropology, University of California, Berkeley
RICHARD TURNBULL	Çatalhöyük Research Project, Cambridge
MEHMET ALTUĞ ULUCEVIZ	Istanbul
SHARON WEBB	Department of Archaeology, University of Cambridge
ANJA-CHRISTINA WOLLE	Çatalhöyük Research Project, Cambridge
NURCAN YALMAN	Istanbul University

As well as those listed above, many other team members contributed to the development of the ideas contained in this book. This book remains above all things, a collaborative effort on the part of the whole team.

Figures

Tables

Appendix

Acknowledgements

Funding for the field research was provided by the Isaac Newton Trust, the British Academy, the British Institute of Archaeology at Ankara, the McDonald Institute, the Kress Foundation, the Dayton Foundation, Stanford University and the National Geographic Society.

The project is extremely grateful to the Ministry of Culture, General Directorate of Monuments and Museums (especially to the current Director, Kenan Yurttagül) and to the government representatives for their help and support. Generous assistance was also given by Ilhan Temiszoy, Director of the Museum of Anatolian Civilisations at Ankara, by Konya Museums (Director Erdoğan Erol) and the Çumra Belediye Başkan. An enormous amount of logistical help and advice was provided over the years by the Director, Dr Roger Matthews, and staff of the British Institute of Archaeology at Ankara, to whom we are extremely grateful.

I would like to thank especially the local men and women who work with us on the site, led by Ismail Yaşli. We are well looked after by Necati and Nazmiye Terzioğlu and their family and by Ismail Salmanci and protected by Sadettin Dural and Mustafa Tokyasin.

Special thanks are due to the Istanbul Friends of Çatalhöyük, especially Reşit Ergener. It is a great pleasure to acknowledge our continued debt to James Mellaart, his wife Arlette and their son Alan. Increasingly the project has become dependant on the energies and support of Ömer Koç. His interest in and intellectual engagement with the site will provide the basis for many future generations at Çatalhöyük. I also wish to thank Evren Artam of the Koç Foundation, and Cem Kozlu.

The project is sponsored by Koçbank, Visa International, Boeing, Merko, Glaxo-Wellcome, British Airways and Shell. The IT sponsor is Koçsistem, and the official tour company is Meptur. Other support has been provided by Lloyd Cotsen, Eczacibaşi Holding, Feyzi and Arup.

IAN HODDER

Author Biographies

Meltem Ağcabay has been working at Çatalhöyük since 1996 with the archaeobotany team. She completed her undergraduate degree in the Prehistory Department, Istanbul University in 1997 and has worked at the Zekirdağ Menekçe Çatağı excavation (1996) and on the Kastamonv Survey (1997). Currently she is studying for her Masters degree in the Archaeometry Department, Çukurova University. She will be analyzing a set of midden samples from the southern part of the Çatalhöyük site and using statistics to sort out groupings based on the botanical assemblages for her thesis.

Banu Aydinoğlu has been working at Çatalhöyük since 1996 as an excavator and for the last two years with the archaeozoology team. She has participated in the Zekirdağ Menekçe Çatağı excavation for the two study seasons (1996–97). She has worked in Greece at the Thessalloniki-Tumba excavation for one season in 1998 and is presently focusing on fauna from flotation samples by resorting them and visualizing the results with graphs.

Ayfer Bartu is an Assistant Professor of Anthropology at Koç University in Istanbul, Turkey. Her areas of interest include anthropology of tourism, urban anthropology, heritage studies and social theory. She has published several articles on the politics of historical preservation in Istanbul. In addition to the Çatalhöyük project, she has been working on a research project on emerging forms of urban segregation in contemporary Istanbul.

Adnan Baysal was born in Istanbul and studied archaeology at Istanbul University. He received his graduate degree from the Protohistory and Asia Minor Archaeology and Art History Department of the Faculty of Letters, Istanbul University. He continued studying in the same department and prepared his MA research on Southern Anatolian Neolithic Cultures and Ceramics. He has been involved in the Çatalhöyük project since 1993 and is currently studying ground stones from the sites as part of his PhD research at University College London. He lives and works in the UK in contract archaeology.

Åsa Berggren is a post-graduate student in Lund, Sweden. Her PhD subject is the spatial relationship between settlements, burials and offering sites during the Neolithic in southern Scandinavia. She is currently employed in contract archaeology in Malmö, Sweden. She participated in the Çatalhöyük project during the 1998 and 1999 seasons, as an excavator.

Peter Boyer started his involvement in archaeology as an undergraduate at the University of Wales, Lampeter, in 1983, during which time he excavated sites in Wales, Somerset, Sussex and Northumberland. Following graduation he worked extensively for Leicester University and the Leicestershire Archaeological Unit between 1987 and 1993. This work involved excavation, environmental archaeology and survey. During this period he was also involved in overseas projects in Libya, Turkmenistan, Italy and Spain and completed his Masters degree at Leicester University. During 1994 he was the environmentalist for a large project in Essex, employed by Essex County Council Field Archaeology Group.

In December 1994 he began his PhD thesis, entitled 'A Geoarchaeological Approach to Late Quaternary Environmental Change in South Central Turkey'. This examined the archaeological and sedimentary sequences of the Çarşamba alluvial fan in the Konya basin of Central Anatolia. He was awarded his PhD in 1999. He first became involved with the Çatalhöyük project in 1995 through the work of KOPAL (Konya Plain Palaeoenvironmental Project). This involved the analysis of geoarchaeological sequences from a number of archaeological mounds in the area around Çatalhöyük including a concentration of sequences from, and in the direct vicinity of the two mounds at Çatalhöyük. The fieldwork element of this work continued until 1997 and the material recovered provided the bulk of data for his thesis. In 1998 he excavated on both the East and West mounds of Çatalhöyük. In 1999 he again excavated on the East mound and also supervised an off-site excavation as a further element of the work of KOPAL. He currently holds a post-doctoral appointment based at the universities of Cambridge and Plymouth, and funded by the Çatalhöyük Research

Project and Plymouth University. This appointment involves post-excavation work for the Çatalhöyük Research Project and the analysis of sediments recovered from various aspects of work by KOPAL. This also furthers his current research interests which are concerned with the investigation of Neolithic and later prehistoric geoarchaeological and alluvial sequences on the Konya plain, and the wider implications these have for prehistoric environments, societies and early agricultural systems.

Başak Boz has been working at Çatalhöyük since 1996 with the Human Remains team. She graduated from the Palaeoanthropology Department in Ankara University in 1992 and has a Master's degree from the Physical Anthropology Department in Hacettepe at Ankara in 1997 and worked at the British Institute of Archaeology at Ankara in 1998 and 1999. She currently works as a freelance anthropologist and is preparing to do a PhD. Başak has participated in several palaeontological excavations and surveys as well as archaeological excavations in the past nine years in Turkey. She is particularly interested in researching the Çatalhöyük population's dietary habits using microwear features on teeth. She also uses information gathered from ethnoarchaeological, botanical and archaezoological work.

Jenny Bredenberg currently works for the Cambridge Archaeological Unit at the University of Cambridge. Previously she took her MA in Archaeology at Stockholm University. As well as being involved in the Çatalhöyük Project she has also been involved in archaeological projects in Ireland, Jordan, Iceland and South Africa.

Dorothée Brill has studied Contemporary Art and Media Theory at the HfG (Staatliche Hochschule für Gestaltung) and the ZKM (Centre for Art and Media) at Karlsruhe and History of Art in Tübingen and Toulouse. Her research interest is focused on the influence of new image technics on art. At Çatalhöyük she was working on the permanent video documentation and the setup of the video data base, as a part of the Çatalhöyük Archaeology & Media Project (CHAMP), a project co-operation between the University of Cambridge, HfG, ZKM and the European Institute of Cinema Karlsruhe (EIKK).

Tom Cawdron is an undergraduate in Archaeology and Anthropology at Churchill College, University of Cambridge. He excavated at Çatalhöyük during the 1998 season.

Craig Cessford studied archaeology at Newcastle University at both undergraduate and Masters levels. Since 1991 he has been a full-time contract field archaeologist working for a number of organizations in Britain. He joined the Çatalhöyük project in 1997 and supervised excavations in the North area of the site since 1998. His main interests in the site are concerned with developing practical methodological approaches to the excavation of complex stratified sites and the interpretation of intra-building spatial patterning. His other research interests include Pictish art, Old Welsh poetry and clay tobacco pipes on which he has presented conference papers and published a number of articles.

James Conolly is a lecturer at the Institute of Archaeology, University College London. He received his degrees from the University of Toronto (BA Anthropology) and the University of London (MA Archaeology, PhD Archaeology). His research interests are lithic analysis and spatial analysis (particularly GIS). He has been a member of the Çatalhöyük Project since 1993.

Anwen Cooper has recently completed an MA in Landscape Archaeology and has worked professionally as an archaeological surveyor and excavator. She first came to Çatalhöyük in 1996 as a student and has returned to dig twice since then. Her main interests in archaeology are British prehistory, landscape perspectives and community archaeology.

Martin Emele studied history and rhetorics at the University of Tübingen from 1984–90. From 1988–95 he produced video documentation and press releases for 'Projekt Troia', archaeological excavation in Troy, Turkey as well as annual video documentation for the Institute of Scientific Film Göttingen, Germany. In 1994 he created the experimental film *Laokoons Rueckkehr — Die Landschaft Troas als Mahnmal des Krieges* (18 min.) for Stunde der Filmemacher, SAT 1 (Prize for greatest innovation and originality, AGON, international meeting of archaeological film Athens, Greece 1996 prize of the jury at AKRAI Catania, Italy 1996). Since 1995 he has been a lecturer and senior researcher at the film department at the Hochschule für Gestaltung Karlsruhe (HfG). From 1996–98 he was involved in project coordination for the 'Çatalhöyük archaeology and media project' (CHAMP) in co-operation with the University of Cambridge and the Centre of Art and Media Karlsruhe (ZKM), supported by INFO2000 of the European Union. He received his PhD in 1997 on the subject 'Neue und Alte Mythen in den deutschen Medien — Heinrich Schliemann und Troia' ['New and Old Myth in German Media — Heinrich Schliemann and Troy]. At Çatalhöyük he is involved with nonlinear documentation for CD-ROM, Internet and Real-Time-Machine; Project management video, audio, content (prize of the jury 'Interaktive Projekte' 2. Forum Hochschulfilm Baden-Württemberg 1997; special prize 'bestes Nachwuchsprojekt' MFG Medien- und Filmgesellschaft Baden-Württemberg and MILIA '98 Cannes at the Multimedia Transfer '98). He also produced the documentary film *Çatalhöyük — Voices of the Past* (45 min.) English (Italian 1998) (Prize for the best Educational Film, International Meeting of Archaeological Film of the Mediterranean Area, Crete, Greece 1998).

Begümşen Ergenekon is a sociologist and social anthropologist who was trained at the Middle East Technical University, University of Bergen (Norway), and Ankara University. Her fields of specialization are rural and urban anthropology and ethnoarchaeology. Since 1990 she has taught in the Department of Modern Languages in the Middle East Technical University, and since 1992 she has taught in the Archaeometry programme there.

Aylan Erkal studied Social Anthropology at Ankara University(1993–1997), before going on to METU for her MSc in Archaeometry (1998–2000). In 1996 and 1997 she was a ethnoarchaeological fieldwork assistant, in central Anatolia. In 1998 and 1999 she undertook ethnobotanical fieldwork on the Çatalhöyük excavations as part of her Master's thesis. She has undertaken extensive fieldwork carried out in plain and mountain villages around the Konya Basin, based on botanical collections and interviews with villagers. She has also carried out experimental work at Çatalhöyük in 1999 on wetland tubers. In June 1999, she received a British Council scholarship to visit England for three weeks and visited researchers and libraries at Cambridge and University College London. She also gave a talk concerning her current research at University College London. In August 2000, she will be starting a PhD program in Anthropological Archaeology at University of California, Berkeley.

Shahina Farid gained a BA Hon. degree in Near Eastern Archaeology from the University of Liverpool. Since graduating she has been a full-time contract archaeologist working in Britain, Turkey, Bahrain and the United Arab Emirates. She has

worked in Turkey seasonally since 1985 joining the Çatalhöyük Research Project in 1995 and has been site director since 1997.

Carolyn Hamilton is an anthropologist and historian, and is currently the Director of the Graduate School for the Humanities and Social Sciences, University of the Witwatersrand. She is the author of numerous publications on the production of historical knowledge. Her most recent book is *Terrific Majesty: the Powers of Shaka Zulu and the Limits of Invention*, 1998, Harvard University Press.

Naomi Hamilton is an archaeologist based at Edinburgh University, where she is carrying out research on methodologies for understanding gender as a social structure in prehistory. Previously a field archaeologist in Britain, she undertook post-graduate study at the Institute of Archaeology, University College London on the Prehistory of Turkey and the surrounding regions with James Mellaart. She joined the team at Çatalhöyük in 1993 when field research was renewed and has been involved both in the field and the laboratory throughout the life of the project. Her particular areas of responsibility are the study of figurines and burials, data sets commonly used as the basis of statements about gender roles in prehistory. Her approach to this material is based on a feminist critique of assumptions prevalent in archaeology and in society in general, and is informed by extensive involvement in the Women's Movement.

Christine Hastorf is currently an Associate Professor in the Department of Anthropology, University of California-Berkeley. She has been involved in anthropological research of human–plant relationships since 1979. Her training and PhD from UCLA was within Anthropology but focused on Archaeobotany and human uses of and relationships with the natural environment. Concentrating in archaeology, she has focused on long-term plant use in the South American region, especially on highland societies of later prehistory within the pre-Inka and the Inka political world. More recently she been directing a project on the shores of Lake Titicaca where we are studying the Formative site of Chiripa. The interest there is in studying the domestic daily world of the residents, but also their ritual world. On the Çatalhöyük project, she is in charge of the plant collection and interpretation, beginning this in 1996. Her laboratory expertise in archaeobotany is with macro remains, the visible plants that are recovered from the site matrix. Within that capacity she has been involved in developing sampling strategies, processing methods, as well as issues of contextual interpretation and forms of feedback with all of the other specialists involved in the site. She is currently the director of the UCB McCown Archaeobotany Laboratory where a series of projects are ongoing, ranging from social theory of past human social life to new methodologies to understand past plant use. She has written on gender relations surrounding plant collection, cooking, agricultural production change through time, the onset of complex society, on political change and the symbolic use of plants in the legitimation of authority, fuel use and symbolism, and the origins of plant domestication as it is involved in developing social identity. She is particularly interested in methods and interpretations of plants to better 'see' wild taxa use as well as the stages in plant processing. All of these methods will help to approach the larger questions about past social realms, especially cultural and symbolic, and the concept of culture in a natural world.

Lucy Hawkes took a BA in Archaeology at Cambridge University and started her MA in South East Asian Art and Archaeology, Tibetan Art and Buddhism at The School of Oriental and African Studies in September 1999. She has been involved with the Çatalhöyük Research Project for three seasons. During her first season at Çatalhöyük she had her first experience of excavating skeletons and began to develop an interest in the treatment of the body during burial, especially in the meaning of the postures and relationships between bodies in the ground. For the last two seasons she has been doing reconstruction illustrations and interpretative work with the human remains team from the Natural History Museum at Çatalhöyük. Her artistic training comprises an A-Level in Art and Design and personal work in her own spare time. She has had freelance commissions for illustrations and design work. She is particularly interested in the human form and has been able to draw upon her experience of life drawing in interpreting the skeletons at Çatalhöyük. She spent the 1999 six month season at Çatalhöyük doing the video recording of the project. After her MA she plans to do a PhD in some aspects of Southeast Asian or Indian Archaeology and is specifically interested at present in the material culture of Buddhism.

Ian Hodder teaches in the Department of Cultural and Social Anthropology at Stanford University. His interest in Çatalhöyük partly stems from his involvement in symbolic and contextual approaches (e.g.

Symbols in Action (1982), *Reading the Past* (1986), *The Domestication of Europe* (1990), and partly from an interest in field methodology and its social context in a global environment (*The Archaeological Process* (1999)). But it also stems from the fact that he was taught by James Mellaart as an undergraduate in London. He began planning to re-open the site in 1991 and has been director of the overall project since fieldwork began in 1993.

Mark Knight is currently employed as Project Office for the Cambridge Archaeological Unit, Department of Archaeology, University of Cambridge, specializing in Neolithic and Bronze Age landscape projects. From 1986–92 he was Project Officer for Exeter Museums Archaeological Field Unit and in 1992 started his undergraduate degree, Prehistory and Theory & Methodology, at the University of Cardiff. Since graduating in 1995 he has worked for the Cambridge Archaeological Unit. His fields of interest focus on material culture theory — in particular the fragmentation/disarticulation of objects and the creation of assemblages in the past (at the point of deposition) and the subsequent fragmentation of the same assemblages in the present (at the point of categorization and specialist analysis); addressing the interrelatedness of different kinds of objects that form an assemblage, and its particular place of deposition against the examination of objects based primarily upon category or type. Similarly, he is also interested in the actual relationship between people and things, and especially keen to develop a kind of contextually informed phenomenological approach to excavation dependent on being there at the point of encounter. This could be seen as an attempt to reclaim the empirical. He is also interested in *visual representation in archaeology* — deliberately embracing ambiguity or the trickery of the visual to contest conventional/rational presentations (both visual and textual) to encourage the possibility of other interpretations. He worked for the Çatalhöyük Research Project during the 1998 season — North area, Building 5.

Mine Küçük received her BA degree from Istanbul University in prehistoric archaeology and worked three seasons as an Early Bronze Age specialist at Troia, Turkey. She received her MA degree in Ancient Studies and Museology from the University of Minnesota, preparing a thesis comparing Neolithic chipped stone assemblages from central and southeastern Anatolia. She interned at the Istanbul Archaeology Museum, the Science Museum of

Minnesota, and the Bermuda Maritime Museum. Her archaeological specializations include lithic illustration and the Early Neolithic of central and southeastern Anatolia, and she has illustrated artefacts in Poland, Turkey and America. She has also assisted with an obsidian sourcing project for central Anatolia.

Since 1994 Mine has been working for the Science Museum of Minnesota as a content specialist, exhibit developer, and project manager for the Çatalhöyük Project. She currently directs production of exhibit components in Turkey for the Çatalhöyük Visitor Center. She also writes articles about museums all over the world as a freelance writer.

Jonathan Last received his PhD from Cambridge in 1995; the subject of his thesis was Neolithic settlements in Central Europe. He has been involved with the Çatalhöyük project since 1994 as an excavator and pottery specialist. He is currently employed as an Archaeological Project Officer with the Hertfordshire Archaeological Trust.

Su Leaver attended Amersham College of Further Education and Art from 1978–80 specializing in Foundation Art and Ceramics. She got her BA Hon. in Silversmithing, Jewellery and Blacksmithing from 1980–84 at the City of London Polytechnic. Since 1987 she has worked in archaeology doing excavation or post-excavation work. She started work at the Museum of London and since has worked all over Britain, Italy and the Lebanon. She was an excavator at Çatalhöyük in the summer season of 1998. Her interest in the project was the prospect of working in Turkey and with on-site contact with so many specialists, something that rarely happens in rescue archaeology. In her spare time she is a ceramicist and whilst there she become involved with experimental pottery firings using local clay and fuel (dung).

Nessa Leibhammer is the curator of African Art at the MTN Institute of Art in Johannesburg, South Africa where she is also in charge of the overall research component of the Institute. After obtaining a Fine Arts Degree from the University of the Witwatersrand in 1990 she held the position of curator of Traditional Southern African Art at the Johannesburg Art Gallery. Her experience includes working as a curator at the University Art Galleries and in the Anthropology Museum at the University of Witwatersrand. She has published mainly in the field of African Art with a special interest in the way visual images inform cultural texts. Currently registered for a Master's degree in Pre-colonial Studies at the University of the Witwatersrand her thesis investigates the role of the visual record in archaeology with particular reference to the Çatalhöyük project.

Louise Martin is a lecturer at the Institute of Archaeology, University College London. Her research is concerned with the role of animals in past societies, particularly the evidence for hunting practices, livestock management and domestications, and she has worked on a number of prehistoric sites in the Middle East. She has been involved in the Çatalhöyük project since 1994 and is part of an international team of zooarchaeologists on the project studying the animal bone remains. Her interest in Çatalhöyük is in attempting to understand the social, dietary and symbolic importance of animals and their products, using an approach which contextualizes zooarchaeological data with the rich body of archaeological and palaeoenvironmental evidence.

Frank Matero is Associate Professor of Architecture and Chair of the Graduate Program in Historic Preservation at the Graduate School of Fine Arts, University of Pennsylvania and Director of the Architectural Conservation Laboratory and Research Associate of the University Museum of Archaeology and Anthropology. He also serves on the faculty as course lecturer at the International Centre for the Study of Preservation and the Restoration of Cultural Property (ICCROM) in Rome. From 1981 to 1990 he was Assistant Professor of Architecture and from 1985–90, Director of the Centre for Preservation Research in the Graduate School of Architecture, Planning and Preservation of Columbia University. He received his MSc from the Graduate School of Architecture, Planning and Preservation of Columbia University in 1978 and attended the certificate program in conservation at the Conservation Centre at the Institute of Fine Arts, New York University from 1981 to 1984. His teaching and research is focused on building technology and on the conservation of historic building materials, with an emphasis on masonry and earthen construction, and on issues related to preservation and appropriate technology for traditional societies and places. Publications include articles in various professional journals, conference proceedings, and two forthcoming books on the technical history of the stone industries of North America and a history of archaeological site preservation in the American southwest. He is regional editor for the journal, *Conservation and Man-*

agement of Archaeological Sites and a member of numerous professional boards including US/ICOMOS, the Frank Lloyd Wright Building Conservancy, the AIA Historic Resources Committee, and the Fairmount Park Historic Preservation Trust; a Professional Associate of the American Institute for Conservation of Historic and Artistic Works and former Co-chair of the Research and Technical Studies Group. Current work includes the development of conservation plans for the Neolithic site of Çatalhöyük, the Al-Dard-Al Ahmar district of Cairo (with the Historic Cities Support Program of the Aga Khan Trust for Culture), and various sites in North America including Mesa Verde National Park and Casa Grande Ruins National Monument.

Wendy Matthews is a fellow at the McDonald Institute for Archaeological Research, University of Cambridge. She studied Near Eastern Archaeology at the University of Edinburgh, and wrote her doctoral dissertation at the University of Cambridge. She has taught as a visiting lecturer at the Department of Anthropology, University of California, Berkeley. Her doctoral and post-doctoral research is focused on microstratigraphic traces of uses and concepts of space in complex settlements and landscapes. The sites investigated include complex early agricultural settlements of Ašıklı Höyük and Çatalhöyük in central Turkey, and Bronze and Iron Age cities in northern and southern Turkey, Syria, Iraq and Bahrain. She has been associated with Çatalhöyük since the first day of renewed investigations, and is currently living in Turkey with her husband Roger Matthews who is Director of the British Institute of Archaeology at Ankara.

William Middleton was born in Istanbul Turkey in 1961 and has lived in the US, Korea, and Japan. He has a BA in Anthropology (University of California-San Diego 1984), an MA in Anthropology (San Francisco State University 1991) and a PhD in Anthropology from the University of Wisconsin (Madison 1998). Research and area interests include transition to agriculture and agricultural intensification, complex societies, domestic archaeology, ethnoarchaeology, Mesoamerica (Mexico, Guatemala) and Anatolia. He is currently a Post-doctoral Fellow at the Field Museum of Natural History, Chicago and Associate Scientist at the Laboratory for Archaeological Chemistry, University of Wisconsin-Madison.

Theya Molleson is a researcher in Physical Anthropology at the Natural History Museum, London in the Department of Palaeontology. She is particularly interested in skeletal variation and the impact of the environment and society on bone morphology. She was responsible for the analysis of the skeletons of documented age and sex from Christ Church, Spitalfields, a study which was furthered our understanding of the ageing process as well as the relationship between chronological age and biological age in cemetery material. Markers of restricted activities associated with food production and sport have been established in skeletons from the Near East dating from the Neolithic (Abu Hureyra) and Bronze Age (Ur, Kish); and the indications of postural preferences have been recognized at Çatalhöyük.

Julie Near has been a member of the Çatalhöyük Palaeoethnobotanical team since 1995 and has conducted four field seasons of archaeobotanical research in Turkey. Currently a PhD candidate at University of California at Berkeley, Near completed her MSc at the Institute of Archaeology at the University of London. Her dissertation work at Çatalhöyük has involved the study of plant-related activities at this site with a focus on the use of plants in the complex daily domestic and ritual lives of inhabitants of the Neolithic tell.

Nerissa Russell is Assistant Professor of Anthropology at Cornell University. Her research focuses on human–animal relations, inequality, and gender issues in the Neolithic of southeast Europe and Anatolia. She has a particular interest in the social and symbolic uses of animals in feasting, sacrifice, bridewealth, etc. She has studied several Balkan animal bone assemblages and has been a member of the Çatalhöyük zooarchaeology team since 1995. She also has a strong interest in bone technology, and has studied bone tools from southeast Europe and Pakistan, as well as those at Çatalhöyük .

Orrin Shane received BA and MA degrees in Anthropology from the University of Michigan, and aPhD in Anthropology and the History of Science and Technology in 1967. His dissertation dealt with the definition of archaeological phases of the Early Woodland in northern Ohio. He taught at Kent State University from 1967 to 1977 before joining the Science Museum of Minnesota in 1978. He is currently affiliated graduate faculty in Anthropology and Museum Studies at the University of Minnesota, and adjunct Professor of Anthropology at Macalester College. He has worked as a research archaeologist with the Çayonu project in southeastern Anatolia, the Incinerator site (33MY57) in Ohio, and he is currently collaborating with the Archaeological Conservancy to preserve and interpret the Native American Grand Meadow quarry in southern Minnesota. His interests are public presentation of archaeology and the cultural implications of agricultural intensification. Competencies in archaeological sub-disciplines include zooarchaeology and remote sensing. In 1965 Shane applied to work with James Mellaart at Çatalhöyük, planning to write his doctoral dissertation on the chipped stone industry in comparison with Early Neolithic industries in south-eastern Turkey and the Levant. He has served as curator-in-charge and content curator for several national touring exhibitions created by the Science museum of Minnesota and funded by the national Endowment for the Humanities, National Science Foundation, and private corporate foundations. Dr Shane has also served as design and content consultant for six major cultural interpretative centres, including Sun Watch in Ohio, the Trail of Tears Interpretative centre in Missouri, and the National Museum of the American Indian (Smithsonian) in Washington, DC. Over the past twenty years the Science Museum of Minnesota has become the leading producer in America of touring interactive science exhibitions and science-based Omnitheater films. Shane has participated since 1993 in the heritage management and public presentation of Çatalhöyük, developing exhibits for the Visitor Centre, directing the development of the Mysteries of Çatalhöyük website, co-directing Window on Çatalhöyük, and working to develop related exhibits and museums in Turkey.

David Shankland read Social Anthropology at the University of Edinburgh, and then moved to Cambridge to study under Professor Ernest Gellner. For his doctoral fieldwork (awarded 1993), he specialized in religion and social change in Anatolia, conducting fieldwork in an Alevi village. During this time he was successively Research Assistant at Hacettepe University, and Lecturer at the Middle East Technical University, Ankara. In 1990, he spent a term in Paris, working with Professor Altan Gökalp. In 1992, he became Assistant and the Acting Director of the British Institute of Archaeology at Ankara, when his work at Çatalhöyük first became envisaged. In 1995, he returned to Britain to take up a lectureship in Social Anthropology at the University of Wales, Lampeter. He is the author of numerous articles, and also the forthcoming monograph *Islam and Society in Turkey*.

Mirjana Stevanovic is a Research Fellow at ARF, Anthropology Department, University of California, Berkeley, where she has been administering the Berkeley Archaeologists at Çatalhöyük (BACH) project and acting as a Visiting Lecturer. She received her BA and MA from the Department of Archaeology, University of Belgrade (Former Yugoslavia) and PhD in Anthropology from the University of California at Berkeley. At Çatalhöyük she is the Field Director for the UC Berkeley Research Project. Her previous work focused on Southeast European prehistory and is marked by extensive participation in the Yugoslav and international archaeological projects, including those at the prehistoric sites of Vinca, Gomolava, Bosut, Rudna Glava (Former Yugoslavia); the Joint American-Yugoslav Archaeological Projects at Selevac and Opovo (Former Yugoslavia); Jezreel Valley Project (Israel), and the Podgoritsa Project (Bulgaria). This research produced numerous publications.

Since 1995 at Çatalhöyük Mirjana has been conducting research on architecture by integrating the analysis of prehistoric houses, with ethnoarchaeological study of traditional house construction in the Konya plain, and experimental reconstruction of Neolithic houses. She has also acted as the Field Director of the Berkeley Archaeologists at Çatalhöyük (BACH) project since 1997.

Mirjana's research interest lies in early agriculturists of the Old World, in origins of sedentism and architecture and the social and cultural conditions in which these developments took place. In addition, method of archaeological excavation, more precisely, the archiving of evidence has been part of her research.

John-Gordon Swogger graduated from Liverpool University in 1992 with a degree in Archaeology of the Eastern Mediterranean. His interest in archaeological illustration developed while digging in Chester and Liverpool after graduating and eventually resulted in a variety of archaeological illustration jobs. By 1996 he was illustrating full time, doing freelance finds illustration, building recording and reconstructions. His particular interests are the integration of archaeological illustration into the various and disparate aspects of the project, and the way in which the fairly traditional techniques and methods it employs have responded and adapted to the new demands of the project and its archaeology.

Ruth I. Tringham is Professor of Anthropology in the Department of Anthropology, University of California, Berkeley, USA, where she has taught and carried out research since 1978. She was awarded a PhD in 1966 in the Department of Archaeology at the University of Edinburgh, UK. After a short period in the Department of Anthropology at University College London, Ruth Tringham took up a position as Assistant Professor of Anthropology at Harvard University, Mass., USA, before arriving at her current destination in California.

Throughout her career until 1996, Ruth Tringham's research focused on the prehistory (specifically Neolithic and Eneolithic periods) of Central and East Europe. She directed two international excavations in Yugoslavia at Selevac and Opovo, and one at Podgoritsa, Bulgaria. In these research projects she collaborated closely with Mirjana Stevanovic. Her first experience with Anatolian prehistory, specifically Çatalhöyük, was in 1996. Since 1997 she has directed the NSF-funded Berkeley Archaeologists at Çatalhöyük (BACH) Project, under the 'umbrella' of the main Çatalhöyük Project, directed by Professor Ian Hodder.

Her early research focused on lithic analysis including experimental research in use-wear on the edges of stone tools. From the late 1970s, her research has focused increasingly on the analysis and interpretation of architectural remains within the context of Household Archaeology. Since the late 1980s, this focus has broadened to include an increasingly feminist and post-processual perspective. Part of this trend has been her current activities in developing interpretive hypermedia presentations of archaeological research and teaching through the incorporation of multimedia authoring. She sees her involvement with multimedia authoring as more than a passing whim — it is the future direction of both her research and teaching.

Richard Turnbull has spent ten years working in contract archaeology in Britain, France, Peru, Turkey and the UAE. He joined the Çatalhöyük project as an excavator in 1998.

Sharon Webb graduated from the University of Sheffield after receiving a BA in archaeology and prehistory in 1994. She then completed an MPhil in archaeological heritage management and museums in the Department of Archaeology at the University of Cambridge. She has also, at various times, worked for the Cambridge Archaeological Unit, and in the University Museum of Archaeology and Anthropology.

Currently she is working on a PhD thesis at Cambridge on museums as social institutions, the interpretation and representation of the past, issues of contestation, and how these are negotiated in the museum. Also of interest are the ideas non-archaeologists have about the past, and how they relate to it through the museum, and other media representation. Her interest in the Çatalhöyük project began with the site museum which forms the basis of one of the case studies for the thesis. She worked in Turkey for her own research in 1997, and was part of the team excavating the North area in 1998.

Anja-Christina Wolle joined the Çatalhöyük Research Project in 1996 as Computing Officer. Since then she has actively developed the web site, and the data base of excavation and specialist data whilst providing general computing support to project members. She studied Archaeology and Computer Science at the University of Newcastle upon Tyne, and gained an MSc in Archaeological Computing from the University of Southampton. She obtained her PhD in Archaeology from Southampton, where she focused her research into the application of electronic publication and archives. In her current post her goal is to support the Project in its endeavour to publish and make accessible all of its excavation data by electronic and conventional publication methods. She has published several papers on electronic publication and archives in archaeology.

Nurcan Yalman obtained her MA degree (1994–98) from the University of Istanbul, History of Art, Prehistory Department, on 'A Contribution of Çayönü Neolithic Site to the Problem of the Earliest Pottery in Near East'. Her undergraduate degree (1987–90) was at the same university as well.

She has participated in the Çatalhöyük excavation and research project since 1994 and is currently undertaking ethnoarchaeological research within the Çatalhöyük Research Project as a freelance researcher. The outline of this research is 'Ethnoarchaeological research on the dynamics of settlement processes in order to discuss better the internal dynamics of the Çatalhöyük settlement pattern'. In 1996 she visited Cambridge to undertake library work to improve her knowledge of Theoretical Archaeology, Social Anthropology and Ethnoarchaeology. She aims to concentrate on this research as a PhD study in the near future.

Introduction

Chapter 1

Developing a Reflexive Method in Archaeology

Ian Hodder

The aim of this chapter is to situate the methods used at the site into the contexts in which we work. This contextualizing of method is one of the key struts of a reflexive method. Rather than the emphasis on universal method seen in positivist archaeology, the emphasis is on developing methods sensitive to context and problem.

Where is Çatalhöyük?

The first and simplest answer to this question (see also Chapter 8 by Ayfer Bartu) is that Çatalhöyük is in central Turkey, near Çumra in the Konya region. The East mound is largely Neolithic in date and has a range of radiocarbon dates for its 20 m sequence from 6400 BC to 5600 BC (Hodder 1996). Çatalhöyük was first excavated between 1961 and 1965 by James Mellaart (Mellaart 1967) and became of international importance because of its size and complexity at an early date outside the Fertile Crescent — i.e. outside the heartlands of animal and plant domestication in the Near East. But the importance of the site transcended these factors because of the sculpture and painting found at the site. Indeed, the site has retained a central significance despite the discovery in the last thirty years of large complex sites at earlier dates in Turkey and the Near East. It is the art which has won for Çatalhöyük this continued reknown. Mellaart understood the art to have been produced in a priestly quarter of the city and he suggested a social and political organization of some complexity.

The site was abandoned in 1965 and the present project began work in 1993. The first three years of work concentrated on the study of surface features using non-intrusive techniques. These studies *On the Surface* were published in 1996 (Hodder 1996). From 1996 the project has had three components. First, archaeological excavation has concentrated on continuing the work of Mellaart in the southwest of the East mound and it has begun to expose buildings on the north part of that mound. Regional survey has been undertaken by a team led by Douglas Baird and palaeoecological work by a team led by Neil Roberts. Second, conservation research has been led by Frank Matero from the University of Pennsylvania and his team. This has concentrated on methods for the conservation and lifting of paintings and sculpture. Third, a team led by Orrin Shane from the Science Museum of Minnesota has dealt with various aspects of the public presentation of the site, including educational programmes, CD-Rom (also produced by a team from Karlsruhe), and a visitor centre.

The context in which we work

One immediate context is the people from the local village and town, several of whom work at the site. Their interests in the site are varied, from the commercial desire to set up a shop, to the desire for labour, to the sets of local beliefs in the mounds. These latter include the idea that the ancient mounds in the Konya plain contain the spirits of the dead, which can sometimes be seen at night moving from mound to mound (for these and other local beliefs see Shankland 1996). But local communities also use the mounds of the plain (although not Çatalhöyük which has been fenced and is continually guarded) to obtain earth for making mud-bricks. The mounds are also used for picnics and leisure pursuits.

Whenever we hold a press day we get massive press coverage, in both local and national media. This is at least partly because Çatalhöyük is taught in schools and in the press as one of the 'origins of Anatolian civilization'. The exhibit about the site in the Museum of Anatolian Civilizations at Ankara has recently been re-installed as a major feature.

The project caters for this national interest by developing a programme for schools. This involves local schoolchildren who come to do activities at the site. Another version is the British Airways competition in collaboration with the national newspaper Yeni Yüzyil. Schoolchildren were asked, through the newspaper, to write an essay on the title 'Why is Çatalhöyük important for Turkey?'. Those who won the competition were brought to the site and then to Cambridge.

The nationalist emphasis has a different flavour locally. The site is located in a conservative area of Turkey in which Islamic fundamentalism and nationalism are strong forces. Many local politicians and officials are members of religious fundamentalist parties (e.g. *Refah*, now banned) or of nationalist parties such as MHP. When these politicians talk to the press at the site they drape the podium in the Turkish flag and talk of the importance of the site for the Turkish nation. But their relations with the site are often ambiguous. After all, the site is pre-Islamic and clearly pre-Turkic. In addition it is being excavated by an international team funded by international companies. But the politicians manage to twist these features of the site to their advantage and they talk of the international focus showing the importance of the site, region and nation. They talk of the gift they are making to the world. They point to the long tradition of achievement in Anatolia.

When the European Union Ambassador to Turkey visits the site, his rhetoric in front of the press is very different. In fact it is diametrically opposed to the national politicians. He talks of the contribution made by the European Union to the project and the site. He talks of the Union's interest in Turkey and in its culture. He emphasizes precisely the non-Islamic character of the site in order to argue for a secular state in modern Turkey. He argues that at the time of Çatalhöyük the boundaries between Europe and Asia did not exist, that we are all part of a common culture, that nations had not yet come into being. He links the site to Europe and to international relations and cooperation.

And then there are the sponsors. When they talk to the press at the site, they drape the podium in the logos of their companies. They have their own specific agendas. For example, a credit card company wishes to show that the obsidian exchanged at the site is the origin of the credit card. They wish their sponsorship to be used to further this idea in an exhibit in the Visitor Centre that we are building by the site. Other sponsors emphasize the scientific aspects of the project's work, or an airline company uses the images of flying vultures in the art to advertise 'flying back to the past'. A Turkish bank supports the project because the obsidian was 'banked' in hoards below the floors. In our reports to these various sponsors, different aspects of our work have to be emphasized and given prominence.

There are many other special interest groups.

For example, the nearby city of Konya has long been central to the trade in *kilims* (a type of Turkish carpet). There is a widespread belief that the origins of the designs found in *kilims* can be traced in the art at Çatalhöyük. But the most important group, numerically, with which have to deal are the varied New Age or Women's Groups. Busloads of tourists on Goddess Tours of Turkey make Çatalhöyük the highpoint of their visit. Other Goddess communities visit in smaller groups or interact with the project via the Web. There are several alternative Çatalhöyük websites provided by New Age or Goddess groups. In fact there is a great diversity of groups ranging from hardline feminist, to eco-feminist, to Goddess worshippers, to women simply interested in the role of women in early times. Although for many of these groups Marija Gimbutas and James Mellaart are focal figures, there is no consensus of viewpoint.

So there are a large number of groups of people who want to tell different and conflicting stories about Çatalhöyük. We are in various ways dependent on these different constituencies (financially, administratively, politically, socially, local goodwill, etc.) and have to find ways of working with them if we want to survive. The interactions between these groups are often dangerous and threaten to undermine the project. For example, there is considerable tension between some Goddess communities and the local people as will be described below. There is some doubt about the viability of an international project dealing with pre-Islamic and pre-Turkic remains in a part of Turkey which is religiously fundamentalist and politically nationalist. At the very least, survival of the project, if that proves possible, is enhanced by a fuller attempt to understand and interact with the multiple voices which surround it.

Method: where IS Çatalhöyük?

So how should we respond to the fact that so many groups want to tell different stories about the site? One response in archaeology has been to erect barriers and to police the boundaries of the discipline. Archaeologists have increasingly faced a plethora of alternative voices, especially in a post-colonial context where archaeology is involved in indigenous rights and claims. Many archaeologists have been frightened by this proliferation of voices and have sought comfort in an authoritarian archaeological science; science as objective and untrammeled by politics. But, on the whole, this oppositional strategy has proved less successful than accommodation and compromise, as seen in the passing of the NAGPRA act in the United States.

Another response to multivocality in archaeology is to emphasize the presentation of the past to different communities and constituencies. And certainly, at Çatalhöyük, we have programmes for the presentation of the site and its interpretation in the Visitor Centre, where there will be multilingual displays and a community exhibit. We have obtained sponsorship funding for the experimental construction of replica houses, and the Friends of Çatalhöyük are seeking funds to build other reconstructions. The Friends have also provided a tent over part of the excavations so that they can remain open to visitors all year round. We provide panels which explain our work in the different parts of the site to tourists.

Figure 1.1. *Working in one of the laboratories in the Çatalhöyük dig house.*

But all this emphasis on the presentation of the site leaves untroubled the ascetic and antiseptic calm of the research laboratories in the dig house. Archaeologists readily deal with multivocality at the interface between their work and the outside world. They less easily allow that outside world to interfere into the calm objective world of the scientific analysis of data. But as the outside voices increase their intensity and volume, and as they become ever more sophisticated and well-informed, this monastic desire for closure is threatened. At Çatalhöyük, the confrontation occurred early on in discussions with Goddess groups, often composed of highly articulate and well-educated professionals. They applauded the emphasis on presentation of the past, and they welcomed the idea that alternative voices would be included in the displays about the interpretation of the site. But they pointed out that if we as archaeologists handed over the data to others to interpret, a bias remained. They said that 'the data are already interpreted by you'. This statement confronts the ascetic calm of the laboratory scientist and the self-contained methods of the field excavators. It shows that alternative voices have to be included in the very construction of the data themselves. We cannot just hand over objective data to interested groups. At least some of those groups recognize that interpretation is involved in the very collection of evidence, in the laboratory itself, and at the trowel's edge.

If the project responds to multivocality simply by building a visitor centre and making a CD-Rom, then the authority of archaeological science is retained. The archaeologist acts as the guardian and interpreter who hands over knowledge to a wider world. But once we let these conflicting voices into the construction or discovery of data, the old centres of archaeological authority begin to be eroded. Archaeological knowledge becomes part of a network or flow.

We need different methods to handle this new situation and it is these we are calling a 'reflexive method'. This debate in archaeology is parallel to those in ethnography (e.g. Clifford & Marcus 1986) but the challenge in archaeology is different because archaeology bridges into the natural sciences. The focus in ethnography has been on writing. But in archaeology a critical reflexivity has to deal not just with writing but also with those aspects of method which involve scientific observation and natural science techniques — that is with the laboratory and the excavation trench.

The challenge of introducing multivocality and reflexivity in the laboratory and trench is being dealt with by taking 12 tentative steps at Çatalhöyük. These are only examples in an ongoing process of experimentation with different ideas.

1. Every one or two days during the excavation, the laboratory staff visit the excavation areas on the site. This is possible because faunal, archaeobotanical,

Figure 1.2. *General view of excavation underway in the South area.*

lithic, ceramic, soil micromorphological, ground stone, human remains and other specialists are present on the site during excavation. The aim of the discussions between the laboratory and field staff is twofold. From the point of view of the laboratory staff, information is gained about context. For example, it is helpful for the ceramics specialist to know if there is some uncertainty about the stratigraphical relations and dating of a layer, hearth or other context. From the point of view of the field staff, the tours by the laboratory specialists provide them with information about what they are excavating. For example, a faunal specialist might be able to recognize in the field the animal species and skeletal parts. This might help the excavator to interpret what is being excavated and thus make appropriate decisions about sampling strategies. This takes us to a second part of the Çatalhöyük methodology.

2. Many approaches in field archaeology assume,

despite provisos about 'theory-ladenness', the objective sanctity of the archaeological data. As a result, sampling strategies are often developed which can be applied in a wide variety of different contexts. The codification and systematization of archaeological recording procedures have also been encouraged by the development of cultural resource management. Sampling strategies are adopted 'off the shelf', using pre-set formulae. In practice, archaeologists have a duty to be responsible to what they find. As a result sampling strategies are often changed as a survey or excavation progresses. But even the most codified of sampling strategies involves making interpretive decisions. For example, it may have been decided to excavate 10 per cent of all pits on a site, but 20 per cent of the hearths. It becomes necessary to interpret a feature as a pit or hearth before excavation. And what happens if a new category of feature is found, such as a ritual hearth? In order to avoid these difficulties at Çatalhöyük, we have replaced decisions about sampling with negotiations about priorities. When the laboratory staff tour the excavation areas, they discuss with the field staff which layers and features should be prioritized. Different members of the team argue for this or that layer or feature to be sampled more intensively (wet-sieving as opposed to dry-sieving for example). The percentages of deposits of a particular type which have been prioritized can be monitored. The priority contexts are retained in all further laboratory analysis. In this way, the sampling (prioritizing) can be related to the changing interpretation of the site and its features. It can be moulded to the particular site and adapted to the particular interpretation. But also this process ensures that all specialists look at the same samples so that for those samples studied there is the maximum contextual information available.

3. Another characteristic of many field approaches is that they assume the self-evident nature of 'the archaeological object'. For example, when trays of artefacts are brought into the laboratory from the field they are usually divided into pottery, metal, bone, shell, lithics and so on. These divisions determine how these objects are then studied and published. The artefacts are sent off to the pottery, metal, bone and so on specialists. This common archaeological procedure involves wrenching artefacts out of their context. Decontextualized they become difficult to interpret except in universalist terms. At Çatalhöyük we have recognized that this process does not help the understanding of the site or of individual object categories. The need for interaction and integration lies behind our emphasis on having all the different types of specialist present at the site. But we have also recognized that the categories themselves are arbitrary and dependent on the scale at which we happen to work. At the microscope level small pieces of obsidian might be used as filler in pottery. They are thus not 'lithics' but 'pottery'. At the large scale, we have attempted to define 'objects' which cut across traditional categories. For example, the study of 'refuse' involves all types of materials, as do the 'objects' 'burning', 'decoration', 'food' or 'domestication'. In these ways the interactions between the different types of specialists are again maximized.

4. Another aim of the tours by the laboratory staff is to get information back to the field staff as quickly as possible. The reason for this is to discourage the idea of excavation as a mechanical process of recording objective data. Rather, the aim is to encourage the idea of excavation involving interpretation at the trowel's edge. In order to interpret stratigraphy properly, it helps to know the date of the pottery in the layers. In order to identify a floor it may be helpful to know about the degree of abrasion of pottery and bone. So, as we dig, we need to know as much as possible about what we are digging. This knowledge and our interpretations will determine the sampling strategies we use. At Çatalhöyük, the laboratory staff are thus asked to 'fast-track' the material from some layers and contexts. In other words, they look at this material quickly and feed back the results to the field staff. Other potential ways of speeding up the flow of information include digital recording and planning. In this way plots and plans could be examined immediately. Histograms and comparisons could be made immediately so that excavation can take place with maximum knowledge of what is being uncovered.

5. An integrated and fluid data base is essential for any attempt to link different participants in an archaeological project. At Çatalhöyük we have invested in a computer network so that the field and laboratory specialists can query each other's data and make comments on the provisional interpretations of their colleagues. All the different types of data, from field records to plans and drawings to measurements of lithic and ceramic artefacts to the film and diary data to be described below are available on the same data base. The separate computers are linked by a hub to one central computer to which all have access. The high degree of circuitry that is thus produced means that interpretations can always be in a state of flux, 'data' can continually be reconsidered and transformed, and conclusions are momentary.

6. However much one might want to create a fluid and flexible data base, some degree of fixity and codification is necessary. This is in order to allow comparison and in order to handle very large amounts of data. But any data base is a construct, and it is important that the user understands it as such. The user of a data base has to be able to situate it within its own context of production. In order to do this at Çatalhöyük we have reverted to the writing of a diary. This is written into the data base and cross-referenced. Thus, if a user wants to find out about layer 321, it is possible to find all the diary entries relating to layer 321 as well as the codified lists of animal bones, ceramics etc. found within it. The diary allows the user of the data base to understand what the excavators were assuming as they excavated a particular layer. It allows understanding of why the layer was excavated and sampled in a particular way. It allows the biases and preunderstandings to be explored. But writing the diary too has a beneficial effect. Other people read the entries as they are made and so the circuitry of information is enhanced. Also, the writing of the diary makes the excavator reflect on the excavation process and evaluate that process in relation to the questions that are being asked.

7. In the same way, video recording of the excavation process leads to a reflexive stance. At Çatalhöyük, the discussions by laboratory staff on the tours of the site (see point 1 above) are video recorded, as are summaries of their work by the field and laboratory staff. These video recordings are then digitized and edited into 1- to 2-minute clips which are placed on CD-Roms. The clips can be accessed by a keyword search system. Thus, it is possible to search for layer 321 in the data base and not only find the artefact and field records and the diary entries but also the video clips. These clips may show the excavator of layer 321 describing her or his work, pointing to the layer, and explaining its interpretation. This process allows the user of the data base to understand using visual information. It also allows the user to understand the assumptions and misconceptions under which the excavation was undertaken. The 'data' thus become relativized within a particular context of production of archaeological knowledge. Again, as with the diary, the process of filming itself means that information is circulated around members of the project as recording and viewing take place. Reflexivity occurs as project members are

Figure 1.3. *Investigating different modes of representation: Mark Knight and Nessa Leibhammer engaged in recording the same bins in 'scientific' and 'artistic' modes.*

asked to explain their work and assumptions before the camera.

8. Being reflexive and self-critical involve a considerable amount of energy and commitment to theoretical awareness. In practice, archaeologists may have little time for and inclination for 'navel gazing', despite the benefits derived. In addition, most archaeologists are not trained in the observation of living cultural behaviour. Thus, at Çatalhöyük, anthropologists work with us, dedicated to the study of the construction of knowledge at the site. They participate in our daily lives on the site, observing and conducting interviews. One studies the ways our interpretations are embedded within unrecognized assumptions and pressures. Another explores the visual conventions through which we see and record the site (in the form of plans, section drawings, artefact drawings, photographs and video clips, and see Fig. 1.3). Another studies the impact of our presence on the local community. The presence of people questioning assumptions has a destabilizing effect on the excavation and research teams. But a lack of stability is necessary if a critical approach is to be taken and if the project is to remain responsive to a changing world around it.

9. In order to facilitate maximum participation in the interpretation of the site from a variety of different communities, steps are being taken to place the entire Çatalhöyük data base on the Web. The aim is to provide a data base which is accessible and multimedia. This type of openness may conflict with the interests of individuals and groups with special access to the site. For example, the career paths of younger members of the project may be threatened if others have access to, and publish, primary data. Indeed, it is conceivable that alternative Çatalhöyük Web sites be set up by competing groups. However, while the rights of individuals and groups need to be protected, such concerns cannot justify the long-term secreting of archaeological information. Immediate accessibility encourages participation and engagement in the research process itself. It enhances multivocality.

10. The linearity of most archaeological narrative restricts the complexity of the stories that can be told. It also encourages the separation of evidence and interpretation. The latter is usually presented after the evidence has been set out. Hypertext, on the other hand, allows accounts with multiple pathways and incorporating multimedia. Thus a narrative account can be given and links provided between the narrative and pictures, plans, and coded artefact data. On the computer, the hypertext user can 'click' from narrative text to data base evidence in order to check the basis on which interpretations are made.

11. Archaeologists have always made plans, drawings and models of the buildings they excavate. These and other reconstructions allow hypotheses about original construction techniques to be experimented with. They also allow wider public participation in the understanding of a site. Today, the techniques of virtual reality allow greater speed and flexibility in the reconstruction experiments. The construction of a virtual world on the computer allows visualization and the experimentation with alternative reconstructions. Also, the virtual world can be made interactive so that the user can ask questions about a site and explore it from a non-specialist point of view. At Çatalhöyük the aim is for a virtual reconstruction of the site to become the 'front-end' to the data base. Non-specialist users can thus 'travel' to the virtual site and then find out about the archaeological information to a required level of detail. Virtuality allows experimentation with different ways of experiencing the site. Also, virtual reality allows us to break down the separation of 'plan' or 'architectural drawing' from 'artefact' and 'activity' (Small pers. comm.). Rather than the plan or wall elevation being seen as mere backdrops, virtual techniques can be used so that distributions of artefacts or chemical readings from floors can be placed in a three-dimensional

context which includes architecture, sculpture and painting. The underlying idea here is that the whole (the overall visual impression of patterns and relationships in a three-dimensional environment) is greater that the sum of the parts (the plans, artefact distributions, microdebitage plots, and so on).

12. At Çatalhöyük teams from different parts of the world are encouraged to excavate their own parts of the site. Equivalent recording and data systems are used, but each team uses its own traditional techniques of excavation and analysis. The assumption here is that the different teams, using different methods, will produce different results. By looking through different windows each team will see and find different Çatalhöyüks. Rather than being decried as chaotic, this diversity is welcomed since it is preferable to a single perspective and monolithic approach. The latter would produce a coherent account but that account would be based on the taken-for-granted assumptions of a particular archaeological tradition.

There are four themes underlying the 12 reflexive strategies being used at Çatalhöyük:

Reflexivity

By this I mean the examination of the effects of archaeological assumptions and actions on the various communities involved in an archaeological process, including other archaeologists and non-archaeological communities. Examples of this type of emphasis at Çatalhöyük include the work of anthropologists who study the impact of the project on the local community as well as on national and international groups interested in or visiting the site. Reflexivity is also engendered by the diary writing and video filming, since these processes encourage those on the team to examine their own assumptions. The diaries and videos also provide contextual information about the excavation process so that others can look back and critically evaluate the claims that have been made. The results of archaeological research are reflexively related to the context in which knowledge is produced.

Relationality or contextuality

The notion here is that meaning is relational. This emphasis is seen in the reflexive attempts to relate findings to a specific context of knowledge production. But the emphasis is also visible in the interrelations of contextual and artefactual information. Thus the date of a layer depends on the artefacts found in it. But in some cases, the date of the arte-

facts may depend on the stratigraphical relationships of the layers. In another example, at Çatalhöyük the interpretation of a building as a house rather than a shrine depends on the artefacts within it. But the interpretation of the artefacts partly depends on whether the building is seen as a house or shrine. So, usually in archaeology, everything depends on everything else within an hermeneutic whole. Our aim at Çatalhöyük has been to facilitate this circuitry, for example by having information about artefacts available to excavators as they dig contexts in a trench. The interpretation of artefact and context depend on each other and so it is necessary to have many artefact and context specialists present together on site so that information can be mutually available, especially for the excavators themselves. The aim is to be highly integrated and inter-disciplinary. Relationality also implies flexibility in the research process. If everything depends on everything else, then as I change one variable in my analysis so there are knock-on effects on all other variables. Thus the data base at Çatalhöyük is as open to change and as flexible as possible; conclusions are seen as momentary and always subject to change.

Interactivity

The aim here is to provide mechanisms for people to question and criticize archaeological interpretations that are being made, as they are being made. During the excavation process, interaction between laboratory and field staff is encouraged by the tours of trenches. The prioritizing (sampling) procedures are arrived at by negotiation between staff members. Interactivity is also facilitated at Çatalhöyük by the provision of the data base on the Web and by the provision of access routes (e.g. virtual reconstructions) that are 'user friendly'. It is also facilitated by the provision of information in diary and video form that situates the data base and opens it up for critique and alternative interpretation. The aim in the on-site museum is to have a community section in which a display about the site is constructed by members of the nearby village. In the museum too an interactive CD-Rom will be provided with hypertext and Virtual Reality components so that visitors and students can find out about the site in a non-linear way.

Multivocality

A wide range of different groups often have conflicting interests in the past and wish to be engaged in the archaeological process in different ways. The same point is often made in feminist archaeology (Conkey & Gero 1997). Mechanisms need to be provided so that different discourses can take place. For example, at Çatalhöyük different teams excavate different parts of the site and present their own 'windows' into the site. While the Web site may allow interaction with international, educated and networked groups, the local rural community is best able to interact through museum displays and visits to the site itself. In the future it may be conceivable to provide a modern shrine so that religious groups such as Mother Goddess visitors can pray at the site.

Behind the 12 strategies and 4 themes there is *one theme* which can be described as *non-dichotomous thinking*; that is the breaking down and questioning of categories and boundaries. Archaeologists have always built clear boundaries around the discipline, and in recent decades they have policed its boundaries very carefully, especially as various 'other' claims on the past have proliferated in a postcolonial and global world. In this new context, it is necessary for archaeologists to break down categories and boundaries, for example, the boundaries around the discipline, the author, around lithics, or Classical Archaeology, or faunal analysis. It is necessary to bridge the divide between archaeology as either science or humanity, as either history or anthropology, as either objective or subjective.

One clear example of this move towards non-dichotomous thinking is the breaking of boundaries around the site. The notion of 'the site' is one of the main building blocks of archaeological knowledge and archaeological authority. Archaeologists talk of 'my site'; they say 'come and visit my site', or 'what site are you digging at the moment?' There is some notion in these statements of ownership, and indeed the discipline is full of unstated rules such that individuals hold the 'rights' to dig a site or to survey a region and to publish the findings.

But at Çatalhöyük we see the site disperse. Different teams produce different Çatalhöyüks. Archaeologists and religious experience different sites, as do the different local, national and international constituencies. Different Çatalhöyüks can be visited by accessing different Web sites. Numerous people interact in the interpretation of the site so that it becomes unclear who is in and who is not in 'the team'.

So, another answer to the question 'Where is Çatalhöyük?' is to say that the one place Çatalhöyük is not is at Çatalhöyük. By this is meant that as varied groups, with their different interests and expectations approach the site, they construct different versions of it which are only partly rooted in the finds made at the physical location called Çatalhöyük.

These varied interpretations are located at other sites, globally distributed. They are grounded in different locales, away from the archaeological site itself.

This idea of dispersing the archaeological site is parallel to Marcus' (1995) notion of multi-sited ethnography. In archaeology the main fear has been the loss of authority that seems to be implied as bounded categories become dispersed into networks. But in the daily practices surrounding the Çatalhöyük project, we are, willy-nilly, seeing a shift from the archaeological site as a source of knowledge and authority to the archaeological site as mediating between many sites. The archaeological authority can no longer be assumed — it has to be argued for within a diverse network. The archaeologist contributes to this network but does not dominate it.

In the practices surrounding Çatalhöyük, archaeologists increasingly act as providers or mediators. A common experience has come to be the following. A TV producer approaches the project. They wish to make a film which includes the site and the project. They want to know what we have to say on some theme, often something to do with New Age movements, the Goddess and alternative religions. The archaeologists get interviewed and are politely listened to, but the agenda of the producer is clear and cynical. Whatever the specialist archaeological perspective, the programme makers have to make a film that will attract public attention. In the editing process, the archaeological perspective is placed on an equal footing with other points of view. The archaeological view is seen as one among many. The archaeological statements may get re-interpreted within a quite different story.

We can decry this situation and lament the loss of archaeological authority. Or we can embrace such experiences as a function of the erosion of boundaries between 'high' and 'low' culture. In the latter case, the archaeologist welcomes the wider public appeal and recognizes the need to speak to different communities and to argue a case in relation to a variety of different points of view. The boundaries around the discipline are eroded, and the enclosed self-sufficiency of the archaeological academy is punctured, but as mediator and provider, the archaeologist enters into a wider debate, often full of dissonance and frustration, but in which active social engagement becomes possible.

Taking a stand

As the archaeological site becomes involved in a negotiation with many other sites, it is impossible to try and remain neutral, objective, distanced. As one's words and as the data get taken and reinterpreted within other sites, there may be a desire to scream that 'there is no evidence for that'. But in that same desire to produce the evidence as objective, one recognizes the desire of others to do the same, from a different point of view. One recognizes that it is impossible to remain simply a service provider or a mediator. The message that is provided is not neutral — it is immediately picked up in the interests of one or other group at the expense of others. As a professional archaeologist and as a member of society one has to be responsive to the impact of one's work.

One is forced, then, to take a stand. As the evidence is taken by others to show that a matriarchy existed at Çatalhöyük, the archaeologist is drawn into an opinion, for or against. For example, in my view the evidence that we have gained at Çatalhöyük suggests not an all-powerful Goddess and a priestly élite, but daily domestic rituals and a set of beliefs and myths in which both men and women play a role. When talking to Goddess groups, many of whom have provided, or have the ability to provide, funding for the project, this alternative perspective has not always been well received. In my lectures to such groups, I have had members of the Goddess community walk out in anger. I argue that Goddess or other groups sometimes make claims that cannot be supported by any evidence. But I recognize that counter claims can also be made.

Indeed, negotiation with such groups has had an impact on our own research agendas and strategies. For example, the interests of the Goddess communities have provided an impetus to explore the role of women at Çatalhöyük. One response has been to develop a research strategy based on the analysis of ancient DNA. In a female-centred society one might expect that the inhabitants of houses would be linked through the female line. Thus as house is built above house and as family members are buried beneath the floors of the successive houses, one should find that daughters of daughters of daughters would be found. Analysis of ancient DNA should be able to distinguish such a pattern from one based on male household lineages. There are of course many difficult assumptions here (such as that those buried beneath a house lived in that house, and so on), but the example is presented to show how research directions in the scientific analysis of the material from the site can be designed to respond to questions from multiple sources and interests.

Negotiation with multiple voices is being undertaken on the project's Web site where a dialogue between myself and Anita Louise, a member of the Goddess community, has been posted. There is also the facility on the Web site to make comments and to enter into dialogue with project members. On the whole, there has been a positive response to the provision of as much information as possible on the Web site, including data files and diary entries. These are certainly read and we hope that a more informed debate may gradually take place. It is possible to provide data while at the same time taking a stand. It is possible both to mediate and to participate in debate, as long as a reflexive context is provided — i.e. as long as attempts are made to involve multivocality, reflexivity, interactivity and contextuality. It is possible to break down boundaries but still take a stand in a dispersed debate.

The impact of our work on the local communities is less easy to evaluate and is on-going. Certainly tensions have arisen. In particular, the support of Goddess communities has had a negative impact locally. There is local suspicion of some of these groups. A traditional society in which women are covered and expected to be deferential is likely to look askance at New Age feminists, naked Goddesses, and groups dancing and chanting on the mound. Many in the local community are wary of newcomers and outsiders.

At some moments it has been important to take a stand and not to participate in Goddess events so as not to confront local feelings. It is important to respond to the local interests in the site and a community exhibit is to be incorporated into the Visitor Centre and people from the local community have been asked to make a video about their own interpretation of the site and about the work of the project. But local views have also been important in understanding the site itself. Our various ethnoarchaeological projects have depended very much on local practices in their attempts to understand micromorphological information about the use of floors etc. The local women have suggested uses for the ovens found on the site which had not occurred to the foreign members of the team.

It has also been necessary to take a stand in relation to sponsors and local and national political interests. Many of these groups want our work to prove that the site is the biggest, earliest, most original, and so on. Much of our renewed work at the site has led to a 'normalization' or 'de-mystification' of some of the more exorbitant claims that have been made for it. This tendency tends to disappoint many of these groups and there is a concomitant danger of a loss of support and revenue for the project. But it is

On 11/08/97, Gavin wrote:

Arrived almost two weeks ago but the first week was taken up with the construction of the steel shelte

and in the end a professional construction team had to be brought in from Konya to complete the job

building had been protected by plastic sheeting and some spoil infill and had survived very well alth

the walls a — very littl — last s

Naomi ha — Mellaa — has c

working in — ces to rem — e ain.

1 such as t — nd F.37, — 8 an(

still taking — le infant — e wa

disarticul — remnants of F. 38 and a lower one, beneath

mostly wor — h has just l — — eletal remains, they app

Unfortunately F.44 has just been shown — 5 which is now being rem

moulding (F.26) and step (F.46), some — still continues un

H — — — ructi — ary element of th

r — rticu — ppeared at the bas

p — ds a — ims to have found

t — e bui — ls the same, inclu

d — een fc — der F.41 - this may be o

is — e the extent of the cut was never fully resolved last year — there

was helping. Some of the floors from here have also been taken down — ost fi

rem — king off some of the wall plasters — ow

the — me re-acquainted with the phasin — — re

I — and it almost certainly needs refin — — f.

I a — k. This is further beset by the pro

onl — e whole building - and with othe fet(

to be checked, the big problem is not so much the stratigraphic relationsl

relationships are crucial. Moreov — ch a

year some on site interpretations a — think

whether it is over-emphasising dis — s one oj — antages of a

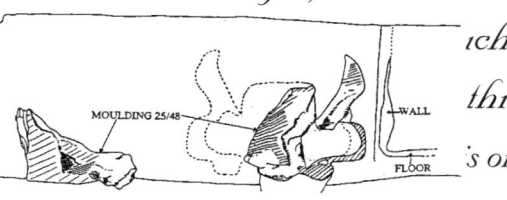

Figure 1.4. *Photomontage: Building 1 representations.*

uth's area, just adjacent to the North; unfortunately, this took a m

ay.   began on the North area just o

e p.   ps a little too damp as a thin fi

e D. who, as last year, will onl

'had and Charlotte. At the moment this is a good size as we are

'hen begin the removal of the architectural features of Building

'layers below. Less burials than I thought were remaining which was a relief although they are

, F.40 another double infant t   removed last year, disturbed/

burials (F.29) under platform   e team has been up helping and

y solid but are extremely brittle   suffered much over the winter.

Charlotte; also some skull fragmen   f the fill for F.44 under the wall

'suggests t   ial which perhaps F.44 has cut.

, we have fairly conclusive evidence of at least one burial like this; after the

mation with its head lying well south of F.   y floor

corroboration; my worry is that more may   want is

s under platform F.13 are being fairly r   early,

arliest under the platform and has a greenstone pendant associate   F.37

e groups/individuals at least, one of which has now come out. Na   arlotte

ins. Although then, most   d on the burials,   remove

mpleted mor   hese. In terms of the interpretive issues surrounding

ed out. Th   r Building 1 was done in almost a day by Roger and

e studied m   onjunction with the drawn sections, something which

floor units)   stratigrap   usually

ion of the bur   eeds to be   t needs

ing or broad   urials and   ct floor

nterments, how   t a sequen   re last

haps check Roger's diary?). Beyond this, ther   elf and

es not need phasing. Having said that, there are   'ding 1,

13

necessary to take a stand and point to alternative ways in which the site can be seen as appealing. In doing so, the interests of sponsors and political groups can be catered for, in partnership rather than opposition.

So we cannot simply act as neutral mediators — providing a service to varied communities so that they can access the past. Rather, it becomes necessary to accept that our 'mediation' involves a particular perspective which has to be negotiated in relation to other perspectives. The aim has been to provide mechanisms so that others can engage in a debate. But such a process means that we have to enter into the debate ourselves. We cannot impose an authority based on an objective science. Rather, we have to argue an authority in terms of a well-informed understanding of the data. We have to recognize that that understanding is better informed if opened up to alternative voices. But we also have to act as members of society, aware of the conflicts and tensions between diverse perspectives, and aware of the benefits and dangers of specific uses of the past. We have to take a stand as archaeologists and as members of society, but we can do so in an inclusive and non-confrontational manner.

Conclusion

The archaeological site at Çatalhöyük does have an impact on diverse communities in the present. It mediates between these various groups and individuals and their constructions of the past. The archaeological site at Çatalhöyük is one site among many Çatalhöyük sites and it is dispersed into those sites, not existing independently of them. Yet the archaeological site impacts on the diverse communities which are networked to it. By breaking down boundaries, and by involving people in the construction of data, people's experience of the world changes. The archaeologist is involved in an on-going negotiation, one that penetrates into the laboratory and into the trench. It does seem possible to argue for a certain authority but be involved in a plural, multivocal debate. It does seem possible to break down boundaries, and move to networks and flows, without losing impact and purpose.

Postscript: the 1999 season

This book describes mainly the early seasons of excavation at Çatalhöyük from 1995 to 1998. During this time the methods discussed in this volume were experimented with. But during 1999 a six-month season took place, prompted by the need to evaluate potential damage to the lower levels of the site caused by a dropping water table. A team of 20 professional archaeologists, half field and half laboratory, were recruited. During this long season, the methods which had been developed in previous years became a routine and the problems faced in earlier seasons were not as apparent.

The aim of the long season in 1999 was to reach natural at the base of the mound in the South area, which involved the excavation of about six metres of stratigraphy and much shoring. The season was a success not only in reaching the base of the mound and keeping within budget, but also methodologically and communally. The success of the methodology is probably largely attributable to the use of a smaller and wholly professional team so that the close interaction between specialists in different fields was easier. Individuals had enough experience to cope with the integration of large amounts of information and with the detailed recording and sampling.

Continuity over six months resulted in efficiency and team stability, and familiarity lessened inhibitions in group discussion and interaction. The process of excavation, recording and interpretation was familiar to everyone. Methodologies were adopted with relative ease, and time was not needed to train students.

With a smaller team and more computer terminals, field data entry was more efficient allowing quicker data querying. This was possible as with more than one competent excavator in an area individuals were able to spend time in the laboratory on paper and computer work. Video records were made by a trained excavator who had closer contact with daily activities in the trench and was better equipped to know what was archaeologically important both whilst filming and editing.

References

Clifford, J. & G.E. Marcus (eds.), 1986. *Writing Culture: the Poetics and Politics of Ethnography*. (A School of American Research Advanced Seminar.) Berkeley (CA): University of California Press.

Conkey, M.W. & J.M. Gero, 1997. Programme to practice: gender and feminism in archaeology. *Annual Review of Anthropology* 26, 411–37.

Hodder, I. (ed.), 1996. *On the Surface: Çatalhöyük 1993–95*. (McDonald Institute Monographs.) Cambridge: McDonald Institute for Archaeological Research; London: British Institute of Archaeology at Ankara.

Marcus, G., 1995. Ethnography in/of the world system: the emergence of multi-sited ethnography. *Annual Review of Anthropology* 24, 95–117.

Mellaart, J., 1967. *Çatal Hüyük*. London: Thames & Hudson.

Shankland, D., 1996. Çatalhöyük: the anthropology of an archaeological presence, in Hodder (ed.), 349–59.

Part A

The Integration of Methods

Part A: The Integration of Methods

With apologies to Clifford Geertz (1973, 19) 'What do archaeologists do? — they write'. Archaeologists dig, certainly. But increasingly they write, draw or record as they dig. The process of digging is surrounded by paper, drawings, clipboards, pens and pencils, graph paper, tapes, masking tape, cameras, total stations etc. (Fig. A.1). This paraphernalia of writing and representation involves a 'turning away' from the excavation process, away from the bodily engagement with the soil, and away from the interpretive process. The trowel is set down and the engagement with the dirt is objectified in writing.

It might even be argued that the writing has become the primary focus of excavation. It is almost as if it is the digging that is the 'turning away' from the writing. The digging is done in order to record or represent. It is structured in a certain way so as to produce sections, profiles and plans that can be recorded and written down. We dig towards taking a photograph or completing a phase plan. We sculpt the earth in order to fulfil the demands of representation.

Most archaeologists would accept that data collection has become highly codified. It aims to be objective and distant from the vagaries, uncertainties and impressionistic experience of excavating itself. The processes of writing and encoding determine the way we see what we excavate. And so the material that is excavated is immediately incorporated into an abstract code. This code divides up and dissects. Following the code, we excavate a 'unit' or a 'context' — that is something unified or integrated in its setting — and then we break it up and decontextualize. Bones, seeds, pots and soils are dispersed, analyzed, disaggregated. The different bags with their different labels lie waiting by the trench or by the sieve to receive the broken-up fragments from the whole. 'Archaeology is destruction', but primarily in the sense of destroying the units, contexts, wholes which make sense of the fragments or parts.

The records drive us in this partitive enterprise. But they are incomplete in themselves. As field notes in ethnography (Clifford 1990), they act as mnemonics, as prompts for the later writing up. Memory will recontextualize the records to make them intelligible. So a separation occurs between the interpretive moment and the record which is written for later 'writing up'. So in the trench the excavator is in split time; subjectively interpreting in the here and now, but objectively writing/recording for later interpretation.

And this later 'writing up' may even be handed over to someone else. A split may occur between the professional trench technician and the later analyst, interpreter or synthesizer. Someone will recontextualize the dispersed and fragmented evidence and 'put it all back together again'. But what can be put back together will not be 'all'. It will only be what has been recorded. It will only be those parts that were selected by the disciplinary codes. So the recontextualizing is done at a distance, partially.

As the excavator works, he or she is split in time, engaged in a process of fragmentation.

The turning away to write also involves a turning away from the group. In most excavations there are conflicting interpretations, changing views, contradictory evidence, uncertain stratigraphy. In turning to the coded form (e.g. unit or context sheet) there is also a retreat into an ordered world which sorts out for us what is relevant. It tells us what to record.

The coded form results from disciplinary codes — it frames our perspective. It guides us by asking questions and offering choices of response. The codes which guide us derive from the discipline as a whole. But there are also specific codes relevant to each region or site (the Çatalhöyük conceptual archive is described in Chapter 7.) The baggage which we bring to the site channels the questions we ask and the recording methods we use. The codified forms are structured less by what we find, by our engagement with the soil, and more by a discipline that is already written.

The distant, objective fixity of the recording process is perhaps reinforced by the metaphor of 'the field' which so pervades archaeological excavation. The idea of 'the field' is common to geographers, geologists, biologists, ethnographers, missionaries, military officers etc. 'Field' of course suggests associations with agriculture and with the separation of village from field. When we go 'into the field' we go away. We make records and 'return'. The field is 'somewhere else'. Perhaps this 'elseness' is important in creating an objective distance. The excavator goes out, away, into the field, perhaps struggling with difficult circumstances. The distance helps to make the record incontestable, decontextualized and so 'objective'.

Particularly in excavations abroad, we come in from the outside. We have a generalized gaze. And so we talk of ourselves in contrast to 'the locals'. So again, our writing deals with general, universal, knowledge, separate from specific, historically grounded and local interpretations.

The separation of an archaeology carried out 'in the field' sets up oppositions between descriptive recording and later writing up in the laboratory. It helps to reinforce

Figure A.1. *Excavation in progress in Building 1 on the north part of the East mound at Çatalhöyük.*

binary opposites: us and them, self and other, objective and subjective, general and local (Gupta & Ferguson 1997). To counter this hegemonic, colonial perspective, there is a need to disperse 'field' and 'site'. In fact, the 'field' is everywhere there is a stakeholder interest in particular archaeological remains. The 'field' extends through networks of interaction which include the 'home', the laboratory, the sponsors, and public-interest groups. There is a need to integrate 'field' method and 'field' staff within a multiscalar, multivocal and multi-sited (Hastrup & Olwig 1996) process.

But the process of integration is not an easy one in archaeology as it is presently organized, at least in Britain. The gulf between the 'two worlds' of the academic and field professional is considerable. Many of the issues discussed in the chapters in this section relate to this underlying issue. The long-term solution is perhaps in the restructuring of archaeological knowledge acquisition so that the divide is transcended. Such restructuring might involve the up-grading and re-centring of fieldwork practices. Professional field archaeologists already engage in background research in contract archaeology. At the evaluation stage, the significance of sites has to be argued against a wide range of criteria, including existing research. At the publication stage, research syntheses may be produced. But despite the renewed emphasis on training in professional field archaeology, fundamental changes are needed if the divide between field and research staff is to be removed.

Ideally, field professionals should have a good knowledge of the Babylonian texts relevant to the sites they are working on, in the same way that researchers should know about the details of find contexts. The problems of integration have increased with rising specialization within the discipline. While such specialization is unavoidable, bridges need to be built if trowel's edge interpretation is to be enhanced.

Experimentation with reflexive methods at Çatalhöyük is not presented here in order to persuade other projects to do the same. In other contexts, different responses will be needed. A research project such as that at Çatalhöyük will require different strategies from a rescue or cultural resource management project. But if different methods will often be needed, many projects today face similar problems. However heightened at Çatalhöyük, the problems of the globalization, dispersal and contesting of archaeological knowledge are widely found. Solutions to these problems will always be local and specific, but at least knowledge of the responses tried at Çatalhöyük, and the problems experienced in implementing those responses, may be of value to other projects in finding their own solutions.

This section and this volume discuss methods which have been experimented with at Çatalhöyük. There has been little attempt here to provide substantive results. These will be presented in later volumes. For example, much of the reflexive methodology at Çatalhöyük aims at integrative discussion amongst specialists in different fields. While the attempts at integration are described in this section, and an example given in Chapter 5, the full fruits of an interdisciplinary thematic integration will have to await further publication. It is method rather than results which is in focus here.

References

Clifford, J., 1990. Notes on (field)notes, in *Fieldnotes: the Makings of Anthropology*, ed. R. Sanjek. Ithaca (NY): Cornell University Press, 47–70.
Geertz, C., 1973. *The Interpretation of Cultures*. New York (NY): Basic Books.
Gupta, A. & J. Ferguson, 1997. *Anthropological Locations*. Berkeley (CA): University of Califonria Press.
Hastrup, K. & K. Olwig, 1996. *Siting Culture*. London: Routledge.

Chapter 2

The Excavation Process at Çatalhöyük

Shahina Farid

with contributions from Craig Cessford, Åsa Berggren, Anwen Cooper, Richard Turnbull, Adnan Baysal, Su Leaver, Peter Boyer, Tom Cawdron, Naomi Hamilton, Lucy Hawkes, Mark Knight, Sharon Webb *and team members*

Since the onset of excavation in 1995, the methodologies introduced at Çatalhöyük have been discussed and argued at many venues: in the public arena at the 1996 Theoretical Archaeology Group Conference in Liverpool, as the subject of published papers (Hodder 1997; Chadwick 1998), and as the topic of much informal discussion, not least of all, by team members themselves. Not all the methodologies are new or revolutionary, rather their combination and means of implementation are new.

Ian Hodder has defined 12 tentative steps towards 'multivocality' and 'reflexivity' (Chapter 1, this volume). This chapter could be subtitled '*the reaction of the field team to the methodologies introduced at Çatalhöyük*' as it details the responses of the field team to the practicalities of employing these methods in a demanding and challenging environment and the resulting tensions between the field and laboratory teams. Only numbers 1–8 of Hodder's steps have been discussed here as these were pertinent to our work and, although we have opinions on steps 9–12 they were deemed inappropriate for our chapter.

The methodologies have adapted and changed over the last three seasons and will no doubt continue to develop with the project, in line with Hodder's adage '*always momentary, fluid and flexible*'. For the field team the uncertainty and discontinuity can be disconcerting, frustrating, and disempowering, but also a challenge. We are also aware that the methodologies employed here do have a lasting impact and an influence on future work, and for us nothing is taken for granted or goes unchallenged after Çatalhöyük.

The excavators

Currently the five areas under excavation at Çatalhöyük are the BACH area excavated by an American team, the Summit area excavated by a Greek team and the North, West and South (formerly known as Mellaart) areas excavated by British teams. This chapter tries to represent the views of the teams working in the North, West and South areas and as such represents the reactions from a British methodological viewpoint only. The team consisted of a few professional excavators, mostly from Britain, and international students of varying experience, some of whom had a few weeks excavation experience and some none at all.

The methodologies

1. Priority tours
On alternate workdays the laboratory team visited the areas under excavation and was given a guided tour by the area supervisor. The latest excavated deposits were described along with the latest interpretations, problems and anomalies, as were the next areas to be investigated and any further information on the previously excavated deposits.

Discussion was encouraged from all team members: as the supervisor guided the laboratory team around the trench each excavator of individual rooms or buildings was encouraged to partake and contribute. This was not always successful, as some of the field team were inexperienced, lacking English as a first language or found speaking in front of a large

Figure 2.1. *Priority tour in the South area.*

fore in the 1998 season the system was changed. It was agreed that at the end of each priority session one or two of the laboratory team along with the relevant field member or supervisor would summarize the discussion and conclusion of the priority unit. The summaries would take place either in the field or, if better illustrated, in one of the laboratories. The next priority unit was also defined and summarized on video as it had been found in previous years that by the time the unit was analyzed and discussed there was nothing of it left to see or film *in situ*.

and eager audience difficult. Nonetheless confidence grew through the season brought about by familiarity with the archaeology and colleagues as well as gaining more of an interest in entering debates.

Throughout the tours, the laboratory team asked questions, discussions took place, ideas and theories were exchanged, and notes taken (Fig. 2.1). The laboratory staff drew parallels with all other excavation areas as they regularly visited all trenches whereas the field staff, along with all Çatalhöyük team members, took part in an end-of-week site tour of the other areas. At the end of the tour after further discussions and compromises, certain deposits were chosen as priorities for discussion at the next tour. Occasionally individual laboratory staff prioritized samples of no particular value to others, for example a charcoal-rich layer potentially full of charred seed remains was of interest to the archaeobotanist but not necessarily to the faunal or obsidian analyst.

In order to record the results of the relevant tours within their contextual environment, the video recording team filmed a three-minute summary given by the field team after the tour was completed. In the earlier seasons the characteristics and reasons for the prioritization of the chosen deposit were briefly described, followed by a summary of the laboratory team's results and conclusions. This method of summarizing was found to be unsatisfactory because the responsibility to recount was on the field team and it was felt to marginalize the laboratory team. There-

As described above, this multivocal input should be a new and positive addition to excavation practices. It should produce direct contact, interflowing ideas, views and discussions by all concerned with the excavation, analysis and interpretation. Whereas on most excavations specialists are required to toil through endless data in isolation and in the peace and quiet of the laboratory, here the laboratory team took part in the excavation on a daily basis, invited into the trench, given a voice and the opportunity to contribute to the excavation process. Although this happened at Çatalhöyük, it was not a smooth process primarily because it is unusual for field and laboratory teams to work in close proximity during the excavation stage of a project. Ordinarily the 'trench' is considered the domain of the field archaeologist who is used to working independently and in total control of the process from identification to execution of the archaeology, coming together with laboratory analysts at the end of the project, at the 'writing up' stage. Tensions arose in the trenches as the field team felt delayed and intruded upon, unable to carry out procedures normally undertaken following self-made decisions, without the need for prior group discussions. Tensions were exacerbated because the excavators felt belittled and mistrusted, and felt that their skills were not recognized as 'specialist' skills in their own right, especially by those with little or no excavation experience. Through time a collaborative relationship developed when an understanding was reached that the laboratory team were not there to find fault in the archaeological data nor to tell the excavator what they were digging but that the process was an exchange of information between the field and laboratory teams which was to contribute to overall interpretations.

Frustration was felt as the summarizing of results by the laboratory team of the analysis of priority units lacked cohesion because a nominated laboratory person was not appointed to take responsibility to synthesize the results and the discussion often lacked direction and quality. The results were often presented in lists with percentages, size and weight often in terms not familiar to the field team, and also without a final conclusion. Some laboratory teams realized and addressed the issue by concentrating more on examining whether all material came from a single source, whether it had been exposed and weathered and / or affected by water etc., which did lead to more helpful information and resulted in a change to the specialist working methods.

Some field members felt that the choice of priority units was laboratory-led. This, however, was not always the case as it was up to the field team to raise specific issues and it is likely that the laboratory team felt that the choice of priority units was field-led! Sometimes the field team felt that a 'Catch-22' scenario developed in the exchange of information on priority tours. The laboratory team were unable to offer an interpretation of a deposit on the basis of the finds alone; the field team had to give descriptions of deposits and working interpretations, the resulting laboratory interpretation tended only to confirm the original field interpretation. Sometimes the time lapse of one to two days between the excavation of the deposit and the analysis of its content was also problematic, and the 'ideal' of interactive interpretation in the field was therefore lessened.

This methodology should not only be stressed as beneficial for the field team but also for the laboratory team who are in a unique position of being involved 'at the trowel's edge'. For practical reasons most excavations abroad include some specialists in their field project because of restrictions in transporting or exporting archaeological material from host countries. However it is also common practice for specialists to work on material at their convenience out of season. Some conduct their analysis during a study season, when no excavation takes place and some even after the excavation of the project is complete and therefore it is quite common for a specialist never to see the site, let alone the excavation in progress. Even when part of the field team, they

may not necessarily take part in the daily events of the excavation, but work independently on their material in the relative calm of the dig house. Having specialists on site at Çatalhöyük therefore was not a new thing but the novelty was in the number of specialists present, and the fact that they were 'on call', took part in daily discussion and input into the process of excavation. Therefore the emphasis should be stressed as a twofold empowering exercise. Through the interaction, discussion and the results of the priority tours the post-excavation analysis was brought into the field and conducted concurrently with the excavation.

2. Sampling strategies

It is misleading to compare 'off-the-shelf' methodologies such as those used on rescue excavations in Britain to the methodologies being introduced at Çatalhöyük. Rescue excavations are part of a reflexive process involving archaeologists, analysts, curators and even clients. Interpretative decisions affecting sampling strategies are made during the evaluation stage of the project, as a result of interactions on site and during post-excavation assessments. Such rescue excavations tend to at least begin with 'off-the-shelf' strategies and pro-forma recording sheets because of the parameters within which archaeology has to operate. Presently these parameters include the legislative and commercial framework of rescue excavation, funding, time (on site), internal operating procedures within local and national excavation units and the large volume of work requiring to be undertaken.

Research excavations also have to work within their own parameters which include funding, academic timetables, availability of staff, research interests of the project director (such as the practical application of a theoretical approach to excavation methodologies), and the need to work out project specific and appropriate strategies. Sampling and analysis strategies will be as much affected by the prioritization within project budgets of travel, accommodation and wages as by academic goals.

Çatalhöyük should be regarded as a project unique in its ability to experiment and use new approaches and methodologies for sampling. The site itself and the results of Mellaart's excavations in the early 1960s, attract academic, popular, commercial and even spiritual attention. Not only does sponsorship allow basic project requirements to be covered, but also many research projects, grants and funded individuals have been attracted bringing the widest available range of current and experimental specialisms to bear on the project. It must therefore be stressed that the choice of sampling procedures available and the on-site attendance by relevant specialists is unusual.

The intention of fluidity in the sampling strategies introduced at Çatalhöyük was therefore a positive innovation and an uncommon opportunity for research. The reality of the sampling strategy at Çatalhöyük, however, is that despite the fluidity introduced in the priority tours, for the most part a more defined sampling procedure has actually been adopted, becoming more 'off-the-shelf' in that everything is sampled with little element of choice. Routinely a 30 litre flotation sample and an archive sample (for sub-sampling for other possible analysis) were taken from each deposit excavated, the remaining material being dry-sieved. With each new research project and experimental analysis, additional samples were taken and these often then became routine. Examples of some of the procedures which have become routine include samples for cattle and

Figure 2.2. *Sampling for chemical analysis of floors in Building 5, North area.*

human DNA, additional flotation samples collected from large deposits, samples from hearths and ovens for archaeomagnetic dating, seed-rich deposits (sampled up to 100 per cent for archaeobotanical analysis), obsidian microdebitage samples, gridded micromorphological blocks, phytolith, chemical, phosphate and organic residue samples as well as 30 litre flotation and archive samples from each 1 m grid on floor deposits. Less routinely pot sherds or clay balls were sampled for residue analysis and organic residue samples taken from possible coprolite deposits. An updated list of all types of sample taken in the field at Çatalhöyük is distributed to each field archaeologist at the beginning of the season (see Appendix 2.1), and although all possible types of sample are covered, there does tend to be a bias in favour of sampling for the laboratory staff present at the site.

Most samples were taken by the field team with strict guidelines on sample-specific lifting and labelling procedures. Some samples, however, were taken by the relevant laboratory staff, e.g. the micromorphological blocks and at times the soil chemical analysis or phytolith samples, but always under field supervision (Fig. 2.2).

The reasons for the field team taking most samples were multiple, but foremost was the necessity to reduce the number of people in the trenches or the need to take samples in step with both the recording of the archaeological stratigraphy and other sampling procedures. Recording and cross-referencing all samples had to be done by the field team, as ultimately they would be held responsible for integration of samples into the archaeological record. Samples for laboratory staff who were either not present at the site full time or who were otherwise engaged, had to be taken by the field team anyway, and it soon became apparent that it was more efficient for the field team to take most of the samples routinely, otherwise they were forgotten or overlooked, or delayed because of the restricted availability of the relevant laboratory person (Fig. 2.3).

For the field team the sampling methodologies proved to be time consuming and tedious and could divorce an individual from the original intention of excavation, making them feel they were caught up in a rigid system of excavation imposed by the demands of others. This was compounded by the lack of feedback from some of these samples and the lack of certainty that any secure knowledge would result from the often painstaking procedures of sampling. It may be that the presence of so many specialists on site raised the expectations of the field team who ordinarily would not have experienced such feedback.

A larger problem was how some sampling strategies were perceived as affecting the excavation process itself. The use of gridded baulks (which contained crucial stratigraphical relationships) for micro-sampling, and the consistent increase of work from the routine sampling in each of the gridded squares across floor surfaces, proved to be a problem for the field team as complete phases of activity were never seen, thereby impeding significant interpretations on phasing and associations of floors and features. It was also felt that excavation by 'box-trench' was a mechanical assembly line with the baulks representing a checking device. Furthermore the regular use of baulks at Çatalhöyük (as opposed to their use as mobile tools introduced as appropriate, at times of uncertainty in stratigraphy) represents a further fragmentation of the whole unit which contradicts the breaking down of barriers (see below), but most importantly blocked the view of complete phases. There is a serious danger that the deposits we excavate become so dissipated into their various sampled components that it is impossible to develop any coherent idea of what they were as a whole and what they mean.

3. Breaking down boundaries

Çatalhöyük presents a unique opportunity for specialists involved in all of the many facets of archaeological investigation and analysis to draw together and work towards a common aim. It has created a forum for the growth of individual skills, for learning and interaction, and does indeed break down spatial and practical barriers between professional field archaeologists, academic archaeologists and archaeological data analysts. However this is not the 'breaking down of barriers' that Hodder refers to (Chapter 1, this volume). His concern is with the dismantling of the archaeological unit or context by its separation into various components and the consequent distribution of these components to the relevant specialists who then analyze and report from an isolated viewpoint, the results usually being collated and published by the excavation supervisor. By having all the specialists present on site the emphasis is placed on interaction, integration and upholding the contextual whole.

Despite the presence of specialized personnel on site and the interactions discussed above it has proved difficult to break down boundaries in some areas. 'Wrenching artefacts out of their context' (Hodder, Chapter 1, this volume) began on site during the excavation stage where finds were bagged by the field team into material category and distrib-

uted to different laboratories at the end of the day where they were analyzed by material type. All excavation methodologies involved the process of decontextualization; the sampling process divided the unit, the use of baulks and sections also fragmented units, contradicting the non-breaking down of barriers. Priority tours were the forum where units were reconstructed when all analyzed data was discussed, but as there are limits to the availability of relevant personnel, and because of time restrictions and practicalities, only a few units can be discussed in this manner.

4. Quick feedback

The idea of immediate feedback on results of analyzed data to the field team was welcomed as additional information, which resulted in some collaborative interpretations of field observations. For instance the field team drew the laboratory team's attention to differences in the infilling of certain buildings which led to discussions and the prioritizing of

Figure 2.3. *A busy day in Building 2, South area.*

these deposits. One building showed materially rich infill accumulated by a range of multiple deposition events, and although the impression was that it was built up over a long period of time the field team could not prove or define the time span. It was through the identification of owl pellets by the laboratory team that it was shown that the building must have been abandoned and left to infill over a relatively long period. This was in contrast to other buildings where the infill was sterile and homogenous and interpreted as deliberately and rapidly deposited. Analysis of the material and environmental assemblages supported this differentiation through the study of fragmentation, wear etc., whereby primary deposition was identified in the abandoned building by large and 'fresh' material and secondary deposition of small and worn fragments in the deliberate fill. The size and wear of the latter also suggested that some form of sieving might have taken place prior to deposition. In defining these differences we formed an interpretation whereby as one building was abandoned and left as an external 'midden' area through at least two later phases, other buildings were deliberately infilled with fine sieved material to create a foundation raft for the immediate construction of the next building. This then led to questions on why the building was abandoned and whether it reflected pre-planning. Was it for structural reasons or practical in that an 'open' space was left, or can it be linked to the people associated with the building? However these questions will only be answered with further work. The above interpretation is by no means ground-breaking, rather the process is illustrative of how collaborative input allows interpretations to develop and the immediate raising and addressing of new specific questions by further prioritizing or sampling.

Not all laboratory staff were able to produce immediate feedback because of the inherent restrictions within certain analyses, e.g. time and the availability of certain specialists. Much science-based analysis required time to process, and some could only be processed away from site, meaning exportation to various destinations in Turkey and abroad. Some results were therefore not available until the following season when the 'moment had passed'. However, steps were taken for laboratory staff to develop on-site methodologies for immediate feedback. Having phytolith samples processed on site resulted in sourcing types of vegetation which not only added to the developing picture of the environment during the Neolithic period but could also illustrate distribution patterns. For instance certain plants may only have been used in certain areas and/or associated with certain functions. If the possibility of a pattern were to emerge areas could be targeted to test the theory. Similar steps are also being taken to process the chemical residue analysis on site.

This methodology was another venue for direct contact between the field and laboratory team resulting in interflowing ideas, views and discussions. Hodder concludes: 'placing so much emphasis on the point of excavation may lead to a re-empowering or re-centering of the field excavator' (Hodder 1997). However the empowering tool was already in the hands of the excavator by way of defining the archaeological unit. All data analyzed by the laboratory teams were reliant on the definition of the unit and its stratigraphic relationship as the excavator perceived it. The field person created the unit and this could be regarded as an assumption to be tested by the laboratory staff, but in practice the initial field interpretation was rarely contradicted.

As well as Priority tours, the mechanism for feedback was achieved by requests from the field team for on-site advice from the laboratory team. Similarly the laboratory team required contextual information from the field team in order to contribute to the discussion on the interpretation of a deposit. Rather than the portrayal of specialists as a team of monitors of the excavation processes they came to be regarded as an additional source of information to help develop a more rounded and complete picture.

5. Interactive data base
The aim of this is to allow a great opportunity to cross-examine and question incoming data and interpretations on an immediate and continual basis. The mechanism to achieve this was based upon immediate accessibility for everyone on the project to the data base. Unfortunately limitations of resources meant that there was a shortage of computer terminals, so not all field staff were able to have easy access to terminals. The provision of immediate data entry was a real resource issue which had to be balanced against so many other demands such as completing daily records, diary entries and other finds or data base related jobs. It was also not always possible for the field staff to complete records immediately as a unit was often not totally completed until sometime after its excavation when it could then be put into its proper overall context. With these restrictions it was at times difficult for the laboratory team to interrogate and use the data base as freely as required. However, the fact that this was

seen as a restriction proved the potential value the interactive data base was viewed with by the team.

One of the advantages the data base will provide is the ease with which to conduct archival research by anyone at any time across the world. Every aspect of any unit can be analyzed from the field record to the faunal reports, plans, drawings, photographs and diary entries, and the aim is that video entries, dimensions and analysis of different artefacts, the location of and any conservation treatment made to, should also be accessible in the future. As aspects are studied the data base is duly updated so that the latest information is available at any time. Specific deposits can be called up by area, room, or building in order to cross interrogate, all burials from a particular phase or, a particular type of pot-sherd from the whole site. In order to achieve this a certain amount of inflexibility is introduced for coding in order for the data base to recognize and match but this is a necessary building block for the construction of a fluid, flexible and usable data base.

6. Diary

As an addition to the formal recording sheets, the diary was generally regarded as a positive medium by everyone. It has proved to be very useful to new researchers joining the project, and for individuals who have never visited the site but may intend to study some particular aspect. It provides informative background reading in addition to the dry and 'coded' recording forms. For the field team it was a means by which a particular thought process or interpretation at a wider scale than the individual unit could be narrated. It also assured individual field members that their deliberations were recorded in the public domain rather than just being the sole prerogative of the area supervisors. This way all team members enter the arena of multivocality. In the 'pseudo-privacy of typing at a terminal' (Hodder 1997), and relative calm away from the pressures of the trench, team members gave a more personal account of the archaeology. The diary proved to be a good means of 'off-loading' a day's miseries, problems and frustrations in a sometimes impassioned and personal narrative form. However after some negative experiences not all individuals felt comfortable with this medium and became self-censoring, which may then not have been an accurate reflection of their thoughts and ideas. These entries were avidly read by other team members, which resulted in positive feedback, e.g. it opened debates and sometimes led to resolutions, but also led to some acrimony and tensions.

Unfortunately once again the diary has resource implications, which means that it could not be fully utilized because of lack of time and time restraints on computer accessibility. This is exacerbated if, as should happen, the diary writing is extended to the laboratory team. There was also a danger that the diary was seen to be a 'checking up' device rather than serving as a positive contribution by all to the interpretation process. In the end the many demands placed upon the field team meant that they became self-selective and addressed what was personally most urgently required, invariably the digging and site recording.

In British contract archaeology virtually all recording is done on pro-forma recording sheets with prompts to ensure that all essential data for post-excavation analysis is recorded. The use of diaries for more narrative recording (even if only by the supervisor) is not widespread as the emphasis is now on the excavation and the creation of an immediately usable archive. Narrative essays are seen as unnecessary and those who have tried to publish from notebook records of the past have sometimes found them to be unwieldy narratives which Barker characterizes as 'prose whose loose format invites the writer to confuse the stages of recording, deduction, interpretation, and speculation' (Barker 1993), and are sometimes totally lacking in any data or interpretation. The inevitable time constraints, both on site and the end of the waged working day, limit additional forms of recording. This has, however, led to a lost awareness by contract archaeologists of the importance of their impressions and interpretations and, how they came to their conclusions.

At Çatalhöyük a debate occurs in which some people advocate the abandonment of pro-forma recording and the use of narrative records only. However even the most experienced excavators have to be reminded of all the categories of information that are required to be recorded, and within an excavation team with variable levels of experience, and one that changes from year to year, a base recording standard is needed more than ever. The process of extracting relevant data from a narrative for particular tasks and for data bases would be daunting, difficult and perhaps unachievable.

The use of both at Çatalhöyük is perhaps the best of both worlds. The use of pro-forma recording ensures the basic level of recording and is easily checked, accessible and recorded on computer for availability and analysis. The use of computerized diaries enables further reflection and interpretation to be attempted and recorded in the public domain by all of the excavation team. The ability to archive this level of recording must be at least partly attributable to the nature of the project in its search for better and new ways of approaching archaeology.

7. Video

A working visual account of the excavation and its progression was regarded as an enhancement to the standard recording tool. As well as summaries of the Priority tours, a daily video record was made of excavation in progress. When filming was first introduced at Çatalhöyük in 1995 the whole project team was conscious and conscientious about participating in the video documentation; it was somehow impromptu, possibly because there was no time limitation, everything was new and exciting and many discussions were filmed on site between laboratory and field staff. As time went by this was no longer viable because of time constraints. It was not possible to film individuals in all trenches, nor was it possible for the film crew to be everywhere all the time. A time limit therefore had to be introduced on the amount of footage taken and used; the result was that what was filmed was quite selective. In the early years, not being archaeologists, the film team was unable to define archaeologically important footage as opposed to 'interesting' footage. Filming became the result of discussion between the film team, the area supervisor and the field staff. The filming was therefore pre-selected and at only three minutes long the clips were somewhat staged. From identification of 'something interesting', to discussion about what, how and whom, to film, as well as a rehearsal, the process became intrusive and time-consuming for everyone. People also became less inclined to use the video as a documentation tool because the film clips were edited by the film team who naturally concentrated on the visual as opposed to what the archaeologists considered important. In 1997 editing decisions of the video clips was transferred to the archaeologists but not always to an individual involved at the 'trowel's edge'. This process can also be seen as part of the interpretative mechanism.

Additional difficulties involved individual reluctance to participate in this form of documentation because of a lack of self-confidence. This resulted in the value of the documentation being biased by the confidence of the participant rather than the value of the discussion. The field team was required to summarize immediate interpretations of the excavation for the camera and it was found to be just as important for the laboratory team to do so also. This was increasingly introduced in the latter seasons result-

ing in more wide-ranging and selective footage as individuals were filmed in the laboratory environment surrounded by material under analysis and accounts of on-going interpretations. Summaries of priority tours were filmed as well as the more informal end of week site tours.

In both filming of field and laboratory related work it is important to stress the need to follow-up; to record final interpretations so that incomplete accounts are not fixed on this medium; this also provides a 'history' of how interpretations and conclusions were arrived at. As a tool the video footage would serve to refresh the memory at times of writing up especially for final publication a few years down the line.

This can be set up as a tool to place the units under discussion and excavation within their contextual setting, including more peripheral information than just text, and more of the surrounding deposits within a wider interpretative picture. Of course it can be used to illustrate points of assumptions and mistakes just as the diary and paper record can, but this aspect should not be negatively emphasized as some kind of control device over the excavator and 'assumptions' and 'mistakes' are only seen in hindsight, so further film footage should always be used to explain and illustrate changes in interpretation.

8. Anthropologists

Initially, and much to our shame, the anthropologist whose concern was to study the context of production of knowledge was treated with considerable caution and distance. The field team's reaction was that here was yet another kind of scrutiny, probing, questioning of motives, and even documentation of the language we used. The tension of being on view by a different medium yet again and having our thought processes dissected was inhibiting and unnerving. We were at an all-time low at the onset of this particular study in 1996, feeling ready to be tripped up and exposed; such was the result of continuous questioning, doubting from the rest of the team, the practicalities of the methodologies, and the arrival of the anthropologist. However, over time we overcame our own insecurities and formed friendships. With the lowering of barriers and the development of trust we developed a more informed understanding of the anthropologists' work and it is to be hoped we were able to help and contribute. This contribution to the project certainly added a different dimension to our work and made us aware of our pre-conceived ideas and assumptions.

Unexpectedly certain anthropologists found themselves in the role of 'dig-counsellor' to whom individuals could release tensions by describing their woes, complaints and difficulties, just as for some the 'diary' had become an outlet.

Discussion

A by-product of a large project is the tension created when 100 people or so are corralled together for up to two months in a restricted and isolated area, to work, live and socialize together. Tensions between the laboratory and field teams, however, developed from a tradition away from the site of working separately and independently. Additional pressure was provided by the constant struggle between long-term and short-term goals. Financial pressure and speed are often tied together and common to most excavations, but the legacy of this site, the sensationalizing of Mellaart's results and the implementation of time-consuming methodologies added extra strain. The project is designed for high-quality research, which makes for slow progress. The pressure to meet everyone's expectations with exciting new information and 'finds' to equal the results of Mellaart's excavations of the 1960s comes from sponsors, the public and would-be critics of the project, all of whom await results to justify the cost of the project. The financial support of this project is talked about as much as the archaeology and the methodologies, and often in a much exaggerated way. It should be pointed out that this project commits a significant proportion of its budget to employing professional excavators, who are not employees of Universities, or who take unpaid leave or even severance of contract from archaeological units to work on this excavation.

In addition to the 'normal' workday there were also a number of 'extra-curricular' events. A weekly 'laboratory tour' was introduced in 1998 in an attempt to re-address the imbalance of 'show and tell', whereby the field team paid a return visit to the laboratory teams to view and discuss their work. Also two or three times a week evening seminars were held when various team members discussed their particular subject and results of work so far. Meetings and group discussions were also called on an almost daily basis, slotted into timetables of those involved in relevant new or on-going projects, such as grant applications, publications, changes in methodologies etc. Evening training sessions were also held for students covering all topics.

A successful debating platform for informal laboratory-field discussion was also introduced in the 1998 season, called 'space tours' (at Çatalhöyük 'space' is ascribed to a room, annexe, external area etc.; any number of linked spaces are then ascribed to a 'building'). All team members were welcome to take part and these ended up replacing evening seminars. 'Space tours' were performed in one of the excavation areas, resulting in a more relaxed and informal atmosphere and also a more immediate venue for the discussions.

Although it was generally accepted that 'space-tours' were a success there were still a number of team members who felt inhibited. A greater continuity in the excavation team would certainly solve some tensions and inhibitions, as individuals would gain familiarity with the project and confidence to engage in discussion about the larger issues of the project and its research aims. Unfortunately one of the characteristics of the archaeological profession is discontinuity in team members, as most excavators are employed on short-term contracts and are unable to commit to projects a year in advance, not a problem unique to Çatalhöyük nor of its making. Laboratory staff, on the other hand, are generally better established and can commit themselves to a longer period of time. It is true that as the season progressed and team members interacted on a social as well as work basis, some of these barriers were overcome and generally those who return to the project are more comfortable with voicing opinions.

Instability within the project was seen to result from several factors: the constant change of personnel on a yearly basis, and throughout the season the arrival and departure of different teams working to their own schedule. Also the methodologies themselves, i.e. 'The presence of people questioning assumptions has a destabilizing effect on the excavation and research teams' (Chapter 1, this volume), was found to be unnerving and unsettling but Hodder interprets this as a good thing: '. . . a lack of stability is necessary if a critical approach is to be taken and if the project is to remain responsive to a changing world around it' (Hodder, Chapter 1, this volume). The 'fluidity' in the written record, however, results in big differences in recording from one year to the next, requiring constant revision of previous seasons data and at some stage this process may become incompatible.

Whilst Hodder has attempted to challenge conventional excavation and recording techniques at Çatalhöyük, the nature of the collective team skills must be remembered when comparing the results to other excavations. Rescue archaeology in Britain tends to demand a greater degree of field experience, while at Çatalhöyük the team consisted of a few experienced excavators and a few students with little or no experience. Therefore the accumulated experience that some excavators could bring to help interpretation was limited. In order to achieve 'a reflexive excavation methodology' through the use of postprocessual methodologies a team of more fully proficient excavators should be employed who know/recognize how and when to record information without the loss of crucial links and relationships. There also needs to be a raising of the level of confidence and awareness of their abilities, as well as a theoretical awareness amongst the excavation team, which allows them to feel equal to, and able to question the demands being made on them by the rest of the team. They need to feel able to make suggestions about different ways in which the excavation could be improved rather than feel like 'puppets on a string'.

Finally, there appears to be an unacknowledged difference between rescue archaeology and research archaeology in the many debates concerning the approach and recording of excavations in Britain. In rescue situations contract archaeologists work to tight budgets and schedules with little or no room for experimentation in excavation, recording, and sampling. Rescue archaeology has a duty to document what will be destroyed, and, in the construction business archaeologists are treated as any other contracting firm. The contract archaeologist's responsibility is therefore to minimize information loss which is achieved in the tried and tested fashion used on most rescue excavations in Britain today, with proforma recording sheets and pre-planned methodologies. When correctly implemented it is work to a high standard fulfilling both rescue and academic requirements although some would argue that it is mechanical, partial, inadequate, resource driven and non-academic. Research excavations are training grounds for students in archaeology and testing grounds for new methodologies, approaches and a venue for research and experimentation. Pressures are different but deadlines less final and such projects can attract researchers and funding to experiment with different scientific techniques.

Conclusions

It is clear that an excavator at Çatalhöyük is not only expected to be a fully experienced field archaeologist but must also be equipped to handle pressures of working with new and changing methodologies, scrutiny and criticism that come with this project. As well as undertaking excavation of complex stratigraphy they need to be willing to enter team debate, contribute to interpretation and interact meaningfully with top of their field specialists. The excavator must be able to undertake the massive sampling strategies and adapt to new ones. The excavator must be willing to undertake the teaching of inexperienced students, withstand the pressures of time and balance all this with doing the job well, especially as the project draws so much attention not only from within the team but world-wide.

As with all research projects the methodologies need to be reassessed in the light of the results of the past three years so as to further explore and develop the project aims. For example, the use of laboratory staff interacting with field staff in a variety of ways is very important and positive. In fact the field team would welcome more initial interpretation and debate rather than lists of dry data.

The use of recording media such as diaries and video must be encouraged and further developed. The full potential of the diaries will only be realized when sufficient computers are available for both input and analysis for everyone. Presently, time restrictions have led to an emphasis being placed on data inputting by the field team but diary writing must be fully extended to the rest of the project team to allow all team members access to this important reflexive tool.

Video recording must be followed through to its conclusion. As a means of seeing thought processes develop, change and expand with new data inputs from analyzed results, this is an excellent medium. However, if the full process of interpretation for any given subject is not seen through, then a semi-informed, partly inaccurate interpretation will be left as the archive video record. As this is also for public access and viewing, those on film will feel resentful and unwilling to further participate.

It is realized that the editing done by the film team is an act of multivocality in its own right. However, it is new as a tool to most people involved in archaeology and understanding its potential and limitation is therefore at an early stage. It may be an interesting experiment to see the results of the same footage edited separately by the film crew, the field team and the laboratory team.

If this project stands for anything it is the breaking down of barriers. However it seemed that in trying to break them down other barriers often formed, created by the implementation of the very methodologies designed for their destruction. Some unexpected barriers were created by the very language used in setting out the project methodologies by seeming to down-grade the field team, causing resentment. Barriers were constantly evolving in the interaction between the field and laboratory teams, and were necessarily created by the selectivity caused by the workload, lack of time and lack of resources. While these barriers in themselves may not have been originally envisaged as those to be overcome by this project, they nevertheless can impede the flow of interpretative ideas. They can be addressed and indeed the team as a whole is aware of them and has begun addressing them.

The reaction to the anthropologists changed in the team's mind from resentment of yet another unusual approach to an accepted input. Whilst the anthropologists did cause the field team to think about themselves and their 'baggage' brought to the interpretation process, perhaps the project should also seek to identify and highlight the individual skills the excavators bring to the project. Also in such a large team, with all the resultant tensions, the anthropologists perhaps importantly and unexpectedly, acted as a valve for the team's personal and project problems. The use of anthropologists for studying the construction of knowledge is interesting. It emphasized the rigidity within our system of recording and highlighted the divide between what we record as archaeologists and what the public sees. However although this awareness was interesting and enabled us to 'navel gaze' it has not as yet changed our conventional recording methods.

This is a unique project in that it has been set up to investigate one of the world's greatest archaeological sites using experimental methodologies and giving all team members the opportunity to participate in a multivocal project. Team members return-ing to the project are much more at ease and empowered and able to volubly participate in all activities. The project is a unique opportunity to learn and interact with new skills and is a thrilling experience. Access to all results and data is made immediately available through the internet to team members scattered across the world, other interested researchers, and to the public, to analysis, utilize and yes, even criticize.

Acknowledgements

This seems to be a good opportunity to thank all the excavators who have contributed to the project since excavation began in 1995 and who have participated in enacting the methodologies. We are grateful to all the specialists for their support and enrichment of our archaeological knowledge. Thanks to Ian Hodder for this opportunity to voice our side and finally to Jonathan Last and especially Peter Moore for editing this chapter.

Whilst this chapter has been compiled from the input and contributions of many team members the author takes responsibility for any mistakes, omissions and misrepresentations.

References

Barker, P., 1993. *Techniques of Archaeological Excavation*. 3rd edition. London: Batsford.

Chadwick, A., 1998. Archaeology at the edge of chaos: further toward reflexive excavation methodologies. *Assemblage* (online journal) 3. http://www.shef.ac.ukslahassem/3/3chad.htm.

Hodder, I., 1997. 'Always momentary, fluid and flexible': towards a reflexive excavation methodology. *Antiquity* 71, 691–700.

Appendix 2.1. *Sampling instructions distributed to excavators for 1997 and 1998 seasons.*

Çatalhöyük sampling strategies and procedures
9/8/97
Please X-find all samples, and collect with a clean trowel without touching the deposits or samples with hand.

1. Flotation
Collection methods for flotation samples and archive samples are described in *Çatalhöyük: the Unit Recording Sheet.*

Analysis	Ideal sample size	Collection method
Flotation	30 litres collected blind	Trowel or shovel into 2 flour sacks.
Archive soil sample	250–500 g (see template)	Trowel, A5 paper envelope ($^1/_4$–$^1/_2$ full). Please collect a representative sample of deposit as block lumps if possible, but also include some loose deposit. Air dry on open shelves in shade.

2. Dry-sieving
Collect all ceramics, clay balls, figurines, beads, lithics, other stone, bone, teeth, shell, charred plant remains particularly wood and tubers (see template).

3. Sampling to answer specific questions about different locales or contexts, and materials

3.1. Building in-fill with structural debris

Analysis	Ideal sample size	Collection method
Dendrochronology	50 rings preferably with bark	Wrap in fine string and put in a sealed plastic bag. (See advice sheet.)
Roofing materials	$13.5 \times 6.5 \times 8$ cm block	Wrap tightly in lab tissue and tape.

3.2. Occupation deposits on floors, platforms and benches, and in bins etc.

Analysis	Ideal sample size	Collection method
Botanical sample, dense plant remains	1) dense/special plants or: 2) approx. $20 \times 20 \times 20$ cm block	Put in a plastic bag with some surrounding soil, without cleaning. *Archaeobotanists will collect* in plastic bag/tissue and tape, in a rigid box.
Microarchaeological residues >2.50 mm (for activity residues notably lithic scatters)	500 g	Plastic bag. Stacked Endecott sieves 250 µm, 500 µm, 1, 2, 4 mm.
Micromorphology	$13.5 \times 6.5 \times 8$cm block Including 2–3 cm of collapse/fill on top of latest occupation deposit	*Micromorphologists will collect.* Swiss army knife, wrap in lab tissue and tape. Mark top and orientation.
Organic and inorganic analysis	*c.* 8 cm^3 block for micro-excavation and sub-sampling, in lab	*Micromorphologists will collect.* Cotton gloves, Swiss Army knife, wrap in lab tissue and tape. Mark top and orientation.
Organic residue analysis	50 g	Cotton gloves, 60 ml glass bottle with foil insert in lid/small paper envelope ($^3/_4$ full).
Parasites/insects	*c.* 5 (1–10) litres	Large plastic bag.

Analysis	Ideal sample size	Collection method
Phytolith concentration: bulk	30 g	Small plastic pot.
Phytolith concentration: small block	min. 3 cm³ block	Please collect as a preserved lump in a plastic bag/box, plants uppermost, avoid crushing *or Micromorphologist will collect*. Swiss army knife, lab tissue and tape/lined plastic box. Mark top and orientation.

3.3. Floor plasters

Analysis	Ideal sample size	Collection method
Micromorphology: block	13.5 × 6.5 × 8 cm Including 2–3 cm of collapse/fill on top of latest occupation deposit.	*Micromorphologists will collect.* Swiss army knife, wrap in lab tissue and tape. Mark top and orientation.
Organic and inorganic analysis	c. 8 cm³ block for micro-excavation and sub-sampling, in lab	*Micromorphologist will collect.* Cotton gloves, Swiss Army knife, wrap in lab tissue and tape. Mark top and orientation.
Organic residue analysis	50 g	Cotton gloves, 60 ml glass bottle with foil insert in lid/small paper envelope (³/₄ full).

3.4. Burials
Please collect flotation and archive sample from fill immediately within and around skeleton.

Analysis	Ideal sample size	Collection method
DNA	human 2nd rib or 4–11th rib (not the 1st or 3rd ribs)	*Anthropologists will collect this.* DO NOT TOUCH during exposure of ribs. Use inverted clean plastic bag turned inside out (without touching inside of bag) as a glove and lift sample, re-close ban over sample.
In situ measurements	scapula and pelvis	*Anthropologists will take these measurements* and assess preservation.
Basket/wrappings: bulk :small block	30 g min. 3 cm³ block	Small plastic pot. Please collect as a preserved lump in a plastic bag/box, plants uppermost, avoid crushing *or Micromorphologist will collect*. Swiss army knife, lab tissue and tape/lined plastic box. Mark top and orientation.

3.5. DNA cattle

Analysis	Ideal sample size	Collection method
Cattle DNA	1) loose cattle teeth (not in a jaw) must be relatively complete 2) cattle metapodials	DO NOT TOUCH. After exposure call faunal person to identify bone/tooth if necessary. If confident about identification, use inverted clean plastic bag turned inside out (without touching inside of bag as a glove and lift sample, re-close bag over sample. Please label with X-find number, take to lab ASAP.

3.6. Fire installations: in situ fuel and structure (p4)

3.6.1. In situ fuel

Analysis	Ideal sample size	Collection method
Botanical sample, dense plant remains: or: if layered and dense	1) dense/special plants 2) approx. 20 × 20 × 20 cm block	Put in a plastic bag with some surrounding soil, without cleaning. *Archaeobotanists will collect* in plastic bag/tissue and tape, in a rigid box.
Dendrochronology	> 50 rings preferably with bark	Wrap in fine string and put in a sealed plastic bag. (See advice sheet.)
Micromorphology: block	13.5 × 6–5 × 8 cm Including 2–3 cm of collapse/ fill on top of latest occupation deposit	*Micromorphologists will collect.* Swiss army knife, lab tissue and tape. Mark top and orientation.
Organic and inorganic analysis	*c.* 8 cm × 3 cm block for micro-excavation and sub-sampling in lab.	*Micromorphologists will collect.* Swiss army knife. Cotton gloves, wrap in lab tissue and tape. Mark top and orientation.
Organic residue analysis	50 g	Cotton cloves, 60 ml glass bottle with foil insert in lid/ small paper envelope (³/₄ full)
Phytolith concentration: bulk	30 g	Small plastic pot.
Phytolith concentration: small block	min. 3 cm³ block	Please collect as a preserved lump in a plastic bag/box, plants uppermost, avoid crushing *or Micromorphologist will collect.* Swiss army knife, lab tissue and tape/lined plastic box. Mark top and orientation.
Pollen	100 g	Plastic bag.

3.6.2. Fire-installation structure

Analysis	Ideal sample size	Collection method
Standard archive sample	250–500 g	A5 paper envelope (¹/₄–¹/₂ fill)
Magnetic susceptibility	>1 cm³ block	*Micromorphologists will collect.* Orientation (compass). Swiss army knife, wrap in lab tissue and tape. Mark top and orientation.
Micromorphology: block	13.5 × 6.5 × 8 cm Including 2–3 cm of collapse/ fill on top of latest *in situ* fuel/plaster.	*Micromorphologists will collect.* Swiss army knife, wrap in lab tissue and tape. Mark top and orientation.

3.7. Deposits rich in botanical remains: middens, pits etc.

Analysis	Ideal sample size	Collection method
Botanical sample, dense plant remains: or: if layered and dense	1) dense/special plants 2) approx. 20 × 20 × 20 cm block	Put in a plastic bag with some surrounding soil, without cleaning. *Archaeobotanists will collect* in plastic bag/tissue and tape, in a rigid box.

Analysis	Ideal sample size	Collection method
Dendrochronology	>50 rings preferably with bark	Wrap in fine string and put in a sealed plastic bag. (See advice sheet.)
Micromorphology: block	13.5 × 6.5 × 8 cm Including 2–3 cm of collapse/fill on top of latest occupation deposit	*Micromorphologists will collect.* Swiss army knife, lab tissue and tape. Mark top and orientation.
Organic and inorganic analysis	*c.* 8 cm³ block for micro-excavation and sub-sampling in lab	*Micromorphologists will collect.* Swiss army knife. Cotton gloves, wrap in lab tissue and tape. Mark top and orientation.
Organic residue analysis	50 g	Cotton gloves, 60 ml glass bottle with foil insert in lid / small paper envelope (³/₄ full).
Phytolith concentration: bulk	30 g	Small plastic pot.
Phytolith concentration: small block	min. 3 cm³ block	Please collect as a preserved lump in a plastic bag/box, plants uppermost, avoid crushing *or Micromorphologist will collect.* Swiss army knife, lab tissue and tape/lined plastic box. Mark top and orientation.
Pollen	100 g	Plastic bag.
Parasites/insects	*c.* 5 (1–10) litres	Large plastic bag.

3.8. All contexts: grindstone, lithic, pottery and clay ball residues

Samples should be collected wearing cotton gloves, and should not be touched with bare hands nor washed. Please collect an adjacent sample of soil.

Analysis	Ideal sample size	Collection method
Grindstone residues:		
grindstone	grindstone	Cotton gloves. Put unwashed sample in paper envelope.
adjacent soil sample	50 g	Cotton gloves. Glass bottle with foil insert lid or small paper envelope.
Lithic residues:		
lithics	lithics in burials or sealed caches	*Consult lithic analyst.* Cotton gloves. Put unwashed sample in paper envelope.
adjacent soil sample	50 g	Cotton gloves. Glass bottle with foil insert lid or small paper envelope
Pottery residues:		
sherds	*in situ* untouched sherds or top, middle, base of whole profile	*Consult ceramicist,* particularly before sampling whole profiles. Lift with cotton gloves and place unwashed in paper envelope
adjacent soil sample	50 g	Cotton gloves. Glass bottle with foil insert lid or small paper envelope
Clay balls:	incomplete examples only	Cotton gloves. Place unwashed sample in paper envelope.
adjacent soil simple	50 g	Cotton gloves. Glass bottle with foil insert lid or small paper envelope.

4. Architectural materials

4.1. Wall plasters

Analysis	Ideal sample size	Collection method
Standard archival sample	250–500 g (see template)	A5 paper envelope ($^1/_4$–$^1/_2$ full). Please collect block lumps.
Architectural block sample	20 cm² block	Wrap in lab tissue and string.
Micromorphology: block	13.5 × 6.5 × 8 cm	*Micromorphologists will collect.* Swiss army knife, wrap in lab tissue and tape. Mark top and orientation.
Organic and inorganic analyses	15 cm² block	*Micromorphologists will collect.* Cotton gloves, Swiss Army knife, wrap in lab tissue and string. Mark top and orientation.
Conservation samples of all plasters: Analyses may include:		*Ask conservation team for advice.*
particle size mineralogical:	150 g	Paper envelope.
XRD, XRF	2 cm³	Plastic bag.
clay fraction: XRD	1 cm³	Plastic bag.
pigments: XRD		Cotton gloves. Tissue and string / glass bottle with foil insert in lid.
organic media: fluorescence staining GC / MS		Cotton gloves. Tissue and string / glass bottle with foil insert in lid.

4.2. Mud-bricks and mortars
Please collect as separate samples unless otherwise indicated.

Analysis	Ideal sample size	Collection method
Standard archival sample	250–500 g (see template)	A5 paper envelope ($^1/_4$–$^1/_2$ full). Please collect as block lumps if possible.
Architectural block sample	c. 20 × 15 × 10 cm block though complete thickness of one brick and one layer of mortar	*Please consult architect/researcher.* Swiss army knife, wrap in lab tissue and tape.
Micromorphology: block	13.5 × 6.5 × 8 cm Including 2–3 cm of collapse / fill on top of latest *in situ* fuel / plaster	*Micromorphologists will collect.* Swiss army knife, wrap in lab tissue and tape. Mark top and orientation.
Organic residue: loose to compare to living floors and middens (particularly naturally sterile bricks / mortar)	50 g	Cotton gloves, 60 ml glass bottle with foil insert in lid / paper envelope.

Analysis	Ideal sample size	Collection method
Conservation samples		*Ask conservation team for advice.*
Analyses may include:		
particle size	150 g	Paper envelope.
mineralogical:		
XRD, XRF	2 cm^3	Plastic bag.
clay fraction: XRD	1 cm^3	Plastic bag.

Bulk chemical and physical analyses
Calcium carbonate
Differential thermal analysis
Isotope
Loss on ignition
Organic content
Particle size
Phosphate
Resistivity
Elemental analysis for organic C, H, N
X-ray fluorescence

Organic residue analysis
Chromatography: thin-layer chromatography (TLC), liquid chromatography, gas chromatography (GC), pyrolisis gas chromatography
Mass spectrometry (MS), Pyrolisis gas chromatography mass spectrometry
Isoelectric focusing
Radio-immuno assays

Small block chemical and physical analyses
Infrared spectroscope, Fourier transform infrared spectroscope (IR, FT-IR)
Microspectrophotometry
Optical microscopy and staining techniques
Scanning electron microscopy with energy dispersive X-ray analyzer (SEM with EDXRA)
X-ray diffraction

Chapter 3

Integrating Archaeological Science

Wendy Matthews & Christine Hastorf

with Peter Andrews, Theya Molleson *and other members of the team*

In one of the first manuals on techniques of archaeological excavation, Philip Barker expressed as an ideal
goal the presence of laboratory field staff during field
excavation. He suggested that 'Only if the scientist . . .
can discuss on site the problems raised by the samples
can he [sic.] be expected to give a full appraisal of their
significance rather than a mere identification and tentative interpretation' (Barker 1979, 206).

In this chapter we discuss some of the practical
and conceptual issues which are arising in integrating archaeological science 'at the trowel's edge' during the excavations. We consider how different
sub-disciplines within archaeological science inter-
relate both with excavation practices, and with one
another. Some of the subject areas and substantive
points discussed in this chapter overlap with those
in other chapters, but this is symptomatic of our
approach in general.

We consider first the ranges of objectives integrating archaeological science at Çatalhöyük. We then
discuss methodologies and issues arising from
implementation of these objectives in practice. We
conclude with specific examples of integrating archaeological science at Çatalhöyük. Substantive and
theoretical issues relating to integrating archaeological science are being explored more fully during
current preparation of publications on the first phase
of excavations, in the light of our own experiences.

Objectives

The principal objectives in integrating archaeological science at Çatalhöyük are closely inter-woven
with the general aims of working towards reflexive
and postprocessual methodologies at Çatalhöyük,
which are discussed in an earlier review and in the
introductory chapter to this volume (Hodder 1997;
and Chapter 1, this volume).

In this chapter we consider four of the principal
objectives in integrating archaeological science during the excavation process. These are: 1) to develop
sampling strategies which are sensitive enough to
detect diverse traces of human behaviour and micro-environment; 2) to enable reflexivity with richly
networked data that can inform excavator's ongoing
decisions and interpretations 'at the trowel's edge';
3) to enable laboratory staff to be aware of the nature
of the deposits and the contexts as they are being
excavated; and 4) to facilitate integrative inter-disciplinary discussion at all levels during all stages of
the project.

The first of these objectives is to develop appropriate and practical sampling strategies that will furnish information at the required degrees of precision
including spatial intervals for detecting different traces
of behaviour and meaning in different contexts within
the settlement and surrounding landscape.

All archaeologists are concerned about the units
in which they excavate as well as the sampling strategies in collecting material. Excavation units and
sample sizes often create the initial boundaries within
which data are collected and interpreted. The issue
of where to divide the excavation universe both horizontally and vertically is critical to interpretation.
These divisions include consideration of the complex three-dimensional characteristics of deposits,
features and spaces as they are being revealed, initially partially, during excavation. Selection of some
units for excavation and sampling includes considerations of whether to sub-divide thicker depositional
units, or to lump together thin microstratigraphic
lenses. In subsequent analyses of the context and
associations of many artefactual and bioarchaeological remains, it is always possible to amalgamate
results from smaller units of excavation and sampling, but impossible to separate results from larger

Table 3.1. *Sampling strategies: scales of analytical focus, and sample type and average size.*

Sample type	Field sample size	Sample nature
Excavation	Unit of excavation	Intact > disaggregated
Micro-excavation: field laboratory	Large block *c.* 50 cm³	Intact > disaggregated
Micro-excavation and sub-sampling: specialist analytical laboratory	Small block *c.* 10 cm³	Intact > disaggregated
Monolith: organic, inorganic & microscopic analyses	Monolith *c.* 50 × 8 cm	Intact
Archive block	Small block *c.* 10 cm³	Intact
Micromorphology	Slice 13.5 × 6.5 cm 25–30 µm thick	Intact
Flotation and screening	30 litres	Disaggregated
Archive bulk	250–500 g	Disaggregated
Specific samples for organic, inorganic and microscopic analyses	500–0.5 g	Disaggregated

units (Lennstrom & Hastorf 1992). Excavation practicalities and objectives are equally critical in determining unit and sample size (see Farid *et al.* Chapter 2, this volume). Further aims and issues relating to sampling are discussed in relation to practice, below.

A second objective, is to provide information 'at the trowel's edge', furnishing the excavators with a range of additional data to employ during excavation and in interpretation of the unit, feature or building. Feedback from rapid processing of selected samples on site can help inform sampling strategies whilst excavation is still underway, both to speed up excavation where possible, and not to miss opportunities for retrieval of additional materials or samples in the field.

A third objective is to provide those working in the laboratories with vital visual, spatial, tactile and experiential records and impressions of deposits and features as they are being excavated, which are greater than the sum of the unit sheets, photographs, and stratigraphic matrices. These experiences will enable those working on materials in the laboratories to be aware of changing field techniques, recording systems and stratigraphic complexities. This interaction will provide crucial aid in understanding the original context of samples and materials, and the potential meaning of results with regard to these points of reference. Such personal experiences will also help stimulate contextual thinking and empathetic interpretation of materials when they are being examined within the confines of the laboratory. Many of these experiences are partially recorded in personal notes, photographs and occasionally video footage taken during a range of visits to the site,

diaries where these are kept, priority tour and archive reports, and in the shifting sands of personal memories.

A fourth objective is to provide a range of different opportunities and media for integrative interdisciplinary discussion. This will encourage thinking and interpretations which transcend material boundaries and different scales of analysis. It will also furnish reflexivity and fluidity. New information can lead to new avenues of inquiry. Different material remains and sub-disciplines can furnish evidence that is not represented in other classes of materials, due either to nature of materials involved in different activities, or to taphonomic processes. These interdisciplinary discussions occur both during and after the field season, as considered in the second part of this chapter.

Practice

Barker (1979, 189) suggested interpretation in the field should be based on:

i. initiation of a dialectic by opposing any initial interpretation with the opposite view or views of its meaning (although 'alternative or multiple' may be more appropriate: current authors' opinion);

ii. lateral thinking;

iii. functional and practical common sense interpretations, whilst being sensitive to possibility of impractical situations (such as sacred or symbolic activities).

He did not go on to suggest specific ways in which such dialectic could be initiated or actively recorded in archaeological practice. In moving towards reflex-

Table 3.2. *Comparison of analyses conducted in the field laboratories at Çatalhöyük with those conducted in more specialized laboratories, and time spent in the field by each analytical team.*

Analyses conducted in field laboratories	Analysts in field	Analyses conducted in specialized laboratories
Preliminary archaeobotanical sorting	Full time	Full archaeobotanical identifications of seeds, wood
	Short visit	Dendrochronology
	Short visit	DNA charred plant remains
	Short visit	14C and AMS dating
Preliminary phytolith analyses and identification	Medium visit	Full phytolith analysis and identifications
Sorting of heavy residues from combined flotation and screening	Full time	
Archaeozoological	Full time	
	Short visit	DNA
	Not yet visited	Cementum analysis
	Not yet visited	Keratin analysis
	Not yet visited	Fish identification
Human remains	Full time	
	Short visit	Isotope
	Full time	Tooth microwear
Microstratigraphic analysis	Full time	Micromorphology
Microscopy of loose sediments in	Full time	Additional microscopy
different mounting media, and	Medium visit	Organic and inorganic analyses, including ICP-AES
staining techniques	Short visit	Phosphate
	Not yet visited	Organic residue analysis (GC/MS)
Micro-excavation	Medium visit	
Geological identifications	Short visit	Geological petrology
		Geochemical and mineralogical analyses
	Not yet visited	Organic residue analysis (GC/MS)
Palaeoecological analysis of	Full time	Pollen
sedimentary sequences and cores	Full time	Diatoms
(KOPAL)	Full time	Geochemical, sedimentological and mineralogical analyses
Conservation	Full time	
Microscopy of loose sediments in	Medium visit	Pigment
different mounting media, and	Medium visit	Geochemical and mineralogical analyses
staining	Medium visit	Micromorphology
	Not yet visited	Organic residue analysis (GC/MS)
Pottery and clay ball form	Full time	Petrology
and fabric groupings	Short visit	Petrology
	Short visit	Geochemical and mineralogical analyses
Obsidian typology	Full time	
	Short visit	XRF
	Short visit	ICP AES

ivity, dialectic elements are being recorded at Çatalhöyük both in the unit sheets (Farid *et al.* Chapter 2, this volume) and in multi-media recording (Tringham *et al.* Chapter 17, and Brill Chapter 19, this volume). This chapter considers some of the ways in which laboratory results are being interpreted and involved in a hermeneutic dialectic.

The title of this chapter refers to integrating 'archaeological science'. The practice and meaning of science generally, and in archaeology, is much debated (Wylie forthcoming). In this preliminary chapter we consider how we are trying to integrate research which predominantly involves analyses conducted in laboratories, whether in the field, or subsequently in more specialized institutions, with archaeological practice 'at the trowel's edge' during excavation. We are trying to open up and inter-relate the approaches and information from each of these analyses.

Before considering practice, we should also attempt to define who is involved in this laboratory-based research. In particular we would like to try to break down any dichotomy between terms such as 'field staff' and 'laboratory staff'. In practice all of our experiences and interests are inter-related and focused on richly networked data and interpretations of the past. Some team members are involved in both field and laboratory work. A considerable amount of the bulk processing of materials in the field laboratories involves the participation of a range of team members who are involved in excavation in the morning and early afternoon. Some of the students periodically help with recording of heavy residues from combined flotation, in collaboration with local women who sort these residues. Some of those who study pottery or artefactual remains at Çatalhöyük also work in the field excavations. Many of the members of the team participating predominantly in the excavations or the laboratories have, at other times in their careers, worked in these other locations. The characteristics and experiences of each individual are diverse, changing and context-specific, and create exciting interactions.

Table 3.2 illustrates the range of analyses which are currently conducted within field laboratories at the site, and those which are conducted in more specialized laboratories. It gives some indication of the current duration of visits to the sites by those involved in each analysis. Some of those who conduct laboratory analyses on materials from Çatalhöyük, have either never visited the site, or do so for only very brief periods of time. Those who visit the site less frequently or for shorter periods of time tend to be those involved in more complex laboratory procedures, a wider range of projects, or in more senior academic positions. The project does have plans to increase the range of analyses that can be conducted at the site. In particular, it aims to develop a well-equipped field laboratory and centre for training, in collaboration with the Middle East Technical University, Ankara, and the conservators. Table 3.3 illustrates some of the additional analyses that could be conducted within field laboratories.

The project is trying to make available as much information as possible to all participants, including those who are not able to visit the site for the entire field season. A range of media through which those participating in laboratory science are able to convey and access information and ideas, and engage in discussions with each other and with other aspects of the project is listed in Table 3.4. Each of these occasions varies, involving different subjects and aims of discussion, different voices and different physical situations and environments. These occasions include instances both during and after field excavation, throughout the year.

Many of these occasions are very structured, focusing on specific issues in order to make most efficient use of time that is otherwise spent in the field on excavation or recording of materials in the field laboratories. Some of the more innovative and less inhibited discussions probably arise during more informal discussions between co-workers within laboratories or on site, although both serious and more imaginative ideas are not restricted to these less formal forums. Stevanovic explores ways in which these less formal ideas can be recorded (see Chapter 20, this volume).

Table 3.3. *Proposed additional analyses to be conducted within field laboratories.*

Field equipment needed	Materials analyzed
High-powered optical polarizing microscope and thin-section preparation facilities	Geological samples Pottery sherds Clay ball fragments Sediments
Photospectrometer for colorimetric analysis of phosphate and other specific compounds	Sediments and organic remains
Soxlet extractor for extracting organic residues and a thin layer chromatography tank and plates for assessment of residues	Sediments and organic remains
pH meter, with an ion specific electrode	Sediments
Hydrometer and graduated cylinders for particle size analysis	Sediments
Resistivity meter	Sediments and salts

Table 3.4. *Media through which those participating in laboratory science are able to convey and access information and ideas and integrate with other aspects of the project.*

Discussion media	Location	Frequency	Discussion group	Focus of analysis
Structured				
Priority tours	Excavation area	Every 2–3 days	Area excavation team Member(s) from most field laboratory teams	1) Excavation units and contexts currently in progress 2) Sampling strategies 3) Results from field laboratory analyses
Specific visits	Excavation area	Random	Area excavation team Specific members from one or more excavation teams	Immediate consultation on: 1) treatment of specific materials such as human or animal bones, concentrations of plant remains, obsidian hoards, unusual deposits, conservation issues 2) sampling or positioning of sections and baulks
Space tours	Excavation area or seminar room	Weekly	Most of the excavation and field laboratory team members	Range of issues larger than individual units of excavation or material remains, e.g. types of spaces, sets of activities, theoretical concepts
Laboratory tours	Field laboratories	Every 2 weeks	Small groups of excavation and field team members	Specific material remains
Evening seminars	Seminar room	Every 1–2 days	1) Some excavation and field team members and students 2) Specific discussion groups	1) Teaching of excavation and laboratory analyses 2) Wide range of specific subject which often integrate analyses of different material remains, e.g. palaeoecology group, ethno-archaeology group, forthcoming publications 3) Theoretical and practical issues
Creative story-telling session	Seminar room	Only held once	Most of the excavation and field laboratory team members	Forum for more creative thinking
Discussion meetings	Cambridge	6–12 months	Many excavation and field laboratory team members	1) Excavation and laboratory reports 2) Forthcoming plans and publications
E-mail discussion groups		Throughout the year	Many excavation and field laboratory team members	
Computerized information: reports, data base		Throughout the year	Many excavation and field laboratory team members	
Non-structured				
Daily interactions	Within and between field laboratories	Daily	Field laboratory members, most frequently within same laboratory	Specific material remains or wide-ranging issues
	Anywhere			

The range of voices participating in any discussion and their empowerment in construction of knowledge must always be considered (Bartu Chapter 8, this volume; Hodder 1997; Longino 1987; Wylie 1996). The ideas and interpretations being generated in all of these occasions are fluid and changing in a hermeneutic way, which is aimed at drawing us closer to richer reconstructions of the past. These changes involve the introduction of additional scientific and contextual information and associations that shift analytical perspectives and theoretical frameworks as the project proceeds.

Practical problems and considerations in integrating archaeological science

A number of practical problems and considerations have been encountered in integrating laboratory science. In addressing these we are trying to develop critical awareness of the reasons for sampling and the nature of the questions addressed, comparability of materials and sample size and scales of analysis, time-lags in preparation and analyses of materials, and presentation and accessibility or transparency of results to other readers and audiences.

Sampling
At all stages from excavation through to laboratory analyses we are aware that we are continually sub-sampling the site and its archaeological components. Variation in occurrence and preservation of specific archaeological materials in different realms of human behaviour and micro-environments, although axiomatic, significantly increase the complexity of sampling procedures and integration of results from different analyses. There cannot be a standard uniform sampling procedure for each context. In practice the range of samples collected tends to vary according questions relating to the materials present, and the perceived interpretation and importance of the context, whether a floor or fill for example (Hodder 1997).

Sampling strategies at Çatalhöyük are being designed to enable study of depositional components at a range of scales of analytical focus, and in different sample types and sizes (Table 3.1; Matthews 1998). Such diverse sampling schemes are designed through group discussion both on the site during the priority tours as well as at specific meetings to discuss sampling and recording procedures. The combined different strategies are designed to be flexible enough so that they can meet the needs of the investigators as well as provide systematic information for the future. Although there is some targeting of sampling for current research projects, we drew up lists of analyses and sampling procedures to include materials not yet studied by current members of the team, and archive samples of deposits (see Appendix 2.1).

Issues surrounding sampling have been em-

phasized, in particular, in discussions relating to application of statistics in archaeology (Shennan 1988, 298). Despite the shifts in fashion within sampling and what it can reveal about the past, any archaeologist must be concerned with the partial universes they are collecting (Clarke 1973). One of the aims in deciding which sampling strategy to employ is to try and establish what size, intervals or levels of information from a part of a universe can be applied to make inferences about the whole universe. What part of this universe we collect will colour our interpretations. Our aim is to have a sample that represents the population that we are studying. Many statisticians have written on this subject. The main goal of a sampling strategy that statisticians put forward is to gather a probabilistic sample, in other words to choose a strategy that will provide a representative sample of the whole (Blalock 1972). This can be done in many different ways and can be tailored to the research issues at hand. We strive for representative strategies by emphasizing systematic sampling across different contexts and time periods for example, but also use random, stratified and judgemental sampling strategies where appropriate.

Adding greatly to this basic but distancing probabilistic approach is the implementation of exploratory data analysis (EDA) (Tukey 1977; Tufte 1983). Such creative presentations of data allow for effective exploration of complex data. One aspect of systematic sampling that has been incorporated at all levels of sampling at Çatalhöyük is a desire to have concurrent multiple levels of sampling. This means that there is a running systematic collection of all major artefact types, in addition to more intensive collections in certain designated settings. These additions are determined by any one involved in the work, the field staff (excavators), the director, or the laboratory staff. Such multiple sampling strategies have been helpful in previous projects (Lennstrom & Hastorf 1992). The systematic and detailed sampling strategies together help towards providing representative results. In addition, applying EDA to the material that has been analyzed allows for this complex set of data to be seen more closely. The results are evident in current analyses of Buildings 1, 3, and 5, and in the contexts discussed in Chapter 5.

The flow of questions and approaches employed in sampling strategies at Çatalhöyük can be summarized as follows. From all units of excavation are collected bulk 'whole-earth' samples for archive storage and matrix flotation water with a mesh size of 0.5 mm (Popper & Hastorf 1988). Remaining deposits that are not sampled further are dry screened with a mesh size of 7 mm.

The most intensive sampling strategies are generally applied to questions relating to behaviour in contexts which are considered to be primary activity areas, notably on floors in all buildings, and on roof segments found in Building 3. From these contexts, in addition, three spot bulk samples are routinely collected at 50–100 cm intervals, to detect traces of organic and inorganic remains and phytoliths. Microstratigraphy and micromorphology of floor sequences are studied and sampled in strategic baulks or plinths set at 1–2 metre intervals, which are located according to both a grid-system and the topography of features within spaces.

Few midden or fill contexts appear to include possible activity surfaces. These are generally only sampled more intensively when specific research questions arise or specific materials or deposits are encountered. One example of such changes in strategy was the detection of a possible activity surface or horizon in an open area, Space 115, that was sampled at 50 cm intervals for inductively coupled plasma-atomic emission spectroscopy (ICP-AES) elemental analysis, for comparison to surfaces within buildings, following approaches at other sites (Middleton & Price 1996). Phytoliths and areas of organic staining associated with this possible surface were also sampled more intensively, where these specific materials were particularly evident and well-preserved. Many midden sequences, however, include fine lenses of deposits rich in bioarchaeological and artefactual remains from single depositional events and are potentially rich sources of information on diverse sets of activities and meanings of discard. Large blocks from some midden contexts will be sampled for micro-excavation and sub-sampling in the near future.

Additional samples from all contexts are also collected in response to questions relating to:

1. the origin or deposition of particular units;
2. comparisons with other deposit and context types, such as variation in types of room fill;
3. representative ranges of deposit and context types, for study of materials by specific analyses, although each analysis may in addition tend to focus on particular deposit and context types;
4. specific material types, both in order to investigate materials of unknown origin, and to analyze materials which relate to a wide range of specific investigations and analyses (listed in Table 3.3) such as:
   a) DNA of human, faunal and botanical remains;
   b) isotope analysis of human, botanical and faunal remains to study diet;
   c) a range of dating techniques including dendrochronology, AMS and optically stimulated luminescence dating;
   d) organic residue analysis of areas of orange staining, possibly relating to coprolites (Evershed & Bethell 1996) or food (Evershed *et al.* 1992);
   e) pottery thin-section analysis of source materials and technology, organic residue analysis of vessel use.

Once again, analyses of specific material types will be particularly intensive in contexts of perceived importance that may vary according to different participants in the project. In such contexts, particularly floors, it may be noted that excavation rates may also be a little slower.

In practice, excavators have tended to collect many of the samples within the excavation areas as:

a) some laboratory staff are only at the excavation for 1 day to 4 weeks;
b) it proved easier for the excavators to keep track of sample number allocation and 3-D recording if they collected the samples themselves;
c) space within the trenches could be crowded.

Exceptions to this include block samples for micro-excavation and micromorphology, and those for ICP-AES analyses.

When a wide range of analyses are potentially applicable, each with different sample collection procedures, the excavator is presented with a difficult and complex range of choices in addition to those made during excavation (Farid *et al.* Chapter 2, this volume). To try and aid these decisions, we compiled two sampling strategy advice sheets (see Appendix 2.1). One sheet lists types of analysis and sample collection methods in alphabetic order, drawing upon instructions from each laboratory team. This sheet currently includes forty different sample collection procedures. The other sheet lists a range of key contexts and questions likely to be encountered during excavation, such as room fill, floors, fire-installations, and plant-rich deposits. This sheet advises which sample types might be most relevant to questions relating to each context or material type, and provides information on collection procedures in an adjacent column. Priority tours and specific calls to the site provide frequent occasions for discussions on sampling as excavation contexts change.

Material and analytical comparability
One of the principal considerations in integrating results from diverse analyses is sample type, size and scale of analytical focus (Canti 1995). The smaller

the sample size, the greater the potential bias in characterizing only some aspects of heterogeneous archaeological deposits, but conversely, the greater the potential accuracy if individual material remains are being spot-sampled for specific analyses. Many of the lenses on floors and in middens at Çatalhöyük are often less than 5 mm thick and may be thinner than 0.5–0.2 mm thick. It may be difficult in many bulk organic and inorganic analyses to be certain what materials and components are present in the sub-sample analyzed. Integration of micro-excavation and controlled sampling or small blocks within the laboratory, however, is aiding precision sampling. Micromorphology of thin sections and scanning electron microscopy coupled with electron microprobe analysis of resin-impregnated blocks is also contributing to micro-contextual analysis of the diverse sediments and bioarchaeological and artefactual components in archaeological deposits. These techniques are enabling analysis of a wide range of their individual visible and elemental characteristics, depositional associations and post-depositional alterations (Courty *et al.* 1989; Jenkins 1994; Matthews *et al.* 1996; 1997).

As discussed earlier, components that are both available and selected for analysis vary according to material, deposit and context type, and sample size and degree of intactness or disaggregation (Table 3.1). They also vary according to complex taphonomic processes and their visibility and invisibility in different types and scales of analysis, and field and laboratory extraction procedures (Hastorf forthcoming; Carbone & Keel 1985; Evershed *et al.* 1992).

Diverse sediments, bioarchaeological and artefactual remains may be analyzed and recorded as:
a) visible sediments, aggregates, bioarchaeological and artefactual remains in depositional sequences during excavation and in micro-excavation and micromorphological samples at increasing degrees of magnification. Bisdom and Barham have examined the different ranges of materials which are detectable in different light wave frequencies, and even ultrasound (Bisdom *et al.* 1990; Barham 1995);
b) visible bone, plant, shell and artefactual components in floated and screened residues;
c) isotopic, elemental and biomolecular components detectable in extracted solutions, during organic and inorganic analyses, such as those listed in Table 3.5.

It is important to re-emphasize that the nature, visibility and presence of materials in these different stages of investigations varies. Some materials and characteristics are only detectable in the field. These include materials which do not survive screening, including mud-brick and plaster aggregates, and information on their nature, diversity, abundance, size, and form. These components are essential to understanding the origin of deposits and thereby the contexts of all other remains. Similarly the orientation and distribution of artefacts, bioarchaeological remains and constituent aggregates can only be recorded in the field. Many of these components and depositional characteristics are being recorded during excavation at Çatalhöyük, using visual descriptions adapting those employed in soil science (Barham & Macphail 1995; Hodgson 1976; Matthews 1992; 1995), which need not involve three-dimensional recording of each item and its angle of dip. Many of these features are also recorded by video, photographic and audio records.

Analyses also vary in their ability to answer particular questions, and the degree to which they can furnish non-specific and specific identifications of archaeological remains (Canti 1995; Gratton 1997). Some of those analyses that furnish less specific identifications particularly in complex occupation sequences include phosphate, total CHN (carbon, hydrogen and nitrogen) elemental analysis, and particle size analysis. Those analyses with greater potential for furnishing specific identifications include: organic residue analysis using combined gas chromatography / mass spectrometry (GC/MS) which can detect diagnostic biomolecular coumpounds, micromorphology as discussed above, and palaeoethnobotanical, phytolith and faunal analyses. Each analysis, however, has inherent problems in identification, some of which relate to available reference materials and taphonomic processes (Popper & Hastorf 1988; Bethell & Maté 1989; Evershed *et al.* 1992; Rosen 1992; Canti 1995). These different degrees of specificity and resolution, however, can be employed in strategic sampling strategies, with reservation. Total CHN analysis, for example, can be used as a preliminary, rapid and comparatively inexpensive search to test for deposits with appreciable quantities of organic carbon, to aid selection of deposits for organic residue analysis using GC/MS which is much more complex and time consuming. It should be borne in mind, however, that some deposits with low CHN content may include sparse but well-preserved lipids or other diagnostic organic residues. Such residues may be potentially informative in relation to very specific questions, such as presence of resins in plasters or paints, or incense in ritual contexts, for example.

Despite potential pitfalls, richly networked data

are emerging to aid understanding and re-examination of individual data sets in a continually evolving hermeneutic (see also Martin *et al.* Chapter 5, this volume). Current results from phosphate analyses show consistent variations in character of different deposit and context types in both the North and South areas of the site. These variations correspond generally with micromorphology and quantitative analysis of screened remains (Jenkins, in Matthews *et al.* 1997). Low phosphate readings correspond with natural sediments, mud-bricks made from alluvial materials, and clean plastered areas, at <200–1000 parts per million. Moderate levels of phosphate correspond with areas around hearths and ovens, at 5000 ppm. The highest phosphate readings occur in middens and a potential animal stable/pen area rich in herbivore dung, at 10,000–12,000 ppm. Some of the exciting potentials in integrating archaeological science in multi-scalar research programmes have been highlighted by Renfrew (1992) and Pollard (1992).

Analytical procedures and time-lags in presentation of results
Whilst priority tours and specific calls to those working in the laboratories have been able to bring diverse information from laboratory sciences to the trowel's edge during excavation, there is still a range of different time-lags between material or sample excavation and analysis and presentation of results. Whilst larger units may still be in the process of being excavated two days after selection of contexts for Priority analysis, some units will have been completely excavated. It is not always possible to view the deposits at the time of presentation of results at the edge of the excavation trench, nor to alter any sampling strategies if necessary. It is difficult to see how this time-lag can be much improved, however, as many materials have to be cleaned or processed as well as analyzed and recorded. The image of the context at least, will be fresh and results can be evaluated in excavating other deposits of the same or similar characteristics or contexts. Field laboratory staff present during the excavation season, moreover, are available for immediate consultation at any time with regard to materials still in the ground.

Whilst it is hoped that an increasing range of analyses can be conducted within field laboratories, a range of analyses require expensive, sensitive and technical equipment, or hazardous materials, which can only be located and maintained in specialized laboratories. This category includes equipment for scanning electron microscopy and electron microprobe elemental analysis, organic residue analysis by gas chromatography/mass spectrometry, induc-tively coupled plasma emission spectroscopy; isotope analysis, and impregnation and preparation facilities for large micromorphological thin sections. Many of these analyses also involve prolonged sample preparation times, which extend beyond the duration of field seasons. Additional problems encountered in specialized laboratories include availability of funds and personnel to conduct the analyses, technical problems and funds for maintenance or replacement of equipment, scheduling in laboratories which serve a wide range of projects, and development of procedures which are both applicable and sensitive to the specific nature materials from each site.

Recording and presentation of results
Data base categories, statistics, and representations of data visually, are all selected by each analyst. These decisions affect the results that are discussed and interpreted. They will also influence the degree to which different analyses can be fully integrated, especially when examining multiple scales of resolution and data sets at the same time. Multivariate statistics and a range of graphics can allow for more flexibility in presentation of data and interpretations and hence for the viewer to integrate diverse and complex material (Conolly Chapter 4, this volume; Martin *et al.* Chapter 5, this volume; Tufte 1983; Tukey 1977; Kvamme 1992).

We are designing a range of ways for results and interpretations to be transparent, comprehensible and accessible to non-specialists outside the sub-discipline, and the public (Shane Chapter 16, this volume). Visual representations of scientific traces of activities and their spatial and socio-cultural contexts are being more fully and systematically explored.

At the time of writing, prior to preparation of the first final excavation report, integration of laboratory results has most frequently occurred at the trowel's edge in priority tours during the excavation season. The archive reports written at the end of each field season that present interim results from each analytical team, however, are often still divided into sections relating to each sub-discipline, largely owing to exigencies of time. In practice, it is the excavators' archive reports that tend to draw more heavily on priority tour discussions and integrative multidisciplinary results. The chapter by Martin *et al.* (Chapter 5, this volume), is one of the first attempts at intensive correlation of integrative multidisciplinary data, and raises specific points relevant to considerations in this chapter. A range of multidisciplinary analysis were applied during study of surface materials at Çatalhöyük (Hodder 1996).

Practical benefits of integrating archaeological science

Palaeoecological research

Palaeoecological and regional archaeological survey projects in the Konya Plain run concurrently with the excavation season at Çatalhöyük (Roberts *et al.* 1996; Merrick *et al.* 1997; Baird 1996). Palaeoecological coring and trenching has been conducted in close collaboration with those involved in both regional survey and excavations in order to study spatial and temporal variations in landscape and environs of Çatalhöyük and the Konya Plain (Roberts *et al.* 1997). Current palaeoecological research suggests that the landscape around the Neolithic settlement was wetter than at present. Backswamp deposits have been identified both to the south and north of the site.

Sets of diverse resources and materials that are likely to have occurred in more mountainous regions surrounding the Konya Plain, have been identified on the basis of both palaeoecological information and laboratory data. These resources include red deer, wild boar, hackberry fruits, juniper wood, red ochre and obsidian. Current archaeological and ethnoarchaeological research is examining potential timing, duration, season and sociocultural context and meanings and associated with these resources (Matthews *et al.* Chapter 15, this volume).

These integrative approaches are enabling study of the nature and transmutations of diverse materials and their meanings in different contexts within landscapes, settlements, buildings, room-fills and middens, for example. Researchers studying pottery, mud-bricks and plasters were able to sample and examine buried Neolithic clays and sands, uncovered four metres below the plain in the palaeoecological trench which was dug at the northern edge of the mound in 1997. Excavation of buried Neolithic land surfaces in 1999 is providing an exciting opportunity for collaboration between palaeoecological and archaeological researchers. This project will focus on investigation of the nature and phenomenology of early landscape and agriculture, and land, vegetation, animal and water management.

Microscopic analyses

A range of microscopic analyses is providing new information in the field. Stereo-binocular microscopy at low magnifications of up to ×80, using a Leica MZ8, is enabling field study of charred plant remains, conservation materials, human and animal bone identifications and taphonomy, and geological specimens, as well as the materials, technology and trace-wear of artefacts including figurines, stamp seals, obsidian and ground stone. Data and interpretations from analyses of charred plant remains, in particular, are fundamental elements in the priority tour information discussed throughout the season. Plant densities and frequencies have led to re-assessments of the concept of clean and dirty areas within rooms which has been evolving on the Priority Tours, such as in Space 150–151 or in Building 5. Feedback on wild plants versus domesticates, and on the presence of specific taxa such as fruits and nuts in certain corners of Building 3 has helped enrich the ongoing interpretation of those areas especially as these co-occur with large deposits of bone and hence are hypothesized to be associated with feasting.

Loan of an optical polarizing microscope from the University of Cambridge is enabling study of phytoliths, sediments, and micromorphological thin sections in the field, at magnifications from ×40–400. A range of exciting results from phytolith analyses is emerging. Many of the cereal phytoliths examined are large, multicell forms which suggest that cereals were cultivated in the wet marshlands or periodically inundated alluvium around the site and near the marshes rather than in better-drained fields such as those which may have been present in more elevated areas (Rosen & Weiner 1994; Rosen 1999). Large reed grasses such as the common reed (*Phragmites* sp.), have been identified, and may have been used in the construction of building roofs. Cyperaceae stalks, the local edible reed that grows in the marches, were used for matting that had been placed on at least one floor. Other phytolith identifications include sedges that line storage bins in Building 5, and traces of barley and wheat husks in front of the access hole to one of these bins suggesting it was used to store cereals.

Microscopic analyses of spot bulk samples of sediments and deposits in different mounting media and with staining techniques is enabling identification of a range of organic and inorganic remains, including starches, calcareous spherulites from dung (Matthews *et al.* 1996; Canti 1999), and distinction between yellowish organic deposits and yellow ochres. Micromorphological thin sections from previous seasons are also being re-studied in the field laboratory, using an optical polarizing microscope. This is enabling direct comparison with extant and new deposits during excavation, and is furnishing direct links between field and laboratory characterizations. It is hoped that once thin section facilities are acquired in the field laboratory, small samples of pottery, clay balls, stones and resin-impregnated deposits and plasters may be submitted for microscopic analysis in the field.

Integrative archaeological science during field excavation
A range of specific identifications of materials in the field by those working in laboratories during excavation has added considerably to interpretations of the significance of these materials and the nature of their depositional and socio-cultural or micro-environmental contexts.

On close inspection a thin orange lens in room fill in Space 116 in the South Area proved to consist of dense micro-fauna and phytoliths. These were identified *in situ* in the ground as remains of owl pellets, by Dr Peter Andrews of the Natural History Museum. On the basis of this identification, these remains were sampled at 10 cm intervals in order to record density and distribution of microfauna. In subsequent microscopic analysis in the laboratory he was able to identify the pellets as those from barn owls (*Tyto alba*). The distribution of the bones and the way the concentrations decrease away from the wall, as well as the fact that some bones are present on the other side of the wall in Space 117, all suggested that the owl was roosting on the top of the wall with access to both spaces as well as the outside. Two inferences arise from this: one is that the building must have been unoccupied at this time, for owls do not usually cohabit with humans to the extent of roosting in an occupied building; and secondly, that the wall separating Spaces 116/117 must still have been standing to its full height and part of the roof must still have been present, for barn owls do not roost in the open and require perches above the reach of predators with cover for concealment. The conclusion is that during the time of accumulation of the rodent bones, therefore, Spaces 116 and 117 were unoccupied, but the walls and roof of the building were still largely intact. If these remains had not been detected and identified in the field they would have just been found as disaggregated micro-faunal bones within the screened heavy residues, and we would not have been certain of the context of their deposition, nor the architectural and socio-cultural implications. It enabled a refinement in the field of the nature and rate of abandonment and infilling of this building, which was surrounded by elaborate buildings in the southern excavation area.

Animal bone is abundant in a wide range of contexts at Çatalhöyük, within buildings on floors and in fills, and in middens. The faunal analysts are able to obtain measurements of bones, particularly those that are fragile, in the ground, which are critical to a range of identifications and interpretations relating to age, sex and domestication, and to identify which bones should be collected for DNA analysis and sampled accordingly. Their observations and discussions of the distribution of bones in the field have greatly informed subsequent interpretations of this and other data types and contexts (Russel & Martin 1998).

Understanding the nature of the accumulation of human skeletal material has been greatly enhanced by close collaboration between field and laboratory staff during excavation, recording and laboratory analysis in the field. This is taking our knowledge of burial practices so much further than has been possible in the past. Excavation techniques identify grave cuts and associated groups of bones, be they skeletons or clusters of bones. In the field laboratory the number of individuals represented can be evaluated in collaboration with the excavator, and the nature of the accumulation interpreted. Thus in Building 1 in the North area where more than 70 individuals were buried, it is possible to distinguish between single primary inhumations of an intact articulated body (e.g. 1378 in the east platform); double burials (e.g. 1955 and 2169, a male and a female, in the northwest platform); inhumations that were disturbed by later reopening of the grave; and secondary burials. Superposition of skeleton plans from several of the multiple burials using a standard grid-system has revealed that there was knowledge of exactly where previous burials lay and there was a minimum of disturbance by later burials.

Bodies were generally tightly flexed before burial. Surviving phytoliths noted during excavation suggest that in at least some cases this was achieved by binding with cord made of plant fibre, such as for 1378. In other cases there are traces of a braided basket in which the body was placed. The lay-out of the torso and limbs of infant burials suggests that some young children were placed in a cloth before inhumation.

The significance of the only burial yet discovered outside buildings in Space 115 in the South area, in a midden/open area (Mellaart's Level VIII) was further emphasized whilst the bones were still in the ground during excavation. The bones were identified as those of a young individual with a chronic bone pathology which left his bones swollen, soft and porous, who had been placed in a shallow grave in the middle of the area. The condition would have been evident in life, although the disease has yet to be diagnosed. The special treatment of this unusual case must be significant in terms of the social attitudes to disease in the community.

Close collaboration during excavation of a wide range of other material remains such as obsidian hoards, pottery, clay balls and ground stone is ena-

Table 3.5. *List of co-ordinating institutions contributing to laboratory analyses of materials from Çatalhöyük. Participants' names are listed at the beginning of each chatper in the annual Çatalhöyük Archive Reports.*

Co-ordinating institutions	Sample type	Analysis
University of California, Berkeley	Charred plant remains	Archaeobotany
Çukurova University		Archaeobotany
Middle East Technical University, Ankara		DNA charred plant remains
University of Cambridge, University College London	Wood	Anatomy
Cornell University	Charred wood	Dendrochronology
Cornell University	Bone tools	Identification and use
University College London	Phytoliths	Anatomical identification
University of Cambridge, University College London Cornell University	Animal bone and teeth fragments	DNA, cementum analysis, keratin analysis, fish identification
University of Cambridge, The Natural History Museum, University of Oxford	Human bone and teeth fragments	Isotope, microwear
Istanbul University	Burnt plaster	Archaeomagnetic
Middle East Technical University, Ankara	Mudbricks and mortars	Optically stimulated luminescence dating
Middle East Technical University, Ankara	Sediments	Phosphate, geochemical and mineralogical analyses
Middle East Technical University, Ankara	Stone	Geological, including petrology
University of Cambridge	Sediment	Micromorphology
University of Cambridge, University of Bristol	Sediment	Organic residue
University of Wisconsin	Sediment	ICP AES
University of Philadelphia	Sediment	Palaeoecological analysis, including pollen, diatoms
University of Philadelphia	Sediment	Conservation
University of Cambridge, University of Bristol	Non-museum worthy fragments: clay ball, pottery, stone	Organic residue
University of California, Berkeley Middle East Technical University, Ankara	Non-museum worthy fragments of: clay ball, pottery	Petrography and mineralogy
University of Liverpool	Non-museum worthy fragments of pottery (Survey project)	Petrography and mineralogy
University of Cambridge	Non-museum worthy fragments of pottery	Petrography and mineralogy
University of Cambridge Middle East Technical University, Ankara CNRS	Non-museum worthy fragments of obsidian	XRF, ICP-AES

bling both maximum feedback of information to the excavators, as well as vital information on context for those studying specific materials in the laboratories. Close collaboration is also vital to all of those studying deposits, particularly microstratigraphy and micromorphology, where the location of baulks and blocks for analysis is critical to recording and sampling significant temporal and spatial variations in occupational sequences. All of this close collabora-

tion and coordinated sample collection is greatly appreciated by those working in the laboratories.

Integrative discussions during Priority tours are diverse and documented in the archive reports. The origin of mud-bricks in Building 1 walls was characterized on the basis of sparseness of charred remains and other artefactual remains, and presence of water-rolled fish bones, unworked water-laid aggregates detectable by close examination in the field, and in later thin-sections. The diverse origin of a range of room fills was characterized by co-occurrence of burnt and unburnt bones, heterogeneous plaster, mud-brick and burnt aggregates, and well- and poorly-preserved charred plant remains of diverse species. Remains of possible feasting in a massive dumped unit in Building 3 were identified on the basis of animal parts and remains of charred nuts. Discussions ranged as to whether some of the lenses of gently sloping deposits in Space 115 (units 3115, 3181, 3314) represented remains of *in situ* activities in an open area or lenses of dumped remains, and will be considered in further analyses of deposits and components which include large fragments of reed phytoliths, traces of burning and obsidian micro-debitage.

Discussions during Space tours, which are designed to transcend specific material and unit or context boundaries, have been wide-ranging and included integrative discussions and diverse information on partitioning of spaces within buildings, abandonment of buildings, indications of feasting, locations of activities on and off site, and production (Conolly Chapter 4, this volume).

Additional results from analyses conducted in specialized laboratories are presented in specific reports when they appear throughout the year and are made available electronically and in the annual archive reports, others are still pending.

Conclusions

This chapter has largely considered how the team tries to integrate field and laboratory analyses during the excavation season. It has outlined the media and timing through which interactions take place, and through which information and interpretations are made available during other times of the year. More specific examples of integration of different data sets can be examined in Chapter 5. A greater sense of integration of the wide range of laboratory results with information from excavation and other analyses can only be evaluated during and after preparation of the first final report during the study season of the year 2000. In the meantime, a range of sample types, including micro-excavation blocks and archive samples, have been selected for examination at a range of different scales of analysis to try and maximize opportunities for integrating information on bioarchaeological, artefactual and depositional remains both 'at the trowel's edge' as well as in field and specialized laboratories. There are theoretical aspects to integrating archaeological science which

are not embraced in this chapter. As we integrate information from multi-disciplinary analyses, we are exploring more fully substantive and theoretical issues relating to complexity of multiple data and approaches, which are currently a focus of discussion in the natural and social sciences (Wylie forthcoming).

References

Baird, D., 1996. The Konya plain survey: aims and methods, in Hodder (ed.), 41–6.

Barham, A.J., 1995. Methodological approaches to archaeological context recording: X-radiography as an example of a supportive recording, assessment and interpretative technique, in Barham & Macphail (eds.), 145–82.

Barham, T. & R.I. Macphail (eds.), 1995. *Archaeological Sediments and Soils: Analysis, Interpretation and Management*. London: Archetype Books.

Barker, P., 1979. *Techniques of Archaeological Excavation*. London: Anchor Press.

Bethell, P. & I. Maté, 1989. The use of soil phosphate analysis in archaeology: a critique, in *Scientific Analysis in Archaeology*, vol. 5, ed. J. Henderson. Los Angeles (CA): UCLA Institute of Archaeology Publications and Oxford University Committee for Archaeology, 1–29.

Bisdom, E.B.A., D. Tessier & J.F.T. Schoute, 1990. Micromorphological techniques in research and teaching (submicroscopy), in *Soil Micromorphology*, ed. L.A. Douglas. Amsterdam: Elsevier, 581–603.

Blalock, H.M., 1972. *Social Statistics*. New York (NY): McGraw-Hill.

Canti, M., 1995. A mixed approach to geoarchaeological analysis, in Barham & Macphail (eds.), 183–90.

Canti, M., 1999. The production and preservation of faecal spherulites: animals, environment and taphonomy. *Journal of Archaeological Science* 26, 251–8.

Carbone, V.A. & B.C. Keel, 1985. Preservation of plant and animal remains, in *The Analysis of Prehistoric Diets*, eds. R.J. Gilbert & J.H. Mielke. London: Academic Press, 2–19.

Clarke, D.L., 1973. Archaeology: the loss of innocence. *Antiquity* 47, 6–18.

Courty, M.A., P. Goldberg & R.I. Macphail, 1989. *Soils and Micromorphology in Archaeology*. Cambridge: Cambridge University Press.

Evershed, R.P. & P.H. Bethell, 1996. Application of multi-molecular marker techniques to the identification of fecal material in archaeological soils and sediments, in *Archaeological Chemistry: Organic, Inorganic and Biochemical Analysis*, ed. M.V. Orna. Washington (DC): American Chemistry Society.

Evershed, R.P., C. Heron, S. Charters & L.J. Goad, 1992. The survival of food residues: new methods of analysis, interpretation and application, in Pollard (ed.), 149–59.

Gratton, J., 1997. High definition archaeology: ideas and

evaluation. *World Archaeology* 29(2), 151–71.

Hastorf, C.A., forthcoming. Making the invisible visible: the hidden jewels of archaeology, in *Fleeting Identities: Perishable Material Culture in Archaeological Research*, ed. P.M. Drooker. (Center for Archaeological Investigations Occasional Paper 28.) Carbondale (IL): Center for Archaeological Investigations.

Hodder, I. (ed.), 1996. *On the Surface: Çatalhöyük 1993–95.* (McDonald Institute Monographs.) Cambridge: McDonald Institute for Archaeological Research and British Institute of Archaeology at Ankara.

Hodder, I., 1997. 'Always momentary, fluid and flexible': towards a reflexive excavation methodology. *Antiquity* 71, 691–700.

Hodgson, J.M., 1976. *Soil Survey Field Handbook.* Harpenden: Soil Survey.

Jenkins, D.A., 1994. Interpretation of interglacial cave sediments from a hominid site in North Wales: translocation of Ca-Fe phosphates, in *Soil Micromorphology: Studies in Management and Genesis*, eds. A.J. Ringrose-Voase & G.S. Humphreys. Amsterdam: Elsevier, 293–305.

Kvamme, K., 1992. Spatial statistics and GIS: an integrated approach, in *Computing the Past: Computer Applications and Quantitiative Methods in Archaeology*, eds. J. Andresen, T. Madsen & I. Scollar. Aarhus: Aarhus University Press, 91–102.

Lennstrom, H.A. & C.A. Hastorf, 1992. Testing old wives' tales in paleoethnobotany: a comparison of bulk and scatter samples from Pancán Peru. *Journal of Archaeological Science* 19, 205–29.

Longino, H., 1987. Can there be a feminist science? *Hypatia* 2(3), 51–64.

Matthews, W., 1992. The Micromorphology of Occupational Sequences and the Use of Space in a Sumerian city. Unpublished PhD thesis. Department of Archaeology, University of Cambridge.

Matthews, W., 1995. Micromorphological characterisation of occupation deposits and microstratigraphic sequences at Abu Salabikh, Southern Iraq, in Barham & Macphail (eds.), 41–76.

Matthews, W., 1998. Report on sampling strategies, microstratigraphy and micromorphology of depositional sequences, in *Çatalhöyük Archive Report 1988*, ed. I. Hodder. http://catal.arch.cam.ac.uk/catal/Archive-rep98/matthews98.html.

Matthews, W. & S. Farid, 1996. Exploring the 1960s surface: the stratigraphy of Çatalhöyük, in Hodder (ed.), 271–300.

Matthews, W., C.A.I. French, T. Lawrence & D. Cutler, 1996. Multiple surfaces: the micromorphology, in Hodder (ed.), 301–42.

Matthews, W., C.A.I. French, T. Lawrence, D.F. Cutler & M.K. Jones, 1997. Microstratigraphic traces of site formation processes and human activities: high definition archaeology. *World Archaeology* 29(2), 281–308.

Merrick, J., P. Boyer & N. Roberts, 1997. Archive report on work by the KOPAL team 1997. *Çatalhöyük 1997 Archive Report.* http://catal.arch.cam.ac.uk/catal/Archive_rep97/roberts97.html.

Middleton, W.D. & D.T. Price, 1996. Identification of activity areas by multi-element characterization of sediments from modern and archaeological house floors using inductively coupled plasma-atomic emission spectroscopy. *Journal of Archaeological Science* 23, 637–87.

Pollard, M.A. (ed.), 1992. *New Developments in Archaeological Science.* Oxford: Oxford University Press.

Popper, V. & C.A. Hastorf, 1988. Introduction, in *Current Paleoethnobotany: Analytical Methods and Cultural Interpretation of Archaeological Plant Remains*, eds. C. Hastorf & V. Popper. Chicago (IL): University of Chicago Press, 1–16.

Renfrew, C.A., 1992. Meeting summary: the identity and future of archaeological science, in Pollard (ed.), 285–94.

Roberts, N., P. Boyer & R. Parish, 1996. Preliminary results of geoarchaeological investigations at Çatalhöyük, in Hodder (ed.), 19–41.

Roberts, N. *et al.*, 1997. Archive report on work by the KOPAL team 1997, in *Çatalhöyük 1997 Archive Report.* http://catal.arch.cam.ac.uk/catal/Archive-rep97/kopal97.html.

Rosen, A.M., 1992. Preliminary identification of silica skeletons from Near Eastern archaeological sites: an anatomical approach, in *Phytolith Systematics: Emerging Issues*, eds. G. Rapp & S.C. Mulholland. New York (NY): Plenum Press, 129–47.

Rosen, A.M., 1999. Phytoliths as indicators of prehistoric irrigation farming, in *Prehistory of Agriculture: New Experimental and Ethnographic Approaches*, ed. P.C. Andersen. Los Angeles (CA): UCLA Institute of Archaeology, 193–8.

Rosen A.M. & S. Weiner, 1994. Identifying ancient irrigation: a new method using opaline phytoliths from emmer wheat. *Journal of Archaeological Science* 21, 132–5.

Russel, N. & L. Martin, 1998. Animal bone report. *Çatalhöyük 1998 Archive Report.* http://catal.arch.cam.ac.uk/Archive_rep98/martin98.html.

Shennan, S., 1988. *Quantifying Archaeology.* Edinburgh: Edinburgh University Press.

Tufte, E.R., 1983. *The Visual Display of Quantitative Information.* Cheshire (CT): Graphics Press.

Tukey, J.W., 1977. *Exploratory Data Analysis.* Reading (MA): Addison-Wesley.

Wylie, A.M., 1996. The constitution of archaeological evidence: gender politics and science, in *The Disunity of Science: Boundaries, Contexts and Power*, eds. P. Galison & D.J. Stump. Stanford (CA): Stanford University Press, 311–43.

Wylie, A.M., forthcoming. Rethinking unity as a 'working hypothesis' for philosophy of science: how archaeologists exploit the disunities of science. *Perspectives on Science.*

Chapter 4

Çatalhöyük and the Archaeological 'Object'

James Conolly

This chapter is an attempt to identify the reasoning and mechanisms for redrawing analytical boundaries between different types and categories of object. The purpose of this is to emphasize the importance of object scalarity, object connectivity and object fluidity, and the effect this has on archaeological interpretations. The origins of this concern lie in recent thinking connected with the ongoing excavations at Çatalhöyük, and the idea that any archaeological object, be it an artefact, a structure, or a single depositional event, can be broken down into further analytical categories (such as a thin-section of a pot sherd) or used as a building block to construct larger objects (such as refitting debitage to make a core). Indeed, whatever the analytic scale — be it microscopic or macroscopic — one discovers objects, and wherever a scale is drawn one creates data and defines the type of interpretation that can be drawn. Within the framework of a contextual archaeology this is important for the critical self-awareness of the ways in which data are created. The sections that follow examine the meanings and implications of the concepts of scalarity, connectivity, and fluidity on the method and practice of archaeological data creation and interpretation.

Scalarity

Scalarity of analysis is not a novel concept for, at least since the late 1960s, archaeologists have recognized the importance of scale in their data collection. Chang (1967) argued that archaeologists needed to move from an artefact-scale approach to the scale of the 'site' or settlement and, similarly, Binford (1964) maintained that the 'region' was the most appropriate scale for understanding human behaviour. More recent discourse on the elements of archaeological analysis have pointed out that concepts such as 'site' are increasingly ambiguous, perhaps to the extent that the site concept is a 'methodological remnant,

the product of an archaeological paradigm that is certainly not dead, but needs to die' (Ebert 1992) and the basic element of analysis is merely where our units of measurement are drawn. At the same time, we have issues of chronological scale to take into account when assessing patterns over time, as Bintliff (1991) and Knapp (1992) have pointed out. For those of us who work on 'sites' — as we do at Çatalhöyük — our units of measurement define how we take samples, how we record depositional events, features, architectural units and artefacts and how we interpret change over time.

It is relatively clear that our objects of analysis are therefore multiscalar in scope. At Çatalhöyük alone, our level of measurement ranges from the microscopic scales of soil chemistry and thin-sections of microstratigraphic sections through occupation deposits, to macrodeposits such as floor surfaces, pits, obsidian microdebitage, pot sherds, bones, figurines, wall-paintings, up to and including the macroscales of the site itself and the region beyond. All the above 'objects', as well as many others, form the focus of attention for analysis and interpretation by groups of field or laboratory-based material specialists and archaeologists. At this level we are all united as being interested in the wider context of the 'site' of Çatalhöyük, together with a range of other contexts ranging from the level of the individual microstratigraphic lens to single depositional events, spaces, buildings, and areas.

A useful contrast can be made between the scale of questions asked of things like microstratigraphy, and macroscopic things like pits or dumps. In the case of the former, although stratigraphic layers are composed of several disparate types of things — grains of sand, plant fragments, trampled plaster, and so on — the 'layer' only really exists in its contextual composite. While there are discrete particles of matter, everything blurs together to create something interpreted as a 'layer', where boundaries between things are vague and dependent on the level of magnification. A similar situation can be proposed for macroarchaeological deposits such as pits or dumps, etc.: these also exist in a contextual composite of events of cuts, fills and artefacts. The essence of the problem is that these all blur into each other and form a context or contexts that are really greater than the sum of their constituent parts, but the analytical process pulls this unity apart. By way of illustration, the interpretation of microstratigraphy is concerned with process and context of the larger whole:

> Interpretation of microstratigraphic sequences both in the field and in thin section is based on internal and comparative analysis of the type, frequency, morphology and structural relationships of depositional components and boundaries in each sequence, and their spatial, temporal, and socio-cultural contexts within settlements. These observations and interpretations are at the same time part of dialectic working hypotheses based on (i) other artefactual and organic and inorganic information from the same context, and (ii) comparisons with sets of information and theories relating to activities and depositional agencies, processes and forms in settlements and environments from other studies in archaeology, ethonoarchaeology, and the natural sciences. (Matthews et al. 1997, 285)

So not all of us seemed to be faced with disintegration and fragmentation of context; indeed, in this example the 'dialect' between object and context can be seen as the hermeneutic spiral of contextual interpretation. In the example above, scalarity is built into the interpretative process, simply because the interpretation of thin-sections necessitates an interpretation of the context of their origin and the processes which can lead to patterns visible at the microscopic level. The same can also be said of those of us at Çatalhöyük involved in the excavation process. In these cases, the object is a depositional event. This object may well contain a host of other objects and microstratigraphic variability, but these constituent components cannot *independently* say anything about the macroevent of the pit-infill, the dump, the midden layer, etc. To the excavator these are contributors to a unified object, which define its eventual dismemberment, as suggested in the prompts from the Çatalhöyük unit sheet under the 'discussion' section:

> Record how and why you have reached certain conclusions and what evidence there is to support your analysis. Discuss what type of activity or activities the unit may represent, the reasons for your interpretation and the events that may have led to the presence of the unit. Give general thoughts on

the unit's location within the space, building or feature. Note any contemporaneity with units under excavation in the vicinity, and also mention any additional details on artefacts, including any clusters within the unit. Any change or variation in the deposit composition across the unit must also be noted. What post-depositional alterations are there? How have they affected the nature or preservation of the unit? (Farid et al. 1997, 8)

In both the above examples the focus is on interpreting 'composite' objects — whether thin-sections of microstratigraphy or depositional events like pits — yet the contexts within which these composite objects sit, together with their micro-contents, are needed to construct the interpretation. Understanding the relationship between the 'whole' and the 'parts' is dialectical, and fundamental to the interpretative process.

In terms of artefacts, any 'whole' from which they may come is difficult to see, as so many of our interpretative boundaries are scaled to material composition. Although a seemingly reasonable way to divide material into categories, all 'objects' and 'things' are defined by arbitrary boundaries, and it is these boundaries that then direct the scale and target of any analysis (Heidegger 1968). Others have pointed this out in a slightly different way, by showing that patterning is entirely dependent on what scale we look at something (e.g. Ebert 1992, 174). In other words, despite the logic of materially-defined categories this may, arguably, be rather limiting, as the boundary of the 'object' is also drawn at this level. This may hinder the process of integration and holistic synthesis — or more simply the 'making-sense' of contextual relationships that cross-cut material categories.

Part of this is undoubtedly because we have difficulties in finding patterns and associations between things at different scales at the same time (Ebert 1992, 174). This, however, is not to dispute the value of the work of the lithic analyst, archaeozoologist or ceramic specialist in their separate examination and interpretation of their particular categories of objects. By themselves, however, they are not particularly holistic, as bones are disassociated and analyzed separately from the pots, which are analyzed differently from the lithics, and so on. The end result is that the categories of objects are interpreted in entirely disparate and *a*contextual ways stemming from a decision to scale down a context into classes of material. In the same way, we may consider that something does not exist, simply because a scale has been drawn at a level that excludes some forms of objects. The easiest example to use is the decision not to sample non-floor deposits for lithic microdebitage because they are believed only to exist on or near floor surfaces. As non-floor deposits are not sampled, microdebitage data do not exist in these contexts. Alternatively, if one considers organic residue sampling on stone tools, this type of data only exists in special circumstances where preservation and sampling procedures permit. At Çatalhöyük, we have sampled bifaces from hoards found under floors as both the type of object and the context suggested the possibility of residue data being preserved. The data on tool use do not exist for other tools; not all can be sampled nor are most contexts suggestive of *in situ* deposition. As such residue data may exist only for 'special' contexts and give us a distorted understanding of what tools may have been used for. In other words, at the macro-scale, an object is one thing; look a bit closer, and the object becomes something else.

Inter-connectivity

The inter-connectivity of archaeological data was considered nearly 20 years ago by Binford, although in a manner that was predominantly concerned with energy, behavioural adaptation, and causal relationships (Binford 1981, 27):

> The archaeological record is a structure of relationships between the distribution and form of matter as caused by energy sources acting on matter in the past. In one very important sense, all properties of matter, whether they be chips removed from a flake of flint, mixing of soils betraying the former location of a pit, piles of debris from meals, or the remnants of a construction such as a mud-brick wall, are the mechanical consequences of the actions of forces on matter.

The search for patterning within and across contexts through spatial analysis, correlations between object distributions, observations and investigation of specific depositional events between rooms, buildings and areas, and extrapolation from ethnoarchaeological observations and experiments are but a few of the ways archaeologists try to make sense of the objects collected through excavation and observation. This process of pattern exploration has been *de rigueur* in archaeology for some time, although the process of making sense of, or interpreting identified patterns, has ranged from formalized middle-range verification (and construction of uniformitarian assumptions), to the generation of (relative) multivocal narratives.

One of the observations that arose from the contributions of our on-site anthropologist (see Chapter 10) was that the moment of object definition was a crucial stage in the analytical process, as it more often than not determined the direction and scope of the scale of the interpretation. Although our objects are by definition multiscalar, she was under the impression that the analytical component was not necessarily so. In other words, the focus of analysis often (but not always) remained at the level of the object as it was first defined. This is perhaps most easily seen when we consider the most traditional objects of analysis, artefacts such as bone, stone tools and pot sherds, which, particularly in the case of the latter two, are arguably the most enduring portable objects of archaeological enquiry. What is also clear is that these traditional objects of analysis are materially constructed, and are viewed implicitly as bounded, discrete entities. Arguably it is a combination of the western primacy of the material object and the historical circumstances of archaeology which has led to material analysts such as lithic analysts, ceramic analysts, archaeobotanists and so on, who record, analyze and interpret these materials to the exclusion of other types of data while, *generally speaking*, we do not employ analysts in things like 'decoration', 'fire', 'food' or 'exchange' that cross-cut the traditional categories of artefacts. If the latter occurs, it is mostly an exercise that occurs during the off-site analytical or interpretive period. Given this, primacy is often bestowed on the artefact as a bounded entity, and its cross-cutting relationships, although recognized as important, in practice are often treated as secondary at the point of analysis and at the point of entry into what is essentially the 'primary' record.

Interesting parallels can perhaps be drawn between the emphasis on artefacts, and the behaviour of collectors to the extent that the act of collecting seems to legitimize the process itself (Belk 1994). In the same way, collections become extensions of self (Belk 1994, 321). I am a lithic analyst: my archaeological training was geared around the study and interpretation of stone tools, and thus I define myself partly by the material I collect, study, put into bags, and interpret. This problem was first raised by Carolyn Hamilton's work (see Chapter 10, this volume), particularly her research into the context of identifying the mechanisms and processes of the practical creation of archaeological knowledge. The central basis of this was that whenever object definition occurred, interpretative barriers (although not necessarily impenetrable ones) were also constructed. As so-called 'artefact specialists' some of us were unwittingly experiencing interpretative boundaries solely because of the definition of what was an artefact.

What in practice seems to occur is that some objects are by default given primacy, and undergo disparate types of analyses. Indeed, in the most extreme, some artefacts become the start and end point of analysis — they become bounded entities on the basis of their material being — despite the blurred boundaries that existed between them within their original context. In a sense the context has been lost through the attrition of its objects to the specialists. As one alternative, we can, perhaps *conceptually* more easily than practically, attempt not to separate things in this way, and retain a sense of object relativity. Although, ideally, everyone recognizes the need to maintain this contextual integrity, *in practice*, as I have said, it is often difficult to recreate once the context has been excavated and the components parcelled out to specialists for a variety of reasons, some of which no doubt are specific to the particular circumstances and pressures under which we work at Çatalhöyük.

If, for example, we take the example of some of the meticulous work done at Franchthi Cave in Greece, it is possible to see how the divisions were made between the objects of analysis, and how this has determined the interpretations of the archaeology. The site is remarkably well published: there are eight volumes, consisting of a pottery volume (Vitelli 1993), two volumes of lithic analysis (Perlès 1987; 1990), a palaeoethnobotany volume (Hansen 1991), one on the marine molluscan remains (Shackleton 1988), a volume on the landscape and people of the Franchthi region (van Andel & Sutton 1987), and a summary account of the excavation which includes the plans and section drawings (Jacobsen & Farrand 1987). One needs only to look at the volume titles to see the divisions in the analytical process. The purpose of the publication method is stated clearly by Jacobsen & Farrand, where three 'tiers' or 'levels' of publication are envisioned:

> Level One is intended for a specialist audience. It will be a series of separate reports prepared by individual specialists describing in full detail their material and their interpretation of it. (Jacobsen & Farrand 1987, 9)

> Level Two is intended for the 'general' archaeologist . . . The results of the specialist studies will appear in a more digested or synthetic form in Level Two . . . A major objective of the Level Two publication will be to tie together those specialist reports and arrive at a reasonable overview of the site as a whole (Jacobsen & Farrand 1987, 10).

> Our third level of publication is intended to be a

brief and well-illustrated synthesis in a single small volume written for the student and informed layman. It will aim to make sense of a very important and complex site in language understandable to the non-professional. (Jacobsen & Farrand 1987, 10)

The idea here is that one starts with the contextual composite of the site, breaks it into analytical components (lithics, ceramics, seeds, etc.) for the first-tier publication, then recreates context for the subsequent publications. For example, the first-tier specialist pottery analysis contains accounts of the phases from which the pottery was derived, followed by a detailed description of the different types of wares, concluded with diagrams and drawings showing distributions and shapes of the various types of pots unearthed. The other specialist reports follow this format insofar as they are primarily concerned with the characteristics of the objects that have been analyzed. The exception to this is the 'Landscape and People' volume, which deals primarily with the environs of the site, rather than the site itself. Undoubtedly this is useful information, and pottery specialists will find the detail presented in the pottery volume useful. What is lacking, however, is something that describes the archaeology of the cave itself. There are copious drawings of sections and plans of features, but there are no interpretations of the features found in the cave *in terms of their contents* and thus the social milieu in which they were constructed. Understanding the context of the excavated units was apparently not a specific objective:

> The purpose of the schematic drawings [of the excavation] . . . is twofold: first, they provide a record of the excavation stratigraphy and, as such, are useful to our colleagues on the project in ordering their artefacts and other excavated materials, and, secondly, the schematic drawings can be overlaid on the section drawings found in the fascicle in order to compare excavation and natural stratigraphy. (Jacobsen & Farrand 1987, 25–6)

As such, the specialist reports can be read independently and, although one gains a detailed understanding of the objects under discussion, one does not really come to understand the site as a whole, but rather has to try to reconstruct it through the details presented in the specialist reports. It may not be fair to use this as an example of de-contextualized recording and interpretation, as the depositional sequences of cave sites are notoriously difficult to understand. Notwithstanding this, I would contend that something is missing in this style of recording, analysis, interpretation and presentation, owing to an overemphasis on the material object, and not on multiscalar context. However, the latter is not easily obtained as it involves breaking down some rigid barriers in archaeological praxis that define how data are collected and analyzed.

Fluidity

In the case of artefact analysis, and possibly all forms of object analysis be they micro- or macroscopic, a potential solution may be to destabilize the object as the focus of analysis, and redraw the boundaries of the object from material to phenomenal. Again, we can refer to the processualist school as seeing this as a goal of archaeology insofar as it recognized both the challenge of unifying the archaeological record with our ideas about the character of the past, and at the same time recognized that people with identical experiences may ascribe different meanings to things (Binford 1981, 21, 24). One solution to this was to search for accurate and unambiguous knowledge of the relationship between a static archaeological record and a dynamic human past (Binford 1981, 25). Our solution differs by harnessing the dynamic nature of the archaeological record, constantly redefining the boundary of 'things' to encompass artefact and context, event, or phenomenon. In doing so we can, at least conceptually, work towards maintaining this blurring in the way that bits of sand, plant remains and plaster blur together to form a layer — a contextual coherency is, at least in theory, encouraged. For example, we have started to do this by looking at specific *phenomena* as a route towards contextual synthesis. At a practical level — i.e. in the field — this is, in part, facilitated by large-scale relational data bases where contexts can to some degree be recreated and relationships explored electronically (although this has brought its own problems). Although the data base (and now a GIS interface) provide a tool to facilitate information flow, in practice a starting point is needed to begin the process of contextual thinking and the exploration of data relativity. For example, if a normative concept such as 'rubbish' is taken as a non-object or context-specific phenomenon that is worth exploring, it is possible to examine the relationships between things in light of the idea of 'rubbish'. This prompts us to begin asking questions such as, 'what is rubbish and does it exist at different scales' and if so, how is it constituted at these scales, what are its associations, and how does it change over time. In doing so we begin not to define contexts by the objects they contain, nor objects by the context they are in, but rather each becomes both structured by, and contingent upon,

the other. The result is, in theory, interpretation that stretches beyond any particular type of artefact or individual depositional event, and encompasses a wider contextual whole.

Conclusion

On the one hand it would appear that specialists are more often primarily concerned with 'their' particular categories of objects while, on the other, excavators are concerned with stratigraphically defined contexts. As a group we are attempting to move towards a process that emphasizes inter-relationships and contingencies at an early stage in the data collection process. Redrawing boundaries and attempting to destabilize the primacy of the artefact and the stratigraphic context is a step towards this. In practical terms there are regular established meetings between excavators and finds analysts to discuss data at levels ranging from the individual deposit and its contents, through to spaces, buildings and areas. At times, these discussions are taken to the level of the level of the phenomenological — such as 'feasting', 'abandonment', 'death' or 'pyrotechnics' — which incorporate many types of data and context. Alternative paths to interpretation of objects and groups of objects and the facilitation of their transition to a paper record are the outcome. As an example of this sort of method, the next chapter takes a multiscalar, fluid object — rubbish — as the focus of analysis. It should, however, be considered as a work in progress, an entry point into continued data collection and interpretation.

When all is said and done, the objective as presented here is not to attack epistemological process but to show how, through a process of negotiation, data can be created at and within several different scales, levels, and contexts. The origins of such debate perhaps lie in the recognized fragmentation that occurs in a large project where information overload often results in decreased information exchange. The mechanisms through which we attempt to become contextual are perhaps telling of 'Çatalhöyük Methodology', and the way we approach archaeology. The chapter which follows can be seen as efforts to think in this way *during* — and I think that is a point worth emphasizing — the process of data creation, assimilation and interpretation.

References

Belk, R.W., 1994. Collectors and collecting, in *Interpreting Objects and Collections*, ed. S.M. Pearce. London:

Routledge, 317–26.

Binford, L., 1964. A consideration of archaeological research design. *American Antiquity* 29, 411–25.

Binford, L., 1981. Middle-range research and the role of actualistic studies, in *Bones: Ancient Men and Modern Myths*, ed. L. Binford. New York (NY)/London: Academic Press, 21–30.

Bintliff, J. (ed.), 1991. *The Annales School and Archaeology*. Leicester: Leicester University Press.

Chang, K.C., 1967. *Rethinking Archaeology*. New York (NY): Random House.

Ebert, J.I., 1992. *Distributional Archaeology*. Albuquerque (NM): University of New Mexico Press.

Farid, S. *et al.*, 1997. Guide to Recording Soil Deposits. Unpublished Çatalhöyük field prompts: on file, Çatalhöyük Research Project.

Hansen, J.M., 1991. *The Palaeoethnobotany of Franchthi Cave*. Bloomington (IN): Indiana University Press.

Heidegger, M., 1968. *What is a Thing?*, trans. W.B. Barton Jr & V. Deutsch. Chicago (IL): H. Regnery Co.

Hurst, D.T., 1975. Non-site sampling in archaeology: up the creek without a site, in *Sampling in Archaeology*, ed. J.W. Mueller. Tucson (AZ): University of Arizona Press.

Jacobsen, T.W. & W.R. Farrand, 1987. *Franchthi Cave and Paralia: Maps, Plans, and Sections*. Bloomington (IN): Indiana University Press.

Knapp, B.A., 1992. Archaeology and Annales, in *Archaeology, Annales, and Ethnohistory*, ed. B.A. Knapp. (New Directions in Archaeology.) Cambridge: Cambridge University Press, 1–21.

Matthews, W., C.A.I. French, T. Lawrence, D.F. Cutler & M.K. Jones, 1997. Microstratigraphic traces of site formation processes and human activities: high definition archaeology. *World Archaeology* 29(2), 281–308.

Perlès, C., 1987. *Les Industries Lithiques Taillées de Franchthi (Argolide, Grèce)*, vol. I: *Présentation Générale et Industries Paléolithiques*. Bloomington (IN): Indiana University Press.

Perlès, C., 1990. *Les Industries Lithiques Taillées de Franchthi (Argolide, Grèce)*, vol. II: *Les Industries du Mésolithique et du Néolithique Initial*. Bloomington (IN): Indiana University Press.

Shackleton, J.C., 1988. *Marine Molluscan Remains from Franchthi Cave*. Bloomington (IN): Indiana University Press.

van Andel, T.H. & S. Sutton, 1987. *Landscape and People of the Franchthi Region*. Bloomington (IN): Indiana University Press.

Vitelli, K.D., 1993. *Franchthi Neolithic Pottery*, vol. I: *Classification and Ceramic Phases 1 and 2*. Bloomington (IN): Indiana University Press.

Chapter 5

Trashing Rubbish

Louise Martin & Nerissa Russell

with contributions from Mehmet Altuğ Uluceviz, Adnan Baysal, Jenny Bredenberg, Craig Cessford, James Conolly, Shahina Farid, Naomi Hamilton, Jonathan Last, Wendy Matthews & Julie Near

The process of tell formation almost intrinsically means that people and rubbish are in close proximity, which is only one of many possibilities when considering rubbish deposition in human settlements. For instance, people could move away from rubbish as it builds up (they could rebuild houses slightly away from old rubbish), they could move their rubbish away (to a dedicated place for rubbish outside the living area), or they could have rubbish areas within the settlement, but maintain the spatial separation of house and midden through time.

At Çatalhöyük, Mellaart's 1960s excavations showed that some rubbish dumping occurred in areas (which Mellaart termed 'courtyards') among the nested mud-brick houses, and houses were built on top of middens. The present excavations allow us to explore the nature of rubbish and refuse a little further. Analysis is still at an early stage, and what is presented here is based on preliminary observations and intended chiefly to exemplify the methodology (see Chapter 1).

Rubbish, refuse, garbage, discard, trash

> 'Refuse has become a widely appreciated category of archaeological evidence in its own right, rich in significance for many aspects of social organization.' (Needham & Spence 1997, 77)

Archaeologists who have considered discard in recent years have generally taken one of two tacks. Those in the processual school have built on Schiffer's (1976; 1987) seminal work in trying to define the factors that affect discard behaviour. Most of the attention has been focused on what Schiffer terms 'secondary refuse', as primary refuse deposits, things that are discarded at their point of use, have seemed easier to interpret. Through archaeological and especially ethnoarchaeological studies, these archaeologists have sought to define different types of secondary refuse deposits and the variables that affect decisions about what gets deposited where (e.g. Halstead *et al.* 1978; Tani 1995; Wilson 1994). In particular, Hayden & Cannon (1983) have argued that decisions regarding the treatment of refuse relate largely to three characteristics of the refuse: the effort required to gather it up and dump it, its potential reuse value, and the hindrance it offers if left where it is. These approaches, then, see discard as a universal human activity that conforms to a uniform set of rules. Materials discarded are seen as refuse, things that, while they may have some residual value for reuse or recycling, are essentially a nuisance that needs to be removed from the places where people do things.

The other approach, which may loosely be termed postprocessual, seeks to problematize the notion of rubbish itself. Whether one speaks of rubbish, garbage, refuse, or discard, the implication is that this material, unless it can be reused, has no further significance for the living community except as a potential problem. Yet it is possible that some things that leave the realm of daily life may still carry meaning, positive or negative, for the people who used them. In practice, all archaeologists recognize that certain things that leave the living sphere do carry continued meaning, such as burials, hoards, and votive offerings. It is simply assumed that remains that are assimilated to our category of 'rubbish' have as little meaning to those who deposited them as our rubbish does to us. Working from an ethnoarchaeological case, Hodder challenges this assumption:

> ... [T]here can be no general theory and no universal method for measuring and interpreting activity residues, except in relation to physical, nonhuman, processes of decay and deposition.... [T]he meaning of settlement organization and discard can only be derived from the context (present or past) within which settlement use and artifact discard take place. (Hodder 1987, 424)

He proceeds to outline the many dimensions of meaning associated with the locations where ash is discarded by the Ilchamus of Kenya (see also Moore 1982; 1986).

Since the notion of rubbish is culturally specific, is it appropriate to continue using it? Should it be abandoned altogether? Or if maintained, can it serve as an exploratory label, as a starting point in analysis and discussion? We will take this last approach here, but do not treat 'rubbish' as a unitary category. It is differing treatments of 'rubbish' that are particularly interesting.

How then do we distinguish 'rubbish' deposits that are created simply to dispose of unwanted waste from those that carry additional meaning? The usual approach has been to seek some sort of patterning that marks certain deposits as special. The concept of 'structured deposition' introduced by Richards & Thomas (1984) argues that repeated associations and regularities of placement of materials that would ordinarily be considered rubbish indicates ritual treatment of items of symbolic significance.

> Ritual communicates rules and categories that reproduce social and metaphysical relations in a manner which is closed to any form of evaluation. One way in which this might be expressed archaeologically would be in particular forms of deposition, with specific sequences and rules applied to the contexts and associations of different objects. (Richards & Thomas 1984, 191–2)

Similar arguments have been made for what are usually termed 'special deposits' of animal and human bones in British Iron Age pits (Cunliffe 1992; Hill 1996). However, Hill sees the existence of structure in 'rubbish' as insufficient in itself to indicate ritual deposits; this simply reflects symbolic behaviour, which may occur in a variety of contexts (Hill 1996, 21; see also Needham & Spence 1997, 85). McOmish (1996) suggests that large, bounded midden accumulations may represent the deliberate saving and piling up of feasting remains; most ordinary 'rubbish' is scattered, consumed by dogs, and so on, and does not enter the archaeological record. Ullén (1994) examines a similar bounded midden accumulation that contains special animal bone deposits and human burials, and argues that such middens may be seen as analogous to graves, suggesting a concept of death that included non-human, non-animate things.

Thus close attention to the construction and composition of rubbish deposits may reveal signs of special treatment. We might question, however, whether it is ever appropriate to think in terms of rubbish that is without meaning. As noted above, even to label material as rubbish carries a sense of uncleanness and distaste. It may be more pertinent to ask what meaning any deposit may have carried by examining it in the context of other deposits and materials from the site and elsewhere. 'Refuse is linked to culturally specific and highly charged notions of dirt and pollution . . . so that the definition and disposal of refuse is structured by (and structures) a range of other relationships through which a society is daily reconstituted . . .' (Hill 1996, 21). Our task, then, is to examine the patterning and variability in rubbish deposits in the context of the particular society that produced them — in this case, the Neolithic inhabitants of Çatalhöyük — to attempt to define the cultural rules regarding purity, pollution, and symbolic contrasts that structure this aspect of daily life.

Approach

This chapter aims to explore ideas about the discard, movement, recycling and redeposition of materials at Çatalhöyük. It presents some preliminary thoughts on the concept of 'rubbish' at the site: why materials are identified as 'waste' by archaeologists; whether this coincides with the evidence for treatment of particular materials on the site by the Neolithic inhabitants; whether there seem to be 'rules' for the disposal of material; how discarded material moves around the site, and whether some materials move from spheres of use to discard and back into a use sphere again. The deposits selected for discussion in this chapter hopefully 'sample' some of the cycle, even if they do not form a coherent whole.

Discussion focuses on two separate areas that have been excavated since 1995: the North area, where until 1998 excavation centred on Building 1 (Fig. 5.1); and the South area (where work has continued down from Mellaart's 1960s excavations), which provides examples both of buildings and external areas, tentatively referred to as 'middens' (Fig. 5.2). Within these, a range of contexts of various types have been selected for examination (Table 5.1). These are not necessarily linked in space or time, but simply chosen as examples. The contexts (units) have been selected in part because they have been the focus of Priority tours (see Chapter 1), and hence analyses of different categories of material are available.

At Çatalhöyük we try to avoid fitting deposits into rigid typological schemes in order to maintain a sense of 'fluidity' between and within categories (see Chapter 4). Still, we find the need for working definitions and labels for various types of deposit in order to make excavation decisions. For example, archaeologists tend to define a deposit as rubbish if it has some or all of the following characteristics: if it occurs outside versus inside buildings; if many different materials are mixed together; if there is a high density of material (sherds, bones, charcoal, lithics); if the finds tend to be broken, 'used up' or considered waste; or if they are ashy, but not *in situ*. Implicit in this is an assumed distinction between clean and unclean, pure and impure, useful and not useful, desirable and undesirable.

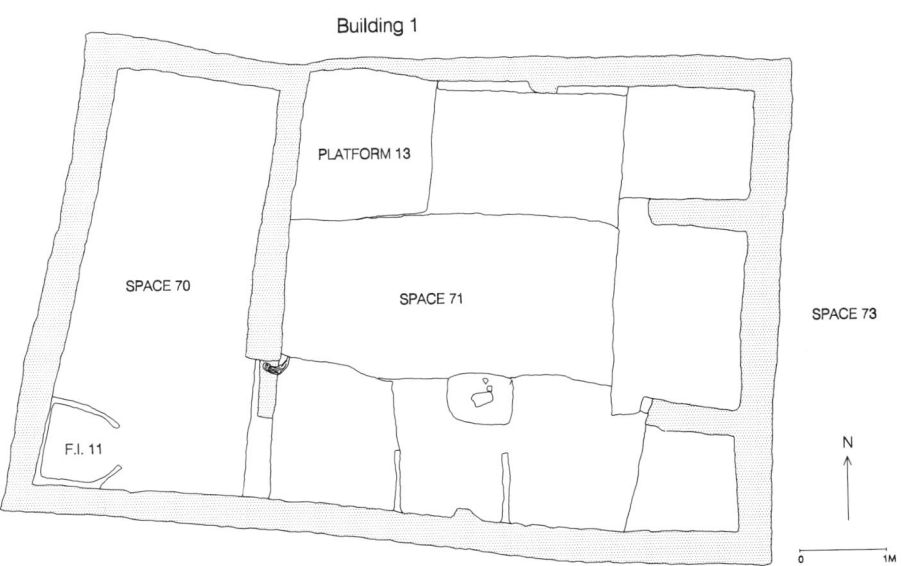

Figure 5.1. *Plan of Building 1, North area, showing features discussed in the text.*

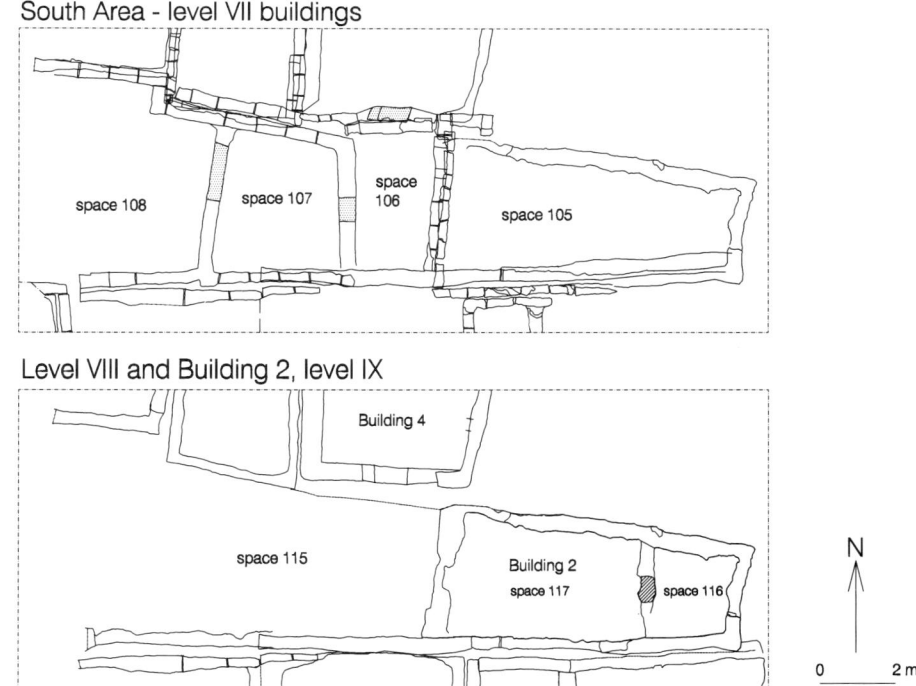

Figure 5.2. *Plan of the South area showing features discussed in the text.*

As discussed in Chapter 4, such characterizations of deposits are not final. The data base has been structured so as to incorporate the interpretations of the various materials from each unit by those studying them, as well as discussion and re-interpretation by any project member. It is in this spirit of reflexive encounter of data and interpretation that we offer the observations that follow. The eventual

Table 5.1. *A summary of the units referred to in the text, with their locations on the site, and working descriptions.*

UNIT	Building number, Space and feature number; with occupation phases for Building 1, and building levels (following Mellaart) for South	Working description of unit
NORTH		
1114	Building 1, Space 70, fire installation 11, phase B1.7	Upper phase of ashy infill of oven (fire installation 11) in southwest corner of Building 1
1118	Building 1, Space 70, fire installation 11, phase B1.7	Upper phase of ashy infill of oven (fire installation 11) in southwest corner of Building 1
1123	Building 1, Space 70, fire installation 11, phase B1.7	Final phase of ashy infill of oven (fire installation 11) in southwest corner of Building 1
1315	Building 1, Space 73, phase B1.5+	Between-wall deposit from narrow space to east of Building 1
1347	Building 1, Space 73, phase B1.5+	Between-wall deposit from narrow space to east of Building 1
1363	Building 1, Space 71, platform 13, phase B1.6	The latest plaster surface of platform in northwest corner of space 71, Building 1
1416	Building 1, Space 70, phase B1.2	'Dirty' floor/rake-out next to fire installation 33 in southwest corner of space 70, Building 1
1488	Building 1, Space 71, phase B1.3	'Clean' white plaster floor
2574	Building 1, Space 70/71, phase B1.1	Mud-brick from upper part of preserved wall of Building 1
2575	Building 1, Space 70/71, phase B1.1	Mortar from upper part of preserved wall of Building 1
SOUTH		
1084	Space 107/108, level VII	Sequence of floors
1668	Space 115, level VIII	Fine lensed ashy midden from external area
1873	Building 2, Space 117, level IX	Mixed infill within the walls of Building 2
2006	Building 4, Space 113/151, level VIII	Inter-phase infilling within Building 4

aim of these analyses is to provide rich and perhaps varied syntheses of the various results, to draw on large samples of feature types, and to make rigorous comparisons of data. This chapter attempts nothing so grandiose, but is simply a preliminary exploration of possibilities at an early stage of analysis, using the concept of 'rubbish' as a framework for the narrative.

To this end, we have selected a variety of contexts (units) for examination at different scales of observation (see Table 5.1). The aim is not to produce a coherent view of discard practices at Çatalhöyük, since, as yet, we do not have enough of any one feature type (e.g. hearth, floor, midden, infill) for comparison. Rather, we wish to explore how the

density and distribution of different materials varies among different context types (see Table 5.2), and to show how this variation, viewed alongside the excavation records that describe the deposit, the heavy-residue data, and the micromorphological information, may inform on ideas of 'rubbish' at Çatalhöyük. The approach taken here is based on the conviction that each part of the process of excavation and analysis is impoverished in itself, as opposed to integrating all materials together: excavation records, stratigraphy, observations, inclusions, deposit matrix, obsidian, pottery, clay balls, ground stone, figurines, beads, worked bone, plant remains, animal remains, flotation residue, micromorphology, and so on.

It should be stressed that while many people

Table 5.2. *The densities of the various materials found in each unit discussed in the text. The third column shows the volume of deposit (in litres) excavated for each unit (including both dry-sieve and wet-sieve samples where taken). For different categories of finds, the density of finds per litre of deposit is shown. In most cases, the density is expressed as numbers of finds per litre (n). For chipped stone, pottery and animal bones, densities are also given for grams of material per litre (g). Plant remains are only expressed as grams per litre (g). x indicates a density of less than 0.005/litre.*

UNIT	Description	Volume of deposit (litres)	Chipped stone		Pottery		Clay balls	Worked stone	Figurines	Beads	Worked bone	Plant remains	Animal bones	
			n	g	n	g	n	n	n	n	n	g	n	g
NORTH														
1114	oven fill	2.50	0.4	0.02	0	0	0	0	0	0	0	–	4.0	5.0
1118	oven fill	0.25	0	0	0	0	0	0	0	0	0	–	4.0	4.0
1123	oven fill	5.00	0.2	2.40	0	0	0	0	0	0	0	–	1.0	1.0
1315	between wall	260.00	0.07	0.03	0	0	0	0	0.01	0	0	0.042	1.9	4.0
1347	between wall	80.00	0.09	0.02	0	0	0.03	0	0	0	0.04	0.205	5.8	13.0
1363	platform surface	54.50	0.06	0.05	0	0	0	0	0	0	0.04	0.008	0.3	0.3
1416	'dirty' floor	25.00	0	0	0.16	0.22	0	0	0.08	0	0	0.828	0.0	0.0
1488	'clean' floor	24.00	0	0	0	0	0	0	0	0	0	0.147	0.2	0.1
2574	mud-brick	30.00	0	0	0	0	0	0	0	0	0	0.339	0.7	0.4
2575	mortar	30.00	0	0	0	0	0	0	0	0.03	0	0.009	10.7	3.0
SOUTH														
1084	floors	110.00	0	0	0	0	0	0.03	0	0	0	0.064	0.0	0.0
1668	ashy midden	821.00	0.15	0.18	0.02	0.02	0.04	x	x	x	0.01	1.433	5.5	17.0
1873	infill	2905.00	0.07	0.06	0.01	0.01	x	0	x	0	0.004	0.302	1.4	5.0
2006	infill	360.00	0.06	0.06	0.01	0.03	0.01	0	0	0	0	0.083	0.4	2.0

have contributed data and ideas to the discussion below, the synthesis has been drawn together mainly by the first two authors. Not all the contributors agree with all interpretations presented here. It is expected that there will be varied interpretations of these same contexts, both from different authors, and resulting from further analyses.

The house

Building 1 in the North area is a typical rectangular mud-brick structure, measuring roughly 8 × 5 m, which saw several phases of use. Characteristic of buildings at Çatalhöyük, Building 1 was entered through the roof, and had several internal partition walls that altered over time. Part-way through the life of the building, the southern half burnt down, was walled off, and was subsequently uninhabited. Internal features included white-plaster floors, raised plaster platforms against the walls, burials under the floor and platforms, and ovens and hearths.

In terms of what was found in the house, there is very little that seemingly represents discard. There are some items that are perhaps deliberately placed: a grindstone set in a hollow in the floor, a cache of obsidian blades beneath it, a worked cattle shoulder-blade on top of a small hearth, a bin full of lentils. There are also things that appear to have fallen from the walls and ceilings during destruction of the house: a group of acorns, a boar's tusk, a cattle skull, several sheep's hooves and most of a broken pot. These, too, probably do not represent discard, but things present in the house when the southern part burned down and sealed them.

For a close look at the floors, unit 1488 serves as an example. Excavators described this deposit as a clean white plaster floor with no inclusions, which reflects what was visible to the naked eye. But while no finds came from either hand collection or the dry sieve, the flotation residue shows low densities of animal bone fragments, mollusc shells, obsidian chips and plant remains, meaning that the floor was not quite so clean at the micro-level. These tiny fragments probably reflect some of the actual activities that took place on the floors, such as food preparation, cooking and obsidian working. They may have been dropped, and trodden into the floor (the animal bones have surface abrasion that could indicate trampling), but did not 'lift off' the floors during house cleaning.

Another sequence of floors, this time from the South area, shows a similar cleanliness. Unit 1084 represents a 50 mm thickness of multiple plaster floors in Spaces 107/108, with a mud-plaster basal make-up. Again they appeared clean during excavation, which explains the general lack of finds in Table 5.2, but micro-finds of bone, shell, obsidian and plant remains are present embedded in the matrix of the plaster floors. Does this also show that discard material was cleared away, and floors kept clean? Three pieces of unworked stone are present, though, at the latest floor horizon, which might indicate that this had not undergone cleaning, or maybe that as the last floor in the sequence, it was not scoured for replastering, a process that would also have redistributed dropped material to other locations.

Back in Building 1, analysis of the surface of the white plaster from platform 13, unit 1363, shows a similarly low density of most finds. The platform was a special place in a corner with painted plaster walls around it. It would have been repeatedly reopened and replastered for the placement of the mul-tiple burials beneath (see Fig. 5.3). There are, however, obsidian pieces and animal bones from here, which might represent activities on the platform that had not been cleaned away, or may be incidental, having been incorporated during replastering. Two complete and apparently still useful worked bone points lend support to the former idea.

The impression, in brief, is of some house floors that are cleanly maintained, and although observations do show that there are spatial distinctions of cleanliness/dirtiness within structures (see unit 1416 below), we might imagine cleaning as a regular, perhaps daily, activity. But from the few deposits examined here, there is evidence that food preparation and stone tool production was taking place inside, and most of the waste was being removed elsewhere.

Deposits from an oven (fire installation 11, Fig. 5.4) built into the southwest corner of Building 1 hint that floor sweepings were sometimes, at least, dumped here. Units 1114, 1118 and 1123 for example, represent the ashy infill of the oven, and contain abundant fragments of white plaster that was not used in the construction of the oven itself, and are likely to derive from the cleaning of the plaster floors. Oven contents appear to be dense in plant remains (representing dung used as fuel, cooking accidents or the burning of domestic debris?) but there are also small animal bone fragments and chips of obsidian, which are likely to result from the regular, small-scale, brushing of the floors. The upper phase of the oven, unit 1123, includes larger pieces of bone and obsidian, and less plaster, and perhaps these were thrown in by hand. Whatever their derivation, it is interesting to note the association of bone and obsidian with the fire, and the absence of other finds such as clay balls and pottery.

These two last categories are present in a deposit termed 'dirty floor', unit 1416. This is a patch of ashy deposit next to an oven (fire installation 33) that was from an earlier phase than that discussed above (fire installation 11), but in the same area of Building 1. It contains pot

Figure 5.3. *Platform 13 in Space 71, Building 1, North area, showing the white plaster with burial cuts.*

sherds, clay ball fragments, a figurine fragment, two broken beads and charred plant material, and finds are in relatively high densities although the volume of the deposit itself is very small. A likely explanation for this accumulation is that it is rake-out from the fire, since the pot sherds are red in colour and have the appearance of being re-fired (after their initial firing) post-breakage. The high density of plant remains, too, is characteristic of those found in fire installation deposits. Clay balls may represent refuse from cooking activities, and it is interesting to note the figurine seemingly discarded here.

Figure 5.4. *Oven (fire installation 11) in the southwest corner of Space 70, Building 1, North area.*

We therefore see all sorts of household materials in this 'dirty' area of the building, although not all of the household waste can be left here. The accumulation is too little to account for the lifetimes of activities that would have taken place in the house, and material must be going out. We should remember that this house has no door but was entered by a ladder from the roof. Taking out the rubbish — as well as bringing things in — and maintaining the general cleanliness of the house becomes something of a task. This may have been formalized, an act repeated (by whom?); they could not just sweep things out the door.

Some things from this house (or the house next door) may have been dumped from the roof into a narrow between-wall space to the east of the building. Deposits in the north half of this space are rich in animal bone with much bigger chunks than found in the house, almost the inverse of what is found inside. But the picture of this between-wall space as just a dump is not straightforward. In its southern part, units 1315 and 1347 do not resemble the dump, midden or infill contexts we see in the South area of the site. The high degree of burning and the presence of building materials in the deposits, argue against it being material fallen from the roof, as suggested during excavation. Rather these units appear to represent clearance, in part at least, perhaps from the southern half of Building 1 after it had burnt down.

The two deposits are of varied character. For example, 1315 includes large amounts of brick lumps and ashy building debris, while 1347 has layers of charcoal. Both, however, contain rather rare and unusual finds. Unit 1315 includes 15 pieces of unworked stone of various raw materials, almost like a cache waiting to be worked. All the stones were then burnt and fire-cracked before being moved here. Three figurines were also found here, all broken and one burnt, the only one recorded as such. The animal bone from these two units is high in density for the North area, all heavily burnt and includes several items that we tend to think of as 'special': a complete wild cattle horn core (Fig. 5.5), wild goat horn cores, a complete dog skull, and a wing of a large bird showing a great number of cut marks. Might these be the remains of former structural installations from the southern part of Building 1 that lost their 'special' meaning when that part of the house was destroyed? The story is not so simple, however, since there are bones mixed in that seem to be food remains: small fragmented pieces, and even some that are digested, perhaps by carnivores or humans, hence representing a different kind of waste. These deposits also contain obsidian pieces, some tools and some debitage, that suggest production debris. Obsidian in general has an association with ashy deposits, and perhaps some material here comes from contexts like the oven infills. The mix of finds is not at all straightforward and suggests a varied derivation of deposits.

Figure 5.5. *Cattle horn from Space 73, the narrow between-wall area to the east of Building 1, North area.*

If part of the material, though, represents clearance from the south part of Building 1, it raises the question of why this part of the house was partially emptied when it was only to become walled off and go out of use? Are we seeing a practice where it is inappropriate for certain 'special' materials to stay? Did these wall installations and symbolic pieces lose their meaning once the structure was destroyed, allowing them to be cleared away? Or was it a stage in preparing for a future rebuilding which never happened?

To sum up for Building 1, it seems that different finds were leaving the house in different ways. Bone food remains may be taken outside, except for the tiny fragments that are not cleaned up. These, and bits of obsidian seem to have a life inside in ashy places, swept into ovens and hearths, but some, perhaps eventually most, are also taken outside and dumped. Pottery is rather enigmatic because it is generally scarce. We see it going through the oven and being refired, but then it is absent from the external between-wall space. Does it get re-used, recycled inside in some way?

There is no simple inside:outside dichotomy. Some parts of the house are clean, some are dirty. Some materials leave the house, others stay in. Some things remain inside for a while, and may be taken out later. The external area is not so simple either. While part of it seems to represent rubbish and household waste, there are the horn cores and dog skull, which may have had symbolic meaning while inside the house, but this appears to have been lost, transformed, as they lost their architectural context.

Two further context types that have been analyzed relate to the story of the house: the bricks and mortar, the building materials of the structure. Unit 2574 represents a mud-brick from part of the wall of Building 1. It contains relatively dense plant remains, particularly from cereals, and a small proportion of bone fragments. The accompanying mortar, unit 2575, is devoid of plant remains but very dense in animal bone. These are mostly very small fragments, although some are actually diagnostic. A high proportion show signs of having been digested, that is, having passed through the gut of an animal and this is also true of those in the mud-brick. Perhaps this indicates that manufacture of both bricks and mortar sometimes takes place in open discard areas where dogs had defecated, or maybe dog faeces were intentionally put into the mix. Perhaps bone was needed in the mortar to 'key' it, or as a temper, as chaff is needed in mud-brick manufacture? Whatever the reason, whether dog faeces were intentionally or unintentionally included, they were clearly not excluded. Hence, as with other kinds of architecture (e.g. wattle-and-daub), we see excrement being taken up into the very fabric of the house.

The South Area

In the South area of the mound, excavations show a very different kind of external space to that yet encountered in the North. There are large open areas of midden deposits that occur on top of earlier houses, with later structures built directly on them: certainly the sense of place at Çatalhöyük did not require the separation of houses and rubbish. Yet it is not only open areas that become filled with rubbish-like material: some disused structures have similar materials in them, too. Yet other abandoned structures are filled with a different type of deposit, which, at first impression, has very little cultural material in. The rest of this discussion is concerned for the most part with a comparison of three contexts — a 'midden' deposit, a house infill that is seemingly 'sterile', and another that is dense in material — in an attempt to trace the derivation of materials in these deposits and to understand variations between them.

Unit 1668 is described as an ashy midden in an open area, or 'courtyard' following Mellaart's terminology. It is bounded by a row of structures on one side, buildings or shrines (now removed) on another, and it extends over the top of another house — Building 2 — in another direction. In a succeeding phase, the area was redeveloped and structures were built on top of part of the midden, thus reducing it in size.

The deposit consisted of fine interdigitated layers of ashy and silty clay lenses (Fig. 5.6), with inclusions of small brick and plaster fragments, and it typically yielded rich bio-archaeological and artefactual remains within discrete depositional events. The ashy nature of these lenses suggests the primary source as oven and hearth rake-out, which seems to have been deposited fairly rapidly since there is no indication that either weathering or activities had taken place on the surfaces.

In terms of finds, the highest density of obsidian is found in this unit, which fits with the general depositional association of obsidian and ash. Maybe chips of obsidian are sharp and dangerous to have around, and hence are safer in ash, which gets thrown out on a daily basis? Pottery is not very common, but the sherds that are present are not broken as small as they are in some units, perhaps indicating less movement and reworking of deposits here. The number of clay balls is high, but their density is not great. They are mostly broken, perhaps suggesting that their use is over. Of the worked stone, too, the axe is broken and blunt, also ready for discarding.

Plant remains are very rich here, and represent mixed activities: food preparation, processing, consumption. Interestingly, the mix of materials is most similar to those found in the dirty floor sample, unit 1416, in Building 1. This confirms the idea that the middens represent, in part at least, accumulated dumping events from household activities. Animal bones are present in fairly high densities, and a wide range of taxa is represented. Cattle bones are common, as are equids, which is different to the usual sheep- and goat-dominated deposits seen most frequently elsewhere. It is also notable that most of the bone is not burnt, indicating that it does not arrive here as part of the ashy matrix, but maybe it gets dumped directly out into the middens — a pattern suggested also by the discussion of Building 1.

In sum, the evidence does point towards unit 1668 representing dumped accumulations from inside (or from the roofs of?) structures: food remains,

Figure 5.6. *Ashy middens in Space 115, South area, shown in section.*

ash from hearths, discarded obsidian and debitage and broken tools, pots and clay balls. A single humanoid figurine is also broken with its head missing, although since this is the normal condition of this class of find it is more difficult to interpret. There are some complete objects, however, such as the two stone beads and worked bone points. These still seem to have life and use in them, although whether they were intentionally or accidentally dropped into the midden, of course, cannot be told.

How different, then, are the deposits of 1668 from those that are used to fill up disused buildings nearby? Unit 2006 serves as an example and represents between-occupation phase infilling within Building 4. Neighbouring buildings were also noted to have similar infill deposits. 2006 consisted of a homogenous silty clay, with sparse inclusions of small charcoal and plaster fragments, totally unlike the ashy midden seen, for example, in 1668. There was no trace of internal bedding and the material seemed to be rapidly deposited, with little or no time lapse during the infilling process. Upon excavation the material was described as almost sterile, and was thought to derive either from a source not yet encountered during excavations (maybe an off-site one?) or from some kind of screening or cleaning of a deposit.

Examination of the finds assemblages, however, shows that the deposit is not sterile, although obsidian, potsherds and clay ball fragments are found only in very low densities. The plant remains are very sparse, but the small quantities of domestic cereal and chaff remains might indicate that it was not from an off-site source, but more likely an on-site one that was carefully prepared before use. Animal bones, too, are in low densities, with few diagnostics, but the range of size fragments, with some over 10 cm long, does not support the idea of fine screening. In terms of derivation of this material, though, there are two observations from the bone that may help. First, most of it showed a slightly eroded surface condition, as if it had been reworked or abraded against some deposit. Second, there is a very high proportion of digested bone here, indicating that carnivore faeces are included in the deposit. This is reminiscent of the mortar of unit 2575 from Building 1 described above. Having made this link, maybe the cereal and chaff remains noted for 2006 could derive from mud-bricks, as seen in the brick of unit 2574, also from Building 1.

In sum for unit 2006, we can suggest that the deposit may derive (in part, at least) from on-site building materials, perhaps dismantled mud-bricks, mortar or roof debris, which was partially cleaned, although maybe not screened (leaving bones, plant remains, charcoal flecks and plaster fragments), and prepared for a foundation deposit. Such material would have been instantly available for quick infilling of a house like Building 4, which was to be built on fast, and unlike midden materials, which are rich in rotting organics, it would need little or no time to settle. Apart from this functional explanation, though, maybe the practice of recycling bricks from ancestral homes brings memories and continuity into the foundations of the new.

Building 2 in the South area (Fig. 5.7) is seen to have been infilled in a very different way. Unit 1873 represents a large deposit that extended across the whole space within the house walls, and lay close to (but not directly above) the floors. The deposit consisted in part of ashy lenses, similar in kind to those of the midden 1668 and presumably representing waste from neighbouring households. Finds, unsurprisingly, are similar to those in 1668, but in lower densities because of the lesser concentration here of the ashy refuse with which they are associated. In part, the deposit also contained mixed building debris (brick, mortar and plaster fragments), which may have come from the destruction of the upper parts of the building itself. The question of interest, then, is why this building saw such different treatment from the others, which were rapidly infilled with relatively clean, prepared material?

There are some unusual features of 1873 that may help in understanding this.

First, many of the pot sherds appear to come from the same vessels, suggesting more integrity to the deposit than its midden-like nature implies. Secondly, clay balls are very few, and under-represented if compared to the ashy midden of 1668. This is particularly interesting in view of the dense concentration of clay balls left in a bin in the house, and may imply some kind of sorting between them. Thirdly, the animal remains, while from a variety of sources, show a layer of very large (wild?) cattle bones in which some skeletal elements are still in partial articulation. Some bones are heavily smashed and the concentration has evidently been used for food, but the presence of parts of what is clearly the same animal strongly suggests the remains of a roasting event, in which parts of a huge cattle skeleton had been distributed and feasted upon. That these remains are all in the same basal layer of 1873 implies a feasting deposit laid down soon after the abandonment of the house and probably related to the closure and destruction of the building.

The infilling of Building 2, therefore, begins to look like a more deliberate and staged event. Initially, after abandonment, feasting remains may have been thrown in amongst the debris, and pottery vessels, perhaps used at the same event, smashed onto the pile. Antler tools discarded in deposit 1873 may have been used in picking away at the structures of the house. A huge cattle horn core may have been hacked down from its place of installation in the house wall. The house was then stripped of its assets, seen by the removal its structural posts, and finally but gradually, filled with the mixed deposits of building material and domestic waste, until all signs of the building were covered over. The area then became one large waste-ground represented by the open middens (e.g. seen in unit 1668) and continued as a location for refuse disposal for a fair amount of time, before eventually changing function. So in this case, unlike Building 1, which was left relatively clean (and intact?), and unlike Building 4, which was rapidly infilled and built over again, Building 2 was destroyed, saw some apparently purposeful infilling and was then left buried under layers of rubbish.

How are these distinctions best understood? Is it possible that the infilling of a building was associated with the burial practices of the inhabitants of the site? If, for example, burials were to be placed under-floor, as is seen in many cases at Çatalhöyük, perhaps the foundation deposit had to be laid deep and clean before the house floors and platforms were plastered on top, as in the case of Building 4 where we see rapid reconstruction of the living area. Building 2, on the other hand, seems to have had no plans for rebuilding, and was clearly left for a long time without structures and hence had no need for clean deposits in which the dead could be placed. Instead, the house is slowly filled up with discard of different kinds and left to become an 'external' midden.

The creation of these dedicated midden deposits is worthy of consideration in itself. It is not the only possible way of disposing of household waste,

Figure 5.7. *Building 2 in the South area, after excavation of infill deposits.*

nor the only one practised at Çatalhöyük, as we have seen. Middens may be simply the product of a desire to keep other areas of the site clear, may be regarded as a resource for manuring fields, or may be symbolic, for instance, a large midden representing affluence. 'Refuse has links with fertility where the value of green midden as fertilizer was recognized, and more generally to the cycle of death and renewal' (Needham & Spence 1997, 85). The situation at Çatalhöyük, where old houses are filled with middens and midden is used in mortar to build new houses, has parallels to the Late Bronze Age site of Apalle in Sweden. In the later period at Apalle, houses incorporate lots of fire-cracked rock from earlier rubbish deposits in their foundations, and the later rubbish deposits contain large amounts of house daub, so that the old rubbish is in the houses and the old houses are in the rubbish (Ullén 1994, 255). This seems to indicate a sense of place that is bound up in the houses and their continuity with previous houses and the lives that were lived in them, as materialized in the 'refuse' those lives generated.

Conclusion

In conclusion, through this brief and selective view of deposits, we have tried to trace the paths of archaeological materials and finds. An integrated view of these contexts and their contents allows us to glimpse patterns of the relative densities and distri-

butions of material, and infer activities and practices, and maybe also some rules and meanings.

In some cases, and at some level, the working definitions of deposits seem to hold: some middens appear to be middens, clean floors are supported as being generally clean, and dirty areas of floor can be confirmed as being so. But these are rather static, functional descriptions that lack meaning and action, in the same way that analyses of individual categories of finds tend to.

The integrated analysis presented here hopefully brings more possibilities to the interpretation of the material. It suggests how the inhabitants of Çatalhöyük kept parts of their houses swept clean of discarded material, but had small accumulations of waste in others, reflecting their use and categorization of space. It shows how some materials, like animal bone, may have been dumped outside quickly — perhaps it was considered a pollutant? — while others, like obsidian (more pure?), are moved from the house gradually. Yet other materials, such as broken pots or figurines, may stay in circulation inside, although the treatment of these seems varied. Some animal parts, like skulls, horns, tusks and hooves, come back into the house (probably after preparation) to be inserted into walls or roofs, taking on a symbolic role. But after the south part of Building 1 burnt down, we see some of these items thrown out with the rubbish, their meanings transformed by the loss of their architectural place.

The middens and fills, too, are complex and varied. Some middens seem to be direct repositories of household waste, and while they may be a useful resource in themselves (a communal space? a source of manure?), they also seem to be a sign of an area laid temporarily to rest, an interval in building. Houses that see continuous rebuilding have broken-down bricks and mortar (from old houses?) quickly prepared and deposited as infill, which also serves as the future burial ground. Building 2 had the feasting and destruction layers, where parts of the walls (with plasters and horn cores still attached?) get torn down into the space, before the slower infilling and closure of the house. There is no further building or preparation for burial here for some time.

These examples note the links between cycles of building and rebuilding, death, rubbish disposal and cleaning. It is perhaps difficult to draw generalizations from these isolated cases, but they do suggest how midden gets taken up into buildings, how buildings get reused in buildings, how buildings create and become middens, and how all the time, people are sweeping their floors, clearing up their chips of bone and obsidian, putting them into fires, following the rules. The sweeping into the fire may indicate that fire had a cleansing, purifying function. Or perhaps it was simply a convenient place to sweep things where they wouldn't get stepped on.

Taking a step back from the detail, what we see at the broader (both temporal and spatial) scale is the mound being built up in a continuous way. Materials were brought onto the site — mud, plaster, plants, animals, clay and stones — and it would seem that very little left again. Rather it was kept close, and lived on and in. The constraints of living on the mound where houses are nested together, where access to the middens or indeed *anywhere* must be across other people's roofs, perhaps necessitated codes and practices in themselves. Decisions about how to deal with ash, bones and dung, about where to make bricks and mortar, indeed about how to treat the closure or continuation of a house, is likely to have structured people's lives through rules and practices. Perhaps also the need to build up the mound, to keep houses and roofs at similar heights, was a factor in itself? Maybe rubbish was not something to be rid of at all, but a necessary fill and leveller that maintains some kind of order.

Fuller exploration of these patterns and themes is ongoing at Çatalhöyük, and these ideas may be either supported or overturned, added to or altered. Whatever the case, this discussion has found the movements of materials around the site to be highly

complex events, whether they move in and out of ovens and hearths or houses or walls, whether they are within small localized dumps, large-scale middens or house infills. It is also clear that the deposition and redeposition of materials — whether they seem to be rubbish or trash or redefined — clearly had relevance and meaning for the inhabitants of Çatalhöyük, and they most likely treated them according to rules and practices that we are only just beginning to untangle and explore.

Acknowledgements

We would like to thank everyone working at Çatalhöyük who is involved in the process of excavation, analysis and discussion, both of the particular contexts discussed in this paper, and all others that inform on and enrich the picture. In particular, we have drawn heavily on the field records and interpretations of Shahina Farid, Gavin Lucas, Roger Matthews, and Roddy Regan, who excavated and documented the contexts that are the focus of this discussion.

References

Cunliffe, B., 1992. Pits, preconceptions and propitiation in the British Iron Age. *Oxford Journal of Archaeology* 11, 69–84.

Gregory, C.A., 1982. *Gifts and Commodities*. New York (NY): Academic Press.

Halstead, P., I. Hodder & G. Jones, 1978. Behavioural archaeology and refuse patterns: a case study. *Norwegian Archaeological Review* 11, 118–31.

Hayden, B., & A. Cannon, 1983. Where the garbage goes: refuse disposal in the Maya highlands. *Journal of Anthropological Archaeology* 2, 117–63.

Hill, J.D., 1996. The identification of ritual deposits of animal bones: a general perspective from a specific study of 'special animal deposits' from the southern English Iron Age, in *Ritual Treatment of Human and Animal Remains: Proceedings of the First Meeting of the Osteoarchaeological Research Group Held in Cambridge on 8th October 1994*, eds. S. Anderson & K. Boyle. Oxford: Oxbow, 17–32.

Hodder, I., 1987. The meaning of discard: ash and domestic space in Baringo, in *Method and Theory for Activity Area Research: an Ethnoarchaeological Approach*, ed. S. Kent. New York (NY): Columbia University Press, 424–48.

McOmish, D., 1996. East Chisenbury: ritual and rubbish at the British Bronze Age–Iron Age transition. *Antiquity* 70, 68–76.

Moore, H.L., 1982. The interpretation of spatial patterning in settlement residues, in *Symbolic and Structural Archaeology*, ed. I. Hodder. Cambridge: Cambridge

University Press, 74–9.

Moore, H.L., 1986. *Space, Text, and Gender: an Anthropological Study of the Marakwet of Kenya*. Cambridge: Cambridge University Press.

Needham, S. & T. Spence, 1997. Refuse and the formation of middens. *Antiquity* 71, 77–90.

Richards, C. & J. Thomas, 1984. Ritual activity and structured deposition in later Neolithic Wessex, in *Neolithic Studies: a Review of Some Current Research*, eds. R. Bradley & J. Gardiner. (British Archaeological Reports, British Series 133.) Oxford: BAR, 189–218.

Schiffer, M.B., 1976. *Behavioral Archeology*. New York (NY): Academic Press.

Schiffer, M.B., 1987. *Formation Processes of the Archaeological Record*. Albuquerque (NM): University of New Mexico Press.

Tani, M., 1995. Beyond the identification of formation processes: behavioral inference based on traces left by cultural formation processes. *Journal of Archaeological Method and Theory* 2(3), 231–52.

Ullén, I., 1994. The power of case studies: interpretation of a late Bronze Age settlement in central Sweden. *Journal of European Archaeology* 2(2), 249–62.

Wilson, D.C., 1994. Identification and assessment of secondary refuse aggregates. *Journal of Archaeological Method and Theory* 1(1), 41–68.

Chapter 6

The Conservation of an Excavated Past

Frank Matero

First, of course, there's the things you don't know;
Then there's the things you do know but don't
    understand;
Then there's the things you do understand but
    which don't matter.

Simple Simon, A.E. Coppard

Archaeology, conservation and heritage

Reflexivity as a methodological approach in the production of knowledge takes its primary position from the contextualization of the problem rather than the superimposition of positivist, empirical models. Yet any methodology depends on the interrelationship between theory and practice as expressed through the intersection of principles, practices and procedures. In the case of postprocessual archaeology, ways of approaching past human behaviour are based on contextual, integrated analyses of issues and data derived from the interaction of numerous disciplines and multiple views (multivocality) and the new relationships that arise from such interaction (Hodder 1991).

The validity of such an approach in archaeological theory has already received widespread attention and criticism yet few projects have actually applied the precepts of postprocessualism in field practice, thus providing a self-conscious look at how archaeology constructs and uses knowledge. At Çatalhöyük, reflexivity has provided a useful vehicle for constructing not one, but many versions of Çatalhöyük, as an archaeological site with defined spatial and temporal boundaries as well as a place possessing complex associative meanings and values for many different contemporary groups and individuals (Hodder 1998). Such dichotomies have become common foils for renewed arguments of cultural relativity, ownership and power in the identification, interpretation and control of heritage sites. However the impact of a reflexive method on the

actual organization and interaction of the different members of the project team and non-professional participants has also forced a new way of thinking about the production of knowledge and who is empowered to generate it and benefit from it. The inclusion of comprehensive site conservation and heritage management alongside excavation from the very beginning of the project certainly represents a novel departure from past practices elsewhere.

The primacy of conservation to the Çatalhöyük research project was clearly stated by Ian Hodder, project director, in 1996 in his introduction to the first volume of field research:

> A site of this importance for the Mediterranean heritage needs careful conservation and presentation to the public . . . It poses special problems of conservation of mud brick and wall plaster, and problems of site management . . . The ultimate aim is to provide the Turkish Ministry of Culture with a well-planned heritage site. Visitors will be able to experience the site in a number of ways . . . By providing a range of visitor experiences the full heritage potential of the site can begin to be exploited. (Hodder 1996, 1)

Although issues of heritage and conservation have become important themes in recent discourse on place, cultural identity, and ownership of the past and the political and economic implications posed, few archaeological projects have actually included conservation as a viable strategy in addressing these attendant issues from the beginning. This has been owing in part to archaeologists' ignorance of a long history and tradition of conservation theory and practice, and a general misperception of the preservation field as one concerned with a nostalgic view of the past or focused only on technical issues and solutions. Simultaneously, specialists in conservation and heritage management have been slow to participate in the recent and rapidly expanding discourse on the meaning, use and ownership of heritage for political

71

and economic purposes and have avoided a critical examination of the historical and cultural narratives constructed largely through past archaeological projects and conservation practices. Yet conservation as an intellectual pursuit is predicated on the belief that knowledge, memory, and experience are tied to material culture. Conservation — whether of a landscape, building or wall painting — helps extend these places and things into the present and establishes a form of mediation critical to the interpretive process that reinforces these aspects of human existence.

The practices of archaeology and conservation are by their very nature oppositional. Excavation, as the primary physical method by which archaeologists reveal and read a site, is a subtractive process that is both destructive and irreversible. In the revealing of a site, structure or object, excavation is not a benign reversal of site formation processes but rather a traumatic invasion of a site's physico-chemical equilibrium usually resulting in the immediate deterioration of associated materials at various rates and patterns of change. Conservation, on the other hand, is predicated on the safeguarding of physical fabric from loss and depletion, based on the belief that material culture possesses unique abilities and the power to transmit knowledge as well as inspire memory and emotional responses, often through associated social interaction. Moreover, the fundamental issues of conservation also concern ways of evaluating and interpreting cultural heritage for its preservation and safeguarding now and for the future (Fielden 1982). In this last respect, conservation itself becomes a way of extending and reifying cultural identities and historical narratives over time through valorization and interpretation.

Conservation is a modern concept born out of the notion of history as something which is linear and has been completed and brought to an end. As such, artefacts and sites are divorced from their past by the present's historical consciousness which dictates new motives and methods for their use and preservation. Such motives and methods found various modes of expression through the application of historical and scientific precepts during the late nineteenth and twentieth centuries. The resulting principles attempted to define a new approach that related the aesthetic and historical values of art and architecture with the material form to ensure the transmission of the whole work as both idea and thing. Contemporary theorists such as Vittorio Gregotti have attempted to explain conservation as an antimodernist/postmodernist stance, founded on non-presentist reactions to notions of progress and based on the believed value and legitimacy of all past artistic contributions to society (Gregotti 1996). In the end, all conservation is a critical act in that the decisions regarding what is conserved, and who and how it is presented, is a product of contemporary values and beliefs about the past's relationship to (and use by) the present.

To date, most preservation activity has focused on programmes of survey, inventory, conservation, restoration and rehabilitation of specific sites associated with specific histories and selected pasts. This approach has compartmentalized sites and activities into mutually exclusive alternatives rather than inseparable aspects of the same overall treatment that all cultural property requires for its long-term interpretation, transformation, protection, use and maintenance. Similarly, as a modern construct, such approaches have tended to ignore the continuing and changing significance that places and material culture hold, especially for affiliated communities, in defining and preserving everyday life and beliefs in all their diverse forms and expressions.

Beginning with the first International Congress of Architects in Madrid in 1904 and later with the creation of the Charter of Athens following the International Congress of Restoration of Monuments (1931), numerous attempts have been made to identify and codify a set of universal principles for the intervention of structures and places of historic and cultural significance.

Despite their various emphases and differences, all these documents identify the conservation process as one governed by absolute respect for the aesthetic, historic and physical integrity of the structure or place and one requiring a high sense of moral responsibility. Implicit in these tenets is the notion of cultural heritage as a physical resource that is at once valuable and irreplaceable and an inheritance that promotes cultural continuity in a dynamic way.

Summarized from the more recent documents, these principals are as follows:[1]
- the obligation to perform research and documentation; that is to record physical, archival, and other evidence before and after any intervention to generate and safeguard knowledge of the structures and site and their associated activities;
- the obligation to respect cumulative age-value; that is the acknowledgement of the site or work as a cumulative physical record of human activity embodying cultural beliefs, values, materials and techniques, and displaying the passage of time;
- the obligation to safeguard authenticity; a culturally relative value associated with the genuine

materiality of a thing or place as a way of ensuring authorship or witness of a time and place;

- the obligation to perform minimum reintegration; that is, to re-establish structural and aesthetic legibility and meaning with the least physical interference; and

- the obligation to perform interventions that will allow other options and further treatment in the future. This principle recently has been redefined more accurately as 'retreatibility', a concept of considerable significance for architecture, monuments, and archaeological sites given their need for long-term high-performance solutions, often structural in nature.

As summarized in the Australian ICOMOS (Burra) Charter, the ultimate aim of conservation is to retain or recover the cultural significance of the thing or place and must include provision for its security, its maintenance and its future. Conservation is based, first and foremost, on a respect for the existing fabric and should therefore involve minimal physical intervention. It should not distort the evidence provided by the fabric, especially as this relates to the traces of additions and alterations related to its history and use. The conservation policy appropriate to a thing or place must first be determined by an understanding of its cultural significance and its physical condition. The conservation policy should determine which uses are compatible with the formal and material reality, not the reverse.

Today, contemporary practice has evolved an entire lexicon of intervention strategies based on the degree of intervention. This has resulted in a more sophisticated as well as sometimes confusing definition of approaches, depending largely on the type and context of heritage. In most professional contexts, conservation has become the designated term for 'an objective, scientific approach to the past in the form of historical knowledge, not the same as the continuity guaranteed by former tradition; a modern phenomenon of maintaining living contact with cultural works of the past' (Philippot 1976). In the United States and Australia, the terms *preservation* and *conservation* have come into the professional language as distinct concepts. Explicit and unique to the definition of preservation is the notion of the *status quo* or the means by which the existing form, integrity, and materials of a structure are maintained and deterioration retarded. Conservation, in this same context, has been relegated to mean the whole spectrum of technology applied to the safe-guarding of cultural heritage.

Both terms, in concept and process, have as their fundamental objective the protection of cultural heritage, meaning the transmission of intangible as well as tangible products of culture. However, whereas preservation seeks to control change by maintaining the existing physical state, or at least the illusion of no change, conservation, as a concept, seeks to sustain continuity through controlled changes. Both are ways of maintaining living contact with the past through the identification, transmission, and protection of that which is considered culturally valuable and worthy of retaining. Yet their differences in approach can be explained partly in response to negative attitudes toward past restorations in Europe and North America which by today's standards deprived the work of material integrity and historical and cultural authenticity. Both definitions and their implicit approaches depend on each other for meaning and a clear understanding of their usage is critical.

For some traditional societies the concepts and practice of preservation are often viewed as antithetical to the role of continuing traditions, or those beliefs, actions, and material correlates which are valued by a group and considered worthy of retaining and passing on from one generation to the next. Whereas continuity of tradition may be critical to ensuring cultural identity, it is important to remember that tradition is as dynamic as culture change itself. Only by recognizing the changing nature of tradition as constructed memory and cultural identities, can a community effectively and responsibly manage its present and future through personal and collective interpretations of the past rather than through imposed fictions from the outside. Like history, conservation represents the conscious commitment to cultural continuity where living memory ends.

In the late twentieth century conservation has become a major strategy in shaping and interpreting our physical world. Every conservation measure is a form of argument that touches upon cultural values and our definition, treatment, interpretation and use of the past. Often historical arguments or values for or against the identification, designation, and physical retention of cultural property are based on an epistemology of scholarship and facts. Facts and scholarship, however, are explanations that serve the goals of conservation and are a product of their time and place. Out of this dilemma, our current definition of conservation has emerged as a field of specialization concerned primarily with the material well-being of cultural property and the peculiar conditions of ageing and survival; focusing on the qualitative and quantitative processes of change and degradation. It finds its outlet in minimal but opportune interventions, conducted with both traditional skills and experimentally advanced techniques. It avoids at all costs a generalized irrational renewal of form and materials.

This last point is important as it leaves open for discussion the possibility for more drastic interventions, such as the reassembly, installation or replication of missing or damaged components. Such interventions, common on archaeological sites, are often based on the desire or need for visual legibility or structural re-integration. These interventions become even more critical if they sustain or improve the future performance or life of the site or structure in its environment. Obviously for archaeological sites, changing or controlling the environment by reburial, building a protective enclosure or shelter on site, or by relocating selected components such as murals or sculpture, often indoors, are options which allow maximum physical protection. However, such interventions significantly impact on the contextual meaning and appearance value, an aspect already discussed as significant for many such sites. Similarly, interventions developed to address only the material condition of objects, structures, and places of cultural significance without consideration of associated cultural beliefs and rituals can sometimes denature or compromise their power, 'spirit' or value. In this regard, cultural and community context and dialogue with professionals are critical.

In light of these issues, conservation emerges as the science of safeguarding cultural heritage by observing and analyzing the evolution, deterioration, and maintenance of material culture; the conducting of investigations to determine the cause, effect, and solution of problems; and the directing of remedial interventions focused on maintaining the integrity and quality of the existing historic fabric. Two associated terms — science and technology — are critical to this definition and require some clarification as they are often taken in their most basic or obvious expression to represent the goals of conservation. By science, what is meant is an imposed systematic and structured way of understanding the material world, different from the approaches of history, philosophy, or aesthetics. Technology is the application of science or an entire body of methods and materials used to achieve the stated objectives. If we accept the premise that the practice of conservation began with the relational study of the underlying causes of deterioration and the refining of an etiological approach, then it was in the 1930s and 1940s, along with the development of conservation laboratories and spe-

cialists, that the field was born. Yet within the understood limitations of the scientific method to generate certain kinds of data, conservation still begins and ends as an interpretation of the work. One is not only dealing with material things and places, but with complex cultural questions of beliefs, convictions, and emotions, as well as aesthetic, material, and functional significance. Science helps to interpret, but it cannot and should not be the sole agent to create meanings nor singularly represent one truth when applied to heritage.

Archaeological sites

The conservation and management of archaeological sites is a field of increasing interest as evidenced by a growing number of professional conferences, published proceedings, and international projects (Matero et al. 1998). Archaeological sites have long been a part of heritage tourism, certainly before the use of the term 'heritage' and the formal study of tourism. However, current concern can be attributed to the perception among the public and professionals that archaeological sites, like the natural environment, represent non-renewable resources deteriorating at an increasing rate. This deterioration is attributable to a wide array of causes ranging from neglect and poor management to increased visitation, vandalism, and environmental degradation and pollution, from inappropriate past treatments to treatment life span termination. No doubt the pressures of economic benefit from touristic development in conjunction with increasing global communication and mobility have caused accelerated damage to many sites unprepared for development and visitation.

Despite the global increase in the scale of these problems, issues of recovery, documentation, stabilization, interpretation and display have been at the heart of archaeological conservation since the early twentieth century. One of the first coordinated attempts to codify principles and procedures of site conservation was formulated in the Athens Charter of 1931 where measures such as accurate documentation, protective reburial, and international interdisciplinary collaboration were clearly articulated. In 1956, further advances were made at the General Conference on International Principles Applicable to Archaeological Excavations adopted by the United Nations Educational, Scientific, and Cultural Organization (UNESCO) in New Delhi where the role of a centralized state administration in managing, coordinating, and protecting excavated and unexcavated archaeological sites was advocated.

Other charters such as the ICOMOS (Venice) Charter of 1964 extended these earlier recommendations through explicit practices including the avoidance of reconstructions of archaeological features except in cases where the original components were available but dismembered (*anastylosis*) and the use of distinguishable modern techniques for the conservation of historic monuments. The Australia ICOMOS (Burra) Charter of 1981 expanded the definition of archaeological site to also include place, challenging Eurocentric definitions of value and significance, and notions of authenticity and integrity to include context and traditional use, an idea important for culturally-affiliated indigenous groups. Finally in 1989, the ICOMOS Charter for the Protection of the Archaeological Heritage was adopted in Lausanne, Switzerland, formalizing the international recognition of many archaeological sites as living cultural landscapes and the responsibility of the archaeologist in the conservation process.[2]

Like all disciplines and fields, archaeological conservation has been shaped by its historical habit and by contemporary concerns. Important in its development has been the shifting, even expanding, notion of site conservation to include the stabilization and protection of the whole area rather than simply *in situ* artefact conservation or the removal of site (architectural) features. The public interpretation of archaeological sites has long been associated with the stabilization and display of ruins. Implicit in site stabilization and display is the aesthetic value many ruin sites possess based on a long-lived European tradition of cultivating a taste for the picturesque.[3] With the scientific investigation and study of many archaeological sites beginning in the late nineteenth century, both the aesthetic and informational value of these sites was promoted during excavation-stabilization. In contemporary practice, options for archaeological site conservation include: reconstruction, reassembly (*anastylosis*,) *in situ* preservation and protection including shelters and/or fabric consolidation, *ex situ* preservation through removal, and excavation/reburial with or without site interpretation.

Despite the level of intervention, that is, whether interpretation is achieved through *anastylosis* or reconstruction, specific sites, namely those possessing impressive masonry remains, have tended to establish an idealized approach and desirable end product for the interpretation of archaeological sites in general. Places such as Çatalhöyük at once challenge these ingrained notions of ordered chaos and arranged masonry by virtue of their fragile materials (earth), temporal and spatial disposition (as a tell of

superimposed levels), and relationship with associated foreign, national, and traditional communities and their narratives. Moreover, changing notions of 'site' have expanded the realm of what is to be interpreted (Dunnell 1992) and preserved resulting in both archaeological inquiry and legal protection at the regional and local level. These aspects of site conservation and interpretation become all the more difficult when considered in conjunction with the demands of tourism and site and regional development for the larger physical and political context.

It is for all these reasons that conservation and archaeology at Çatalhöyük must be conceived as an integrated strategy, the aim of which is to link the needs and potentialities at all scales and levels from the artefacts and murals to the buildings and urban plan, from the contemporary local villages to the surrounding region, from objects and site to people and place.

Earthen architecture in the archaeological context

The exposure of earthen architecture at archaeological sites presents tremendous difficulties both during and after excavation. Like all buried structures and artefacts, earthen buildings and their associated features such as wall paintings exist in unique microenvironments created by a wide range of factors including soil type, ground water, buried material, depth and configuration, animal and plant activity, microflora and bacteria. After years of interment, overall thermo-hygrometric equilibrium is usually achieved with the surrounding environment, assuming external conditions remain the same. The destabilization of this environment through excavation can cause structural instability and potential collapse from rain and snow erosion, wind load, seismic and vibrational forces, and plant and animal (including human) activity.

At the micro-scale, a loss of surface pressure and rapid drying owing to surface evaporation inevitably results in the migration of soluble salts to the surface as well as shrinkage cracking, loss of cohesion, and delamination. Through evaporation, accelerated by wind action, salts may crystallize on the surface or within the subsurface pores of the material causing disruptive internal pressures resulting in disaggregation, flaking, and detachment. Immediately upon excavation, all exposed surfaces become a plane of climatic activity. Heat is absorbed and moisture evaporates. Newly exposed walls may be subjected to dramatic temperature changes ranging from the extreme midday heat to cold nights. Slight differences in thermal coefficients between mud-brick walls and plasters may exacerbate plaster and paint failure. Cracks, delaminations, and the natural layered structure of wall and floor plasters facilitate plant root growth and salt formation causing gross macro-failure, detachment and collapse. The more gradual the process of excavation or exposure, the more likely it is to mitigate damage by slowly acclimatizing the buried remains to the variations of the new environment.

While such processes affect all excavated porous materials, the situation becomes particularly damaging for clay-based materials owing to their thermo-hygrometric sensitivity and resultant dimensional changes (expansion/contraction). Highly reactive clays such as smectites, present in the marls used for the plasters, mural paintings and reliefs at Çatalhöyük, are especially problematic. This is critical for freshly excavated walls as rapid desiccation in the Anatolian summer climate leads to rapid shrinkage, and extreme mechanical stress causing cracking, detachment and collapse. Earlier experiences at mud-brick sites in Iran proved that the period of greatest danger for newly excavated work was the first few weeks (Bruno *et al.* 1968–69, 449), a situation also observed at Çatalhöyük.

Over the past three decades, numerous international symposia and conferences have been held in order to collect and disseminate information relating to strategies and techniques for the temporary protection, preservation and display of earthen sites. The consensus regarding earthen archaeological structures is that every effort should be made to preserve and protect them either through reburial, shelters, or direct material consolidation or surface protection. Where removal is necessary due to excavation safety and the objectives of the archaeological research programme, recording and sampling must be extensive.

Site conservation history at Çatalhöyük

The discovery and excavation of Çatalhöyük by James Mellaart from 1961–65 immediately gained world attention for a site unique in its great size, apparent complexity, and enormous time depth as well as for the amount and quality of finds discovered. Popular and academic coverage of the excavation in the *Illustrated London News* and *Anatolian Studies* quickly established Çatalhöyük's significance. Mellaart labelled Çatalhöyük '. . . a supernova among the rather dim galaxy of contemporary peasant cultures' (Mellaart 1965, 77) and cited among its many 'firsts' were the largest Neolithic urban settlement and most extensive mud-brick architecture found to date as well as

the unprecedented discovery of highly sophisticated mural paintings and painted plaster relief sculpture.

Dwellings were constructed of sun-dried mud-brick with timber posts and beams on a modular rectangular plan. Entrance to each house was gained through flat roofs made of reeds and earth supported by wooden beams and staggered to allow each building access to light. Multiple layers of plaster made from locally available marly soils coated the walls. Many of the interior spaces contained elaborate plaster reliefs and wall paintings, all of which indicate an enigmatic symbolism. The extensive physical evidence revealed at Çatalhöyük has dramatically altered traditional views of prehistoric Anatolia and the Near East in general. Here a civilization existed with sophisticated artistic and technological ability and complex religious beliefs. These monumental components — buildings, paintings and relief sculpture — were immediately understood as significant features of the site; however their physical preservation proved challenging and without precedent.

Excavation at Çatalhöyük lasted for four seasons from 1961–65 with a hiatus in 1964; only a thirtieth of the sixteen-hectare East mound was dug. Minimal site protection was employed both during and after each season and the extreme fragility of the site became particularly apparent in 1965 when the excavation resumed after having been left unprotected for two years. The published field report for the 1965 season stated; 'after two successive winters of rain and snow the remains discovered in 1963 had badly weathered, many walls had fallen, others were dangerous' (Mellaart 1966a, 166). The vulnerability of the unprotected site to the ravages of weather was all the more obvious in 1993 with the re-opening of the excavation after 28 years.

Fortunately, emergency measures were taken on several paintings and plaster relief sculptures during the 1960s excavation. Given the unexpected discovery of the wall paintings and the absence of an integrated conservation programme as part of the project, the only, and preferred, option for preservation at the time entailed the removal of the paintings and reliefs from the site. It is through these early efforts that surviving examples exist today in the Museum of Anatolian Civilizations at Ankara. No efforts were made to preserve any of the structures or their murals *in situ*.

Past conditions, current problems

The existing conditions of the architecture, murals and reliefs during and between excavation seasons from 1960–1965 are difficult to reconstruct from the available information. Nevertheless through isolated observations in the published field reports, limited photographs, interviews, and current excavation experience, it is possible to reconstruct something of the conditions of the walls and their associated art as found in the 1960s. According to Mellaart, wall conditions varied depending on proximity to the surface, plant and animal disturbance and subsidence from upper level compression (Mellaart 1962a, 976). As Todd has pointed out, the difficulties encountered at other archaeological sites with poorly preserved and collapsed mud-brick walls were not normally encountered at Çatalhöyük; in some instances walls had deformed and failed causing plaster to crack, buckle, slump, and fall, but generally the walls were in sound condition (Todd 1976, 19 & 35).[4]

By the third season (1963), as the excavation reached lower building levels, Mellaart was faced with structural concerns and safety issues due to the depth of the excavations and the 'heavy mud brick walls perilously lean[ing] at drunken angles and mak[ing] any work in depth in a restricted space impracticable'. As a result he cautioned, 'If wall paintings are found at any great depth, it is not safe to clean them . . .' (Mellaart 1964a, 158) Partial excavation of the lowest level, X(1), revealed structures in the poorest state of preservation owing to compression damage and moisture. He observed, 'Because of its depth and the tremendous weight of five successive shrines (IX–VIA) built on top of it, the walls bulged, the decoration had been somewhat compressed and its west wall was deformed beyond recognition' (Mellaart 1964b, 73).

During excavation Mellaart and Todd noted that plastered walls began to deteriorate immediately, the exposed plaster developing large cracks upon drying (Mellaart 1964b, 39). This is evident in the published close-up photographs of the paintings after exposure where the surfaces reveal a pattern of fresh parallel vertical cracks typical of shrinkage cracking. Apparently not only did the unprotected walls and plasters suffer, so did several of the colours of the paintings. Mellaart stated that 'upon exposure the flesh-coloured bodies turned brown and the pinks either turned gray or faded completely' (Mellaart 1966c, 24).

Todd further mentions that because of the rapid hardening of the plasters upon exposure and drying in the hot Anatolian climate and the resulting difficulty in removal of the plaster layers overlying the paintings, the use of a gridded excavation system

Figure 6.1. *South area, Building 2/Wall 64. Wall plaster detachment and collapse from root growth, salts, and desiccation during excavation. (Photo: F. Matero.)*

with balks was abandoned as too time-consuming. Instead, excavation was performed by individual building units allowing entire walls to be exposed, conserved and revealed quickly before surface hardening, thus ensuring speedy removal of the outer layers of plaster with dental knives (Todd 1976, 19, 35). Site photographs from the 1960s suggest few if any protective shelters were employed during the excavation to retard rapid drying. Writing a decade after the excavation closed, Todd postulated that if a controlled sheltering system as at Can Hasan III had been employed, the surfaces would not have desiccated so rapidly and the recovery process could have occurred in less haste (Todd 1976, 19).

Immediate desiccation, shrinkage, detachment and collapse of the walls and plaster surfaces have also been observed at the site on freshly excavated walls during the past four field seasons of the cur-

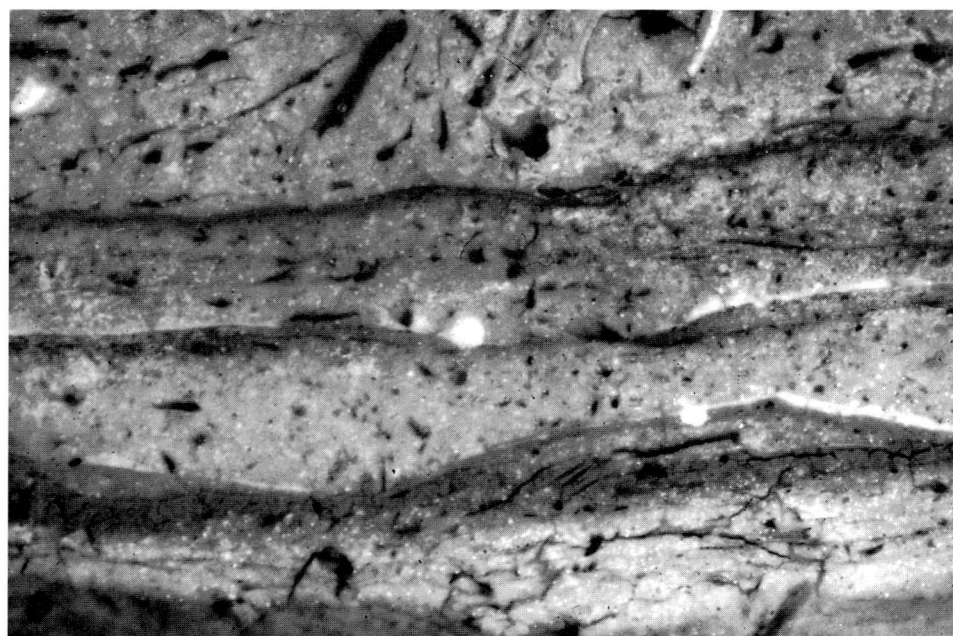

Figure 6.2. *Cross-section of painted wall plaster illustrating typical stratigraphy of porous tan marl base (preparatory) and dense white finish layers with superimposed hematite pigmented design layers, presumably related to painting. [Sample B95, 18.75× magnification, in plain polarized reflected light/Nikon SMZ-U stereoscope.] (Photo: E. Kopelson.)*

rent excavation (Fig. 6.1). Exposed walls protected by sun and wind-screening shelters display lower temperatures and slower desiccation than those exposed without protection. These external protective controls coupled with partial excavation temporarily leaving 5–10 cm of protective excavation fill against the surfaces (floors and walls,) and polyethylene sheeting loosely draped over walls and features during excavation have significantly reduced shrinkage cracking which occurs immediately after exposure and before conservation work.

Plasters, paintings and relief sculpture

By Mellaart's own admission '[Çatalhöyük's] most spectacular contribution to Near Eastern archaeology, as well as to art history, [was] its wall-paintings, the earliest yet found on man-made walls' (Mellaart 1962b, 57). As many as 80 two-part sequences of ground and finish plaster layers, each measuring 0.5 mm or less, have been revealed in the recent examination of representative earthen plaster and mud-brick samples (Fig. 6.2). Paintings, most often executed on the dense white finish plasters and often subsequently plastered over, were observed in cross-section examination between many of the super-imposed sequences. What is perhaps less well-known and buried within the field reports of *Anatolian Studies*, unpublished technical conservation reports, and the anecdotal coverage in the *Illustrated London News*, is their remarkable discovery and the creative efforts to conserve them.

Discovery of the first mural paintings occurred during the first field season (17 May–29 June, 1961) on the East Mound in two 'shrines' in Levels III and IV and in two 'houses' of Level VI. Among these finds were some of the best examples of geometric and figural painting to be discovered on the site including the leopard dancers and deer and bull hunt scenes of Shrine A.III.1 and the so-called mortuary structure images of Shrine VI.B.1 (formerly E.VI.1.) In order to understand the nature and importance of the discovery of these early murals, a contemporary account published in a series on the first field season in the *Illustrated London News* is quoted *in extenso*:

> . . . on the second day of the excavation, a wall appeared in our first trench that was covered with a white plaster. One of the workman knocked against it and part of it fell off, revealing an area of red plaster beneath . . . After cleaning the entire wall, even a cursory examination revealed that the red patch accidentally revealed was not a patch of a red-painted wall but part of an animal, painted in red on a pinkish-white background (Mellaart 1962a, 976).

Given the fragility and importance of these elements, Mellaart arranged for the production of detailed watercolour 'copies' or 'transcripts' of many of the wall paintings and reliefs by artists Anne Louise Stockdale, Grace Huxtable and Raymonde Enderle Ludovici (Mellaart 1963, 43). This graphic record documented the murals both in their as-found condition, exhibiting areas of loss and partial exposure of the various superimposed layers of painting, as well as renderings of individual design levels with their missing portions sometimes reconstructed with dotted lines. Drawings were apparently produced directly from the walls by first tracing them 'in *grisaille* on cellophane' between each painting exposure (Mellaart 1966b, 25). On at least one occasion these 'transcripts' were positioned in place on the wall to illustrate the effect of the restored painting *in situ* (Mellaart 1966a, pl. 42a). As such, these drawings represent a significant, and often the only, record of the extent and condition of the paintings as found prior to their detachment, and occasional loss. Photographic documentation appears to have been limited or at least subsequently compromised owing to the unfortunate loss of Mellaart's field notes and records from fire.

Mural paintings and reliefs were also depicted in their architectural context at first schematically in perspective building views by RIBA architect Peter Winchester (Mellaart 1962b, 42) and later as partial perspective interior room views, illustrating specific period reconstructions ('restorations') drawn by Grace Huxtable. These 'restorations' have had a profound affect on all subsequent interpretations of the interior architecture, especially in relation to the limited number of photographic views that have been available for subsequent study. Limited technical analysis of the paints and plasters was conducted during the second season by S.J. Rees-Jones of the Courtauld Institute in London (Mellaart 1963, 43) and later by Pamela (Pratt) French during follow-up treatments to the mural paintings from 1968–74. Recent analyses by Matthews, Kopelson, Turton, Moss and Myers have extended the knowledge about the plasters, paintings and mud-brick.

Published site photographs of the mural paintings and relief sculptures generally suggest these works were found in a remarkable condition with a clarity of surface and design. What must be remembered, however, is that much of the painted wall art that was photographically recorded and ultimately removed was freshly revealed on site either behind superimposed protective layers of white plaster or subsequently 'peeled' painting layers. Mellaart reported that he spent two days removing the protective overlying layers of white plaster after discovery of the first painting. The poor condition of the panel, attributed to its proximity of less than five inches from the surface, however, prompted the field application of polyvinyl acetate emulsion after cleaning and before removal and transfer to the Archaeological Museum in Ankara (Museum of Anatolian Civilizations.) Paintings considered too damaged or fragile for treatment were reported to be covered up after recording (Mellaart 1962b, 58–9).

The conservation of mural art (wall paintings and sculpture), and in particular detachment and removal, has an extended history beginning with Vitruvius.[5] Long justified as the only means of preserving such works where the building was in jeopardy or the environment harmful, or in the early twentieth century, as a way of studying artist's techniques, the detachment of mural paintings and mosaics has fallen out of favour except in situations of extreme crisis such as the Florence flood of 1966. By the 1960s, conservators, especially those working in Italy, possessed a well-developed *repertoire* of techniques for the removal of wall paintings executed on lime-based substrates. These techniques were based on the extent and level of removal relative to the design layer, substrate, and support interface and employed specific methods and materials depending on the level of detachment. Superimposed multilayered paintings and relief sculpture executed on earthen plasters and mud-brick supports such as at Çatalhöyük represented a technical problem well outside the realm of experience with lime-based paintings, even those in an archaeological context.[6] This is due primarily to the lack of inherent strength and susceptibility of clay plasters to water and other polar solvents necessary for the detachment process.

During the first season at Çatalhöyük, field preparation required cleaning, supporting, removing and packing the wall paintings and reliefs, techniques which were formulated and undertaken by Perry Bialor and Mrs Mellaart under the supervision of Ernest Hawkins of the Byzantine Institute of America in Istanbul. Development of a conservation programme for the wall paintings and reliefs was subsequently undertaken by Henry Hodges, Pamela Pratt, T. Martin, Viola Pemberton-Pigott, Margaret White and later Priscilla Berridge and Anne Searight. Little recorded detailed information on the *in situ* conservation of the wall paintings and reliefs exists; however, according to unpublished conservation reports from 1968–74, paintings removed from the site in 1962 and 1963 were either block lifted, including the mud-brick support (*stacco a massello*) or partially detached removing either the design layers with the underlying base plaster (*stacco*) or the individual design layers alone (*strappo*). Unmounted paintings detached by the block method were surface consolidated with polyvinyl acetate both with and without facings of Japanese tissue, linen and glue size. Mounted paintings detached by 'peeling' the plaster off the mud-brick support (*stacco* or *strappo*) were faced. Depending on their size, paintings and reliefs were removed in sections for ease in manipulation and transport.

Beginning in 1968 previously recovered paintings and reliefs were prepared for treatment and display by Pamela Pratt. Examination revealed a host of problems related to their earlier site preparation for detachment and subsequent storage. Conservation treatments generally included refacing, removal of the mud plaster base coats, and consolidation of the paint layers with polymethyl-methacrylate. A primary backing was then applied consisting of a mixture of the same as a binder with marble dust and glass powder fillers reinforced with strips of pre-washed muslin. The cut sections were rejoined and the whole reinforced with adhesive and aluminium mesh (Pratt 1970, 6). Some of these paintings are currently on display at the Museum of Anatolian Civilizations in Ankara.

Strategic Plan for Site Conservation Program Çatalhöyük, Turkey

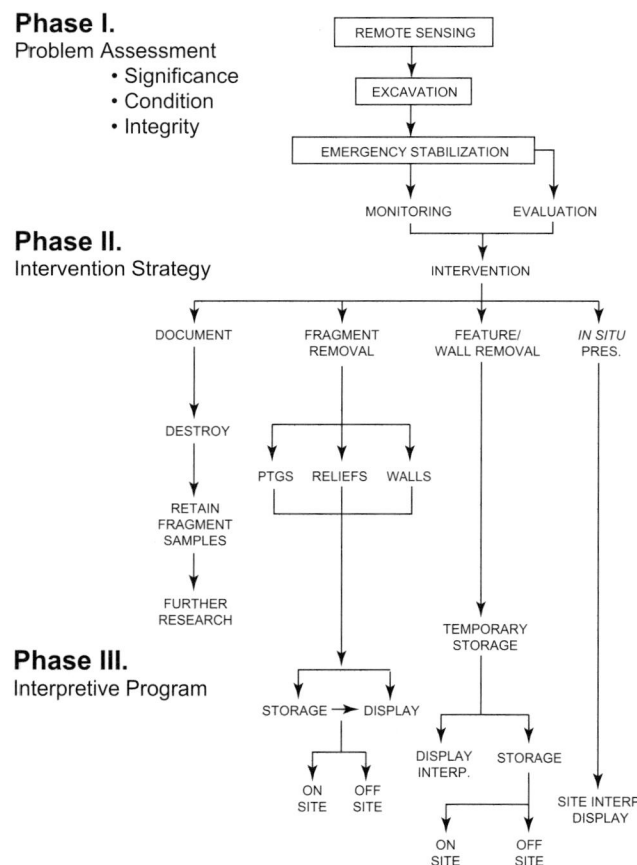

Figure 6.3. *Strategic plan for site conservation programme at Çatalhöyük.*

Summary of the current programme of field conservation and research

In 1993, thirty years after its discovery, Çatalhöyük was reopened by the Turkish government through a 25-year archaeological programme developed under the direction of Ian Hodder of Cambridge University. One of the principal aims of the renewed programme is the conjoining of the archaeological agenda with conservation, cultural tourism and heritage management. Central to this is site interpretation through the public display of the extraordinary architecture, mural paintings and relief sculpture *in situ* as well as the construction of a site museum. Site conservation activities including research and fieldwork are under the direction of Frank Matero, Lindsay Falck, and Catherine Myers of the Architectural Conservation Laboratory of the University of Pennsylvania.[7]

The primary objective of the current programme is to develop sound techniques and interpretive approaches to the immediate and long-term conservation of the site and its architecture, including the monumental art (wall paintings and reliefs). A second objective is the development of standards and guidelines for the examination, documentation, and characterization of earthen materials so that future studies can be conducted against a broader, more consistent data base. A third objective is the opportunity for the practical training of conservators, archaeologists and students in archaeological site and material conservation. This project is key to Turkey's cultural heritage and the development of cultural tourism in central Anatolia and seeks to coordinate applied research on a much-neglected subject in response to actual site conservation needs and field training of local and foreign students and professionals.

A phased programme of research and fieldwork has been coordinated to develop integrated methods for the conservation and management of the site including: the *in situ* stabilization and protection of wall paintings, plaster reliefs, and selected buildings; the development of non-destructive transfer methods for the wall paintings, reliefs, and architectural elements; and the development of techniques for the separation of multiple layers of wall paintings (Fig. 6.3). Activities include: emergency stabilization and protection during excavation and between field seasons, condition survey and environmental monitoring, materials analysis, and conservation treatment development, testing, and application. The methodology employed is *de riguer* for any conservation project involving:

- documentary research on the site's excavation and treatment history to establish previous conditions and subsequent conservation methods;
- technical analysis and characterization of the mud-brick, plasters, paintings and relief sculpture using standard geo-technical and wet-chemical techniques, microscopical and instrumental analyses;
- monitoring and recording of site conditions using developed methods for earthen materials and diagnosis of deterioration mechanisms; and
- the design, testing, and execution of a treatment programme specifically focused on the *in situ* and off-site stabilization of architectural fabric including plain and painted earthen plasters and mud-brick walls and features.

In order to accommodate the exigencies of excavation, fieldwork and research have been guided by emergency issues such as temporary protection and structural stabilization during excavation and between field seasons. Related to this has been the need to develop an understanding of the environment through a monitoring programme designed to measure ambient temperature and humidity and ground and wall moisture. During the academic year between field seasons, research has focused on the characterization of the plasters and paintings, mud-brick, and associated materials using micromorphological, mineralogical and petrographic analysis, as well as instrumental techniques including scanning electron microscopy, x-ray analysis (EDS), and x-ray diffractometry in order to determine composition, layer structure, execution techniques, and overall physico-chemical properties.

Deterioration mechanisms have been hypothesized and studied in conjunction with the environmental monitoring programme for immediate and long-term evaluation of site conditions and intervention assessments (Figs. 6.4 & 6.5). Based on existing condition, and environmental and material characterization studies, a variety of conservation

techniques have been examined and laboratory-tested on facsimile models as well as on site as pilot treatment tests (Fig. 6.6). This has allowed for the gradual adjustment of the developed programme over time and the opportunity to provide advanced training for conservation graduate students and other professionals.

A long-term strategy designed to shape current excavation techniques in conjunction with conservation needs is on going. This involves an understanding of site materials and construction technology, site formation processes and conditions before, during, and after excavation, and field applications of the developed techniques for the conservation of the architecture, mural paintings and relief sculpture at the site. Current research will build on earlier research and experiences developed during the 1960s excavation and 1970s mural conservation and together through feedback from field experience, a site conservation plan can be implemented.

Experimental research

In situ preservation of earthen archaeological sites has received limited study owing to earlier attitudes of expendability of the earthen remains and the lack of research in site conservation techniques. Current research conducted in preparation for site conservation at Çatalhöyük has focused on a range of issues

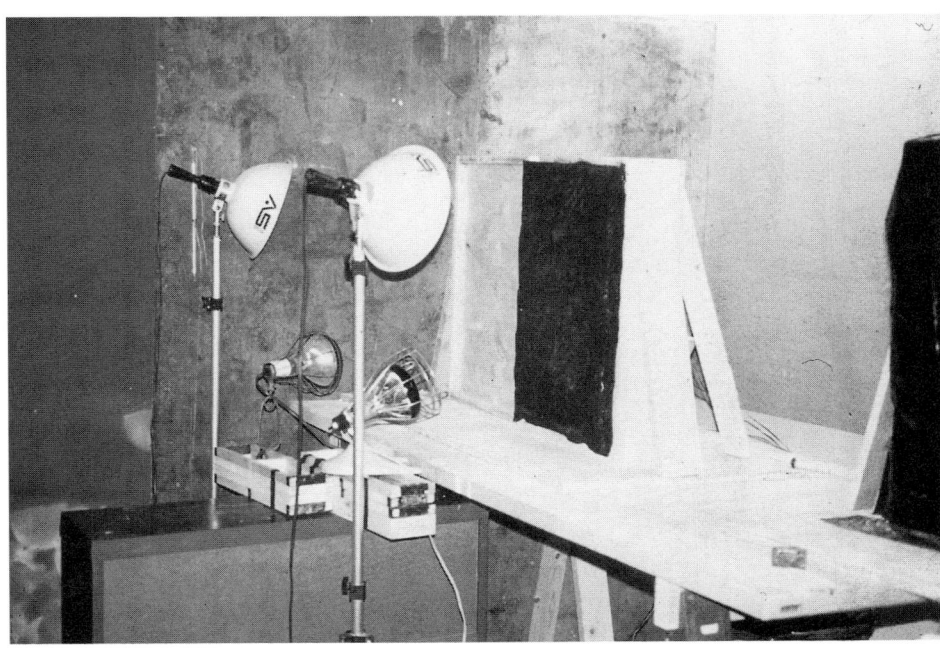

Figure 6.4. *Experimental model of plastered and painted mud-brick facsimile wall with protective geo-fabric batten of perlite-vermiculite during desiccation trial. (Photo: E. Moss.)*

including:

- analysis and characterization of the earthen plasters, paintings and mud-brick;
- treatment testing and assessment of plaster reattachment and consolidation;

- development of lifting apparatus for the detachment, removal, and transport of retained architectural walls and elements;
- development of preventive conservation techniques involving temporary passive environmental control during excavation for mitigating the effects of rapid drying. In addition, a research programme for the removal, and separation of the mural paintings was conducted (Turton 1998).

The major causes of deterioration affecting the murals are: a loss of cohesive strength within discreet layers and of adhesive strength between individual layers of the plaster and mural paintings; salt infiltration, macrobiological growth, and mechanical stresses induced by the drastic ambient changes brought on by excavation. Additionally, continued excavation of the site places remaining paintings at greater risk of destruction, a factor that requires an evaluation of methods for the transfer and reattachment of the painted plasters.

In order to test treatments, facsimile sample types were developed based on material analysis of plaster samples. Executed on 6" × 6" and 12" × 12" gypsum board and terracotta tiles, the samples were made of 14 layers of plaster and paintings of materials similar in character and superimposition of the original painted plasters (Figs. 6.6 & 6.7). The treatment research programme addressed the following issues:

- surface consolidation of

Figure 6.5. *Results of desiccation experiment after 30 hours. Note cracking, flaking and loss on the exposed left side and layer retention on the protected right side. (Photo: E. Moss.)*

Figure 6.6. *Experimental programme to test detachment techniques for mural paintings. (Photo: C. Turton.)*

powdering paint and plasters;
- interlayer detachment/preconsolidation;
- consolidation of the earthen plasters;
- evaluation/selection of facing adhesives for mural detachment;
- evaluation/selection of detachment methods; and
- compatibility of treatments.

Visual assessment and standardized tests developed by ASTM, CRATerre and the Federation of Societies for Coatings Technology were used to evaluate methods and materials.

Site conservation

In view of the high levels of preservation of the site's monumental art and architectural features, including mud-brick walls standing to two metres in height, permanent and temporary shelter facilities and structural and environmental protective methods are required both during and after excavation and treatment. Of particular importance is the interpretation and display of monumental art and architecture *in situ*. A strategy for handling these resources both in place and in the museum is required to allow follow-up research work to occur during and after the excavation period. Techniques already under investigation and trial assessment include *in situ* stabilization, partial removal, and full scale lifting and transport utilizing two special rigs developed in 1997 by Lindsay Falck and Caitlin Moore specifically for the purpose (Fig. 6.8). This latter option will

be especially critical where building features identified for preservation will need to be removed to gain access to the lower occupation levels. Structures preserved *in situ* are being stabilized, interpreted and protected with specially designed shelters, the first one completed in summer 1999.

Figure 6.7. *Results of various detachment methods for superimposed design layers. (Photo: C. Turton.)*

Figure 6.8. *Rig assembly on site (South area) during experimental wall lifting operation. (Photo: L. Falck.)*

Figure 6.9. In situ *plaster layer detachment tests, North area-BACH 1. (Photo: T. Ready.)*

Emergency stabilization of the architecture, murals and relief sculpture

Emergency stabilization refers to temporary measures to arrest rapid and destructive alteration during and between field seasons. Current research and field trials have focused on techniques and materials for mitigating deterioration during excavation by controlling desiccation through decelerated drying. This has proven to be most effective through the use of woven synthetic battens filled with perlite and vermiculite to absorb and pass moisture, stabilize surface temperature and humidity, and provide positive pressure (where needed) for fragile, delaminating surfaces and reliefs during exposure (Moss 1998) (Figs. 6.4 & 6.5). To address larger-scale structural collapse, simple lightweight reusable clamp and truss assemblies provide support and allow excavators easy access to the space and the floors for sampling and excavation.

Removal of murals, relief sculpture, features and buildings

Location, condition and significance of each structure, mural painting and relief will affect the intervention strategies selected (Fig. 6.3). To date no paintings or reliefs of significance or great extent have been uncovered. Specific treatments considered for field application based on the previous conservation work and facsimile tests conducted over the past several years include: separation of superimposed layers (*strappo*), removal of all layers together with a layer of the substrate (*stacco*), removal of all layers with partial thickness of the wall (*stacco*

Figure 6.10. *Wall plaster reattachment using grouting techniques, North area - Building 5. (Photo: T. Ready.)*

84

Figures 6.11–6.13. *North area - Building 5. Sequential phases of reburial for temporary site protection during the winter months between field seasons. (Photos: E. Kopelson.)*

a masello), and removal of all layers with all of the wall (Fig. 6.9). Where whole or partial structures are deemed significant and in an excellent state of preservation, but need to be moved to proceed with the excavation, block lifting of the walls and features will occur using the specially designed rigs for the project. Re-erection can then occur on- or off-site.

Site conservation and display

Methods developed and field tested on sites in the American southwest have been applied at Çatalhöyük with good results.[8] Buildings and features deemed suitable for *in situ* interpretation and display such as Building 5 in the North area have recently been stabilized and exhibited under a protective shelter. Mildly hydraulic lime-based grouts have been developed and employed for consolidating voids and cracks in walls and detached plasters after dimensional stability is reached through conditioning (Fig. 6.10). Specially designed modular shelters have been designed that provide protection and display and allow for future reuse and expandability as the site needs change. Easily reversible reburial methods for site protection between field seasons were also developed based on the above research into environmental control and surface protection during excavation (Figs. 6.11–6.13).

Heritage planning and management

Fundamental to the project is the recognition that integrated, comprehensive strategic planning is crucial for any public archaeological site which must accommodate and help shape any and all potential development in the larger context of the social, cultural and economic forces and the physical realities that define and shape such places. The region of Anatolia in south central Turkey has seen the interaction between human settlement and the natural environment for at least the last 9000 years. Since the recession of the last period of glaciation, some 15,000 years ago, the highly fertile soils of the Konya Basin have supported human settlement and agricultural production in a cyclical but ever increasing way, up to the present time. With the more rapid intensification of irrigation-based agriculture in the post-war period, increased international interest in the cultural history of the region since the excavation of Çatalhöyük in the 1960s, and the subsequent development of Konya and Cappadocia as a recreational destination for the area, increasing pressures of growth and change have occurred, making the need for site and regional planning critical. Increased tour-

ism and heritage development, if not properly managed, could have a seriously negative impact on the historic and cultural landscape of the region and especially the unique nearby village and farm communities.

The site already attracts visitors and their numbers are likely to increase as excavations proceed to provide a substantial income-generating tourist and educational market which needs to be encouraged and accommodated as required by national and regional authorities. A site visitor centre has been constructed and the excavation is now open to the public. In order to accommodate these needs, the programme has not only taken into account the technological issues but also the economic and social value of developing the site for tourism and improvements in access and infrastructure that will be needed to accommodate them. Site planning including a regional survey of the vernacular cultural landscape of the area and the surrounding villages will begin in 2000 in conjunction with the Faculty of Architecture and Preservation at Istanbul Technical University and other local agencies.

Conclusions

Archaeological sites, like all places of human activity, are constructed. Despite their fragmentation, they are complex creations that depend on the legibility and authenticity of their components for meaning and appreciation. How legibility and authenticity of such structures and places are realized and ensured must be understood for effective conservation. Certainly conservators, archaeologists, and cultural resource managers need to know well the theoretical concepts and the history of those concepts pertaining to conservation, and they need to know something of the historical and cultural context of structures and sites, archaic or past building technologies, and current technical solutions. They need to familiarize themselves with the political, economic and cultural issues of heritage management and the implications of their work on local communities, including issues of appropriate technology, tradition, and sustainability.

This problem of integrating established conservation principles into the care, preservation and display of existing structures, sites, and objects is further compounded by the fact that conservation is not routinely involved in the planning, execution, or review of proposed interventions such as archaeological excavation. This is due not only to the constraints already mentioned, but it is also related to the complex professional and legal structure required for many projects, involving archaeologists, architects, engineers, scientists, general contractors, tradesmen, and the public. Decisions involving the selection and extent of any given conservation treatment as well as the actual execution of those treatments by trained conservators are still unlikely for many projects. With rare exceptions, even project development and site supervision and approval of specialized conservation work from documentation to remedial treatments often occur without the involvement of a professional site conservator on the project team.

So within the contemporary field of archaeological site conservation, it is possible to find any number of incompatible and quarrelsome, diametrically-opposed viewpoints and work methods: from the strictly idealist one which hopes for an improbable return of the structure or site to an origin that can never really be established with any certainty, to the pragmatic one which permissively treats as historical values all the alterations made to the site and its structures over the course of time. To this must also be added the recognition of cultural and community ownership and the input of cultural affiliates in the decision-making processes.

The basic tenets of conservation are not the sole responsibility of any one professional group. They apply instead to all those involved in the conservation of cultural property and represent general standards of approach and methodology. From the broadest perspective, archaeology and conservation should be seen as a conjoined enterprise. For both, physical evidence has to be studied and interpreted. Such interpretations are founded on a profound and exact knowledge of the various histories of the thing or place and its context, on the materiality of its physical fabric, on its cultural meanings and values over time, and its role and effect on current local and distant societies. This implies the application of a variety of specialized knowledge based largely on scientific method, but ideally the process must be brought back into a cultural context so that the archaeology and conservation project become synonymous.

Notes

1. The primary general charters include the ICOMOS (Venice) Charter of 1964 and the Australian (Burra) Charter of 1981 (rev. 1988).
2. For a compilation of these and other documents see US/ICOMOS 1999.
3. This long-lived tradition can be found as recently as 1981 in M.W. Thompson, *Ruins: Their Preservation and Display*.
4. This generally good and unusual state of preservation may be due in part to the intentional and swift burial of many structures, thereby reducing the deleterious effects of weathering and collapse through exposure over time.
5. For an historical overview see Catherine Turton, Plan for the stabilization and removal of wall paintings at Çatalhöyük, Appendix B. MSc Thesis, University of Pennsylvania, 1998.
6. Prior to the work at Çatalhöyük in the 1960s and 70s, very few examples of mural painting detachment on earthen substrates or supports can be found in the literature. Two important early examples are the removal of kiva mural paintings from Kuaua (Coronado State Monument) in New Mexico and Awatovi and Kawaika-a Pueblo ruins in Arizona in the 1930s. Both projects dealt with the combined problem of detaching the paintings from the walls and the intralayer separation of individual superimposed paintings.
7. Past and current project team members include: Evan Kopelson (Building Conservation Associates), Caitlin Moore, Elizabeth Moss, Kent Severson, Constance Silver (Co-director 1993–95), Catherine Turton, and Harriet Beaubien (Smithsonian Institution), A. Esin Kuleli (Directorate of Ruins and Monuments), and Latif Özen (Museum of Anatolian Civilizations).
8. Similar situations of environmental control and plaster reattachment have been implemented at Mug House and Cliff Palace at Mesa Verde National Park, Colorado.

References

Australia ICOMOS, 1981. *The Australia ICOMOS Charter for the Conservation of Places of Cultural Significance; (Burra Charter)*. Canberra, Australia. http://www.international.icomos.org/icomos/e_charte.htm

Bruno A., G. Chiari, C. Trossarelli & G. Bultink, 1968–69. Contributions to the study of the preservation of mud brick structures: preliminary report of a survey of monuments in Iraq during the period March–June 1968. *Mesopotamia* 3–4, 445–79.

Dunnell, R.C., 1992. The notion site, in *Space, Time and Archaeological Landscape*, eds. J. Rossignol & L. Wandsnider. New York (NY): Plenum Press, 21–41.

Fielden, B., 1982. The principles of conservation, in *Conservation of Historic Stone Buildings and Monuments*, ed. N.R. Baer. Washington (DC): National Academy Press, 22–30.

Gregotti, V., 1996. On modification, in *Inside Architecture*, translated by P. Wong & F. Zaccheo. Cambridge & London: The MIT Press, 67–73.

Hodder, I., 1991. Postprocessual archaeology and the current debate, in *Processual and Postprocessual Archaeologies: Multiple Ways of Knowing the Past*, ed. R. Preucel. Carbondale (IL): Center for Archaeological Investigations, Southern Illinois University, 30–41.

Hodder, I., 1996. Reopening Çatalhöyük, in *On the Surface: Çatalhöyük 1993–95*, ed. I. Hodder. (McDonald Institute Monographs.) Cambridge: McDonald Institute for Archaeological Research; London: British Institute of Archaeology at Ankara, 1–18.

Hodder, I., 1998. The past as passion and play: Çatalhöyük as a site of conflict in the construction of multiple pasts, in *Archaeology Under Fire*, ed. L. Meskell. London & New York (NY): Routledge, 124–39.

ICOMOS, 1964. *International Charter for the Conservation and Restoration of Monuments and Sites*. Adopted at The Monument for the Man, 2nd International Congress of Restoration, Venice, 25–31 May 1964. Marsilio Editori on behalf of ICOMOS, Padova, Italy.

Matero, F., K.L. Fong, E. del Bono, M. Goodman, E. Kopelson, L. McVey, J. Sloop & C. Turton, 1998. Archaeological site conservation and management: an appraisal of recent trends. *Conservation and Management of Archaeological Sites* 2, 129–42.

Mellaart, J., 1962a. The earliest frescoes yet found on a man-made wall: remarkable discoveries in the excavations at Anatolian Catal Huyuk-part II. *The Illustrated London News, Archaeological Section* (June 16), 976–8.

Mellaart, J., 1962b. Excavations at Catal Huyuk: first preliminary report, 1961. *Anatolian Studies* 12, 41–65.

Mellaart, J., 1963. Excavations at Catal Huyuk: second preliminary report, 1962. *Anatolian Studies* 13, 43–103.

Mellaart, J., 1964a. Earliest of Neolithic cities: the third season of excavations at Anatolian Catal Huyuk, part I: Shrines and images of 9000 years ago. *The Illustrated London News, Archaeology Section* (February 1), 158–60.

Mellaart, J., 1964b. Excavations at Catal Huyuk: third preliminary report, 1963. *Anatolian Studies* 14, 39–118.

Mellaart, J., 1965. *Earliest Civilizations of the Near East*. London: Thames & Hudson.

Mellaart, J., 1966a. Excavations at Catal Huyuk: fourth preliminary report, 1965. *Anatolian Studies* 16, 165–91.

Mellaart, J., 1966b. The leopard shrines of Catal Huyuk. *The Illustrated London News, Archaeology Section* (June 4), 24–5.

Mellaart, J., 1966c. The teasing of the great beasts from Catal Huyuk. *The Illustrated London News, Archaeology Section* (June 11), 24–5.

Moss, E., 1998. Protection and Environmental Control of the Plastered Mudbrick Walls at Çatalhöyük. Unpublished MSc Thesis, University of Pennsylvania.

Philippot, P., 1976. Historic preservation: philosophy, criteria, guidelines, in *Preservation and Conservation: Principles and Practices*, ed. S. Timmons. Washington (DC): The Preservation Press, 367–74.

Pratt, P., 1970. Catal Huyuk wall paintings. *Anatolian Studies* 20, 6.

Thompson, M.W., 1981. *Ruins: Their Preservation and Display*. London: British Museum Publications.

Todd, I., 1976. *Catal Huyuk in Perspective*. Menlo Park (CA): Cummings Publishing Co.

Turton, C., 1998. Plan for the Stabilization and Removal of Wall Paintings at Çatalhöyük. Unpublished MSc Thesis, University of Pennsylvania.

US/ICOMOS, 1999. ICOMOS Charters and other international doctrinal documents. *US/ICOMOS Scientific Journal* 1, 1.

Part B

The Dispersion of 'Site' and the Problem of Representation

Part B: The Dispersion of 'Site' and the Problem of Representation

In this and the next section of the book the question of 'representation' comes still further to the fore. By focusing on the 'dispersion' of site, the second group of papers explores the ways in which the traditional definition of 'site' is inadequate. The archaeological site is today increasingly constructed from a multiplicity of perspectives, situated within diverse locales, and appropriated by different interest groups.

As the dispersion occurs, so the archaeologist becomes more acutely aware that the same site or excavation trench or artefact represents different things to different groups. At one level this is a familiar experience. Archaeologists have come to take for granted the need to produce different accounts of their work for different stakeholder groups.

But at another level, the proliferation of special interest accounts begins to blur the boundary between representation (signifier) and represented (signified), between image and source. The paper by Emele in this volume (chapter 18) prompts us to question the opposition between representation and reality. The notion of 'virtual reality' blurs such boundaries. One of the overall impacts of foregrounding video, film and media at Çatalhöyük is that the centrality of representation in all areas of archaeology comes into focus. The continual presence of the camera eye makes one aware that one is always representing as one 'tells stories' about one's excavation on a day-to-day basis. The presence of video clips within the data base encourages reflection on the degree to which the 'objective' lists and tables of data are themselves representations.

So archaeologists make representations of representations of representations. Especially when multimedia are used, there is an inexhaustable array of representations of any one archaeological object. Take, for example, Building 1 in the North area of the site (see also the collage in Fig. 1.4). There are of course the unit sheets, feature sheets and space sheets or forms which describe the 'primary' data, but there are also drawings, plans, sections, photographs and diary entries. There are paintings (by Nessa Leibhammer) and illustrations (by John Swogger). There are micromorphology slides of the wall and floor plasters and infill deposits. There are three-dimensional plans built from PenMap and AutoCAD. There are plots of microartefact distributions on the floors, and plots of inorganic and organic chemistry residues. And so on.

In particular, there are different representations at different scales. To say 'there are 30 long bone fragments in this unit' is to represent reality at a particular scale of resolution. The statement may refer only to bone recovered in the excavation process and in dry sieving. But smaller fragments of long bones may have been recovered in wet-sieving and sorting, although at this smaller size range they may not have been identifi-

able as long bone fragments. High phosphate readings may suggest the disappearance through taphonomic processes of yet further bones. Thus any description or data entry is itself a representation at a particular scale of analysis.

The danger of such accounts of the archaeological process as representation is that they lead us onto the slippery slopes of relativism. If archaeology deals in representations of representations, is it only representing and never dealing in objective facts?

Certainly the chapter by Matero in Part A forces us to reconsider the notion that we first excavate an object and then represent it. After all, we could argue that all the varied representations of Building 1 described above are simply representations of different aspects of the same stable 'thing' — Building 1. But archaeologists carefully prepare walls, sections and so on for representation (cosmetically cutting grass before taking a photograph etc.). Matero further explodes the myth that we simply find an objective reality which has been hidden from us. When we excavate the walls of Building 1, we unleash an unstable set of interactions.

Earthen buildings exist within the ground in specific microenvironments which are destabilized once excavation begins. Evaporation from exposed walls results in migration of soluble salts to the surface, as well as cracking and delamination so that plasters fall from walls. Newly excavated walls may be exposed to dramatic temperature changes between the heat of the day and the cold of the night. Plant growth and roots may further force cracks to open. The effects of all these processes are especially severe in relation to the highly reactive smectitic clays used in the plasters at Çatalhöyük. Particularly in the first few days and weeks of exposure, the buildings excavated at Çatalhöyük are in a continual process of transformation. Here it is very clear that the process of observation changes that which is being observed.

As a result, there is an immediate need for intervention in order to stabilize walls and plasters and artefacts. The process of conservation involves making choices about which techniques to use and how to represent what is being found. In a very direct way, the conservation intervention means that archaeological sites are always constructed. The walls are sculpted as we dig. Decisions are made as the trowel moves over the ground, about how much dirt to remove from the surfaces of plaster walls and such issues are continued in the cleaning of walls by conservationists. Decisions are made about which phases of building to stabilize and present to the camera eye and to public audiences. The walls are cleaned, grouted, pinned, reinforced, covered and so on. The excavated building is thus not a reality which is then represented; it is always already represented. It is always both reality and representation.

A representation of what? A building in the past. But that past building was continually changing. We excavate a palimpsest resulting from changing uses of the building. At any one time the building itself represents one of many possible social realities (such as a domestic cohabiting unit or a unit of domestic food consumption). But that social reality can itself be seen as a representation of the organization of economic production, and so on.

Thus one can argue that we as social actors, and as archaeologists live in worlds of representation, separate from reality. This hyper-relativist position is caught within a tired opposition between representation and reality. The unity of representation and reality is perhaps most elegantly expressed in this section by Nessa Leibhammer's work. In some of her colour sketches of the walls and buildings at Çatalhöyük she rubs 'real' dirt onto her paper. The dirt is selected so as to capture the colour of the deposits being represented. In this blurring of the boundaries between representation and reality she still chooses which dirt to use — her use of 'real' dirt is still a representation. Conversely, her use of dirt is no less real because the dirt is selected and used to represent itself. Her action unifies reality and representation.

Archaeological production is always simultaneously informed by reality and representation. To say that archaeological realities are constructed is not to say that they are only constructed. We do not need to slip down into an abyss of relativism. Rather, we can explore the positive aspects of a recognition of the pervasiveness of representation in archaeology. In Chapter 18, Emele describes a new form of contemporary society — one increasingly at ease with the manipulation and transformation (the 'morphing') of images. The advantage of such an approach is that it is less bound by single ('tunnel') visions. It is more open to diverse ways of viewing, linked to dispersed perspectives and interests. An openness to exploring representations allows experimentation with diverse ways of looking at the past.

If we posit that reality is always multidimensional then there are clear scientific advantages in prising it open from different angles, exploring and experimenting with different perspectives. The multidimensional argument has increasingly been made in the human sciences. Whether we follow Marx, Freud or Saussure, we see that there are levels of reality not immediately discernible. We have come to accept that much material culture behaviour is non-discursive, and that events are caught up in long-, medium- and short-term processes. We have also increasingly come to see social life as negotiated between multiple interest groups, with many unacknowledged conditions and unintended consequences.

It becomes possible to argue, therefore, that if reality is multidimensional, its anatomy needs to be explored from multiple perspectives. Since we have long recognized that 'the medium is the message', multimedia are needed in order to allow different aspects of reality/representation to be prised open. It cannot be scientific to explore reality through one system of representation only. We can only ever see through representational media. Rather than taking a fixed view (the one, objective, view), a scientific archaeologist needs to be able to manipulate differing images.

But the 'mixing' and 'morphing' of different representational media should not be seen simply as 'play'. There is a danger in an historically blind manipulation of images. It is important to understand how media and representation are situated in present realities. It is important to take a critical stance regarding the relationship between knowledge and power. Why do certain images of Çatalhöyük occur at certain times (see Chapter 7, by N. Hamilton)?

'Playing with' and 'mixing' images have the valuable effect of demystifying the representational process. The ability to tinker with digital images may help to remove some of the fixity, wonder and awe associated with 'final' drawings or photographs. The handling of and playing with images and representations may foster critique. But there is a danger that the 'play' itself becomes the goal. So there is also the need for reflection on image making. Particularly in the context of new digital technologies, we need to ask questions such as 'who has access to the technologies so that they can experience new high-tech representations?' 'Who is excluded?' 'Who benefits from this portrayal of the past?' 'Who has the skills to decode this image?' 'Is mystique being created around these images by the new technologies?' 'At what point does virtual Çatalhöyük simply become another computer game?'

The chapters in this section deal with the dispersal of Çatalhöyük into multiple representations. But they also attempt to situate the images through which different archaeologists and diverse public groups conceive of the site. They attempt to understand the diversity of interests in the site and the inadequacy of any attempt to define 'a Çatalhöyük team', 'a Çatalhöyük site'. 'a Çatalhöyük public' and so on. In this way we can begin to explore how representational media are chosen in the interests of particular perspectives and interests. We can also begin to see how a variety of representations takes us closer to an understanding of complex and multidimensional realities.

Chapter 7

The Conceptual Archive and the Challenge of Gender

Naomi Hamilton

When Mellaart excavated Çatalhöyük in the 1960s he published very full preliminary reports which contained interpretive as well as field data (Mellaart 1962; 1963; 1964; 1966). These reports are notable for the changes in his thinking which occurred over the four seasons of excavation, his readiness to re-interpret as new data were retrieved, and the transparency with which he presented these changes. This is not generally recognized, and it is his 'final' interpretation of the social structures of the Çatalhöyük people which are commonly known. These attained their fullest, and certainly most widely-disseminated, form in his 1967 book (Mellaart 1967). It is largely this version of Mellaart's ideas about Çatalhöyük, including his visual reconstructions, which form the archive into which scholars interested in Çatalhöyük delve, and it is inevitably against the backdrop of this model that the new excavations are taking place.

The influence of the Mellaart archive is immediately recognizable in almost everything written about the site, whether in support of or against Mellaart's interpretations. The huge importance of the site to a number of special interest groups outside the archaeological profession — notably goddess followers (Conkey & Tringham 1995; Meskell 1995), historians of early religion and feminist revisionist historians, as well as more localized or economically-based groups — has led to a dissemination of 'knowledge' about the site matched rarely in archaeology (obvious similar examples are Stonehenge and the Egyptian pyramids). It is therefore inevitable that new work at the site will be measured against the Mellaart archive, and new findings will be viewed in terms of whether they support or reject Mellaart's views. Thus those working at the site need to be aware of the content of the Mellaart archive in all its breadth, in order to know 'which side they are on' in terms of whether their information is new or not. Further, it would be idle to suggest that most of those working at the site were not attracted because of Mellaart's original work. Although re-excavation is currently something of a fashion, the sites are still chosen with a purpose, and there are two purposes which spring to mind where Çatalhöyük is concerned — either to find more of the wonderful things Mellaart found, or to overthrow the Mellaart archive and create a new one.

For the variety of reasons touched on above, it is relevant and indeed necessary to explore the Mellaart archive and to examine its effects both on those working at the site, and on those consuming our 'product'. However, within the Mellaart archive is another archive — the cultural baggage of Western thought and academia — and this too needs to be explored. Although long recognized in its macro-constituents — the well-known bias of the white, Christian, middle-upper class male, which contains a host of diverse elements — there are other broad issues which are less easy to categorize and require a considerable effort of deconstruction.

Recognition or acknowledgement of cultural bias has had little effect on the attitudes of archaeologists in the present, for the bias remains in our everyday life, and extensive self-reflexivity is required to counter it. It is therefore unsurprising that Western culture has generally been regarded by Western archaeologists as both advanced and superior to other forms of social organization and thought, and that concomitantly other forms have been regarded as both backward and inferior. Although few would now state this in such bald terms there has been little change in archaeological attitudes. Concepts such as power, hierarchy, and the determining role of biology have been naturalized in Western culture (and in some others) — that is, they are regarded as 'natural' and inevitable aspects of humankind. Gender-based assumptions and religious concepts dominate Western thought, and thus have a strong influence on interpretations of social structure in the past. These influences are fairly simple to recognize at a basic level, although this does not always occur, but it is often only when new interpretations are attempted that the full range of these ideas is apparent.

It is clear therefore that any attempt at an objective or self-reflexive interpretation of Çatalhöyük requires a central acknowledgement and extensive knowledge of the multiple conceptual archives with which we work. This is a massive task, and in the remainder of this chapter I will examine briefly just a few cultural concepts to explore the impact of our archives on how we interpret social structures at Çatalhöyük.

Gender is perhaps the field in which our conceptual archives have the strongest influence. This may appear obvious in relation to topics such as figurines and burials, but because of the centrality of gender to the way we all view the world (even if we do not all do so in the same way), gender is relevant to other areas of archaeological interpretation which may not be immediately apparent. The aspects of Mellaart's work at Çatalhöyük which have most caught the public imagination, and which have been at the centre of much of the academic debate about the site, are those concerning gender. The Mellaart view of gender at Çatalhöyük, as understood by the interested public, was essentially that women played an important and possibly dominant role in society. This was a result of the introduction of agriculture, and was expressed in the worship of a Mother Goddess linked to the fertility of the earth (evidence for which was found in the presence of numerous female figurines and a number of large female sculptures on the walls), and in the preferential treatment of women during burial (below the main platform, supplied with richer grave goods, and occasionally covered with red ochre). However, the extent of female power was uncertain, as some male figurines were also found, 'bulls horns' were postulated as the male equivalent of female sculptures, and some male burials contained rich grave goods. The only other evidence for a social hierarchy was a number of elaborate buildings regarded as shrines, which Mellaart suggested had housed a priestly class. As both male and female burials were found in shrines, the sex of the priests was unclear. The high percentage of cattle bones among the faunal remains at the site was thought to relate to the importance of cattle in religion, shown by the cattle skulls in some shrines.

This very condensed view of gender at Çatalhöyük has become the battleground of conceptual archives — patriarchy versus matriarchy, hierarchy versus egalitarian society, and Goddess representa-tions versus toys. All these relate to deep-seated beliefs about gender, and scholars have argued on both sides with no further evidence than that supplied already by Mellaart. It has been a battle of ideology rather than of fact, its ideological status made less obscure than usual in archaeology because of the clear-cut issues. However, few protagonists on either side have attempted to tease out the issues and problems, to clarify their concepts — for instance, what do we mean by matriarchy, or egalitarian — and the debate has become entrenched. This relates to our cultural archives, which give meaning to terms for us, and it is only rarely that we question whether our archives are the same. In the unusual case of Çatalhöyük, it has sometimes seemed easier for scholars to recognize that their archives are not the same, and therefore to dismiss the opposition entirely, than to look more carefully at their own influences, prejudices and expectations, and to make explicit what generally remains implicit. Çatalhöyük therefore presents major challenges to a team which aims to work with a reflexive methodology, and requires us to rethink everything we 'know' about society, trying to make sense of the data at the same time that we are dismantling the analytical tools needed to do so.

Western culture offers strong views on gender, so strong that it is difficult for many people to question them. One major element is that there are two biological sexes, and that social roles are 'natural' and immutable extensions of this binary division, resulting automatically in two sex-linked genders. Parallel to this is the assumption that men are innately competitive and violent, and 'naturally' seek dominance over each other and women, and that this is just the way things are. Add these beliefs together, and we get male dominance in a violent hierarchical structure, and since this is 'natural' and immutable it follows that it has always been so. Hence early societies have routinely been assumed to have male hierarchies which go to war to achieve dominance over their neighbours. This is reflected in the traditional archaeological division of cultural periods according to the predominant material used for weapons — i.e. Stone, Bronze and Iron Ages. This is the dominant cultural archive with which most archaeologists have approached Çatalhöyük.

Mellaart's interpretations of Çatalhöyük began within the dominant cultural paradigm. However, the data did not appear to fit, and he sought alternative models — demonstrating a flexibility which is all too rare. It happens that the idea of Mother Goddesses and their link with agricultural fertility had been around since the late nineteenth century, although no longer popular by the 1960s (see Hamilton 1996a), and this offered Mellaart another archive with which to examine Çatalhöyük. The Western belief that the bull is a male symbol helped to integrate the two versions, allowing strong male imagery alongside female sculptures and figurines, with echoes of Classical mythology in support. Thus the Mellaart archive is a hybrid, but remains within broad Western traditions (Hutton 1997). The binary nature of sex/gender, the existence of nuclear families, the concepts of religion and power were unchallenged.

Looking at Çatalhöyük in the 1990s, the field is much wider. Many of the old paradigms are under question, and this creates methodological and archival difficulties. All types of data are not affected equally — Mellaart's work on the East mound pottery was limited, and the chipped stone, bone, botanical and textile reports commissioned from experts are fairly basic. Although their findings may prove to be right, wrong or incomplete, this is largely a methodological issue of retrieval rather than interpretation. The animal bones, however, have wider relevance — the re-evaluation of the percentage of cattle bones and overall cattle consumption at the site, although also a matter of retrieval, has interpretive overtones concerning ritual, symbol and religion, and it is here that the Mellaart archive comes to the fore. The presence of a very high proportion of cattle bones in the faunal remains was linked by Mellaart to the religious importance of cattle skulls found in shrines, although he cautioned that the area excavated in the 1960s may turn out to have been a priestly quarter unrepresentative of the site as a whole. Current work has shown that, with near total retrieval of animal bone through the sieving of all deposits, cattle is far less common than sheep/goat. As one of our trenches is in the same area as Mellaart's, this is clearly a matter of retrieval rather than site variation. How this information will affect interpretations other than those concerning animal management, domestication and diet is unclear: it seems likely that for those who believe cattle imagery represents the human male, there will be a shift to suggest that the comparative rarity of cattle bones reflects the veneration in which the animals were held; for those who believe cattle imagery represents the human female reproductive system (Cameron 1981), it will be largely irrelevant; for those who believe cattle imagery represents the wild, produced by a Goddess and controlled by humans, it will emphasize the symbolic nature of such awe-inspiring creatures. In other words, it is difficult to

change our basic conceptual archives. People are more likely to adapt new information to old paradigms, creating the same explanation for changed data, than vice versa.

The human burials have become crucial to the debate on social structure, yet the human bones are the subject of a double archival burden: from Mellaart they bear a weight of symbolic interpretation which renders their examination more complex than would be expected, while our standard models of sex and gender come from our own cultural archive. The issue of female versus male dominance rests partly on the burial data, and to test Mellaart's data it is necessary to sex the skeletons in the traditional way and to assess both whether female skeletons occur in privileged positions within houses and whether they have richer grave goods and special treatment. However, this also pre-supposes that sex and gender can be equated as they are in modern Western culture — that they are binary, immutable, and inescapably linked, a supposition which has been challenged in recent feminist theory (e.g. Moore 1994, now fairly well-known amongst archaeologists; Baker 1998 is a useful introduction to the issues). Previous analysis of Mellaart's data has shown that, using a traditional binary model, some burials do not fit the pattern — that some female skeletons are accompanied by 'male' grave goods or were buried in 'male' areas and vice versa (Hamilton 1996b, 242–62). It suggests that gender was more fluid and/or less developed than currently, or took a different form from one we can recognize easily; that perhaps there was an element of choice in the assignment of gender, with only two choices; or that there were more than two genders, or none. However, if this were so, it makes current work extremely difficult. The only way of assessing whether a skeleton is in the 'right' place or has the 'right' grave goods for the standard model is to assume that binary gender existed; without this paradigm, every skeleton is simply an individual and patterns do not exist. Perhaps they will be shown to exist when large numbers of burials have been excavated, but at present the questioning of the cultural and Mellaart archives has largely removed the basis of its own critical method. Fortunately there are other techniques which may assist, such as use-wear studies on human bones and the chemical analysis of diet, but large quantities of data are still going to be required to obtain usable results.

The same issue is apparent when considering shrines. The presence of shrines was one of the essential building blocks for the presence of organized religion and a Mother Goddess, and the only evidence of a priestly class. This in turn was the main evidence for hierarchy at the site, while the Mother Goddess provided the second strand of evidence, suggesting female dominance. Current thinking among team members is varied, but while some believe in Mellaart's 'shrines', others feel that the constant changing of structures suggests that shrines were simply buildings which were destroyed at a certain level of elaboration, rather than buildings which were permanently and exclusively more elaborate than the rest. It has also been suggested (Hamilton 1998) that they could be lineage houses rather than purely religious or ritual buildings. If either or both of these last two ideas were accurate (they are not mutually exclusive), the concept of shrines as exclusively religious buildings with a specialist priestly class could be removed. With it would go much of the evidence for hierarchy, religion and female power. However, issues concerning what the elaboration meant, and the presence of apparently female sculptures and female figurines, will not go with them.

Religion is frequently a difficult topic to discuss because of the strong feelings invoked, and at Çatalhöyük the issue has largely become polarized, both among consumers of the site, and among the archaeologists working there. The conceptual archive is to the fore in such territory, although this is not always acknowledged. For some, a society without religion is unimaginable, and any religion is better than none, while for others the existence of organized religion of any sort at that time is a nonsense, and there are many other views filling the gaps between these two extremes. What is certain is that the reaction against the interpretation of female figurines as images of a Goddess was initially cultural rather than intellectual (Hamilton 1996a), although it is currently argued in intellectual terms. Had the figurines been male, the debate over the existence of religion in the Neolithic would have taken a different form, and the alternative interpretations offered for figurines are unlikely to have included pornography, images of sons offered for marriage, or husbands and concubines for the dead (this last not suggested for Çatalhöyük as they are not found in graves), although it might just conceivably have included children's dolls. Controlled by our conceptual archives, the rigidity of attitudes to both religion and gender roles impedes both gradual exploration and rigorous interpretation of the Çatalhöyük figurines — many of which are not sexed — because of the inter-linked beliefs about society which are assumed to follow any interpretation or suggestion.

While arguments rage around the major or obvious topics, others are barely recognized as areas requiring debate. Concepts such as the family and property ownership have been little touched upon beyond speculation as to whether the numerous burials in Building 1 could be accounted for by a polygynous family unit, or were derived from a broader social grouping. It is generally assumed that houses were lived in by groups recognizable as families in the modern world, and that houses would have been family property. Other options, such as houses built and used by larger groupings such as lineages, shared out according to need and re-allocated regularly, with varying uses and purposes, have been little discussed (although see Hamilton 1998). The use of buildings other than for living in has also received little attention, as habitation is the primary use of houses in our cultural archives. However, storage of foods, tools, ancestors and ritual knowledge could also be a primary purpose, despite our own view that such heavy investment in buildings is inappropriate unless they are essentially for human shelter and protection. Use of buildings purely for storage has been noted among semi-nomadic people in Jordan, who continue to live in tents next to their buildings during the winter (Alison McQuitty pers. comm.), and the construction of more substantial homes for the dead than for the living is known, for instance, in the megalithic cultures of Europe.

On a more mundane level, conceptual archives impinge routinely on our thought processes. 'Kitchen' is a term which is readily used but rarely examined. In modern Western culture the kitchen is a gendered space, the woman's domain and the centre of domestic work — although not necessarily of domestic life. However, this is largely a twentieth-century phenomenon. My house in Scotland, now 100 years old, was built without a kitchen; it had just a small scullery attached to the everyday living room, as food was normally brought in from outside. Previously it was only the houses of the rich which contained dedicated kitchens, and these were not gendered spaces, but the workroom(s) of servants of both sexes/genders. Farmhouses and rural cottages had 'kitchens', but may not have had other living rooms, thus kitchens were long used by both sexes for a wider variety of tasks than our modern ones and should perhaps be called general rooms or living rooms. This is still the situation in some village houses in Turkey and in neighbouring areas such as Cyprus, where the same general room might also be used for sleeping in. Therefore a term which appears unproblematic is both tied closely to particular cultural forms, and is gendered in modern Western usage. At Çatalhöyük the western room of Building 1 is sometimes referred to as a kitchen, because it contained an oven and food remains, although the main room also contained these items. Mellaart regarded the southern part of the buildings as 'kitchen areas' because the oven was generally situated there, and Hodder took this further: he added explicit gender by suggesting that the south was female because it was a kitchen area and also contained the entrance to the outer world, while the north was inner, male, and contained more important symbolism (Hodder 1990, 9–10; but see Hamilton 1996b, 252). Although there is an intent amongst the team currently working at the site to question everything, the concept of gendered spaces based upon modern gender roles has not yet been widely problematized.

Challenging our conceptual archives is not a short-term task. While some aspects of interpretation are obvious danger zones, many of the issues touched on above are not restricted to any particular area of study, and apply to topics not normally thought to be influenced by ideology. Moreover, we are all dependent to some extent on others carrying out specialist studies of various data groups, and each has their own cultural archive which informs their work, in addition to the Mellaart archive which we share. Constant self-surveillance is required to ensure that assumptions do not remain within our methodologies, yet the consequent loss of paradigms can be a serious stumbling block. The aim of the team at Çatalhöyük for transparency of thought processes, through a variety of reflexive methodologies, may enable us to overcome these difficulties, but we still need to develop specific methodologies designed to enable constant reassessment of models as well as interpretations. Mellaart's annual reports provide an example of transparency and changing ideas in many ways, and perhaps this is an argument for regular and fairly immediate impressionistic reports, in addition to the periodic production of considered opinions, disregarding the common fear that we will be seen to have changed our minds or made mistakes. This might be a useful tool to demonstrate the power of our conceptual archives, and thus the importance to any interpretation of Çatalhöyük of acknowledging and recognizing the archives which influence our work.

References

Baker, M., 1998. Italian gender theory and archaeology: a political engagement, in *Gender and Italian Archaeology*, ed. R. Whitehouse. London: Accordia Research Institute/Institute of Archaeology, 23–34.

Cameron, D., 1981. *Symbols of Birth and Death in the Neolithic Era*. London: Kenyon Deane.

Conkey, M. & R. Tringham, 1995. Archaeology and the goddess: exploring the contours of feminist archaeology, in *Feminisms in the Academy*, eds. D.C. Stanton & A.J. Stewart. Ann Arbor (MI): University of Michigan, 199–247.

Hamilton, N., 1996a. The personal is political, in Can we interpret figurines?, by N. Hamilton, J. Marcus, D. Bailey, G. Haaland, R. Haaland & P. Ucko. *Cambridge Archaeological Journal* 6(2), 282–5.

Hamilton, N., 1996b. Figurines, clay balls, small finds and burials, in *On the Surface: Çatalhöyük 1993–95*, ed. I. Hodder. (McDonald Institute Monographs.) Cambridge: McDonald Institute for Archaeological Research; London: British Institute of Archaeology at Ankara, 215–63.

Hamilton, N., 1998. Re-thinking Burial and Society at Çatalhöyük. Paper delivered at the Symposium on Mediterranean Archaeology, 21–23 February 1998 at Edinburgh University. *Neo-Lithics* 3/98, 7–8.

Hodder, I., 1990. *The Domestication of Europe*. Oxford: Blackwell.

Hutton, R., 1997. The Neolithic Great Goddess: a study in modern tradition. *Antiquity* 71, 91–9.

Mellaart, J., 1962. Excavations at Catal Huyuk, first preliminary report, 1961. *Anatolian Studies* 12, 41–55.

Mellaart, J., 1963. Excavations at Catal Huyuk, second preliminary report, 1962. *Anatolian Studies* 13, 43–103.

Mellaart, J., 1964. Excavations at Catal Huyuk, third preliminary report, 1963. *Anatolian Studies* 14, 39–119.

Mellaart, J., 1966. Excavations at Catal Huyuk, fourth preliminary report, 1965. *Anatolian Studies* 16, 15–191.

Mellaart, J., 1967. *Catal Huyuk: a Neolithic Town in Anatolia*. London: Thames & Hudson.

Meskell, L., 1995. Goddesses, Gimbutas and New Age archaeology. *Antiquity* 69, 74–86.

Moore, H., 1994. *A Passion for Difference*. Cambridge: Polity Press.

Chapter 8

Where is Çatalhöyük? Multiple Sites in the Construction of an Archaeological Site

Ayfer Bartu

A site of the importance of Çatalhöyük is bound to attract attention within archaeological circles. But archaeologists are not the only group of people interested in Çatalhöyük, and the excavation site itself is only *one* of the sites in which a particular kind of knowledge about Çatalhöyük is being produced. As with any other archaeological excavation, the Çatalhöyük project is embedded within a wider social, political, historical, and cultural context. Being one of the social anthropologists working on the project, my research focuses on the multiple groups and sites through which different kinds of knowledge about Çatalhöyük are being produced and consumed. In this chapter, I will briefly discuss: a) this wider context in which Çatalhöyük is being interpreted, consumed and possibly co-opted by various groups with different interests and agendas; b) the resulting methodological challenges facing archaeologists and the practice of archaeology in the 1990s; and c) different ways in which we are attempting at Çatalhöyük to involve these various groups in the interpretation and presentation of the site.

Multiple sites, shifting contexts

I want to start with multiple and apparently disparate ethnographic sites.

Çumra-August 1998, opening ceremony of the Annual Agricultural Festival
It is the opening ceremony of the Annual Agricultural Festival in the nearby town of Çumra. The town square is decorated with banners, Turkish flags, and the flags of the political party, Nationalist Action Party (*Milliyetçi Hareket Partisi*, MHP), which has been in power locally since 1994. The mayor of the town enters the square among the cheers and the

waving flags of the spectators, accompanied by the head of the MHP who is also in Çumra for the occasion. After a series of folklore performances, the mayor goes up to the stand and starts giving his opening speech. Going through the various 'achievements, and successes' of his party in the region, he highlights the investments made in industry and agriculture, and continues:

> Besides these, we are also making progress in tourism. There is an international team of scientists excavating at Çatalhöyük here. We are making every effort possible to be able to display the artefacts found there in a museum here in Çumra rather than in Ankara or anywhere else. We should be proud of this contribution of the Turkish nation-state to European civilization. We are aware of the importance of having such a site in our region.

Çumra-July 1997, wedding ceremony
It is the garden of a house in Çumra, packed with women and children, celebrating the wedding of a young girl in their neighbourhood. I am invited to this ceremony as a guest of one of the women, N from Çumra, who is also hired at Çatalhöyük. N shows me the golden bracelet on her nine-year old daughter's wrist and asks:

> It is nice, isn't it? I bought it with the money I saved from my Çatalhöyük salary last season. This year I decided to change the refrigerator we have at home. You have seen it, it is very old. Now there are very good deals where you can buy a good model by paying reasonable instalments. I decided that I can pay those instalments with the money I make from Çatalhöyük, so I registered in one of those campaigns to buy a new one.

Istanbul-August 1997, office of a fashion designer
The office of one of the well-known fashion designers in an upscale neighbourhood of the city. It is

101

three months before the fashion show, in which the designer will display her 'Çatalhöyük' collection. The details of the show are being discussed. The designer brings into the room several dresses which are part of her collection and explains:

> I wanted to use as few stitches as possible in these dresses. I wanted them to be really light. The models who will wear these will be wearing no shoes, no accessories. The themes I am using in the show are volcano, lava, earth, mud, and the colours of the plain. I collected a sample of plants from Çatalhöyük and decided to use the colours of that landscape in my collection. Before I start to design any collection, I always write a poem about it. I wrote one after my visit to Çatalhöyük called 'Women of Another Time', and that's what this show will be named. The models will walk out of a reconstructed Çatalhöyük house and in the background there will be flashing images from the site.

Istanbul-June 1998, Opening Session of a 'Goddess' Conference

It is the meeting hall of one of the five-star hotels in Istanbul and it is the opening session of an international symposium entitled 'Earth Shaped by Women, Women Shaped by Earth: Women in Prehistory, Today, and Tomorrow'. The meeting is attended by writers, artists, performers, historians. The room is surrounded by the banners of one of the artists who is attending the symposium, whose paintings are inspired mainly by the wall paintings of Çatalhöyük. Almost all the papers presented make references to Çatalhöyük as the origin of the 'Mother Goddess' cult and as a time when societies lived in 'peace and harmony' both with one another and with nature. The third day of the symposium takes place in Çatalhöyük, where the participants gather in a circle and perform their rituals on the mound as part of their efforts to 'feel the Goddess energy in Çatalhöyük', and form a spiritual connection with the site.

Washington DC-November 1998, World Bank Office

It is the World Bank Office in Washington DC where the proposal for a Bank-supported project at Çatalhöyük is being discussed. The Bank is interested in giving a loan to the Turkish government to preserve and develop the heritage site of Çatalhöyük, a site which is 'listed by the World Monuments Fund as one of the world's 100 most endangered heritage sites and one of 30 most in need of funding to stop further destruction and loss'.

What unites these multiple, apparently disparate sites is the archaeological site of Çatalhöyük. But then the question is which one of these is Çatalhöyük and what does Çatalhöyük really represent? Is it the contribution of the Turkish nation-state to 'European' civilization? Or is it a means to a different end: development of the regional economy through providing seasonal labour to the inhabitants of the area? Does it possess the positive spiritual energy of the 'Mother Goddess'? Is it a 'world heritage site' which needs to be preserved and developed through the aid of international development agencies? In some ways, it is all of these, and I wish to argue that it is actually the simultaneous (re)workings of these multiple sites and shifting contexts that make up the archaeological site of Çatalhöyük.

The existence of this wide range of groups with different interests and agendas, related to the site in various ways, poses a major challenge both for archaeological theory and practice. How do or should archaeologists pursue their work given this diversity of interests in their sites? One immediate and easy answer/solution might be to ignore all these groups, their interpretations, and the ways in which they relate to the site, and retain an archaeological authority in telling the story of the site. Another answer/solution, the one adopted at Çatalhöyük, is to recognize this wider context in which archaeological projects are embedded, to engage in a dialogue with these groups and possibly get them involved in the interpretive process of the site. But this kind of engagement with the wider context requires a reassessment of archaeological theory, and more specifically methodology. What are the mechanisms through which one can capture this simultaneity? At this point I want to suggest that contemporary theoretical and methodological discussions in social anthropology might shed some light on the question and provide archaeology with useful tools for this kind of reassessment.

'Multi-sited' ethnography: implications and potential for archaeology

In recent years, the kind of self-critical and reflexive body of research which has emerged in social and cultural anthropology has been characterized as an 'experimental moment', following similar trends in many other social science disciplines (Marcus & Fischer 1986). The major points of concern of this recent re-evaluation have been the concepts of culture used in anthropological theory (Geertz 1973; Kuper 1994; Ortner 1984; Yengoyan 1986), powerful 'localizing strategies' and the regional traditions of ethnographic writing (Fardon 1990), the ways in which anthropology has created its object of study (Fabian 1983), fieldwork practices (Sanjek 1990; Gupta & Ferguson 1997a,b), textual strategies in the production of ethnographic texts (Clifford & Marcus 1986), the wider context in which disciplinary practices are embedded: the historical relations between world macropolitics and anthropology (Asad 1973; Said 1989), the colonial origins of traditional anthropology and a growing recognition of the power relations embedded within the discipline (Marcus & Fischer 1986).

Similar kinds of concerns have been carried into archaeology through the debates between processual and postprocessual approaches (see Preucel 1991; Hodder 1991a; 1995). There has been an increasing awareness and reflexivity concerning the wider context in which archaeological practices are embedded: the relationship between the practice of archaeology and nationalism (Atkinson *et al.* 1996; Diaz-Andreu & Champion 1996; Kohl & Fawcett 1995), various indigenous claims over the interpretation and uses of the past (Layton 1989), and the need to respond to multiple voices and calls for active social engagement of archaeologists with the wider public.

In anthropology, these various critiques of anthropological theories and practices led either to nihilistic arguments, calling for the end of anthropology, or attempts to take up the postmodern challenge in more constructive ways, by capturing the complex and contradictory nature of social life rather than calling for the end of anthropology or falling into a totally relativist position. Once it was established that the world and the practice of anthropology have always been more complex than we had imagined them to be, there was a need for different ways of conceptualizing culture and the ways to study it. There has been a series of critical re-evaluations of the anthropological project and various suggestions to develop alternative representational strategies.[1] Given these efforts, however, explicitly methodological discussions in the field have been rare. The emphasis has still been on the textual strategies to represent the complexity of the world — on the writing-up phase of the ethnographies. Although there have been powerful conceptual visions of multi-sited processes and spaces for ethnographic research (e.g. Appadurai 1990; Haraway 1991), these have failed to function as guides for designing such research. How could an ethnographic research which would come to terms with these emerging concerns and spaces be designed?

Similar arguments can also be made for postprocessual approaches. In other words 'postprocessual archaeology, in contrast [to processual archaeology], has made less impact on methods but has developed a theoretical critique' (Hodder 1991b, 38–9). Is postprocessual methodology possible and, if so, what does this kind of methodology entail? In recent discussions over postprocessual methodology Hodder (1997; see also introduction, this volume) suggests that this kind of methodology can be based on the following four themes: reflexivity, contextuality, interactivity, and multivocality. I wish to argue that a body of research that has been emerging in social anthropology in recent years, which is characterized methodologically as multi-sited ethnography (Marcus 1995) might also be used as an integral part of postprocessual methodologies. Multi-sited ethnography is described as research 'designed around chains, paths, threads, conjunctions or juxtapositions of locations in which the ethnographer establishes some form of literal, physical presence, with an explicit, posited logic of association or connection among sites that in fact defines the argument of the ethnography' (Marcus 1995, 105). This kind of research can take several forms — following the people, the thing, the metaphor, the plot, story or allegory, the life or biography, the conflict, or choosing a strategically situated single site.

My research in Çatalhöyük is a multi-sited ethnography in the sense that I focus on multiple sites and groups through which different kinds of knowledge about this site is produced and consumed. The groups I focus on include the local community living in the surrounding villages (some of whom are hired at the site), domestic and foreign tourists visiting the site, Goddess groups and worshippers, the local and central government officials, and the fashion designers interested in the site. I follow the story of Çatalhöyük across these sites and through different ways in which these various groups relate, interpret and coopt Çatalhöyük.

Rather than being merely descriptive, I think this kind of research and methodology has two major implications for archaeological theory and practice. First, it challenges archaeologists to reconsider the notion of the 'site'. Rather than one single, monolithic archaeological site, we see the dispersion of the site. C. Hamilton's discussion of the 'faultlines' in Çatalhöyük (Chapter 10, this volume), and Tringham's discussion of different 'windows' onto the site (Chapter 9, this volume), already draw attention to the multi-sited nature of the excavation site itself. The site starts dispersing within the excavation site. But we also see the emergence of multiple sites outside of the excavation site itself in which different kinds of knowledge about Çatalhöyük are being produced and consumed. It might be more apt to describe Çatalhöyük as a site in the sense of a 'spatial vortex, in which complex historical processes come into conjunction with global processes that link such sites together' (Appadurai & Breckenridge 1995, 15). Çatalhöyük is an archaeological landscape in the making, through the simultaneous workings of multiple sites, and situated at the intersection of both local and global processes. Secondly, this kind of research might provide some insights in developing different methodologies for actively engaging with the wider context in which archaeological projects are embedded. This kind of engagement will also enable archaeologists to get multiple groups involved in the interpretation process which will eventually lead to a more inclusive archaeological practice.

In this sense, the multi-sited ethnography that I am involved in at Çatalhöyük is an integral part of the reflexive methodology which is being used at Çatalhöyük. But this research also aims to broaden the boundaries of the themes being pursued. In terms of reflexivity, for example, this research attempts to study the impact of the project on various groups interested in the site, but simultaneously attempts to go beyond an 'impact' model. In terms of contextuality, this kind of multi-sited methodology enables archaeologists to be aware of the wider context in which their projects are embedded. The kind of interactivity which is sought in this process goes beyond the computer-generated, high-tech interactivity and does not only include the interactions between laboratory and field staff, but tries to facilitate interactivity between multiple groups involved in the project in various ways. A series of attempts are made to provide various mechanisms for multiple groups who wish to be part of the archaeological process, enhancing multivocality at different levels of the project. These can be seen as attempts to provide appropriate media through which multiple groups can participate in the making of this archaeological landscape.

Towards an inclusive archaeological practice

As I suggested above, this multi-sited ethnography has the potential to transform archaeological practice, making it more inclusive. One of the aims of the Çatalhöyük project from the start has been to engage in a dialogue with various groups who are related to and interested at the site in various ways, and get them involved in the interpretation and public presentation of the site as much as possible. Since the nature and the interests of these groups are varied, we need to develop different mechanisms for interaction and dialogue.

One of the groups that we interact with is the wide range of domestic and foreign tourists visiting the site. In 1998 season, a questionnaire was prepared in seven languages to get an idea about the profile of the visitors to the site as well as their expectations regarding the public presentation of the site. Visitors were asked to fill out these questionnaires during the excavation season, and this will continue throughout the year. The information we gather from these questionnaires, we believe, will be helpful in thinking about the public presentation and preservation of the site.

Among these visitors, one of the most colourful, and in many ways powerful, groups that Çatalhöyük attracts are the 'Goddess' groups, who are interested in forming a spiritual connection with the site. Although this is also a heterogeneous group, one of the ways in which we interact with them is through participating in the conferences they organize, and engaging in discussions over the kinds of archaeological evidence from Çatalhöyük which are of interest to these groups. More recently, there has been a series of correspondences through the Internet with active members of these groups, and these are shown on the website.

Another group of people that we interact with on a more daily basis are the members of the local community, mainly the local bureaucrats and government officials, and people living in the surrounding villages and the town, some of whom are hired at the site during the two months excavation season.

But it should be noted that what we label as the 'local' is neither monolithic nor static. In particular, our interactions with the bureaucrats and the local government officials are constant reminders of the heterogeneous and dynamic nature of the 'local'. In our various meetings with them, on topics ranging from fixing the water tap at the site to various negotiations regarding the press day, we are constantly reminded of the nuances of the local context and things we need to accommodate. Çatalhöyük also provides the bureaucrats with a medium through which the nature of the 'local' is (re)formulated and (re)confirmed. The existing power structures and hierarchies are confirmed through the (re)workings of Çatalhöyük.

Although some of these bureaucrats never visit the site itself, they are very much involved in the project, and are very keen on using Çatalhöyük especially in the promotion campaigns for Çumra. The Annual Agricultural Festival, which is held every August, is named after Çatalhöyük. The name of the sports club has recently been changed to Çatalhöyük Çumra Sports Club. The 'Mother Goddess' figure appears in the promotional brochures of Çumra. Although many of the bureaucrats are members of the ultra-nationalist and religiously conservative MHP (see above), they do not hesitate to participate in some Goddess groups' visits to the site, even holding hands with them on the mound, participating in their rituals celebrating the 'Goddess energy'.

It can be argued that the mere presence of this kind of vast project in the region will inevitably have some kind of an impact on the local community. But to conceptualize this process through an 'impact' model might be extremely misleading. An 'impact' model assumes a pristine, static community, and people with no history (Wolf 1982), which will start changing through the presence and impact of a 'Western' project in the region. Whereas local inhabitants of the villages have been part of the global flow of the images, objects, and people (through television, and immigration and emigration to and from Europe and the Turkic republics etc.). Given the unequal power relations within these flows, the local inhabitants had some agency in shaping and negotiating the terms of this integration.

One of the major 'impacts' of the excavation project in the region will be its potential to transform Çatalhöyük into a tourist site. Çatalhöyük as a tourist attraction might be considered a mixed blessing. But in this context, the challenge is to use this potential in the most positive terms possible for the local community. This also requires us to think in terms of an interactive model rather than an impact one. One of the aims of the Çatalhöyük project from the start has been to have community participation in the interpretation, management, and public presentation of the site. This kind of participation is crucial in the sustainable development of the area (Smith & Eadington 1992). The idea is to give the local people the initiative and the power in setting the terms of the development of the area and in having some kind of control over the development of the area as a tourist site.

Although it is difficult to generalize, many of the local inhabitants and visitors to the site have a rather utilitarian view of the project. For many of them Çatalhöyük is a means to a different end — development. They are excited about the idea that the presence of this international project so close to

their town and village might lead to improvements in the infrastructure of the area. But they also have their own perceptions of the excavation project and the site, and different ways in which they relate to the site and the landscape in general.

In order to facilitate interaction between the project and the local community and find out different ways in which we can have more community participation in the interpretation, management, and presentation of the site, in 1998 we started experimenting with several projects. One such project involved organizing slide shows in Küçükköy as a way of informing the villagers about the kind of work conducted at Çatalhöyük, and sharing the kind of knowledge produced about this site by the archaeologists with the villagers. Although this kind of interaction is commonly practised as part of anthropological fieldwork, it has been rarely used as part of archaeological excavations. The idea of organizing slide shows in the village was received enthusiastically by the workmen/women at the site. Our foreman suggested that this will help him in his recruitment efforts in the village:

> I bring my whole family to work here with me including my wife and daughter. I do this to set an example in the village, just to show them that it is alright to have your women work with foreigners. When you show those pictures {referring to the slides} in the village, they will see themselves that nothing awkward is going on here, especially with respect to the kind of work that women do here. That will help me in recruiting workers, especially women workers, from the village. Their husbands, fathers, and brothers will feel more comfortable after they themselves see these pictures.

But the women hired at the site, most of whom are from Küçükköy, expressed even more enthusiasm about this possibility. A series of discussions I had with them regarding the timing and the logistics of these shows revealed several reasons for their enthusiasm. Given the rumours that had been circulating in the village about the kind of work women do at the site, the slide shows would provide a powerful means of showing the others in the village what they really do at the site. It would give them a chance to disclaim these rumours. The fact that they insisted that I should use as many slides as possible showing the kind of work *they* do at the site and highlight the importance of this work for the project suggests that, in addition to disclaiming the rumours, these shows would also provide them social prestige in the village. It should be noted that the villagers hired at the site, both men and women, are in many ways the economically and socially marginal ones in the village. They are amongst the poorest families in the village, and one of the women, divorced with one child, came back to the village to live with her mother and brother's family.

We had two separate slide shows in the village. The one for the women took place in the school building of the village in which the discussions were centred around the building techniques used in Çatalhöyük houses and the possible uses of ovens found at the site. The one for the men took place in the coffee house of the village and was mostly attended by the older men of the village, most of whom remember the Mellaart excavations in the 1960s. Slides acted as cues for those memories: the conditions in the village in the 60s; the team members they remember from those excavations; the kinds of techniques used at the excavations. There were also discussions over possible explanations for the use of some artefacts found at the site such as clay balls and obsidian. They also expressed an interest in pursuing these kinds of slide shows. One suggestion offered by an elderly man, something which we are planning to pursue in following seasons, was preparation of a newsletter or a bulletin with updated news and pictures from the excavation, posted outside the coffee house, which can provide a continuous flow of information between the villagers and the excavation project. Both of these slide shows provided information on the ongoing excavations at Çatalhöyük and also provided a forum in which different ways of getting the local community involved in the project could be discussed and formulated.

The second project involved preparing a community exhibit at the visitor centre at the site. The existing visitor centre is designed to create an interactive medium through which visitors can experience different aspects of life in the Neolithic settlement of Çatalhöyük through interactive CD-ROMs, virtual reality etc. The idea is to tell various stories about Çatalhöyük rather than use this centre as a storehouse of artefacts excavated at the site (see Shane & Küçük Chapter 16, this volume). The idea of including a community exhibit in this centre is very much compatible with this notion of interactivity but uses a broader definition of this notion. It goes beyond computer-generated, high-tech interactivity and aims to capture the different ways in which the local people relate to the ongoing archaeological research and to the landscape in general. This was partly inspired by the 'ecomuseum' concept; museums which are different from the conventional in the way they relate to their audiences, in terms of their collections, and the nature of the exhibitions in them (Poulot 1994; Fuller 1992). The key issues in ecomuseums are their orientation toward the community and their emphasis on community participation and empowerment. The activities and collections of ecomusuems reflect what is important to the community, not necessarily conforming to mainstream values and interpretations. They are institutions which value local knowledge, rather than serving as a storehouse which isolate objects from ordinary people, and require professional assistance for access and understanding. They provide a medium to develop community autonomy and identity. The exhibits in these museums are designed through a dialogic approach, i.e. instead of having a group of expert curators preparing the exhibits, a group of curators or specialists work in a dialogue with various parties involved in the content of the exhibition in an interactive medium.[2]

Experimenting with these ideas, I started working with the local women hired at the site in putting together a community exhibit which would be part of the visitor centre. The major challenge was to find an appropriate medium through which these women could express their perceptions and interpretations of the project and the landscape. Photography, something that many of them enjoyed a lot, seemed to provide such a medium. They were given cameras and took pictures of the parts of the project and the landscape that they found interesting during the alternative tours of the site in which these local women were the guides. Along with the pictures they took, the stories and narratives they provided during these tours formed the basis of the community exhibit. Once the pictures were developed, we had a series of discussions with them where they picked the ones they wanted to be displayed as part of the exhibit and elaborated on the reasons for their selections.

These discussions and their selections reveal a set of issues regarding their interests, perceptions and interpretations of the project and the landscape. The kinds of questions which came up during these discussions suggest an overlap with their interests and those of the archaeologists regarding the people who inhabited Çatalhöyük: 'What were they eating? How did they prepare their food, how did they store them? How were they dressed, were they really dressed the way we saw in the slides of the fashion show? Did they have a religion, what did they believe in? Were the women really superior?'. The pictures they selected to be displayed point to three specific interests: building materials and techniques used in Çatalhöyük houses; the burials; the tedious work that archaeologists do at the site. But other interests and concerns also came up during these discussions which do not necessarily overlap with the archaeologists' concerns, nor were directly related to the excavation. One of them was the abundance of pictures they had taken of dried-up trees and wells, and they insisted that these images should be part of the community exhibit. In one of our sessions, one of the woman, picking up the picture of a dried-up well among dried-up trees, commented:

> We want the old things, like this well, to be preserved. This well is preserved just because it was next to the road, otherwise it would also disappear. In the old days there were wells like this one in each field. Now none of them are left with the onset of this drainage system. We want a green environment. It is said that there is no green left in the cities, but now the villages are like that, too. Just look around, most of the trees died because of dryness. There is no water left since the opening of the canals. After this drainage thing, there is no water left here. Before this, all of our water would come from these wells. One cannot help but wonder and worry whether everything will eventually dry up here.

Although they had long arguments and disagreements among themselves about which pictures should be part of the exhibit, there was an immediate consensus on the selection of these particular images. All were extremely concerned about the environmental disaster which has been caused by the falling water table under the Konya plain, and wanted to draw attention to this problem in any possible way they could. This exhibit would provide such a means to express a serious concern they have about this pressing environmental problem.

Another set of interests which dominated our tours of the mounds concerned the plants. The story of the mounds was told mostly through the plants on them, and even the routes the women chose to go from one mound to the other were mainly determined by the location of certain plants on the mounds. There were frequent stops during our tours to talk about these plants: plants they use for medicine, plants they eat, plants they use as brooms, plants they use for makeup, plants they use to protect themselves from the evil eye.

At the end of these tours and discussions, the community exhibit we put together consisted of a panel of collage of the pictures they took and selected with accompanying narratives of these images, and plants they collected from the mounds during these tours. But it is important to note here

that the idea is to prepare a different set of panels in following seasons working with other groups of people in the surrounding villages. Just like the archaeologists working at the project, ideas and interpretations by the local people regarding the project and the landscape do change over time. We believe that it is important to capture this dynamism in putting together a community exhibit. Therefore we are planning to change and update this exhibit every season, also involving multiple groups.

Although this exhibit was prepared only with the local women hired at the site, through these kinds of exhibits part of the visitor centre has the potential to become an ecomuseum, a community centre, which provides a forum for discussion, a place in which to hold discussions and exhibits about issues of concern to the community. Moreover, by providing a forum for discussion and interaction between different members of the community over shared concerns, these kinds of exhibits go beyond computer-generated, high-tech interactivity in the museum context.

As suggested by other similar projects (e.g. Fuller 1992), these kinds of community exhibits might act as vehicles for community empowerment by putting in place those conditions that enable communities to learn about themselves, their needs, and act upon that knowledge. Although it is too early to suggest whether this is the case of Çatalhöyük, the following comment by one of the local women hired at the site (a sentiment shared by many them) point to this kind of potential at Çatalhöyük:

> We feel more important now. We are also proud of the fact that Çatalhöyük is right next to Küçükköy. People from all over the world come here. This place provides for us both material and spiritual gain. We feel that we are valued here. People care about what we have to say, and express their interest and affection for us. I was working for a hotel on the south coast at the beginning of the summer. There when people, both foreigners and the Turks, heard that I also work at Çatalhöyük they expressed so much interest in me and what I do here and so on. I realized how important this place is, and I also felt important. If I have a chance I want to make a documentary about this place and the excavation. I am already obsessed with Çatalhöyük anyway. Whatever I do at home, I always think whether people of Çatalhöyük would do it the same way.

The fact that these local women also share their knowledge of the landscape, building materials and techniques, and especially their knowledge of plants with various specialists on the team contributes to this sense of empowerment as the following account

107

by one of the local women suggests:

> We are a team here. Everyone is doing his/her job. Dried dung, for example. We burn them, you examine them. Sometimes we tell you and teach you the things that you don't know about — plants for example. In previous years they found a bunch of acorns. We call them *pelit*, you call them *palamut*. First the plant specialists could not identify them, and they asked me for help. I told them that they are acorns.

It would be naïve at this point to suggest that all this process of interaction, participation and empowerment is smooth. A striking example demonstrating that this is not such a process is the burning down of an old house in Küçükköy in the winter of 1998. Although the details of this event are not yet clear, the sequence of events suggests a series of tensions in the village. This old house, owned by the headman's family in the village, had been sold to a woman from Istanbul. She bought it on behalf of a women's group centred in Istanbul with the aim of restoring and establishing this house as an international research centre in which anyone interested in 'women's issues' could stay and conduct research. The woman who is the head of this organization describes their aim as follows:

> We want to work at the grassroots level for various empowerment projects for the women by using centuries-old indigenous knowledge, wisdom, and culture that women possess. We call these centres HERINN, and of course the one in Küçükköy is especially important since it is so close to Çatalhöyük. This centre has the potential to attract many researchers from all over the world who are interested in women's issues in different historical periods. In Küçükköy, we want to be able to work both with the local women here and bring in all these people interested in doing this kind of research.

But the house which was bought and restored for these purposes burned to the ground. It can be argued that the potential of this kind of a centre to attract many 'foreigners' to the village might not be welcome by some of the villagers.[3]

Concluding remarks: de-centring the archaeological project

The multi-sited ethnography is an integral part of the reflexive methodology which is being developed in Çatalhöyük, complementing the four themes on which this methodology is based: reflexivity, contextuality, interactivity, and multivocality. *Presenting* Çatalhöyük, in the sense of bringing it to the present and understanding it in its living context, and recognizing the reworkings of the site by multiple groups, is crucial if we want to move towards an inclusive archaeological practice. This conceptualization and methodology also has implications for *presenting* Çatalhöyük to the public. The multi-sited nature of the site and the simultaneous workings of these multiple sites require a non-linear and multimedia presentation of the site to the public (see Tringham and Wolle's discussion Chapter 17, this volume).

The wider context in which the Çatalhöyük project is embedded and the concurrent dispersion of the site suggest that archaeologists increasingly find themselves as one of the many actors in the 'public culture . . . a zone of contestation, where private and state interests, low and high cultural media, different classes, groups formulate, represent, and debate what culture is and should be' (Appadurai & Breckenridge 1992, 38). This process not only de-centres the archaeological project but also provides an opportunity for an active social engagement of archaeologists with the wider public.

Notes

1. For more recent collections on 'rethinking', 'recapturing', 'reinventing', and 'rereading' anthropology, see Fox 1991 and Marcus 1992. For some earlier work on this kind of reevaluation of the anthropological project, see Hymes 1969, and Leach 1961.
2. Chinatown History Museum in New York and Ak-Chin Indian Community Ecomuseum in Arizona are two of the recent successful projects designed with these concepts. For a detailed discussion of these projects see Tchen 1992 and Fuller 1992.
3. Some of the 'Goddess' tours to Çatalhöyük have been organized by this women's group. One of the highest points of these tours is visiting this centre in Küçükköy. One of the tours which was organized after the burning of the house also included a visit and performance of a ritual in front of the house with the aim of 'turning the negative energies in the house to positive ones'.

Acknowledgements

This research was made possible by the support of all these people in Küçükköy and Çumra who so kindly made me part of their lives and so willingly shared their insights with me. I am extremely grateful to them for their enthusiasm and trust in this project.

This chapter has been presented in various forms in WAC 4 conference in Capetown, South Africa, and in seminars at Koç and Boğaziçi Universities in Istanbul, Turkey. I am indebted to the participants of these meetings for their comments and criticisms. I am particularly indebted to Esra Özyürek and Han Tümertekin for their insightful comments and support. I also wish to thank all the team members of the Çatalhöyük project for their encouragement of my work at the site. My deepest debt is to Ian Hodder for his constant inspiration, patience, and interest in this project.

References

Appadurai, A., 1990. Disjuncture and difference in the global cultural economy. *Public Culture* 2, 1–24.

Appadurai, A. & C. Breckenridge, 1992. Museums are good to think: heritage on view in India, in Karp *et al.* (eds.), 34–55.

Appadurai, A. & C. Breckenridge, 1995. Public modernity in India, in *Consuming Modernity: Public Culture in a South Asian World*, ed. C.A. Breckenridge. Minneapolis (MN): University of Minnesota Press, 1–21.

Asad, T. (ed.), 1973. *Anthropology and the Colonial Encounter*. New York (NY): Ithaca Press.

Atkinson, J.A., I. Banks & J. O'Sullivan (eds.), 1996. *Nationalism and Archaeology*. Glasgow: Cruithne Press.

Clifford, J. & G. Marcus (eds.), 1986. *Writing Culture: the Poetics and the Politics of Ethnography*. Berkeley (CA): University of California Press.

Diaz-Andreu, M. & T. Champion (eds.), 1996. *Nationalism and Archaeology in Europe*. London: UCL Press.

Fabian, J., 1983. *Time and the Other: How Anthropology Makes its Object*. New York (NY): Columbia University Press.

Fardon, R., 1990. *Localizing Strategies: Regional Traditions of Ethnographic Writing*. Edinburgh: Scottish Academic Press.

Fox, R.G. (ed.), 1991. *Recapturing Anthropology: Working in the Present*. Santa Fe (NM): School of American Research Advanced Seminar Series.

Fuller, N.J., 1992. The museum as a vehicle for community empowerment: the Ak-Chin Indian Community Ecomuseum Project, in Karp *et al.* (eds.), 327–65.

Geertz, C., 1973. *The Interpretation of Cultures*. New York (NY): Basic Books.

Gupta, A. & J. Ferguson (eds.), 1997a. *Anthropological Locations: Boundaries and Grounds of a Field Science*. Berkeley (CA): University of California Press.

Gupta, A. & J. Ferguson (eds.), 1997b. *Culture, Power, Place: Explorations in Critical Anthropology*. Durham & London: Duke University Press.

Haraway, D.J., 1991. *Simians, Cyborgs, Women: the Reinvention of Nature*. New York (NY): Routledge, 149–82.

Hodder, I., 1991a. *Reading the Past: Current Approaches to Interpretation in Archaeology*. 2nd edition. Cambridge: Cambridge University Press.

Hodder, I., 1991b. Postprocessual archaeology and the current debate, in Preucel (ed.), 30–41.

Hodder, I., 1995. *Theory and Practice in Archaeology*. London & New York (NY): Routledge.

Hodder, I., 1997. 'Always momentary, fluid and flexible': towards a reflexive excavation methodology. *Antiquity* 71, 691–700.

Hymes, D. (ed.), 1969. *Reinventing Anthropology*. New York (NY): Pantheon Books.

Karp, I., C.M. Kreamer & D. Lavine (eds.), 1992. *Museums and Communities: the Politics of Public Culture*. Washington (DC) & London: Smithsonian Institution Press.

Kohl, P.L. & C. Fawcett (eds.), 1995. *Nationalism, Politics, and the Practice of Archaeology*. Cambridge: Cambridge University Press.

Kuper, A., 1994. Culture, identity, and the project of a cosmopolitan anthropology. *The Journal of the Royal Anthropological Institute* 29, 537–54.

Layton, R., 1989. *Conflict in the Archaeology of Living Traditions*. London: Unwin Hyman.

Leach, E.R. (ed.), 1961. *Rethinking Anthropology*. London: Athlone Press.

Marcus, G. (ed.), 1992. *Rereading Cultural Anthropology*. Durham: Duke University Press.

Marcus, G., 1995. Ethnography in/of the world system: the emergence of multi-sited ethnography. *Annual Review of Anthropology* 24, 95–117.

Marcus, G. & M. Fischer, 1986. *Anthropology as Cultural Critique: an Experimental Moment in the Human Sciences*. Chicago (IL) & London: University of Chicago Press.

Ortner, S., 1984. Theory in anthropology since the sixties. *Comparative Studies in Society and History* 26, 126–66.

Poulot, D., 1994. Identity as self-discovery: the ecomuseum in France, in *Museum Culture: Histories, Discourses, Spectacles*, eds. D.J. Sherman & I. Rogoff. Minneapolis (MN): University of Minnesota Press, 66–84.

Preucel, R.W. (ed.), 1991. *Processual and Postprocessual Archaeologies: Multiple Ways of Knowing the Past*. Carbondale (IL): Southern Illinois University.

Said, E., 1989. Representing the colonized: anthropology's interlocutors. *Critical Inquiry* 15, 205–25.

Sanjek, R. (ed.), 1990. *Fieldnotes: the Makings of Anthropology*. Ithaca (NY) & London: Cornell University Press.

Smith, V.L. & W.R. Eadington (eds.), 1992. *Tourism Alternatives: Potentials and Problems in the Development of Tourism*. Chichester: John Wiley & Sons.

Tchen, J.K.W., 1992. Creating a dialogic museum: the Chinatown History Museum experiment, in Karp *et al.* (eds.), 285–326.

Wolf, E., 1982. *Europe and People Without History*. Berkeley (CA): University of California Press.

Yengoyan, A., 1986. Theory in anthropology: on the demise of the concept of culture. *Comparative Studies in Society and History* 28, 368–74.

Chapter 9

Different Excavation Styles Create Different Windows into Çatalhöyük

Ruth Tringham & Mirjana Stevanovic

The aim of this chapter is to point out that important contextual variables occur in the process of retrieval of the archaeological materials through excavation. The excavation methodology at Çatalhöyük has tended to be treated in the literature (Hodder 1997) as relatively uniform. We shall show, however, that there are in fact multiple excavation methodologies. This has been implied in an earlier chapter in this volume (Farid *et al.* Chapter 2, this volume) in which the excavation strategy and opinions of the British team excavating at Çatalhöyük are voiced. This chapter will draw attention to the voices of the other excavation teams at Çatalhöyük, specifically the 'American' team.

Joan Gero has demonstrated the nature of some of the variability of excavation strategies along gendered and regional lines (Gero 1996). Farid *et al.* have also suggested that regional variability is present by referring to the 'American team' and the 'Greek team'. In this chapter, however, we are interested in exploring some of the interesting implications and complexities of training, organization, and status/power that, to a certain extent, are the result of regional methodologies, but are also the result, we believe, of variation in the field experience and intellectual histories of the individual researchers. Joan Gero (1996) and Margaret Conkey (1997) have both set these implications of the 'constituting context' for the practice and routines of archaeological research in a more theoretical context than we shall do here.

Is the BACH team American?

Mirjana Stevanovic and Ruth Tringham — who together direct the Berkeley Archaeologists at Çatalhöyük (BACH team, or 'the American team') — through working together for fifteen years in Yugoslavia and Bulgaria have developed a strategy which was designed to retrieve information on the use-lives of Neolithic houses (Stevanovic & Tringham 1998). Neolithic houses in southeast and central Europe are rectangular detached houses of wattle-and-daub with a gabled roof. In southeast Europe these are universally burned at the end of their use-lives.

Ruth Tringham's first experience in excavation was gained (after a couple of seasons in Britain and Scandinavia) at the Linear Pottery settlement of Bylany in the then Czechoslovakia with Bohumil Soudsky (Soudsky & Pavlu 1972). This excavation was without vertical stratigraphy, but involved large-scale horizontal exposure of post-hole patterns (the ghost of large wattle-and-daub buildings) using earth-moving equipment, and an early use of computerized recording of ceramics. Subsequent excavation experience was of large exposure of architectural features (although on a smaller scale than at Bylany) at Neolithic settlements in the Soviet Union and northern Yugoslavia. At none of these was there any form of continuous occupation leaving a deep stratigraphic record.

Ruth Tringham's first experience of such a site was during the excavation of the site of Selevac which she directed with Dusan Krstic (Tringham & Krstic 1990). This was later supplemented by participation with Mirjana Stevanovic in the research at Gomolava (Brukner 1988), which has deep, though not necessarily continuous, occupation deposits. In this research we were guided by our Yugoslav colleagues into recognizing and working within the framework of building horizons.

Mirjana Stevanovic was trained in Yugoslavia at the University of Belgrade and in the field at such projects as Bosut, Vinca and Gomolava. We first worked together at Selevac in the detailed study of architectural remains in small 4 × 4 m trenches (Tringham & Stevanovic 1990). This was our strategy for retrieving information on resource utilization through the 500-year history of Selevac's occupation, but did not give us information on architecture.

Through a growing interest in architecture and addressing questions about use-life of houses which had previously only been addressed to movable artefacts, we subsequently worked together at Gomolava (Brukner 1988), Opovo (Tringham *et al.* 1992), and at Podgoritsa Tell, Bulgaria (Bailey *et al.* 1998). Mirjana Stevanovic meanwhile carried out postgraduate research at the Agricultural University of Wageningen, Holland, Belgrade University and the University of California at Berkeley that involved experimentation and the analysis of architectural materials from these sites (Stevanovic 1996; 1997).

The point of this preamble is to point out that 'the American team' is directed by two people who have never excavated in 'America'. Having said that, however, we should point out that in the Selevac project and later, we have excavated with the aid of archaeologists and students from the USA. At Çatalhöyük, where we have excavated since 1997, the BACH team comprises graduates and undergraduate students from the University of California at Berkeley, some of whom (but not all) have experience excavating in the USA. Many of these students and archaeologists, however, only have experience excavating in Europe and/or west Asia. Our team, moreover, also includes archaeologists from Yugoslavia, some of whom worked with us in the Selevac and Opovo projects. It is also true, more importantly, that we excavate with funds from the US which involve peer review in that country.[1] We should not forget to mention, however, that every semester, our research strategy is put into the intellectual framework of 'American' archaeological practice through graduate seminars and other public meetings in the US.

The 'American' aspect to our research is its intellectual content, and in the practice of explicating research aims, strategy, and interpretation in the public arena. The style of our 'performance' of the site probably owes much to this experience (Tilley 1989). There is little in the 'American team's' excavation strategy, however, that could be described as typical of the American style of excavation practice. Nor is it typically the practice of southeast European archaeology, although much of what we do is recognizable as stemming from our experience in Yugoslavia (Tasic & Jovanovic 1979).

What the BACH team brings from the Balkans

In southeast Europe, where architectural units are distributed as discrete units, separated from each other by equally large areas of deposits that may have no obvious fixed architectural remains, our horizontal/spatial reference was always the grid oriented according to cardinal points (Bailey *et al.* 1998; Tringham *et al.* 1992). At Opovo, Yugoslavia, for example, a 16 × 20 m block was divided into 2 m quadrants which would form the main units of excavation and recording of the archaeological materials throughout its stratified deposits. Through the seven years of excavation, the same basic strategy was maintained, proceeding by 1 m units in and around the structural features and by 2 m units in the cultural layer itself. Excavation proceeded by 10–15 cm thick arbitrary levels by spade and shovel and screening with 1 cm mesh screens. In and around features, however, such as primarily and secondarily deposited burned clay rubble, ovens, and pits, excavation proceeded according to their natural stratigraphy by trowelling. Constant stratigraphic control baulks were retained from 1983–89 (Tringham *et al.* 1992; in press).

In contrast to standard Balkan excavation practice, we tended to create a profusion of temporary baulks which served to record the relative stratigraphy of the structures and other domestic features, rather than record the main transition from one building horizon to another. A crucial difference in the excavation strategy that we developed from standard Balkan practice is that our aim was to excavate each house as though its life-history was a priority rather than being subordinated to the history of the settlement (or building horizon) as a whole.

We developed a strategy in which the remains of the burned wattle-and-daub houses were more carefully excavated and more systematically and fully mapped, recorded and sampled than on any other Neolithic site yet excavated in southeast Europe. Each burned building was carefully cleaned, lifting up the rubble and mapping it layer by layer, and taking systematic samples for later analysis of fabric composition and temperature of firing. Recording was carried out according to cells (each 1 × 1 m) in and around the structural features (Stevanovic 1996; Tringham *et al.* 1992).

Computerized recording was by locus, which may be equivalent to a 2 m square in the cultural layer, or a 1 m square screened unit, or a 1 m square unit within a feature. Features could also be designated as a separate locus. Some features, however, were divided into several loci, depending on their size and the significance of detailed spatial recording within them. In every case, loci were always oriented and located according to the main grid of the site.

The detail, care and large scale of the excavation and analysis of building construction materials at Opovo is considered to be an important innovation in the investigation of the Neolithic architecture of southeast Europe (Stevanovic 1996; 1997; Stevanovic & Tringham 1998). The number of loci that were assigned to the structural remains is much higher than any other loci assigned to the associated materials. It may seem logical to those unfamiliar with southeast European Neolithic archaeology that the largest quantity of material, such as construction remains, would reflect numerically the most attention. Nevertheless, it had not been the case in the treatment of Neolithic architecture of southeast Europe prior to the Opovo Archaeological Project. The most typical treatment of rubble as constructional remains had been to discard it readily in the course of excavation as an obstacle to reaching the most valued part of a house, i.e. the house floor with all the artefactual remains on it.

We should mention at this point that the 'locus' was similar but not identical to the 'unit' used in the Çatalhöyük recording system. The use of the Harris matrix and the terms 'context' or 'unit' were not incorporated consciously into our excavation of houses until the excavation of the Eneolithic tell at Podgoritsa, in northeast Bulgaria (Bailey *et al.* 1998). This project was the one that we carried out in 1995 and had planned for subsequent seasons. The project was cancelled, however, and we moved our interest in the life-history of houses to the project at Çatalhöyük in 1996.

Bringing southeast Europe to Çatalhöyük

By the time our project at Podgoritsa developed, there were many features in our strategy of research that we had in common with that practiced at Çatalhöyük by the Cambridge team. In fact we have been delighted to collaborate with the Çatalhöyük team because it has given us a chance to put into practice the ideal strategies to investigate the physical and social formation of the settlement that we had always in some way or another had to compromise in our previous research in Yugoslavia and especially Bulgaria.

- We share an interest in the investigation of the formation of the tells as a composite of the histories of individual buildings in contrast to the traditional viewpoint of a tell as a sequence of the replacement of one village by another in a stratified sequence of building horizons.

- So we share a desire to examine the construction, modification, abandonment, filling in, and destruction of individual buildings in relation to that of the buildings around them by slow and detailed excavation.

- We share an interest in maintaining a standardized digitized detailed recording of multiple lines of evidence using Harris matrices, standard forms, and a detailed visual image recording by photography and line drawing. We welcomed the sharing of this data base amongst the different teams at Çatalhöyük and on the Internet.

- We share an interest in putting a reflexive methodology advocated by Ian Hodder (1997) and others into practice. At Opovo we were one of the few teams in the Balkans whose final report has a conclusion written by the multiple voices of the team and whose strategy was designed by a core research team rather than the individual authority of the directors. We have noted that at Çatalhöyük such a methodology with its many opportunities for discussion and debate at many different levels leads to a much more vocal enterprise than is experienced on most projects; this definitely slows down the pace of removal of deposits, but in the end we believe that the results will reflect the amount of thought and effort that go into the interpretation of the archaeological data of Çatalhöyük. As noted above, we welcome the slower pace of excavation after the sense of urgency that often characterized our Balkan efforts. Even at Çatalhöyük, however, there may be pressures exerted for speedy results.

- Finally, we share an interest in, and a sense of responsibility to, the broader scale of multivocality advocated in the Çatalhöyük project, in which audiences from the surrounding villages and towns as well as much further away share in the data that we are recovering. Here we face the same dilemmas that face archaeologists everywhere with standing architecture and other features that could be preserved *in situ*, thus preventing further excavation, or preserved in an external context in a museum or interpretive centre. This is an aspect of research that we rarely had to deal with in our previous research in southeast Europe, but as with some of the other aspects of this project mentioned below, we have had to face for the first time at Çatalhöyük.

How the Balkan (BACH) window on Çatalhöyük is different

In spite of this profound sharing of methodological principles and aims of the Cambridge-directed Çatalhöyük project, there are some important differences that our (the BACH team) intellectual and field histories bring to the project at Çatalhöyük. One of these that I (RET) think is worth mentioning but not elaborating in this chapter is the fact that I have been thinking about and discussing the feminist practice of archaeology for a number of years with colleagues at Berkeley and elsewhere. The U.C. Berkeley graduate students may not necessarily agree with these practices, but they have certainly been exposed to them in a variety of ways through seminars and less formal instruction. I feel that although for many the feminist practice of archaeology may seem to be identical to the reflexive methodology and postprocessual practice of archaeology that forms the basis of the Çatalhöyük project, there are important differences that are probably part of the 'BACH window' on Çatalhöyük, in addition to the more obvious Balkan background.

There was a sharp learning curve for both Mirjana Stevanovic and Ruth Tringham in order to adapt their excavation strategy and interest in the use-life/life-history of houses to the very different architectural context of south-central Anatolia.

• In the BACH area we have tended to continue to use the site grid as a basis for dividing up Building 3, within which we identify features. Within Building 3, we still regard the use of the 'space' (e.g. platform, room) as a unit subordinate in usefulness to features, building and the grid.

• We had been accustomed to excavating clearly discrete architectural features — buildings — whereas those of Çatalhöyük were a complex web of rooms, some of which might have been discrete places during a part or all of their history, but whose relationship to other rooms was an object of investigation rather than a given starting point.

• We had been used to excavating timber-framed houses, thickly daubed on one or both surfaces, and destroyed by burning, so that all that remained was a heaped mass of burned clay rubble, on top of burned clay floor (hopefully) and wall stumps at most 30 cm high. Under these we would be able to discern postholes and, occasionally, wall trenches. At Çatalhöyük we were faced with mud-brick architecture with relatively sparse use of wood and with well-preserved walls, often more than a metre high, and fixed features. Not only did this mean a very different way of uncovering the architecture, but our expectations of what the architecture would look like in terms of modifications through time were quite different.

• In southeast Europe we had been used to architectural debris being piled up as discrete stratigraphic units within which the primary and secondary occupational debris was buried. Other pockets of occupational debris were concentrated around and within such discrete features as external fire installations and pits. Outside of these architectural and other features, the occupational deposits were visible as soil deposits of variable nature. At Çatalhöyük, on the other hand, there were few concentrations of cultural debris that were not part of the fill of the rooms. For example, pits dug for the deposition of garbage are very rare (unlike pits dug for the burial of the dead). Thus at Çatalhöyük every part of the deposits has relevance for one or other aspect of a building's life-history, whereas in southeast Europe the challenge is to link depositional events and features outside a building to the life-history of that building. In both areas it is a challenge to link the life-history of one building with those of subsequent and earlier buildings. The nature of the challenge is quite different in each area. In southeast Europe, the challenge is again in making a link through distinct stratigraphic layers. At Çatalhöyük, the challenge is in making sense of the mass of data and observations on the sequence of building events whose distinction is often difficult to discern.

• In southeast Europe we had become familiar with and enjoyed the greater horizontal exposure of excavation area, which we believed was an essential step to an important aim of establishing the relationships between houses and the outdoor features (e.g. pits) as well as between the houses themselves. It seems to us that the Cambridge-based teams (except for the large South area, which they have in some sense 'inherited') interest and strategy is to focus their excavation and analysis on specific houses whose vertical replacement becomes the object of investigation by intensive vertical exposure. In this way houses that most likely belong to different generations can be compared. The focus in the BACH area (within the spatial restrictions of our solid-framed shelter) is to excavate on a broader horizontal scale in order to compare the life-histories of different buildings whose histories were overlapping. Thus, whereas the Cambridge-based team studies buildings as self-contained units, the BACH team studies the Neolithic buildings at Çatalhöyük as part of a network (or 'anthill') of rooms in which it is hard to say where one 'building' begins and where it ends.

We have changed some of our excavation strategies to deal with the different conditions of the archaeological record. There are clearly, however, some features of our excavation strategy which we have retained from our projects in the Balkans which contributes to our different attitude to the architecture and thus to our window on Çatalhöyük:

- In southeast Europe the cultural deposits were usually excavated by arbitrary levels, as they are in the United States, with their variability monitored horizontally and vertically by cross-sections which, in the case of a deep stratification might be recorded and then dismantled and re-established at regular intervals. At Çatalhöyük we retained the use of a main cross-section through Building 3, and were quite prepared to use arbitrary levels in the excavation of the cultural debris. As it turned out, the profile has been extremely useful in understanding the sequence of the collapse and filling of Building 3, but we probably could have dispensed with the artificial spits.

- We see a need for different strategies in the excavation of different deposits. We see a need to use arbitrary layers in excavating the deposits that are stratigraphically undifferentiated and yet comprise thick layers of mixed materials (like house fill). This is especially important if one starts excavating from the surface and has remains that have been eroded and disturbed. As soon as we arrive on a 'firm' ground and can define natural layers we proceed excavating in natural layers. Our strategy is time consuming but is safe. After all, this was one factor that

helped us uncover the roof (see below).

- In our projects in Yugoslavia and Bulgaria, the stratigraphic relation of one building to another was recorded through a series of baulks in which the microstratigraphic context would be preserved and linked to the main stratigraphic profile which served to monitor the bulk of the cultural deposits (see below). We diverged from traditional Balkan practice by having a large number of such baulks and profiles, and retaining them throughout the cleaning and lifting of the floor. We have continued to use such small temporary profiles at Çatalhöyük to understand the relationship of one part of the fill of a room to another (Fig. 9.1). Their proliferation has been remarked on and criticized by the Cambridge team as redundant when excavating according to the depositional sequence of units. We feel, however, that the baulks are valuable as a visual way to demonstrate and document stratigraphic relationships, as a supplement to the schematized demonstration of the Harris matrix.

- In keeping with our strategy that we have brought with us from southeast Europe, we do not excavate whole units in their sequence of deposition (Fig. 9.2). We are often excavating several parts of a depositional sequence at once, since we believe that our treatment and interpretation of the later part of a sequence may change as a result of a better understanding of the earlier part. This practice can, of course, test the patience of the

Figure 9.1. *The main cross-sections through Building 3 during its excavation.*

Figure 9.2. *Example of the unsequential excavation of the roof in Building 3.*

to carry out all the tasks needed for the proper excavation and recording of her or his own unit. Thus an archaeologist in the Cambridge-based team is assigned a unit or series of units, and is expected to see the whole process through — excavation, sampling, drawing, form-recording, photographing — from start to finish. In the BACH team, units — new or already open — are assigned and reassigned on a daily basis. Thus each participant while excavating a restricted area had to be reminded constantly of the situation in the whole building. The archaeologist is expected to excavate with the field director looking over her or his shoulder, record and keep track of finds, but the on-going recording of the visual record — drawing, EDM mapping and photography — is done by a 'specialist' for this task. This organization was partly due to the nature of the deposits being excavated in that during the excavation of Building 3 in 1997–98, few internal divisions which could be separately assigned to particular archaeologists were visible. The fill of the house can only now be defined as the roof, midden, screen wall, and mixed remains. In smaller, more clearly defined areas, such as space 88, we actually did experiment with a single archaeologist excavating, drawing etc. but we did not feel comfortable with this situation (although the archaeologist in question — Dušan Borić — may have felt it more satisfactory).

flotation crew and other laboratory staff who are waiting to analyze a complete unit and may have to wait for several sessions of the excavation of that unit.

- In the strategy of excavation that we developed in the Yugoslavia and Bulgaria, the definitive cleaning of a feature is reached very slowly. The feature is cleaned back and forth from its apparent centre to periphery and back again to the centre, gradually going deeper in the level. We are interested as much in the nature of the collapse of the superstructure and debris of the house as we are in the cleaned floor-plan. At each level of cleaning, the feature is recorded by photography and drawing. Our philosophy is that the feature does not have to be definitively cleaned before it is recorded. The excavation is a more on-going process with definition being rarely achieved, but recording being frequently carried out.

- This process of work, with the idea of excavating several levels of a feature and several features at once, and having a large number of units open at any one time is made possible (we believe) by an organization of labour which is very different from that employed by the Cambridge-based team. Ian Hodder (pers. comm.) has referred to the BACH organization of work as a 'centralized system' in contrast to the decentralized nature of the Cambridge-based team. The latter is more characteristic of British practice in general, in which each excavator-archaeologist is expected

- In this regard we draw attention to the apparent contradiction in the organization of labour in the Cambridge-based team, in which excavators are 'universalists' in contrast to the laboratory analysts who are 'specialists'. The implications of this contradiction are explored in much more detail in the article by Shahina Farid and others in this volume.

- This way of working is — yes — undemocratic to a certain extent in that an archaeologist/student is not working independently and there is less con-

Figure 9.3. *Photo-montage: contrasting styles of excavation.*

tinuity of recording (a unit sheet might be filled in by several people). Its advantage is a greater consistency of unit recording across a building, a much greater consistency of visual record, and — an unexpected bonus — excavators can double as 'specialists' for part or a whole day during the work week. For graduate students who might be doing research on a particular body of material, the opportunity for both excavation and analysis is essential. Excavators can also be ro-

tated at more frequent intervals through tasks such as heavy fraction sorting.

Conclusion

It is fairly clear that these different styles of excavating and organizing the work force create different windows on Çatalhöyük. This is where the multivocality begins. But how far can we take this viewpoint? Can we go far as to say that each team finds what it 'deserves' according to its aims and strategies? Perhaps this is taking the theatre too far, but we cannot resist the temptation to draw attention to the contrast between the clearly — almost neatly — defined areas of the Cambridge-based team in the North area, with the mass of complicated fill and history of collapse and destruction of Building 3 — including its roof — excavated by the BACH team!

Note

1. We excavate with the aid of a senior research grant from the National Science Foundation Washington DC (SBR-9805755).

References

Bailey, D., R. Tringham, J. Bass, M. Stevanovic, M. Hamilton, H. Neumann, I. Angelova & A. Raduncheva, 1998. Expanding the dimensions of early agricultural tells: the Podgoritsa Archaeological Project, Bulgaria. *Journal of Field Archaeology* 25(4), 373–96.

Brukner, B., 1988. Die Siedlung der Vinca-Gruppe auf Gomolava (Die Wohnschicht des Spätneolithikums und Fruhäneolithikums-Gomolava Ia-b und Gomolava va Ib) und der Wohnhorizont des äneolithischen Humus (Gomolava II), in *Gomolava: hronologija i stratigrafija u praistoriji i antici podunavlja i jugoistocne Evrope*, eds. N. Tasic & J. Petrovic. Novi Sad: Vojvodanski Muzej and Balkanoloski Institut SAN, 19–38.

Conkey, M.W., 1997. Beyond art and between the caves: thinking about context in the interpretive process, in *Beyond Art: Pleistocene Image and Symbol*, eds. M. Conkey, O. Soffer, D. Stratmann & N.G. Jablonski. (Memoirs 23.) San Francisco (CA): California Academy of Sciences, 343–67.

Gero, J., 1996. Archaeological practice and engendered encounters with field data, in *Gender and Archaeology*, ed. R. Wright. Philadelphia (PA): University of Pennsylvania Press, 251–80.

Hodder, I., 1997. 'Always momentary, fluid and flexible': towards a reflexive excavation methodology. *Antiquity* 71(273), 691.

Soudsky, B. & I. Pavlu, 1972. The Linear Pottery Culture settlement patterns of central Europe, in *Man, Settlement, and Urbanism*, eds. P. Ucko, R. Tringham & G. Dimbleby. London: Duckworth, 317–28.

Stevanovic, M., 1996. The Age of Clay: the Social Dynamics of House Destruction. Unpublished PhD thesis, University of California Berkeley.

Stevanovic, M., 1997. The age of clay: the social dynamics of house destruction. *Journal of Anthropological Archaeology* 16(4), 334–95.

Stevanovic, M. & R. Tringham, 1998. The significance of Neolithic houses in the archaeological record of southeast Europe, in *Zbornik posvecen Dragoslavu Srejovicu*, ed. Z. Mikic. Beograd: Balkanoloski Institut, 193–208.

Tasic, N. & B. Jovanovic, 1979. *Metodologija istrazhivanja u praistorijskoj arheologiji*. Belgrade: Srpska Akademija Nauka i Umetnosti.

Tilley, C., 1989. Excavation as theatre. *Antiquity* 63, 275–80.

Tringham, R. & D. Krstic (eds.), 1990. *Selevac: a Neolithic Village in Yugoslavia*. Los Angeles (CA): Institute of Archaeology Press, UCLA.

Tringham, R. & M. Stevanovic, 1990. Archaeological excavation of Selevac 1976–78, in Tringham & Krstic (eds.), 57–214.

Tringham, R., B. Brukner, T. Kaiser, K. Borojevic, N. Russell, P. Steli, M. Stevanovic & B. Voytek, 1992. The Opovo Project: a study of socio-economic change in the Balkan Neolithic. 2nd preliminary report. *Journal of Field Archaeology* 19(3), 351–86.

Tringham, R., M. Stevanovic & B. Brukner (eds.), in press. *Opovo: the Construction of a Prehistoric Place in Europe*. Berkeley (CA): UCB Archaeological Research Facility Publications.

Chapter 10

Faultlines: the Construction of Archaeological Knowledge at Çatalhöyük[1]

Carolyn Hamilton

On 29 August, 1996, Shahina Farid, supervisor of the South area of the Çatalhöyük excavation, drew the attention of the various teams and specialists conducting a tour of the progress of the excavation to three instances of faultlines on the east walls of spaces 106 and 108. Reflecting the earlier discussions of the excavators as they first uncovered these features, she speculated as to whether the faultlines were the result of an earthquake or of bricks slumping, possibly because they were still moist when removed from their moulds and first placed on the walls.

In much the same way as excavation uncovered these faultlines, so too investigation of the Çatalhöyük project, i.e. of the various activities, methods and dynamics by means of which archaeological knowledge of Çatalhöyük around 6000 BC is produced, reveals interesting faultlines, the causes and implications of which this chapter sets out to explore. Just as Farid drew the touring group's attention to the on-site discussions of these structural features as they emerged, so too does this chapter explore the explanations offered by project participants of the project faultlines as they emerged. In so doing the chapter seeks not simply to account for those faultlines, but to understand the recursive relations between them and the way in which features like the structural faultlines, are observed, discussed, affect and are turned into archaeological knowledge.

Methodology

This preliminary chapter is based on a limited (one month) period of fieldwork, conducted in the middle of the 1996 excavation season. Further fieldwork was undertaken in 1997. While two areas were cleared in 1995, and limited digging begun, the real work of excavation only commenced in 1996. In part, this limited endeavour serves as a pilot study to assess the feasibility and potential value of a longer term project on the production of archaeological knowledge conducted over an extended period of time and in greater depth.

The study is part of the broader concern at Çatalhöyük to develop greater self-reflexivity within archaeological theory and methodology. Indeed, since the late 1980s, considerable attention has been paid within archaeology to the recognition that archaeological practice is always socially and politically situated (Wylie 1994; Pinsky & Wylie 1989; Gero 1996). Close empirical analyses of the conditions under which specific assumptions or forms of practice arise have begun to be undertaken. The Çatalhöyük excavation takes this in a new direction through exploration of what might constitute a postprocessual field project. Effectively the challenge is to consider how greater reflexivity about the way in which archaeological knowledge has been produced in the past can inform, change and improve, or benefit, current practice. These points frame the Çatalhöyük project and underpin my study.

This challenge is currently also being taken up in other projects. On the basis of an examination of what she calls conventionalised narratives, Joan Gero (1996), for example, argues that the routinized accounting for field methodologies ultimately distorts what is done on site. She goes on to suggest developing alternative narratives for accounting for field practice, new (and yet largely untried) ways of revealing what was actually archaeologically undertaken, to produce greater insight into how knowledge is 'in fact' constructed and to emphasize the role of archaeologist as knowledge-producing agent. This present research project is similarly concerned with how archaeological knowledge is constructed, but more importantly also seeks to review how new and experimental methodologies, implemented in response to the recognition of the constructed nature of archaeological knowledge, work. What does an explicitly reflexive and interactive methodology facilitate, and what are its limitations, its sticking points and sites of abrasion? In short, what happens on an excavation where the idea of 'objectivity' is not effortlessly invoked, where scientific procedures are constantly investigated for their poetics and politics, and where more, or at least as many, 'brownie points' are gained for exposing an assumption as a 'find'? How is knowledge produced by archaeologists occupied with postprocessual concerns?

Once operationalized, this study quickly expanded its reflexive ambit from being an attempt by a non-archaeologist to document and analyze procedures and developments within the Çatalhöyük project, to a situation where occasions of interaction between this researcher and the archaeologists created conditions in which the archaeologists were able, and in some instances obliged, to reflect on their daily practices. These occasions fed into broader processes of reflexivity built into the heart of the Çatalhöyük project. In short, the present study does not simply document and analyse developments at Çatalhöyük but also contributes to their shaping.

As such, the study emphasizes in new ways the participant part of the deployed methodology of participant-observation. It involves the studying of not a physically distant and culturally remote society, but the anthropologists' closest kin, archaeologists, many of whom have some training as anthropologists and honed understandings of the powers, implications and limitations of an anthropological gaze as well as the capacity and opportunities to challenge the ethnographer's authority. It is furthermore not an instance of applied anthropology seeking to find solutions to problems, and yet is a case where intervention cannot be withheld. A spin-off of this project will be an assessment of the implications for the broad project of ethnography of this particular exercise in participation.

While the study is in part an ethnography of the production of postprocessual archaeological knowledge at Çatalhöyük and hopefully in the long-run will yield a fine-grained analysis of archaeological practice, it is explicitly not conceived of as an ethnography of the archaeologists at Çatalhöyük. In other words, the full extent of social relations at Çatalhöyük is not the object of study nor is the research method confined to participant-observation.

Deconstructionism, historicization, detailed contextualization and performance analysis are other strategies utilized in diverse combinations. The materials on which this chapter is based were derived from a mixture of informal interviews, analysis of various texts produced by and about the project, in addition to the participant-observation from within the project by being a working member of the project, not as an excavator but as a notebook specialist with the (non-archaeological) brief of doing this particular exercise. The study thus refuses disciplinary or methodological containment as part of its own explicit research strategy.

The present study, an exercise in meta-reflexivity, is itself one device among a host of others built into the Çatalhöyük research project designed to encourage reflexivity, and as has already been suggested, came also to facilitate a degree of interaction among participants. The linkage between reflexivity and interaction is not inevitable, but has been, in other areas, actively structured into the Çatalhöyük project.

In the next section of the chapter I will briefly summarize some of the devices built into the Çatalhöyük project to facilitate interaction and reflexivity. I will rely on the fact that other chapters in this volume have already begun to introduce these features. To extend the metaphor with which I opened this chapter, I liken these pioneering devices to the mud-bricks moulded *in situ* at Çatalhöyük some nine thousand years ago. I will not be focusing on those devices which have been entirely successful — the bricks that have held their shape. Rather, I will focus on the faultlines of the project: I will try to distinguish between methodological 'bricks' which might be thought to have 'slumped' once *in situ*, and those which have been forced out of alignment as a result of structural rupture or contradiction. I will try to account for why some courses 'slumped' and others 'ruptured', and finally and most tentatively, I will seek to assess the significance of the slumpings and ruptures for the methodologies being developed at Çatalhöyük. The focus of this first, very preliminary paper on faultlines was suggested by the work of the French literary theorist, Pierre Machery. The central idea that I adapt somewhat loosely from his approach to textual analysis is that rather than examining a work, or a set of practices, for their continuities, successes or failures, it is often useful to seek rather the points of rupture or contradiction and try to understand why they are present, to see what they say about the matters in hand. This seemed also a way of being able to say some things about a body of research that I must emphasize is as yet in a very early stage.

Moulding the building bricks of a postprocessual methodology

A variety of devices can be identified at Çatalhöyük which constitute the moulds for the bricks that might eventually be built into a postprocessual methodology for archaeology. The excavation diaries kept by the project director, supervisors, and others provide a daily account of the evolving logic of the excavation, its successes and errors, and its suggestiveness. The recording on film of daily occasions of excavation and interpretation also hold out enormous promise for encouraging and facilitating a reflexive approach to the activities of interpretation involved in the processes of excavation and in the generation of the data on which archaeological analysis is based. The imminent integration of the video material into the project's on-line and publicly accessible data base will place it at the heart of the research exercise alongside the data regarding ceramics, faunal remains, lithics and so on.

The data base itself is founded on a commitment to providing specialists in various sub-fields ready access to each other's material and working interpretations, and thereby creating possibilities for breaking out of forms of explanation and analysis limited by the horizons of the various specialities and for thinking critically and innovatively about the conventions of the sub-disciplines.

Another device structured into the field project is the attendance by the on-site but lab-based specialists of regular tours of the excavation areas. These are designed to keep the specialists up-to-date and familiar with developments in the excavation areas and to provide the excavators with rapid feedback on what the laboratory people are discovering.

The location of a social anthropologist in the nearby village of Küçükköy (see Chapter 14, this volume) opens up for consideration the implications and effects of the Çatalhöyük project on the village and vice versa.

Tours and discussions of the site, specially laid on for the local Turkish workers employed on the project, similarly provide an opportunity for consideration of the nature of this mutual impact, and begin to recognize the diversity of knowledges about Çatalhöyük. Acknowledgement of popular knowledges and appropriations of Çatalhöyük, including the concerns of Mother Goddess cultists who visit the site, are thus not ignored because of their lack of scientific underpinnings. A variety of local, visitor and tourist needs of the site already show signs of affecting the development of the site, and the notion of a purely scientific project untouched by the pressures of public, popular and sometimes rival needs and interpretations is eschewed.

A still greater degree of multivocality is invited within the project. Discrete aspects of the project operate with relative autonomy; separate teams with different research agendas are invited to excavate, and diversity of participation and interpretation is emphasized. Mid-season in 1996 at least ten nationalities were present at the site. A storytelling session held in the middle of the season underscored the commitment to multiple interpretations of Çatalhöyük.

Conservation, public presentation of a site and the availability of data often come years after an

Figure 10.1. *Çatalhöyük 1996: James and Arlene Mellaart discuss the 1960s excavations with conservator Connie Silver. Ian Hodder and Carolyn Hamilton listen in while the Karlsruhe team film the group. The whole is being photographed by Shahina Farid, while Orrin Shane who took this photograph captures the entire scene.*[2]

121

excavation is completed, but at Çatalhöyük these features are moved up in time to proceed in step with excavation. A local journalist spent a week on site obtaining a close-up view of its progress and contributed to putting knowledge of Çatalhöyük up-front for the public at an early stage in the history of the excavation. The 'Friends of Çatalhöyük' actively promote public interest in and knowledge of the site.

In short then, the project is characterized by a range of features implemented to promote open, non-authoritarian and multivocal interpretations, wide interaction, and a high degree of reflexivity, and designed optimally to create a setting for a recursive relationship between data and theory enabling innovative thinking while shifting ownership of knowledge of Çatalhöyük out of the hands of the archaeologists currently at work on the project. Investigation of how these features worked in practice in the 1996 season revealed, however, a series of faultlines, indicating that they were not implemented without some form of slumping, and even minor earthquakes. Some of the resultant faultlines are the focus of this chapter; others await long-term assessment.

It is a premise of the approach adopted for this research that these features of the project, and the project as a whole, are fundamentally shaped by the multiple contexts of Çatalhöyük. But, just as object and context on site shift in relation to each other and to the interpretive framework applied to them, so too in the postprocessual methodology of Çatalhöyük are the faultlines and their contexts mutually constitutive.

The multiple contexts of Çatalhöyük

The primary context of the current Çatalhöyük excavation is that constituted by the previous excavation of the site by James Mellaart in the early 1960s (see Chapter 7, this volume). Mellaart's reports and his book emphasized the preservation at Çatalhöyük of what has come to be regarded as an example of 'advanced civilization', a centre of artistic achievement and elaborate ritual. From the point of view of the public, Çatalhöyük became something of a household name in the 1960s while amongst archaeologists it achieved renown not only for its art and rich symbolism, but also for its significance for the understanding of early villages, processes of urbanization and the development of 'complex societies'. Mellaart's excavation was terminated in 1965, following a series of controversies which surrounded this excavation and other of his projects. These included the so-called Dorak Affair in which Mellaart

fell under suspicion of having appropriated jewellery finds from Dorak; a scandal over the illegal sale of antiquities by workmen at his Hacilar excavation, and finally a further uproar concerning problems at Çatalhöyük. The current reopening of the site has demanded that due attendance be given to this legacy and to guarantees regarding the conservation of the finds.

Indeed, the location of the site in Turkey where strict regulations pertain regarding excavation permission, monitoring of excavation, storage and the removal of finds constitutes yet another of Çatalhöyük's contexts.

The Mellaart legacy is by no means confined to the perception of problems around his handling of significant finds. Perhaps more important for the current excavation is the way in which Çatalhöyük became fixed in the popular imagination and thereby set up all sorts of preconceptions, expectations and potential assumptions around the present excavation. As one participant in the project commented, 'Çatalhöyük is almost of mythical significance.' As such there are substantial demands on Çatalhöyük emanating from the Mother Goddess cultists, tourists, museologists and others.

At the same time, the archaeological significance of Çatalhöyük exerts its own pressure. As a high prestige site regarded as especially significant in the emergence of 'civilization', its reopening made it the object of widespread academic attention. The Director commented on how its status made it possible to attract the best people in various fields to work in the project. All participants remarked on what an extraordinary thing it is to work on such a site. One consequence of its status is that everyone concerned with the project brings to it both high expectations and deep commitment. They show themselves to be especially motivated to do the best possible job, with the greatest care, the best methods and the latest technology. A huge range of specialists and highly experienced field excavators congregated at Çatalhöyük — numbers in excess of what any of the participating archaeologists are accustomed to — eager to participate in this exercise. As one participant commented, 'At Çatalhöyük there are more specialists per square metre dug than anywhere else.' As much as many were eager to work at Çatalhöyük so too were other Near East archaeologists perturbed by the prospect of the prestigious Çatalhöyük site being excavated by archaeologists with no experience in Anatolian, and limited involvement in Near Eastern, archaeology.

The contested development of the school of

postprocessual archaeology constitutes yet another context of the present project. An often repeated remark made of the postprocessual archaeologists is that the theory may not be good to dig with; effectively, the Çatalhöyük excavation is made to test the proposition that postprocessual theory can generate better archaeology. This test-case status exerts particular pressures on the excavation that demand consideration.

The final, but perhaps the most important, context is that of funding. The Turkish government was motivated to reopen the site at Çatalhöyük primarily because of the extent of this particular project's intention to invest in the excavation process the latest methods and the best specialists over a projected 25-year period, but, more importantly from the point of view of the Turkish authorities, the project's commitment to develop the site and to present the site to the public early on during the excavation, and to do so in a sophisticated, well-capitalized way.

These commitments, which gave access to the site, in part dictated the scale and shape of the project, and the amounts of funding needed. The demand from the Turkish government for high calibre research matched with the concern of the participating archaeologists to treat this particular site with the maximum care. Other than bodies like the British Academy, funders are not typically committed to the scientific excellence of the process of an excavation, but rather to the value for themselves of the results of the excavation. What constitutes in their eyes 'results' at Çatalhöyük is in part a product of expectations created by the sensationalism of what Mellaart found, and the need for products which resonate with the understanding and the demands of the public at large. In short, the funders are looking for spectacular material finds in the realm of art and architecture, finds which can be preserved, unveiled for journalists and generally shown off.

The next section of the chapter identifies some of the faultlines of the project. I will confine my discussion to three examples, though there are a host of others that could be discussed.

The faultlines

The data base, much-vaunted as a device for interaction, manifested its own faultlines. Participants considered themselves to be under too much pressure to consult through the data base each other's material, the excavation diaries, or even the basic excavation documentation — the unit sheets. This, together with technological hitches, led to the marginalization of the data base in the 1996 season. Furthermore, discussions around the data base, in part but not exclusively facilitated by my research enquiries, drew attention to the way in which the structure of the data base continued to constrain participants within set categories and actively inhibited the interrogation of categories which a postprocessual and contextual approach hoped to facilitate. To some degree, the data base insists on constituting objects and delimiting them from contexts in a manner at odds with the project's emphasis elsewhere on the need for provisionality on this question.

But as much as the data base which was designed to facilitate openness imposed its own new constraints, it must be noted that this tension did not pass unnoticed, but became an object of attention. No one was complacent about the data base. This building brick may have slumped and lost something of its intended form but it was nonetheless a solid aspect of the emerging methodology. What I mean here is that for all that the data base restricts interaction, and may in some respects be reinforcing categories, it was also the focus of anxiety over precisely these features. Let us take another example: the video footage designed to promote reflexivity about on-site interpretation in data gathering.

Entering of filmed clips on the data base initially proved time-consuming and lagged behind daily filming. A need for substantial editing emerged, both at the level of the performance actually committed to film and also subsequently in the photographic lab in discarding footage prior to entering it into the data base. Editing demanded daily decisions as to what was 'important' and what was not. This appeared to compromise the potential of the filmed material to capture aspects of the interpretive process on site which the participants were not conscious of or may have deemed 'unimportant'. In other words, the directing and editing imposes and conceals precisely the kind of interpretive closure that the videoing seeks to reveal.

We can take this point one step further and argue that the videoing and finished works produced by the film crew for public presentation which already present the site to the public through selective use of daily footage and virtual reality reconstruction constrain the visual interpretation and imagining of the site.

But again these constraints, working to exactly the opposite effect of the project's aims, began, in the course of the 1996 season to be revealed, partly through my investigations, and through a host of other developments. As with the data base, the way in which the videoing constrained interpretation as much as it opened it up began to be actively discussed. Likewise, sensitivity began to develop to the range of visual conventions operationalized at Çatalhöyük — in plans, cross-sections, photographs, footage and so on — and to how these conventions themselves constrain both interpretation and the public presentation of the site.

In contrast to my first two examples, my third and final example does not take up a feature designed to facilitate a postprocessual methodology, but a feature introduced to speed-up the excavation, the division of the team broadly into two categories, so-called 'diggers' and 'specialists' (field staff or excavators, and laboratory staff).

One of the most substantial faultlines to manifest itself was initially conceptualized by the project participants as a 'tension between diggers and specialists'. In order to facilitate the sophisticated processing of excavated material on site, professional excavators experienced at speedy contract archaeology were employed to dig, and a range of specialists taken on to handle the finds in on-site laboratories. Where ideally a postprocessual methodology might seek to ensure maximum interaction between the various participants, this structural arrangement potentially enforced segregation. A further range of devices was implemented to counteract any such tendencies, including regular tours of the excavation by the lab-based personnel and the introduction of elaborate sampling procedures designed to provide the lab-based specialists with a wealth of contextual information.

Some three weeks into the season, the specialist tours of the excavations were criticized by field staff for being time-consuming. Laboratory staff demands on field staff were deemed by the latter to be intolerable. In particular, the field staff claimed that the number of samples which they were required to take was so large that it affected adversely the capacity of the excavators to do their job, that of digging. Every time the excavators recognized a new unit, they were obliged to plan it, take spot heights, fill out a unit sheet, take a bulk (flotation) sample from the centre of the unit, an archive sample, and on occasion an average sample, a residue sample, pot sample, a photograph and a host of other possibilities depending on the particular character of the unit (see Chapters 2 & 3). In addition, certain of the excavators expressed frustration about being stalled in their excavation of a space while they waited on specialists to complete particular operations, such as the taking of sections or sampling of bricks. The intensity of the

sampling procedures implemented at Çatalhöyük had the spin-off effect of making excavation with a section or in metre squares especially onerous and time-consuming. What emerged then was that the demand for scientific excellence and for the detailed information needed for contextual archaeology seemed to be putting a strain on the desired goal of interaction. The camera crews, frequent public, funder and promoter tours of the site and the demands of this research exacerbated the excavators' sense of 'wasting valuable time'.

The anxieties of the field staff were summarized in the often heard claim of 'being slowed up'. This claim was initially most vocal from excavators working in the South area. A number of factors contributed to its manifestation early on in this setting. The first is that the major part of the season was spent removing Mellaart's in-fill and digging spaces already excavated in the 1960s. For the most part this meant working through large amounts of material that came to fill in buildings and spaces after their periods of human occupation. This contrasted sharply with developments in the North area, which was, from the start, a pristine excavation, and which quickly reached floors, platforms, burials and other interesting features. Where extreme meticulousness seemed warranted in the North area, speed was prioritized in the South area. The detailed sampling procedure was thus perceived as more onerous and possibly even less rewarding in the South area.

The culture and habitus of the individual excavators fed into this division. Where in the North area, only one of a team of on average seven excavators, worked regularly as a contract archaeologist and the area supervisor was a research archaeologist, the South area was supervised by a professional contract archaeologist and at least four of the team of on average eight excavators worked regularly as contract archaeologists. Contract archaeologists are accustomed to working competitively with tight deadlines and under strict financial constraints. This, it would seem, developed in them a confidence and professional ease about rapid dismantling. An associated tendency appears to be a reliance on thinking through the trowel and with the materials as they are encountered in the field. It could be observed in the South area that excavators often invited each other to comment on current developments in the excavation, asking a colleague to come and 'have a look', and then moving over to accommodate the person trowelling in the area in question. The 'contract archaeologists' were expert in reading the emerging plan [stratigraphy] and at feeling their way around the units being excavated. Characteristically their processes of interpretation were immediate, commonsensical and typically concerned with interpreting relatively gross features and changes.

For the most part, the contract archaeologists favoured excavation in plan over section or in squares, though a minor exception to this needs to be noted. Those 'contract archaeologists' who also carried other portfolios within the project (such as a responsibility for pot sherd processing), did not manifest the same degree of concern with excavating in plan rather than with a section. This suggests that the resistance to sections and to excavating in squares was in part an effect of the intensity of sampling which increased dramatically with excavation in squares or with a section, but was also a consequence of how the confidence of the excavators was established and maintained when pressures for speed were exerted. What emerges is that excavators who rely for their interpretation of a site solely on the emerging logic of the stratigraphy suffer a loss of confidence when a section or squares intervene in their maximal reading of the space in plan. This is expressed most strongly in their stated fear of being 'misled by the section' in the one case, or being unable to link up the squares in the other. As Farid put it in her excavation diary entry of 9 September 1996, '. . . a section can inform on the events in one particular location through time but 5–10 cm further in, the storey [sic., but a great slip for the stratigraphically-concerned] will change, and also sections rarely solve problems over a wide expanse of area'.

The opposite position was held for the most part by research archaeologists, and was most manifest in the North area. In contrast to the contract archaeologists' interpretation through trowelling and feel, the research archaeologists emphasized 'seeing' and 'cleaning'. Characteristically their processes of interpretation were deferred, 'scientific', relatively detailed, even micro, in scale, and concerned on occasion to explain what did not endure as remains, or what might be absent.

As with the data base and the video footage, these faultlines generated their own highly productive spin-offs. Professional excavators and laboratory specialists alike were constantly forced to reconsider their own practices and investigate their assumptions. In all three instances, a condition of destabilization prevailed that might be considered the heart of a methodology concerned to promote reflexivity and interaction. While to a certain extent all three examples evidence the effects of funding and speed imperatives, those effects are the most

threatening and potentially deleterious to the productive tension between the professional excavators and the laboratory specialists.

Çatalhöyük is under considerable pressure from the Turkish authorities and the funders to show results quickly and make spectacular finds, to make the findings accessible, and to present the site to the public. The data base and the videoing service these demands as much as they do the new methodology. The division of the team into professional excavators and lab-based specialists was a huge concession to the need for speed and finds, but had the effect of causing a situation of profound interrogation of archaeological practice by both the professional excavators and the specialists. However, one month into the season in 1996, the effects of the project's mode of operation — the emphasis on detail and meticulous sampling and taking of thin sections — on the rate of excavation was evident. The project director reflected the pressure exerted as a result of this realization in his entry in the excavation diary of September:

> I sometimes wonder whether modern archaeology is possible — there is such an enormous disjunction between the scientific requirements and expectations and the public (or private) purse . . . The people with big money want so much more than microdetail — e.g. reconstructed rooms, museums and car parks. To do that we need to move earth. But we aren't.

Within a week excavation in metre squares which had been implemented in the North area since the beginning of the season was abandoned in favour of excavation in plan. Excavators in the South area were given the go-ahead to judge for themselves when sampling according to the system would impede them, while on-site decisions were taken as to how much variation of deposit could still be accommodated within one unit number. The ideal system was foregone in favour of what was 'realistic'. At much the same time other forms of detailed recording implemented either the previous season or at the beginning of the 1996 season were abandoned. Detailed documentation of lithics became grosser; at one point flotation dropped from 40 litres to 20 litres; while the specialists concerned with faunal remains also contemplated ways of speeding up their procedures.

Where the tension between the two approaches was important early in the season in guaranteeing the co-existence of both logics, towards the end of the season funding and time constraints began to compromise the specialists' situation and to tip the balance in favour of the professional excavators. Financial pressures and the need for speed which follows therefrom is common to most excavations. At Çatalhöyük, the special significance of the site and its particular contexts exacerbated this situation considerably.

Chapters 2 and 3 discuss how this deeper-lying structural contradiction played itself out over the later seasons. From one point of view yielding to the pressures of funding and immediate presentation of finds appears to run the risk of sacrificing the scholarly imperatives of the excavation and the need for painstaking academic research. From another point of view these pressures force the asking of hard questions about the social role of academic enquiry. They ask anew what the purpose of excavation is, what the public responsibility of archaeologists is, and why public money should be committed to an enterprise like the Çatalhöyük excavation. What may in fact be signalled here is a need for review of what the status of university-based archaeology is in relation to society at large, a question which goes to the heart of the issue of the social and political situation of archaeological practice.

Some of the faultlines which I have identified and the attendant if productive condition of destabilization must be recognized as also being points of structural weakness, that may threaten aspects of the enterprise. My suggestion here is that the methodology being pioneered at Çatalhöyük may need to move beyond attempts to promote interaction and reflexivity to think creatively about how to cope structurally with these weaknesses. My point here might perhaps be best illustrated with reference to the commitment to making data immediately publicly available. While data-accessibility is highly desirable for all sorts of reasons, that accessibility runs the risk of affecting adversely the participation of young scholars on the project. The use of the data base and the project commitment to making data widely and immediately available on the internet mitigate against the perennial problem within the discipline of archaeology of researchers sitting on material from unpublished sites for years. The engagement of a variety of different teams in the site, albeit in different areas, further disperses control of interpretation out of the hands of a single powerful director and into the hands of a number of senior archaeologists.

In so doing an informal convention is disrupted. Graduate student labour has long been an important resource in academic excavations which are typically cash-strapped. The 'deal' usually takes the following format: graduate students process excavation data for the team leaders who then pull together overall interpretations. In return the graduate student stakes out a specific area for close attention and earns — by dint of many hours of lab work and seasons of excavation labour — privileged access to the relevant data which then become the basis for a PhD thesis. There is an implicit acknowledgement in this arrangement of a graduate student's need to take time to learn with a body of research material. By making data immediately available the Çatalhöyük project removes this period of protected access from the apprentice archaeologists and indeed runs the risk of allowing their labour to be exploited without due recompense. Even recently qualified younger archaeologists, juggling heavy junior teaching loads and the pressures of tenure track demands, who do not have research money to allow them time off to write up findings rapidly, are disadvantaged by the system. In short, the commitment to data-accessibility may weight participation in the project in favour of professionals employed to dig thereby unintentionally concentrating interpretation in the hands of a few senior archaeologists. The guild basis of archaeology is thereby challenged, which may or may not be a good thing. Either way, it is likely to cause considerable upheaval and the material conditions of participants' existence would benefit from structural attention before they erupt into social crisis. This last point indicates that structural contradictions are not confined to the different circumstances of contract and academic archaeologists, but occur in a host of other locations, such as in differences of status among academic archaeologists.

Conclusion

What then do we make of the faultlines which have been identified in this chapter? From the point of view of structural strength, faultlines are points of weakness. If the aim at Çatalhöyük is to produce a research structure with a strength set in stone, able to withstand all pressures and pulls, then the emerging project is flawed. From a position which is concerned with process and change, faultlines signal points of rupture and shift. If the production of knowledge is viewed as a process, and if the aim of the project is to be responsive to change, the faultlines are a guarantee of flexibility, contingency, provisionality and multiplicity. But structural resilience albeit in a more tensile form remains important and demands attention. It is probably essential in ensuring that a condition of destabilization remains productive and does not tip over into despair or demotivation.

Note

1. This chapter is a slightly modified version of the paper presented at the Theoretical Archaeology Group (TAG) conference in Liverpool, December 1996.
2. Figure 10.1 first appeared in an article by Ian Hodder in *Antiquity* 71 (1997).

Acknowledgements

Special acknowledgement due to Gavin Lucas for his help in formulating some of the key ideas in this chapter.

References

Gero, J., 1996. Archaeological practice and gendered encounters with field data, in *Gender in Archaeology*, ed. R.P. Wright. Philadelphia (PA): University of Philadelphia Press, 258–80.

Pinsky, V. & A. Wylie (eds.), 1989. *Critical Traditions in Contemporary Archaeology: Essays in the Philosophy, History and Socio-Politics of Archaeology*. Cambridge: Cambridge University Press.

Wylie, A., 1994. Evidential constraints: pragmatic objectivism in archaeology, in *Readings in the Philosophy of Social Science*, eds. M. Martin & L. McIntyre. Cambridge (MA): MIT Press, 747–65.

Chapter 11

Rendering Realities

Nessa Leibhammer

In 1997 Ian Hodder and Carolyn Hamilton, one of the anthropologists at the site, identified a need to study the artistic conventions at work in archaeology with particular reference to the Çatalhöyük project. With this brief in mind I visited the site in 1997 and 1998. This chapter, which is a result of those visits, hopes to show how images do not only serve to illustrate texts but, in themselves, shape knowledge in ways of which the viewer, as well as the illustrator, is often not aware. It also seeks to argue for a parity of discourse between the textual and the visual since assumptions made about pictures are often not thought of as critical.

During 1997, while at the site, some team members expressed the feeling that they experienced a sense of loss when recording information according to 'scientific' conventions. Hodder also noted that the 'scientific' drawings did not capture the often powerful 'atmosphere' of Çatalhöyük. My brief was then broadened to include the generation of my own images of the site which are of an 'interpretive' and aesthetic nature and which complement the more 'scientific' recordings generally produced.

Diversity and difference

Visual images produced by both early and current phases of the Çatalhöyük project take many forms. They range from measured drawings of excavated layers, executed in fine black line, to 'artistic' reconstructions of what life might have been like 9000 years ago rendered dramatically in Baroque techniques of chiaroscuro (see Fig. 11.5). This range is not surprising since, as Hodder notes, 'archaeology . . . brings together the "softer" humanities and social sciences with the "harder" physical and natural sciences' (Hodder 1992, 11). Although this diversity exists, different types of rendering currently occur in very separate settings. The 'scientific' illustrations are used to illustrate finds, plans, sections, elevations and to create maps and charts while the more 'aesthetic' images are produced for the public and are found in museum displays, magazine articles and on the web-site. A fusion of these two 'types' of illustration occurred in 1998 when John Swogger, an archaeologist and the site artist, produced a number of drawings of what Çatalhöyük, and the people who lived there in the past, might have looked like (see Chapter 12). He also drew a series which de-

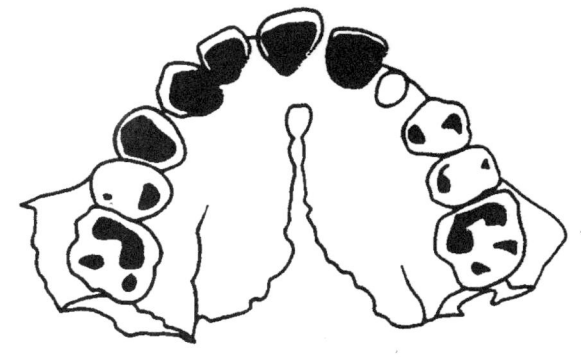

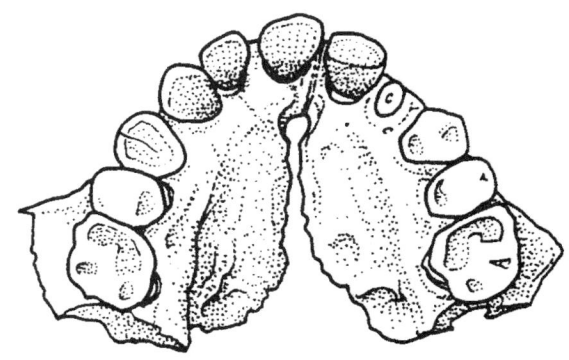

Figure 11.1. *Drawing showing tooth-wear patterns on a male adult. (Published in Çatal News 5, 1998, 19.)*

129

Figure 11.2. *Tentative reconstruction by John Swogger which illustrates what sort of activity might have caused the tooth-wear patterns shown in Figure 11.1.*

picted how change in use over time affected the structure and appearance of one of the spaces. These images are closely based on evidence and data from the site (e.g. Fig. 11.2). It is yet to be seen how these drawings will be used by the project — whether they will be seen as 'scientific' or interpretive.

The neglected image

Postprocessual archaeology has subjected its textual recordings to a great deal of analytic scrutiny. While issues which deal with the way text constructs meaning from material objects have been extensively explored (see Hodder *et al.* 1995; Shanks & Tilley 1994; Bapty & Yates 1990), visual images have not yet received the same amount of attention (see Molyneaux 1997). As Topper comments, *scientific* illustration has either been taken for granted or ignored. In an article on the epistemology of scientific illustration he comments that:

> (f)or several decades, art historians, psychologists, philosophers, and other theorists have been directing much effort towards understanding the nature of visual imagery. Nevertheless, a reading of this literature reveals that little has been directed towards the study of scientific illustration. (Topper 1996, 215)

While illustrations of a diagrammatic nature are recognizable as 'artificial' conventions used to convey information, realistically rendered images assert themselves in the viewer's perception in a different way. Moser points out that less diagrammatic and more 'realistic' reconstructions which illustrate 'scientific' texts:

> achieve much in the way of convincing us that they are a reasonable explanation of the data, because they make use of a range of icons and symbols that draw on our own human experience. They are fundamentally different from other types of archaeological illustration — such as stratigraphic sections, models or diagrams — in the sense they are presented in a naturalistic format that is a highly familiar form of representation. (Moser 1996, 213)

Visual theorists Bryson, Gombrich and Mitchell have written extensively on the nature of images, yet little of this has spilled over into archaeological theory. This is particularly evident with regard to Neolithic archaeology, which lacks a suitably refined and differentiated language of representation capable of speaking about images and the way they codify information in very particular ways.[1] This chapter seeks to develop an understanding of how images create meaning not just explicitly through their iconology[2] but implicitly through their very construction. The chapter will only touch on a few aspects of this vast area of study. It will look at the 'scientific' renderings of plans, sections, elevations, isometric projections, finds and the Harris matrix as well as the use of the photograph as archive. The more 'aesthetic' reconstructions as seen in the *Illustrated London News*, in the Museum of Anatolian Civilizations in Ankara, in virtual reality renderings and my own drawings will also be discussed.

Absence of the original and the importance of the image

Material evidence is the foundation on which the understanding of Neolithic, or any other, archaeology is based. Unfortunately the researcher cannot always have this evidence close at hand and furthermore, once excavated, the evidence undergoes disruption. The mud-brick structures of Çatalhöyük are particularly problematic since, as the site is excavated, the archaeological contexts are destroyed. Not only are they destroyed but the finds are removed to museums displays and storerooms.[3] The recording and documenting of evidence by the excavation team becomes critical as primary material on which to base further research. The visual images, no less than the written documentation, are crucial to the generation and interpretation of theory about the site. The potency of the reproduction is obvious — the 'presence' of the original archaeological object is superseded by its textual and visual rendition. This rendition remains pervasive through the successive replications of the site.

The imperfection of the image

Unmediated access to the 'real' or 'original' object or context through illustration cannot exist. Forms of illustration that are thought of as recording 'fact' or 'knowledge' are always encoded by pictorial convention. The knowledge that they encode is made visible through conventions and techniques, which shape the very nature of that knowledge. The impossibility of achieving isomorphism (an exact replica) applies to all images but the degree of accuracy and the percentage of fact will vary considerably depending on the modality used, the skill exercised, the amount of information available and the kind of information selected in the rendering of a particular image.

Photographs, realistically-rendered images and virtual reality constructions, in particular, have a way of seeming self-evident and sufficient, concealing their status as signs. In a discussion on the nature of images visual theorists Norman Bryson and Mieke Bal hold that:

> the modernist no less than the humanist discourses are constructed in such a way as to prevent realization that when we confront works of art, we enter the field of the sign and semiosis. (Bryson & Bal 1991, 184)

No image has a special claim on reality — no image can 'possess reality or the truth' and, since no 'perfect' reality exists 'out there', no 'perfect replication' can be produced (Bryson 1983, 6). Once it is accepted that no illustration, even those that are 'rendered realistically', has any 'special' relationship to nature and the truth, and that *all* images operate within a system of signs and symbols, then it becomes easier to discuss these as meaningful/meaning-full constructs which interface between the viewer and the world.

Making meaning with marks

The study of technical processes used in the construction of images is an area that seldom receives concentrated attention. In a chapter entitled 'The Essential Copy' Bryson points out that:

> [b]esides the codes of the real, there are codes specific to the material signifying practice of painting;

codes which cannot be mastered, so to speak, simply by inhaling the atmosphere of a given culture. To approach the image from the sociology or anthropology of *knowledge* is to risk ignoring the image as the product of *technique*. If the concrete nature of technique is overlooked, analysis of the image falls into immediate simplification; only its semantic or iconological side is noted. (Bryson 1983, 16)

Artistic conventions deliver specific information — what they do or do not contain can be measured by comparing them with other codes and conventions but more arguably by comparison with the original physical entity. An archaeological line drawing of a ceramic vessel appears very different to, and carries a different set of information from, a painting of the same vessel in the style of a seventeenth-century Dutch master. Each artist uses a unique mark and each medium and aesthetic convention will determine possibilities of representation. The features and relationships the pencil picks out will be different to those of the brush or the pen, the artist always 'seeing' the motif in terms of the medium.

No technique or style existed as a 'natural' way to illustrate the world and its objects. Artists develop styles and techniques as vehicles to communicate information. As the nature of the information changes so will the styles and techniques used. A new medium can also change visual languages and thus the possibilities of depiction. It has been suggested that the development of oil painting in the fifteenth century was responsible for the sumptuous style of Late Gothic and Renaissance realism. The oil medium enabled the depiction of glowing light and the nuanced tones of things in the world such as flesh, fabric, fur and metal in intense detail not previously possible (Gardiner 1959, 356). Gombrich makes it quite clear that the artist, no less than the writer, needs a vocabulary to render an image. For the artist this vocabulary is manifest in their graphic techniques and aesthetic style. It is possible to draw attention to the way information is included and excluded by studying these conventions.

Compression, inflation and exclusion

In *Envisioning Information*, Tufte (1990) writes extensively on the translation of three-dimensional evidence into two-dimensional information. Speculating on the 'loss suffered' when three-dimensional data are 'compressed' onto a two-dimensional surface, Tufte sees this as both a necessary and a strategic loss (Tufte 1990, 13–14). Information is only workable in a format that is usable and practical such as a

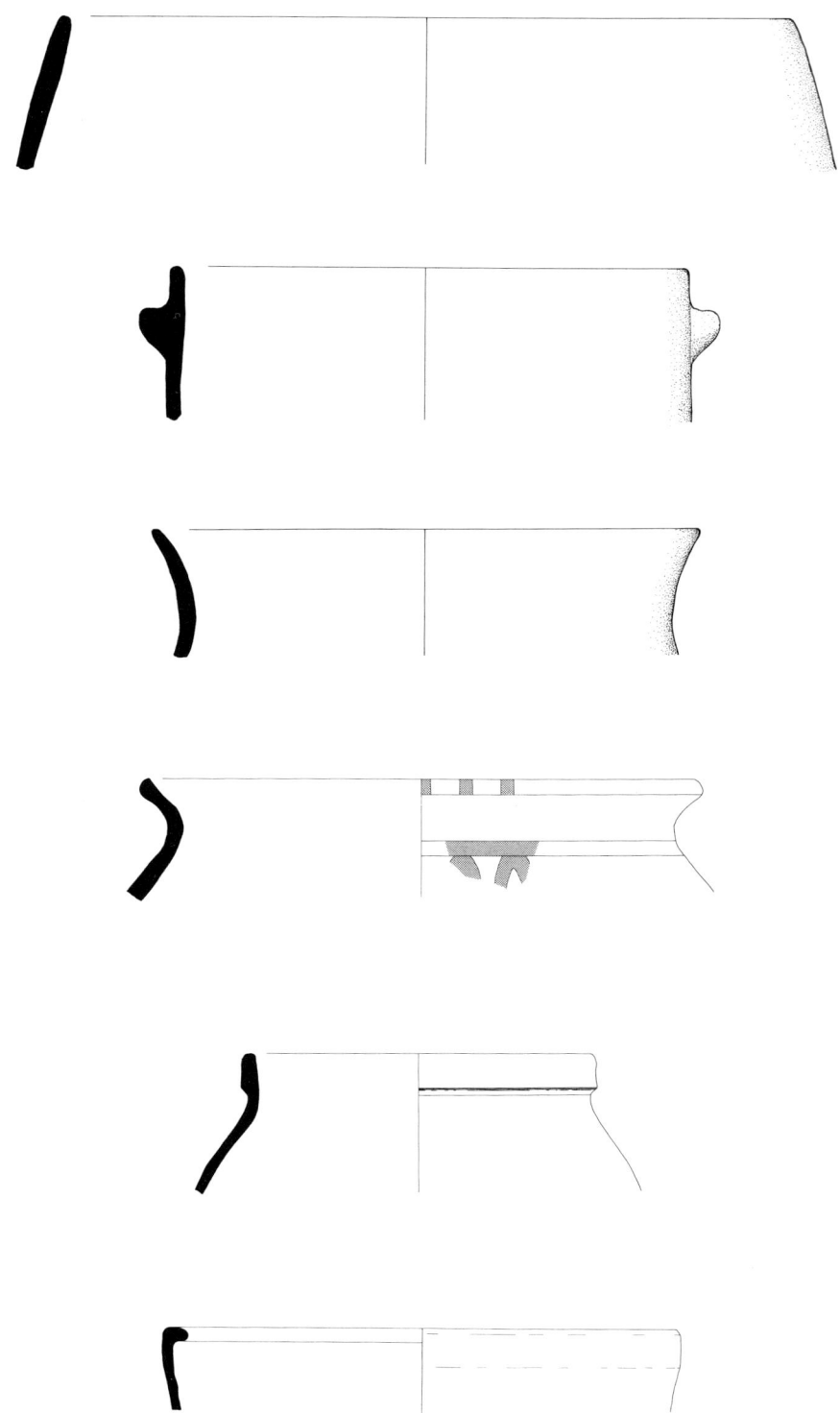

Figure 11.3. *Example of 'scientific' drawing which illustrates handmade and wheelmade forms Çatalhöyük West. (Published in Hodder 1996, 165.)*

flat sheet or screen. Illustrations of very large originals can be reduced in scale and very small originals (even microscopic ones) made large. Another consideration is that an illustration cannot capture the entire 'presence' of the original since this would constitute the recreation of the original. Diagrammatic rendering thus begins the process of shaping and selecting information so that it is 'easier' and 'clearer' to work with. 'Compression' is not always necessary — some archaeological procedures structure evidence so that it approximates the format of the drawing and, therefore, does not undergo volumetric distortion when fitted onto the page format. In rendering sections of the site the archaeologist draws information from a two-dimensional original. The single plane of data — the cut down through exposed layers of the site — is used to plot information across a two-dimensional surface.

Recovering volume

A viewer can recover a sense of volume from a section in two ways. Firstly, the viewer was present at the time of excavation and has a memory of the area beyond the section cut. But memory in this case is not useful for scholarship since it is personal and not available for general sharing. Alternatively the section is viewed together with the appropriate plan enabling a sense of the spatial form of the area to be recreated. This occurs through active mental imagining on the part of the viewer — the reconstruction of those parts that occupied the space between the plan and the section. This 'filling in' of data needs a viewer who is versed in the codes of representation.

Consider how much detail, how much latent evidence, is eliminated in this selective process. Both plan and section are determined and 'designed' by the archaeologist, who selects the sections to plot, who cleans the area and selects what to exclude and what to include in the recording. External factors such as humidity and prevailing light condition also affect what the archaeologist can see and thus what is recorded. These all impact on what information is available for study and what never features in the data base.

But the practice of archaeology is about sampling — it deals with partial information — if it did not it would be impractical. It must be borne in mind that specific diagrammatic configurations such as plans, sections and elevations deliver specific details about a site leaving out a plethora of information not considered important and thus addressing only very selective sections of the site.

Depicting time and space

None of these diagrams engage the complex way three-dimensional shapes of actual sediments and remains interlock with each other at all points of their surface area. The concept of geological time is also implicitly present in sections and elevations — what is below is perceived as being earlier in time, following the principle of sedimentation. To counteract this rather linear concept an alternative system of recording — the Harris matrix — was developed, a system which gives the archaeologist the capacity to include a more accurate reflection not only of the stages of the site deposition but also the sequences of excavation. Fundamental to the construction of this matrix is the concept of the archaeological unit. The boundaries of discrete archaeological elements are decided by the excavating archaeologist who records each one on a separate unit sheet. Each sheet is unique and is given a number, which is part of a sequence. Archaeological features such as bins, walls and ovens are made up of many units and are each given a feature number.

The Harris matrix allows the excavating archaeologist to plot the association of these units with each other and record their archaeological sequences in the underground three-dimensional puzzle. Not only does the Matrix develop a convention by which a third dimension — 'space' — can be indicated but it also allows a fourth dimension — 'time' — to be introduced. Hammond writes that:

> [t]he idea of a stratigraphic diagram which was procedurally rigorous, forcing the excavator to account for every defined context in a spatial and chronological relation to its neighbors (Hammond 1993, foreword).

Although the element of 'time', and change over time, is considered significant and methods are devised whereby its presence and effect can be shown (as in the Harris matrix) other areas of visual rendering practise a systematic excision or 'freezing' of time.

The timelessness and authority of the scientific drawing

'Scientific' drawings, which strive to record accurately aspects of an object or site, present themselves as enduring and absolute. Renderings of particular categories of archaeological artefacts, such as finds or architectural structure, fall under this visually selective convention. Outlined with a single, unbroken, black line on a white surface — the drawings leave no scope for either the imagination or the eye

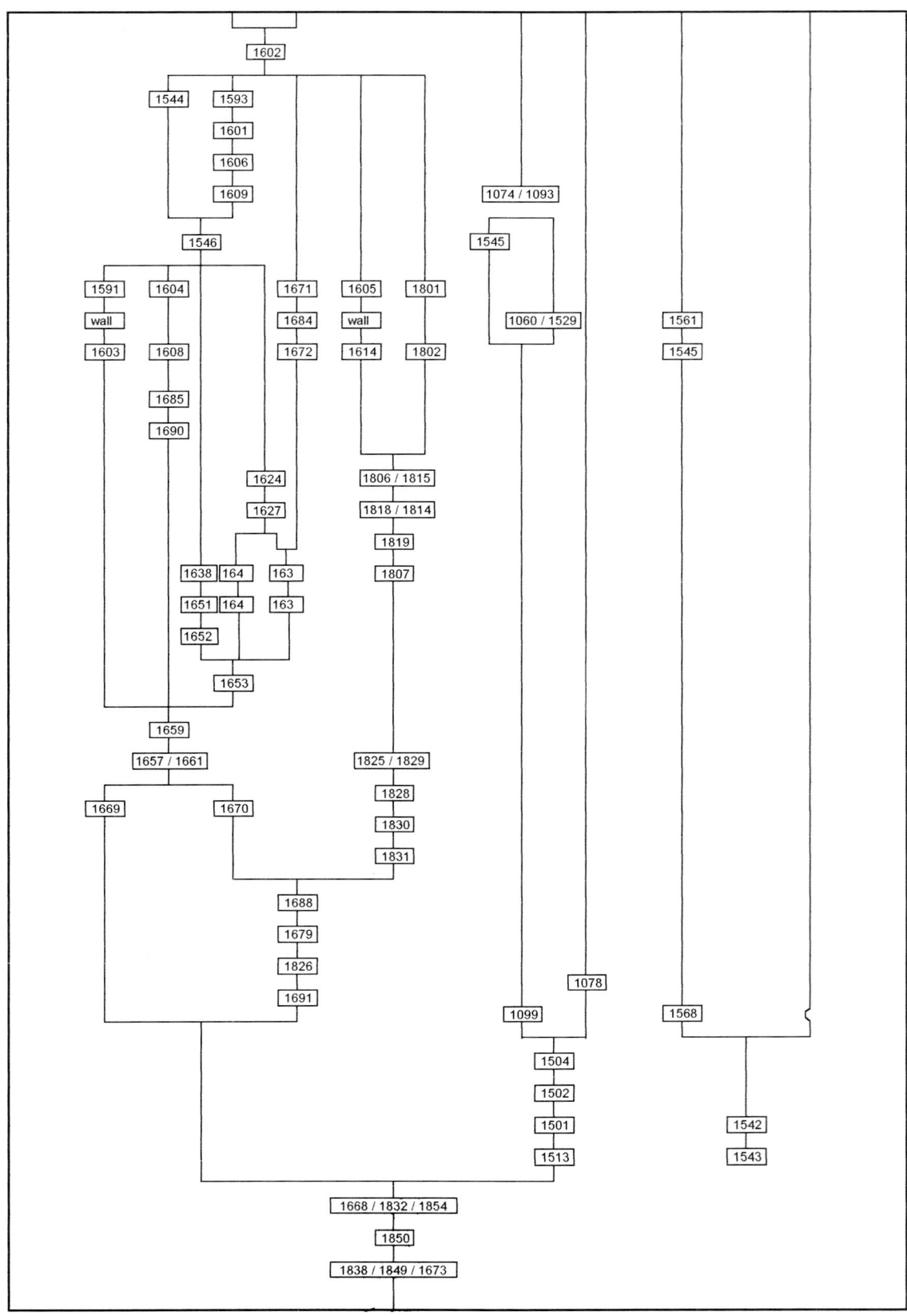

Figure 11.4. *Section of Harris matrix from the South area showing relationships between units.*

to engage the dialectic process of vision between beholder and object. In fixing the image a sense of timelessness, of completeness and factual accuracy is imparted. The linear depiction of a ceramic sherd does not encourage much imaginative interaction between beholder and image.

In contrast, the technique which artists such as Leonardo da Vinci, Rembrandt and Van Gogh used to evoke a sense of volume, movement and the shifting vision of a beholder is one where the edges of objects are neither clearly defined nor of a consistent thickness but are broken, varied and multiple. The eye can never really 'fix' the edge of an object firmly. Bilateral vision keeps the eye and the object engaged in a continuous assessment of the position and appearance of the object in space — each eye 'seeing' the object slightly differently and from a different point. The (one-eyed) viewpoint of archaeological drawing becomes evident in this passage from a manual on drawing finds. It instructs that:

> [i]t is useful, from the start, to develop the habit of keeping your right eye (if right handed) directly over the point of the pencil, and moving along with it. It is very easy to misjudge the position of the outline, even on relatively flat pieces, due to the distortion caused by perspective or the angle of view. (Griffiths *et al.* 1991, 97)

The high contrast rendering of black ink line-drawing further enhances the 'unquestionable', authoritative presence of the illustration. The clarity of the image is embodied not only in the polarities of black on white but also in the thinness and singularity of the line — it appears to have no margins for error. But, however 'thin' the line, it has a 'thickness'. In actuality this thickness of the line gives it two edges. Where radical accuracy is necessary the edge (being two surfaces of a black line) becomes ambiguous. Which is the true surface? Rather than mark the surface of the object or the edge of space — it delineates the point at which these two surfaces meet — between the object and the non-object.

In order to highlight the manner in which different modalities of renderings encode different sets of information it is useful to contrast the style of scientific rendering with the artistic 'styles' of late nineteenth- and early twentieth-century artists such as Cézanne (1839–1906) and Monet (1840–1926). These artists were inspired by nineteenth-century discoveries regarding the nature of light and the complexities of human vision and experience.

Obsessed with exploring the action of human visual perception, many works by Cézanne depict the edges of objects as diffuse and multiple, re-en-acting the shifting and unsecured gaze of the viewer. As the beholder seeks to understand and grasp the painted form in Cézanne's work she re-enacts the process of visual comprehension in physical space[4] where the edge of an object is seldom precisely defined. Compared to a scientific rendering of a find, a painting by Cézanne would engender a greater sense of three-dimensionality of both the object and the context in which it is placed. Much more of the 'visual noise' around the object is captured by such a painting (or drawing). In contrast the 'scientific' linear drawing seeks to offer constancy and clarity — no uncertain edges, no doubt, no ambivalence and constant space and time. There is always loss and gain in translations; clarity of information means absence of complexity.

Monet, less concerned about the nature of edges and more about the passage of time, painted a famous series depicting the effect of changing seasons and transient light on haystacks in a field. The painted haystacks are defined in strokes and swatches of colour — colour which moves from the cold blue and yellow of a winter day to the fiery orange red of a summer sunset. In creating this series Monet stressed the importance of seeing the series as a whole and implied that to isolate a specific moment in the life of an object was to deny an aspect of the experienced world — the passage of time.

Light, shadow and the academic text

A further aesthetic convention, shadow, is used to imply the presence of time and space as it appears in the physical world. But many archaeological drawings assume a constant shadow — one resulting from a single constant light source positioned at the top left-hand edge of the page. Griffiths and Jenner write that:

> [l]ight for illustrative purposes is conceptual; it should not be confused with the real illumination which may fall on the artefact . . . if you attempt to represent the light and shade as it really looks the drawing will end up looking confused (Griffiths *et al.* 1991, 100).

This abstract field, used in the academic text, is the site of clarity and constancy as opposed to the transience and complexity of lived experience.

The corollary of the presence of shadow is the presence of a light source, a source that could be conceptual, natural or artificial. In 'scientific' drawing a conceptual source is used to facilitate clarity and re-enacts an idealized situation. The use of either of the other two demands that the image be perceived as existing in a physical realm. Artificial light (such as a lamp, candle, etc.) assumes the pres-

Figure 11.5. *'In the dawn of religion: a reconstruction of a funerary rite, nearly nine thousand years ago, at Chatal Huyuk in Anatolia' by Alan Sorrel.* (Illustrated London News, *May 9th 1964, 728.*)

ence of human technology and thus human presence and natural light (the sun or moon) give clues as to the time of day or night. Thus with no shadow to mark the time, no context or the implied presence of people to locate it in a physical domain — the image exists in the context of the white page, in the context of academic authority.

Evoking 'other' presences

The 'fixing' of shadow in 'scientific' renditions is generally accepted without question. Why is this convention significant and what does the presence of shadow mean for the image? From a purely practical point of view shadow adds the illusion of three-dimensional volume to the two-dimensional image on a surface. But it does not only do this. In aesthetic discourse light and shadow can be used to evoke 'mood' and 'presence' in an image. Rosenblum discusses the use of light in the work of van Gogh showing how particular light can imbue a work with quasi-religious overtones. He writes that:

Van Gogh's search for the supernatural in the world of the natural gave his interpretation of light, whether solar, lunar, or artificial, an aura of mystery that seems to have more to do with the magical light of Friedrich and Turner than the empirically examined light of the French Realists and Impressionists. (Rosenblum 1983, 91–2)

In 'fixing' the shadow according to an accepted 'scientific' convention archaeological drawings seem to imply that only the clear light of reason is present — no taint of the transcendental, no vicissitudes of the personal, no mood or emotion to effect the documenting and recording of these artefacts.

The black-and-white Mellaart drawings, which reconstruct the appearance of the interior spaces, as excavated during the earlier phase, utilize the high contrast convention of architectural or scientific drawing. Rendered isometrically the features are lit by the artist with an intense contrast of black against white. Light floods in, bathing the interior and casting crisp shadows. The effect of the rendering convention results in surety, having the scientifically desirable effect of brightly-lit architectural features accessible to the investigating gaze.

This is a very different light to the one which illuminates the scene illustrated in Figure 11.5. Included in this scene are mural images that depict vultures attacking headless humans; sculpted bulls' and goats' heads loom large, bathed by dramatic beams of light. Four figures kneel facing a large bovine head and the beams of light. A scattering of human skulls and a smoking fire add 'atmosphere' and drama to the scene.

Not only do the motifs of the image imply a particular kind of event, the chiaroscuro style of rendering, which models form in deep shadow and intense light, obscures edges and creates mystery. The light (and shadow) in this image is clearly not the descriptive light of the previous paragraph — one which seems to assists the 'scientific' gaze — it is a particular Baroque technique which was used to suggest the presence of spirituality and the non-natural or supernatural. By manipulating conventions drawn from Western aesthetic practice the artist has left the beholder with a distinctive 'impression' about the nature of religious practices in Çatalhöyük 9000 years ago, one of animism, idolatry and mystery.

The 'code-less' fantasy

Archaeologists, quite clearly, do not believe that section drawings and elevations capture the full 'reality' of a situation. The enormity of the archive and the ongoing collection of data indicate that, at Çatalhöyük, no complacency exists about 'having discovered the truth'. But the use of particular visual codes and conventions, particularly those drawn from the 'realistic' style, can impart a sense (to those not versed in visual conventions) that some images are 'code-less' and thus occupy a position close to an original. The quote from Moser in the introduction of this chapter draws attention to the fact that archaeological representations can be made to appear realistic when they have little purchase on the truth. It is largely in the aesthetic (re)constructions of what Çatalhöyük may have looked like in the past and in the use of the photograph as a record of the site and the finds that the discourse of realism becomes particularly significant.[5]

Photography

Photographs are used at the site as a complementary record for the archiving of most aspects of the excavation. The photograph is a quick and easy way of capturing data — much faster than any hand-rendered image and, possibly because of this, it is used extensively as a method of building inventories. Because the photograph captures a veracity of appearance with the subject photographed they are valued as satisfactory substitutes for the original. It is clear that the photographic image is believed to capture something close to the 'truth' at a given moment. Mitchell describes how:

> [t]he photograph, like its parent notion, the mental impression, enjoys a certain mystique in our culture that can be described by terms such as 'absolutely analogical' and 'message without code' (Mitchell 1986, 61).

Because of this belief the photograph is able, ultimately, to stand in for the absent thing, either lost through excavation, or made inaccessible by distance or museum policy.

The perception that a photograph in some way captures 'reality' is a pervasive concept. Yet the photographic image is not always able to make particular distinctions that may be needed. On the 1997 excavation I noted that Peter Andrews of the human remains (taphonomy) team systematically photographed the burials *in situ* for his records. In addition to this he drew a sketch of the bones in the same position. This was done because, in his view, the photograph was not able to depict certain essential aspects of skeletons. For example it could not clearly differentiate different individuals in the same burial. Where the actual 'field' is messy or unclear a drawing must be made which is essentially a selective 'map' of the site — inclusions, exclusions and focus all being determined by what information needs to be yielded.

(Re)constructions of the past

Realism as a stylistic convention is based on a belief that a stable entity called the 'real' world exists and that it is possible to observe it and render it in aesthetic form. When reconstructions of the past are created these rely on the genre of 'realism' to produce a convincing image of what the past (might have) looked like. Veracity to conventions of light and shadow, depth of vision, perspective, details of environment and images of things we know well from our own experience such as sky, plants and landscape combine to convince the viewer that what is depicted is the 'real' thing.

An artist's interpretation of what life at Çatalhöyük could have looked like in the past hangs in the Ankara Museum of Anatolian Civilizations.

Threatening clouds gather darkly to the right, overshadowing the mood of the scene. Vultures hover here expectantly, waiting for the corpse (which is being transported on a bier) to be left outside the settlement. A distant, erupting volcano adds drama to the presence of death and impending calamity. None of these phenomena appear to disturb the daily routine of people who are shown going serenely about their daily chores of skinning animals, carrying water and burying the dead.

We, the viewers, recognize the icons chosen for depiction (family groups, houses, vultures). Not only do these images refer to our life experiences but also to those phenomena which we have seen in books and films (volcanoes, corpses on biers, vultures hovering). All these are within our range of knowledge and experience and all are rendered in a realistic style. This scene is largely constructed in the artist's imagination yet appeals to the canons of 'realism' make it believable. With only fragments of information a realistically rendered image which abides by the canons of western representation, and the norms of the familiar, will be convincing.

Seductive images and the public domain

The virtual reality images of Çatalhöyük generated by the Multimedia Project based at the Hochschule für Gestaltung Karlsruhe are seductive and dramatic (see Chapter 18). The lustrous back-lighting of the computer screen allows the image to glow and 'live', enhancing presence . Wall surfaces are smooth, edges are sharply defined and mysterious lighting filters in. Interior atmosphere is powerfully dramatized by bulls' heads with needle-sharp, elongated horns dominating the space and casting multiple shadows on the walls (Fig. 11.6).

Advanced computer technology allows for the creation of much more technically sophisticated images than those generated during the Mellaart period. The images produced are seamless and enticing, inviting the virtual traveller to traverse the smooth silkiness of a finely pixellated surface. But the question is raised whether these images advance knowledge about the site beyond the scope of the earlier Mellaart reconstructions or whether they fix the assumptions of these earlier interpretations more firmly in the viewer's imagination?

The virtual reality images have their register in the graphics generated by animated films of the most sophisticated genre. Virtual reality production relies on the same software as that used to create animated cartoons. Not only does archaeology use resources from the film industry, the animated film industry borrows from archaeology. In the production of *Moses, Prince of Egypt* the animation team based their

Figure 11.6. *Virtual reality image of Çatalhöyük 'Shrine' E VI 8 produced by the Hochschule für Gestaltung Karlsruhe.*

reconstructions of ancient Egypt on the drawings of a British Egyptologist. Thus a close relationship exists between these two seemingly diverse areas of image production. This would explain the suitability and appeal of the virtual reality images as a public front to the graphic dimension of the project. Where these images have a powerful appeal in the public domain the more introspective images of the personal interpretation address a different sensibility.

Artistic rendering — a personal interpretation

Using graphite and coloured pencil I drew a series of interior wall surfaces from the South area of the excavation (Fig. 11.7). The graphite and coloured pencil medium is the antithesis of the smooth surface of the virtual reality image and it avoids the homogenizing authority of the single, decisive, black line of the classical archaeological drawing — the assured mark

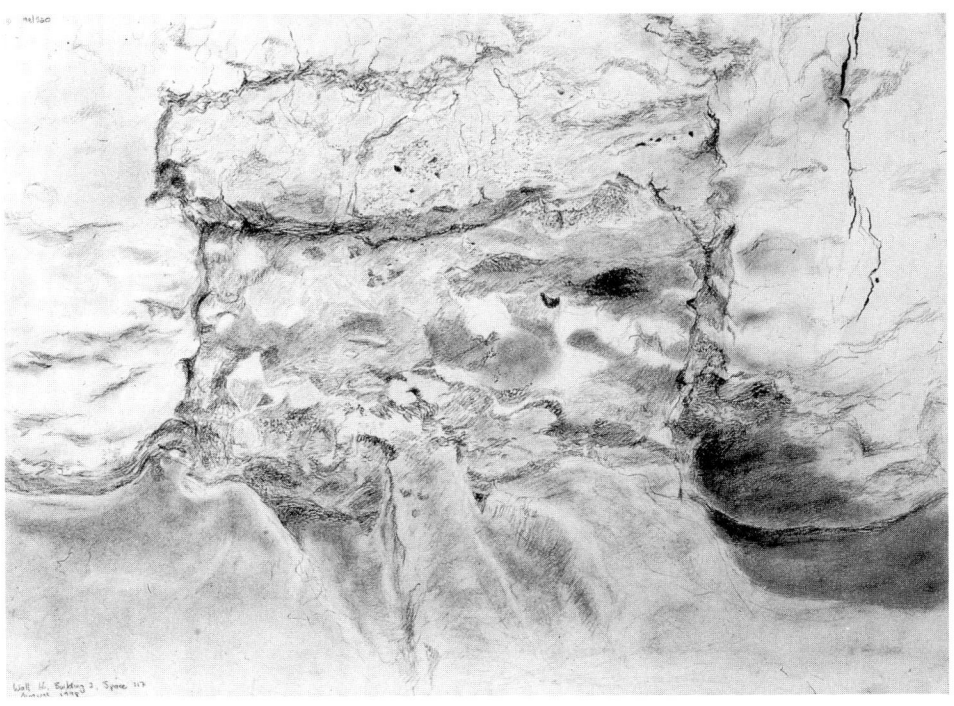

Figure 11.7. *Drawing of Wall 66, Building 2, Space 117 rendered according to 'artistic' convention by Nessa Leibhammer. This is the same wall as depicted in Figure 11.8.*

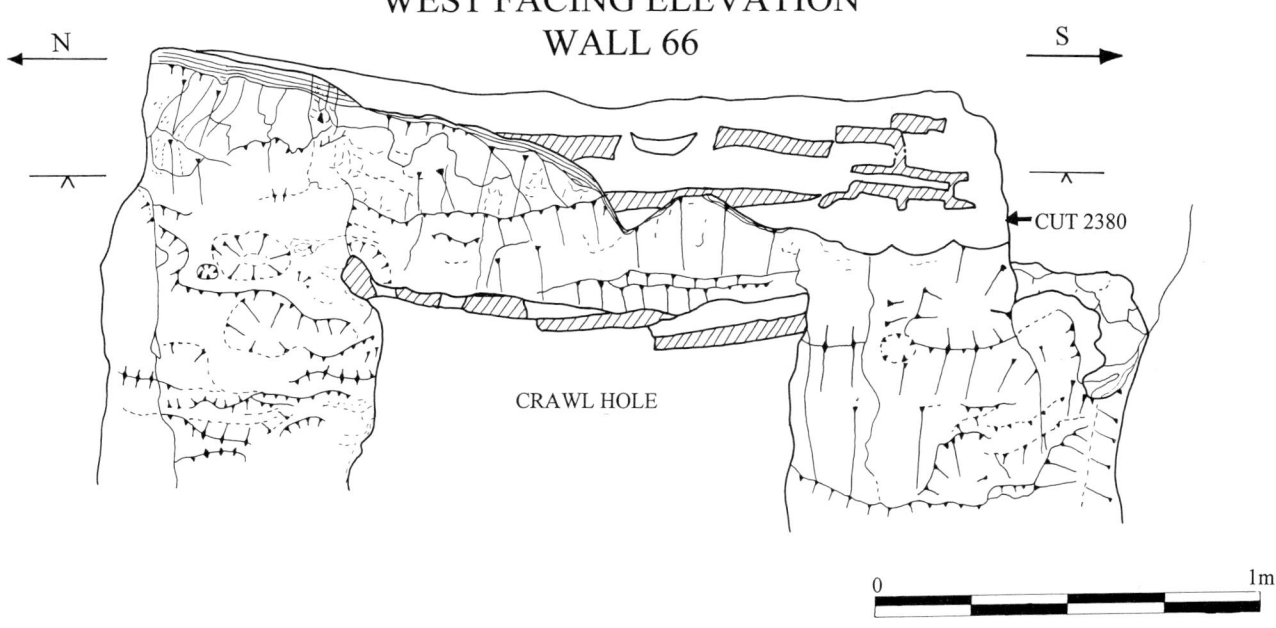

Figure 11.8. *Drawing of Wall 66, Building 2, Space 117 rendered according to 'scientific' convention by John Swogger.*

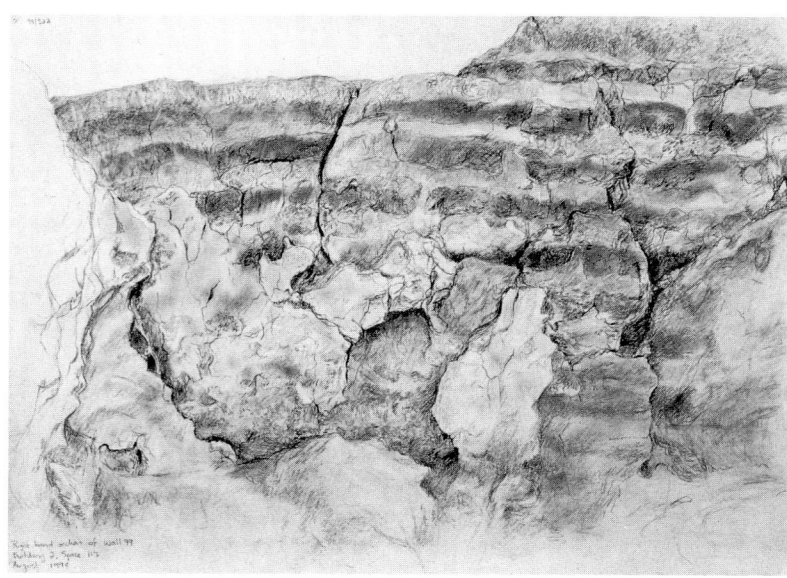

Figure 11.9. *Drawing of a section of Wall 79, Building 2, Space 117 by Nessa Leibhammer.*

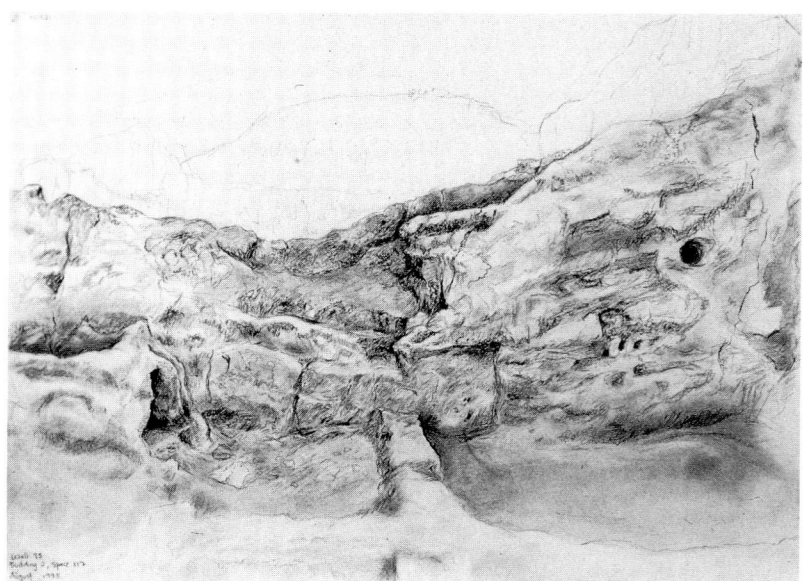

Figure 11.10. *Drawing of a section of Wall 93, Building 2, Space 117 by Nessa Leibhammer.*

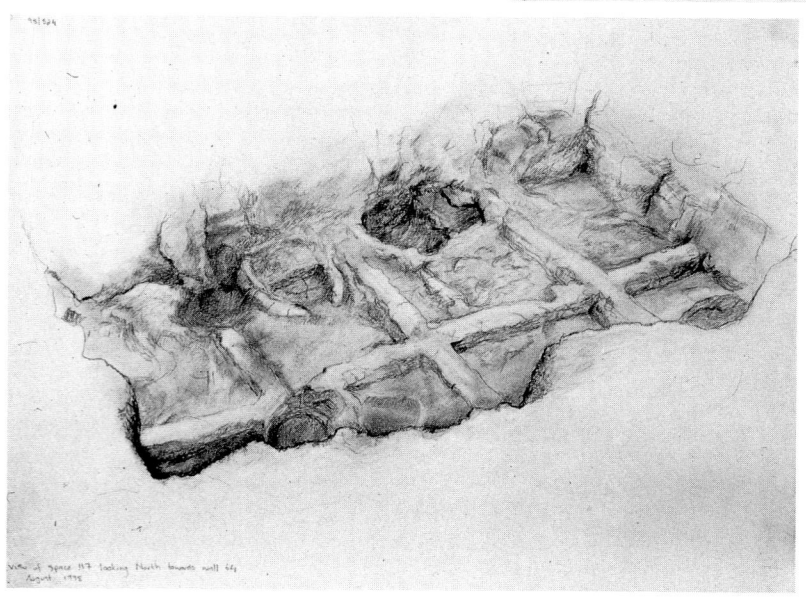

Figure 11.11. *Drawing of Space 117 from above, looking south towards Wall 79, by Nessa Leibhammer.*

of the non-negotiable. Each surface is slowly built up with a series of lines — diffused and broken — which search, seeking to discover. The searching quality of the mark allows the viewer to respond creatively — adding their own 'interpretation' to the drawn surface — filling in where ambiguity is present since the marks do not over-determine the viewer's response. Each drawing took about three and a half days to complete so that what is drawn is also a compound experience of observation over time. I drew not only what I saw at a given moment but also what I knew and learnt about the subject as I was exposed to it. Some drawings included soil from the site rubbed into the paper as background colour — investing the image with the presence of 'original' material.

The drawings are personal and interpretive. Another artist working at the site would produce an entirely different set of drawings not only in terms of style but in choice of subject matter, scale, selection of viewpoints, responses to light, use of medium and many others. Furthermore the drawings capture a set of information different to those usually selected by the conventions of modern archaeology. They record what the latter would consider visual 'noise' e.g. the baulks left for micromorphology sampling, animal holes, roots, cracks, scatterings of unswept soil.

Conclusion

Images are important because they come to replace the original objects and contexts in scholarship and in the public domain. They are rendered according to conventions, which codify the information. Anyone seeking to understand and use the images must know and understand the visual especially when the original is not available. This paper has sought to show how meaning and information are encoded and embodied in certain archaeological images.

Postprocessual archaeology embraces interpretation as a seminal factor in the construction of archaeological knowledge. This approach creates a space for the production of images of a more personal nature not confining archaeology to the visual canons of most mid to late-twentieth century practices. 'Artistic' renderings enrich the archaeological archive, but the full extent of their contribution to the Çatalhöyük project is still uncertain. We the makers of an archive do not know what future generations will ask of it. It is therefore our responsibility to make it as rich as possible.

Notes

1. See *The Cultural Life of Images* by Molyneux (1997) for discussions on other areas of archaeological illustration.
2. Iconology is the study of the symbolic meaning of icons or images.
3. Storerooms are often inaccessible and a large majority of the team are not based in Turkey making it difficult for them to visit museum displays on a frequent basis.
4. I hesitate to use the term 'real space' as defined by perspectival conventions. See Mitchell (1994, 31) for a discussion on perspective as ideology.
5. It is not in the scope of this chapter to engage fully the phenomena of realism as a historical moment in the figurative arts but it should be noted that it was never a constant theme in aesthetic production but was a dominant movement in Euro-American arts from 1840 to about 1880. Its aim was to 'give a truthful, objective and impartial representation of the real world, based on meticulous observation of contemporary life' (Nochlin 1976, 13). Realism is thus defined as a movement in the arts and should not be thought of as free from conventions embedded in aesthetic discourses. It should also not be confused or conflated with the concept 'reality' which raises a plethora of philosophical issues which cannot be dealt with here.

References

Baigre, B.S. (ed.), 1996. *Picturing Knowledge: Historical and Philisophical Problems Concerning the Use of Art in Science.* Toronto: University of Toronto Press.

Bapty, I. & T. Yates, 1990. *Archaeology after Structuralism: Poststructuralism and the Practice of Archaeology.* London: Routledge.

Bryson, N., 1983. *Vision and Painting: the Logic of the Gaze.* New Haven (CT) & London: Yale University Press.

Bryson, N. & M. Bal, 1991. Semiotics and art history. *The Art Bulletin* LXXIII/2.

Gardiner, H., 1959. *Art Through the Ages.* London: G. Bell & Sons, Ltd.

Gombrich, E.H., 1960. *Art and Illusion: a Study in the Psychology of Pictorial Representation.* London: Phaidon.

Griffiths, N. & A. Jenner, with C. Wilson, 1991. *Drawing Archaeological Finds: a Handbook.* London: Archetype Publications.

Hammond, N., 1993. Foreword, in Harris (ed.), vii–viii.

Harris, E. (ed.), 1993. *Practices of Archaeological Stratigraphy.* London: Academic Press.

Hodder, I., 1992. *Theory and Practice in Archaeology.* London & New York (NY): Routledge.

Hodder, I. (ed.), 1996. *On the Surface: Çatalhöyük 1993–95.* (McDonald Institute Monographs.) Cambridge: McDonald Institute for Archaeological Research; London: British Institute of Archaeology at Ankara.

Hodder, I., M. Shanks & A. Alexandri, 1995. *Interpreting Archaeology: Finding Meaning in the Past.* London &

New York (NY): Routledge.

Mellaart, J., 1967. *Çatal Hüyük: a Neolithic Town in Anatolia*. London: Thames & Hudson.

Metropolitan Museum of Art, 1978. *Monet's Years at Giverny: Beyond Impressionism*. New York (NY): The Metropolitan Museum of Art.

Mitchell, W.J.T., 1986. *Iconology: Image, Text, Ideology*. Chicago (IL): University of Chicago Press.

Mitchell, W.J.T., 1994. *Picture Theory*. Chicago (IL): University of Chicago Press.

Molyneaux, B.L. (ed.), 1997. *The Cultural Life of Images: Visual Representation in Archaeology*. London & New York (NY): Routledge.

Moser, S., 1996. Visual representation in archaeology: depicting the missing link in human origins, in Baigrie (ed.), 184–214.

Nochlin, L., 1976. *Realism*. Harmondsworth: Penguin Books.

Orienti, S., 1979. *The Complete Paintings of Cezanne*. Harmondsworth: Penguin Books.

Rosenblum, R., 1983. *Modern Painting and the Northern Romantic Tradition: Friedrich to Rothko*. London: Thames & Hudson.

Shanks, M., 1997. Photography and archaeology, in Molyneaux (ed.), 73–107.

Shanks, M. & C. Tilley, 1994. *Re-constructing Archaeology: Theory and Practice*. London & New York (NY): Routledge.

Thomas, J., 1991. *Rethinking the Neolithic*. Cambridge: Cambridge University Press.

Topper, D., 1996. Towards an epistemology of scientific illustration, in Baigrie (ed.), 215–49.

Tufte, E.R., 1990. *Envisioning Information*. Cheshire (CT): Graphics Press.

Chapter 12

Image and Interpretation: the Tyranny of Representation?

John-Gordon Swogger

The central role of archaeological illustration in the recording and presentation of archaeological information has not changed much in two-hundred-odd years of antiquarianism and archaeology. What has changed, however, is the nature of the archaeological information being used and presented by these illustrations. And as that information has changed, so the practice of illustration has adapted to match these changes in style, preference and direction. Now, once again, as the present nature of our archaeology changes, the manner in which it is recorded and presented is also beginning to change.

The difficulties in creating a well-defined postprocessual approach to illustration at Çatalhöyük stem from the somewhat ill-defined nature of archaeological illustration itself: is it a discipline? A skill? A specialization?[1] A craft? Creating a definition is not just a semantic parlour game: the lack of solid understanding means that, poorly-defined, it has no 'proper' place within archaeological projects and no 'proper' role within the wider conduct of archaeology. Consequently, it is often under-used, and its potential for communicating archaeological information often woefully under explored.

This lack of definition, and perhaps also archaeological illustration's primarily practical nature, has also traditionally excluded it from most theoretical discussions, with the exception of its inclusion in more broad-based discourses on the nature of archaeological sight, reception and image-interpretation (e.g. Molyneaux 1997). Academically also, there persists a prejudice against aspects of the practice of archaeological illustration, particularly with reconstructions, where it is often ignorantly supposed that their 'artistic' nature proscribes any possibility of their being 'scientific' and therefore not subject to the same intellectual or academic rigours as other modes of presentation (James 1997, 24; Moser & Gamble 1997, 185) (see Fig. 12.1). However, it is perhaps

no coincidence that as economic pressures force archaeology to look more closely at the way in which it presents itself, attention is drawn ever more to the nature as much as the manner of the visual presentation of archaeological information — in other words, the theoretical basis for the practice of archaeological illustration. Interest in the development and application of current archaeological theories of practice to illustration has grown within the discipline for many years. For the past decade, archaeological illustrators have been posing questions that have addressed the very nature and practice of the subject (e.g. Moser & Gamble 1997), and have been suggesting ways and means by which the subject might or should become integrated within the changes that were embracing the wider archaeological world.

The Çatalhöyük project provides a perfect environment for the development and implementation in the field of new approaches to archaeological illustration. Archaeology is a construct, and as such, the physical aspects — the finds, the structures, the stratigraphy — are merely hangers upon which we fix individual pictures of a site and its narrative. Images plays such an important and fundamental role in the construction of archaeology that its power is often hidden. In the context of the creation of a reflexive archaeology at Çatalhöyük, the way in which these images are created and those constructs defined must be examined. 'Illustration . . . is taking on new dimensions' (Shanks 1997, 99), and the challenge presented by Çatalhöyük is to move not just the theory, but the practice also of archaeological illustration towards a new approach.

Archaeological illustration has a rich tradition of practices and principles from which it works. Some of these are no longer necessary or appropriate; some are acting as brakes to the progression and evolution of the discipline; some lie for the most part unused and unexplored. A new approach to archaeological

Figure 12.1. *A Çatalhöyük woman tends both a child and a cooking vessel. This illustration includes many details about current ethnoarchaeological ideas concerning food preparation, artefact use, etc. Is this illustration, nestled within 'artistic' tradition, any less or more valid than a couple of paragraphs of text dealing with a similar topic? (Compare, for example, Hastorf 1998) Is it any less or more subject to peer review and comment?*

illustration must involve a thorough examination of what archaeological illustration now is and has, while at the same time investigate new aspects and new avenues of practice and theory. It is not enough simply to adopt new techniques without any reference to the practices of the past.

This chapter will address some of the background problems and considerations of redefining the practice of archaeological illustration, and also examine some of the practical attempts to put some of these redefinitions into practice at Çatalhöyük.

Defining and directing archaeological illustration

I would suggest that archaeological illustration be regarded not as a strictly defined set of traditional media employed to produce a rigidly defined set of end-products, as is implicit in Griffiths *et al.* (1990), but rather as a tool — a mechanism or process for recording and presenting archaeological information in visual form. It is as much a tool as any object used to dig with is a tool: a trowel is simply an object for moving soil from one place to another. If the trowel

does not move the soil in the right way, then another digging utensil is used — a teaspoon, a shovel, a JCB. Good excavation practice depends to no small extent on deciding which thing is best to dig with; so good illustration practice should depend on deciding which method of presentation is best in a particular circumstance. Defining archaeological illustration broadly as a tool can allow it to function so; it has the freedom to embrace any number of media and styles. And as each different medium and style is a complex interrelationship of visual and interpretive restrictions, possibilities and constraints, each one has the certainty of conveying archaeological information in a completely different manner. If, as has been done previously, some of these media are considered the province of 'artists' and some the province of 'archaeological illustrators', then each medium and/or style, depending on its categorization, will have been treated differently. By extending the remit of archaeological illustration so that it embraces all these different approaches, there exists the possibility for more fully understanding and exploiting that potential of each different medium to illuminate a different aspect of archaeological information. New presentations create new archaeologies which in turn create new questions. Destroying the artificial boundaries between media and styles by redefining our understanding of what archaeological illustration is will encourage the creation of these new presentations.

Illustrating at the trowel's edge (I): new media in residence at Çatalhöyük

The Çatalhöyük project is attempting in a very real way to fully integrate post-excavation analysis with ongoing field excavation, so as to combine the results of laboratory analysis with the process and methodology of excavation. Archaeological illustration, traditionally regarded as part of post-excavation analysis, is included in this attempt at breaking down the barriers of procedure within the project design. There are several ways in which illustration at Çatalhöyük either has been, or should be, working outside of its traditional remit.

Although not invited to the site in response to a new definition of archaeological illustration, an 'artist' has already been present at Çatalhöyük, using media and approaches traditionally regarded as lying 'outside' the definition of archaeological illustration to visually represent material more usually regarded as the exclusive preserve of the 'archaeological illustrator'. Nessa Leibhammer describes in detail her own work at the site in Chapter 11 of this volume. In brief, however, what she produced were images of the visible, physical archaeology, but as seen through the eyes of an 'artist'. Nessa's work at the site, the results of her paintings and the reactions from members of the site team to the different visual approaches convinced me, at least, that the application of a new definition of archaeological illustration to the whole question of visual representation must be pushed forward.

There has been increasing interest at the edges of archaeology in the inclusion of the voices of 'artists' within programmes of presentation and interpretation of archaeology, whether through museum exhibitions accompanied by 'art' exhibitions whose themes are parallel to or draw from archaeological content (Hamilakis *et al.* 1998), or in using the experience of art as a mechanism for understanding the experience of archaeology (Renfrew 1998). It has been suggested that Çatalhöyük should participate in a programme of 'Artists in Residence', and in doing so combine the ideas of art drawn from archaeology with an experience of art paralleling an experience of archaeology. My own suggestion would be that a new definition of archaeological illustration must include an active search for new modes of visual expression and understanding in any attempt to use the tool of visual representation to its fullest potential. Rather than

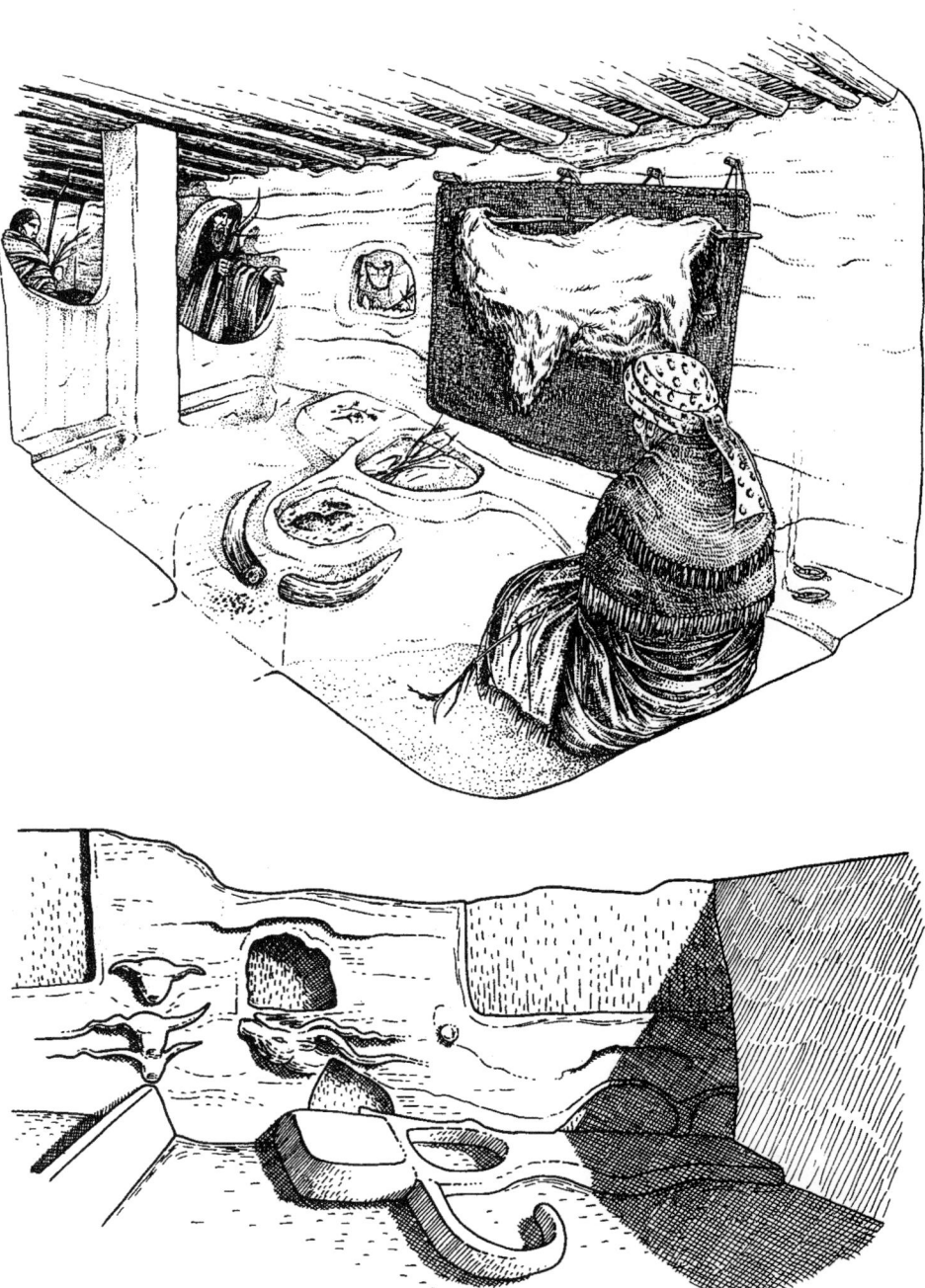

Figure 12.2. *The first illustration (top) is a reconstruction view of Space 155 in Building 5 drawn in a contemporary style, illustrating current theories and interpretations about the use of space, etc. within a Çatalhöyük building. The second illustration (bottom) shows the same Space, but borrows the illustrative style used by Mellaart throughout his Anatolian Studies reports. The simple change in style between the two creates two very different pictures, and consequently, two very different Building 5s and two very different Çatalhöyüks.*

simply invite 'art' and 'artists' to be a sideshow in the main process of presenting visual information within archaeology, I would like to see both more

a

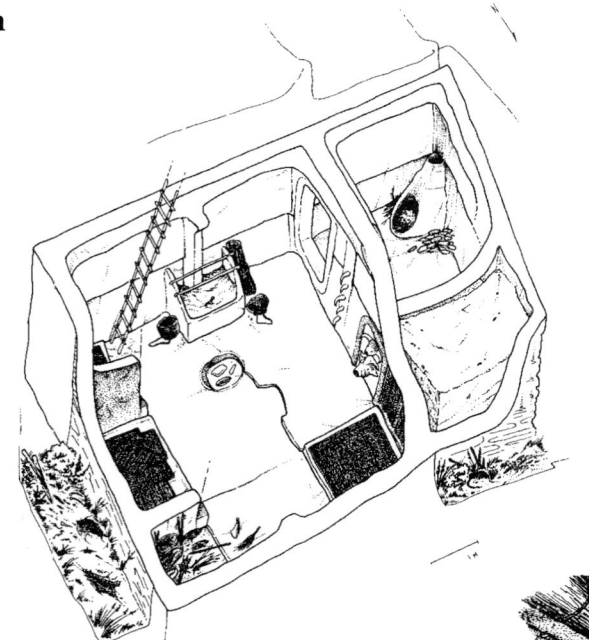

Figure 12.3. *These three illustrations are all reconstructions of Building 1. Figure (a) is a standard axonometric view of the whole building, much loved of archaeologists for its 'cutaway' perspective. Figure (b) is a more 'artistic' view at eye-level, within the building and the main room (Space 71), and Figure (c) is another 'artistic' view of the same space. In each drawing, style and presentation have been altered, although the content of archaeological information in each illustration remains more or less the same. Each of these three illustrations will mean more or less to different viewers. Appreciating and understanding this potential is vital.*

b

c

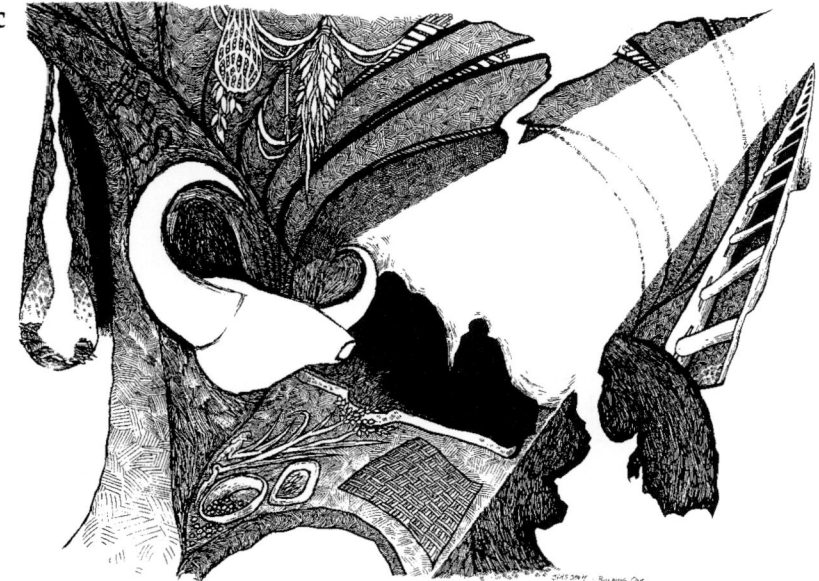

fully incorporated within the recording and presentation process, and their visual approach used within the context of an expanded programme of visual representation of archaeology.

Illustrating at the trowel's edge (II): reconstructions and the power of imagery

A reconstruction illustration is considered to be a visual representation of the archaeology which, as far as possible, attempts to present that information within its original past context. Archaeology has developed very particular and fixed ideas of what is or is not a reconstruction, and how or why they are or are not to be used (James 1997, 24). The historical connection between Çatalhöyük and the use and production of reconstruction images is strong. It is a connection which has inspired the current project's use of reconstructions, and a connection which provides a basis for a discussion of the nature of the presentation of these visual interpretations of archaeological data and the ways in which they might be affected by a new approach and definition of archaeological illustration.

In any discussion of the way in which archaeological illustration is to be included in an on-site, rolling process of excavation and analysis, the use of reconstructions must take a central place. As a means for bringing together the wide and often confusing range of experiences, questions, analyses and interpretations, the reconstruction drawing is often unsurpassed. Yet unfortunately, the process of creating and using these illustrations is often badly misunderstood.

Creating Çatalhöyüks

Archaeologists and non-archaeologists alike approach a visual representation of the past through three windows, each of which will frame that approach in a particular way. The three windows are: style, content and presentation. The style of a reconstruction refers to the media employed in the production of the image, the content is the archaeological information embodied by the image, and presentation relates to the manner in which that image and its content are set before the viewer. The relative importance and significance of each window depends partly on the knowledge, background and taste of the viewer, and partly on choices made by the illustrator (see Fig. 12.3.) — a relationship between ways of representing and ways of seeing mirrored in much of archaeological practice (Bradley 1997, 68–71). In the context of a new definition of archaeological illustration, it must be understood that a reconstruc-

tion is a product of the use and impact of all three of these windows.

These reconstructions are translations into visual formats of often extremely complex archaeological interpretations. They represent the urge to understand and make sense of the behaviours and material culture of the inhabitants of the past in precisely the same way as our text-based interpretations do (James 1997, 33; Sorrell 1981, 21). These images become arresting because they are phrased in the language of the visual, a language ascribed a greater degree of immediacy, comprehensibility and believability to the Western — particularly scientific — tradition (Molyneaux 1997, 2). As such, the drawn, painted or otherwise visual reconstruction can carry with it a power greater than the written conclusion or spoken discussion of archaeological interpretation. Consider as an example, the following sentence, written by James Mellaart in 1961: '. . . One can imagine the presence of light buildings of reed bundles and matting standing in the plain well away from the village as the temporary resting places of the dead' (Mellaart 1962, 68). This was Mellaart's interpretation of a geometric patterned wall-painting (Mellaart 1967, fig. 44) which depicted, so he concluded, charnel houses where the dead of Çatalhöyük were placed to be defleshed through exposure. The sentence is virtually forgettable: in the vast agglomeration of conclusions and interpretations which fill the seasonal reports from the site, this one sentence vanishes among the digressions on goddess worship, bull veneration and other subjects. But the visual image generated from that sentence, using no more evidence than that which created the textual interpretation, inevitably leaves a more lasting impression (see Fig. 12.4). Seeing the reed hut set amongst the grass of the plain sparks off questions and suggestions that the written conclusion never could. How would the hut have been marked? Is the choice of patterning significant? Does the wall-painting depict one hut made into a pattern, or a row of huts? Is there any archaeological evidence that bodies were laid out prior to burial (in fact, as yet, there is none)? What sort of individuals were placed in these huts? And for how long? What rituals accompanied their placement, their recovery and their internment? Where are these huts — or where might they have been placed? Is there any other evidence to suggest their location, form, etc.? Regardless of the veracity of the conclusion or the strength of the logic which creates it, the reconstruction image forces a much closer examination of the interpretation. Indeed, the most frequent comment I received on the

Figure 12.4. *One of several possible visual presentations of Mellaart's '"mortuary" wall-painting' interpretation of a wall-painting from shrine VI.B.1.*

drawing was along the lines of: 'Where on earth did you get the evidence/idea for that? Did Mellaart really say that?'. The interpretation, buried in textual form, had become forgotten and invisible, and an aspect of the textual interpretation, not apparent or seemingly insignificant has suddenly been brought to life, and so illuminated and subject to closer scrutiny. Illustration cannot be entirely divorced from its intimate connection with written presentation — one leads invariably to the other: an analogue hypertext of reading and meaning. Taken separately, image and word can be incomplete: reconstructions without explanations may be as misleading and obscure as discussion and conclusion without illustration.

Monumentality, or the tyranny of representation
But these conclusions about the power of reconstruction images to force debate and consideration are not in any way new (see James 1997, 45). One of the great problems, however, is that these images tend to be only produced when all the talking is finished, the report written and the conclusions reached. Reconstructions produced then are static, fossilized archaeological thoughts, neither able to adapt, nor, owing to their power as visual images, truly able to fade away. Their power remains, even though their content may become meaningless as time passes. If there is a 'tyranny of representation' in archaeology, it is perhaps here.

It is this 'monumentality' that needs to be dispensed with, both inside and outside archaeology

and archaeological illustration. It is generally accepted within the archaeological community that reconstruction illustrations are temporary entities — they are created to illustrate particular ideas, they have a life-span which matches the life-span of those ideas, and then they cease to be useful. Unfortunately, this perception is not generally matched by an enthusiasm for either publishing new reconstructions nor readily discarding the old. The only method that can actively counter the myth that reconstructions are the visual embodiment of definitive conclusions is the active use of reconstruction illustrations as a central tool in the creation and evolution of archaeological interpretation, giving image and visual presence to those transient conclusions that are, at present, only written or spoken. Within the context of a new definition of archaeological illustrations, this reconstruction of the transient becomes even more important. The impact of the introduction of new media, new styles and new methods of presentation to the interpretative process will create new avenues of discourse and evolution: '. . . images can always be disengaged from their meanings and inlayed into new combinations. This disassembly *should* be constant. The discovery of *new* insight depends on a nervous novelty which avoids the settling of . . . accepted equations and identities' (Shanks 1997, 84). Long a goal of archaeological illustration (e.g. Sorrell 1981, 22; James 1997, 27), what is being created at Çatalhöyük is an archaeological opportunity where the process of interpretation is an active and equal combination of the written and the many aspects of the illustrative.

In practical terms, attempts to break down the 'monumentality' of reconstruction images should result in reconstructions being treated somewhat differently than they traditionally have been. As a starting point, it may mean that there is a particular responsibility on any illustrator to ensure that their work never achieves 'monumentality' — rather, that it remains at all times fluid, reflecting the changing and transient nature of interpretation. I would suggest that there are ways in both the production and consumption of reconstructions to achieve this fluidity.

Fluidity of production: the reconstruction of the transient
The most important illustrative weapon in the war against monumentality is volume. With any limited selection of images, the chance that these will form themselves into a fixed view greatly increases. The aim should be to produce as many different reconstructions as possible — and that means as many different reconstructions using as many different approaches to the 'windows' of style, presentation and content. The illustrations in Figure 12.2 demonstrate this quite clearly. But there must be more — in essence, one can never have enough visual 'discussion' in the form of multiple reconstructions, in the same way that one can never have enough verbal or written discussion of archaeological interpretations. Putting artificial limits on the number of reconstructions produced is to constrain their discursive potential, and worse, emphasizes the gulf in primacy and veracity between what has been reconstructed and what has not. Perhaps implicit in this is the necessity of identifying more clearly when a reconstruction fails to be current and informative, and perhaps has become misleading. Increased access to the process of illustration and its archive (discussed below) may be one good way of addressing this issue.

Second, fluidity of discussion in visual reconstructions can further be achieved by using drawing and illustration as a quick and temporary means of capturing or presenting interpretations — as opposed to using the techniques in a permanent or more finished manner. In other words, illustrators should be producing things such as quick fifteen-second sketches in the field to show excavators how an oven may have fit into a wall, or a ladder into a gap in the plaster. These 'instant reconstructions' are invaluable contributions to the informal discussions and debates that characterize field interpretation. Within the context of Çatalhöyük's many 'tours' and evening discussions, these sorts of illustrations should perhaps start to play a bigger role. It might also become a useful tool in bridging the gap between those who dig and those who analyze. One of the concerns of the Çatalhöyük excavation team over the years has been the disconnection between the modes of analysis and interpretation used by them in the field, and modes employed by post-excavation, but still primarily on-site, laboratory teams. The incorporation of more visual imagery into these analyses and interpretations, with an eye towards making the laboratory data more accessible and more tangible to those doing the actual excavation, could help to bridge this divide. Combined with a process of exploring new modes of visual expression and looking carefully at the way 'art' can illustrate the data of 'science', there could be here the potential for creating a powerful and important tool for managing on-site interpretation and analysis.

Third, monumentality is also a process of familiarity. It is not unusual for the visual reconstructions of archaeology on a particular product to be the sole product of one illustrator. However adept such an illustrator may be, there will always be an identifiable 'tone' to their work. Bringing in the work of other illustrators may be a vital 'breath of fresh air' to reconstructions. These illustrators do not have to be specially hired expensive professionals, either. In increasing the scope of reconstructions, the project should actively encourage its excavation and laboratory staff to attempt to put their own ideas into a visual mode. Some present members of the team already do this: Lucy Hawkes, working with Theya Molleson and Peter Andrews, has been using reconstruction overlays to make sense of multiple and disturbed burials (see Chapter 13).

Fluidity of consumption: access and interpretation
But such 'productive' weapons against monumentality are only half the story. Multiple reconstructions are of no use unless they can be viewed and included in an ongoing process of interpretation. What this means is that an illustrator producing reconstructions needs to make their work available at all times for feedback, comment and inclusion in the whole interpretive process.

The first stage is to ensure that all those who have an input into the interpretation understand the various stages through which a reconstruction illustration passes — research, modelling, studies, detail work, composition, emphasis, etc. Understanding this process clarifies the entire web of logic which creates the style, content and presentation of a reconstruction. Such an educative approach can be low-key, but it still needs to be present.

Second, having outlined clearly what each of these stages is, work from each stage should be made as widely available as possible (see Fig. 12.5). Most illustrators and artists feel nothing but horror at the thought that their process of creation should be made open and accessible to anyone but themselves. There is a vulnerability and haunting nakedness in the exposure of the inner workings of artistic creation — part of the myth about the transcendent and magical nature of artistic creativity that still persists. But an inclusive approach to reconstruction illustration must allow for wholehearted scrutiny in order to best benefit from such an approach. During the 1998 season, I made every effort to ensure that my own activities were as accessible and available as possible. Even so, there exists still a palpable gap between my illustrative process and the produced image. I am hoping during the 1999 and subsequent seasons to have all the various stages of my work displayed more frequently, with more accompanied encouragement for comment and observation — however trivial it may seem to the commentator. This would include the collation of rough and preliminary drawings, notes and journal entries as a possible addition to the site's on-line archive, and access to the Web's potential for feedback and comment. Thus any final presentation of the reconstruction should be able to include directions to a large archive of material that reflects the evolution and process of decision-making that has formed any published images. Questions then posed about these images (Why are they wearing those clothes? Why do the buildings look that way? Why is there a woman and not a man in that scene? etc.) can be directed to the archive, and the questioner informed of the chain of logic which has created those elements of the published images about which they have questions. It is essentially the same process of comment and desire for transparency which has been applied to the site's textual interpretation, and it is an implicit part of accepting archaeological illustration as a tool and a process rather than as a narrowly defined method and end-product.

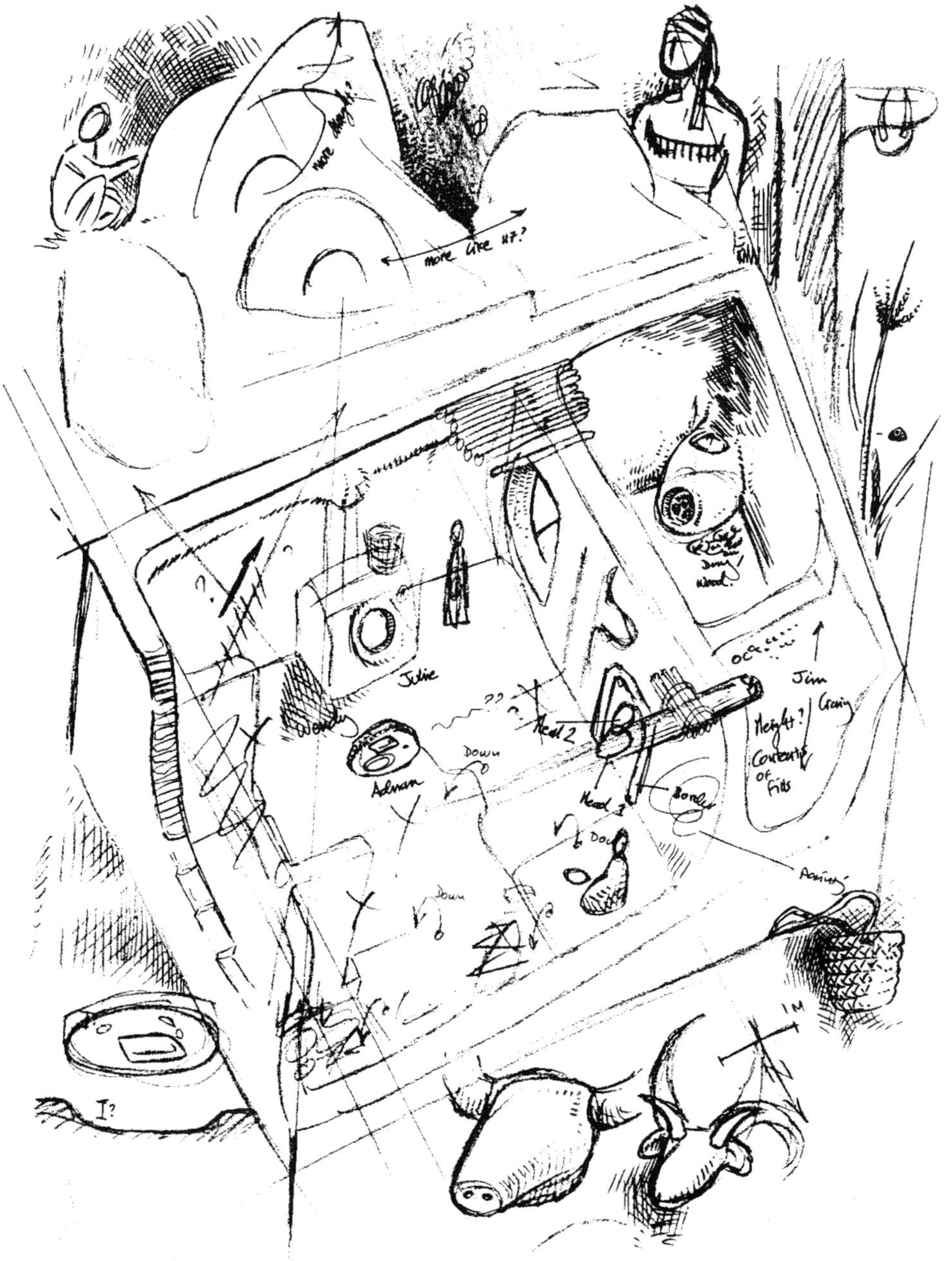

Figure 12.5. *A rough draft of the reconstruction in Figure 12.1. A comparison of the two shows how many elements — stylistic, content and presentation — have changed between rough and published versions. Illustrators are often categorized as 'brave' for displaying their rough drafts in public, but only by doing so can the monumentality and artificial solidity of reconstructions be broken down.*

The future

Unlike other disciplines in use at Çatalhöyük, illustration has not yet had the benefit of several years of field-testing in which to propose, analyze and examine a defined methodology. This present chapter, therefore, must be seen as more of a 'mission statement' than the conclusions of a specific experiment. Nevertheless, the ideas and proposals expressed within, and the stated goal of creating — or at least moving towards — a new approach to the use and function of archaeological illustration are also the result of work that has already been completed at Çatalhöyük, and processes that are already in place. Although this chapter concentrates primarily on the use and production of reconstructions within the project's evolving methodological framework, this is only one of several areas of archaeological illustration that is in the process of being addressed in a new way in light of a new definition: finds illustration and building recording are two further types of archaeological illustration that are being redefined, re-approached and re-understood.[2]

Of course, it should not be imagined that the process of evolution that is being enacted on archaeological illustration is a one-way street; it is not only archaeological illustration that must pay attention more closely to the changes in archaeology, but vice versa. By involving those archaeologists and non-archaeologists not usually included in the process of illustration, both sides can better understand the practice, its theory, and ultimately its full presentational and interpretational potential.

The box

As a final 'coda' to this chapter — a means of drawing together several threads and perhaps looking to the future — I would like to consider the illustration in Figure 12.6. This is a design (and at present not yet even a proposal) for a three-dimensional Çatalhöyük reconstruction based on current archaeological ideas and interpretations. The sculpture would consist of a three-sided glass screen, eight foot to a side, onto which was etched views of the interior of a Çatalhöyük space as seen by someone within that space. Although ostensibly a piece of 'sculpture', it is intended also as a serious attempt to reconstruct some important aspects of Çatalhöyük archaeology. The construction is solid, yet transparent. One cannot look at the images or views on the glass without being aware of what/who is both outside of the box and what/who is inside the box. The box is therefore, visually, a combination of the reconstructed image and the present-day environment. As such, it seeks to embody the curious contradiction of archaeology that our work in the past can never be separated from our position in our present. But in the

Figure 12.6. *The box. This idea for a three-dimensional reconstruction draws heavily from traditions of sculpture and installation art, but uses them to try and present complex ideas about the relationships between archaeology and the present. Is this a valid form of 'reconstruction'? How does something like this alter or affect the way in which we view or consider archaeology and its results?*

context of archaeological illustration, what is this 'box'? Is it a reconstruction? The ideas which have shaped its design and construction are without doubt relevant to a discussion of archaeology at Çatalhöyük, but how exactly is exploring these themes in the form of this structure different to exploring them on paper, whether in print or illustration? Is this merely an example of archaeology and archaeological interpretation getting a bit too clever for its own good, or can such an attempt to reconstruct, interpret and present archaeology bring out something more than other forms of reconstruction and presentation? Excitingly, these are questions to which, at the moment, there are no answers; it must, I believe, be part of the job of archaeology to address and explore them.

Notes

1. See, for instance, Adkins & Adkins 1989, 9, or Griffiths *et al.* 1990, where their introduction leaps right into a discussion of *how* to do archaeological illustration and *why* it is used, omitting any solid references as to *what* exactly it is. Their definition of its role is created only by identifying it as preferable to photography.
2. Unfortunately beyond the scope of this paper, there are interesting possibilities for rethinking our attitudes to the contextual nature of artefacts and their illustrations (Henley 1998), as well as reviving some of the older illustrative practices of building illustration.

References

Adkins, L. & R. Adkins, 1989. *Archaeological Illustration*. Cambridge: Cambridge University Press.

Bradley, R., 1997. 'To see is to have seen': craft traditions in British field archaeology, in Molyneaux (ed.), 62–72.

Griffiths, N., A. Jenner & C. Wilson, 1990. *Drawing Archaeological Finds: a Handbook*. London: Archetype Press.

Hamilakis, Y., S. Pluciernik, S. Tarlow & L. Attala, 1998. Body, Vision and Representation in Archaeology. Paper presented to the Theoretical Archaeology Group Conference, Birmingham 1998.

Hastorf, C., 1998. The cultural life of early domestic plant use. *Antiquity* 278, 756–72.

Henley, C., 1998. Is all Art Quite Useless?: Post-Processualism in Representing the Past. Paper presented to the Theoretical Archaeology Group Conference, Birmingham 1998.

James, S., 1997. Drawing inferences: visual reconstructions in theory and practice, in Molyneaux (ed.), 22–48.

Last, J., 1998. A design for life, interpreting the art of Çatalhöyük. *Journal of Material Culture* 3(3), 355–78.

Mellaart, J., 1962. Excavations at Catal Huyuk: first preliminary report, 1961. *Anatolian Studies* 12.

Mellaart, J., 1967. *Catal Huyuk: a Neolithic town in Anatolia*, London: Thames & Hudson.

Molyneaux, B.L. (ed.), 1997. *The Cultural Life of Images*. London: Routledge.

Moser, S. & C. Gamble, 1997. Revolutionary images: the iconic vocabulary for representing human antiquity, in Molyneaux (ed.), 184–211.

Piggott, S., 1978. *Antiquity Depicted: Aspects of Archaeological Illustration*. London: Thames & Hudson.

Renfrew, C., 1998. Monuments without Phenomenology: Walking with Richard Long, Standing with Anthony Gormley. Paper presented to the Theoretical Archaeology Group Conference, Birmingham 1998.

Shanks, M., 1997. Photography and archaeology, in Molyneaux (ed.), 73–104.

Sorrell, M. (ed.), 1981. *Reconstructing the Past*. London: Batsford Academic and Educational Ltd.

Chapter 13

Refleshing the Past

Lucy Hawkes
with Theya Molleson

Under a juniper-tree the bones sang, scattered and
    shining
We are glad to be scattered, we did little good to
    each other,
Under a tree in the cool of the day, with the
    blessing of sand,
Forgetting themselves and each other, united
In the quiet of the desert.
T.S. Eliot – Ash Wednesday

As archaeologists, we encounter human remains in our everyday work. We are familiar with the image of the skeleton both in excavation and in popular culture. This image can begin to take on a life of its own, disconnected from the human body. Paradoxically, whilst the skeleton is such a familiar image to us, we can never directly see our own, which is perhaps why the image of the skeleton becomes disconnected from our experience of the body.

My particular interest in refleshing the skeleton comes from a personal response to the archaeological material encountered at Çatalhöyük. During excavation of burials I was struck by the postures of the skeletons *in situ*. The integral skeleton seemed to convey something which I can only call 'body language'. This quality of the complete skeleton seemed in danger of being lost owing to the particular excavation methods at Çatalhöyük, which involve removing the skeleton piece by piece rather than *en bloc* in order to preserve the surrounding context. To further situate my response to the skeletal remains within my experience, it was my earlier study of life drawing and particular interest in line and rhythm in the figure which allowed me to perceive the skeleton in this way.

This initial personal response found expression in my reconstruction work with the human remains team. The ideas, techniques and interpretations outlined in this chapter were developed jointly. As dif-

ferent case studies were tackled, new aspects of burial began to be explored. A method was developing as a practical response to specific problems, each study broadening the approaches used. An outline of the major case studies will illustrate some of the problems which stimulated these developments.

The first piece of work was produced for an in-the-field seminar on reconstructing Building 1 in the North area. Its purpose was merely to represent the cumulative burials on the east platform, providing a visually accessible form of information. Through the use of overlays it was possible to study patterns of spatial organization which had not been seen before, and to ask new questions. To what extent were these spatial patterns relevant? What did they tell us about the relationship between burials? Why were some bodies fragmented and some complete? Was the final headless burial originally interred with a head?

The next major case study was skeleton 3368 in the South area (see Fig. 13.1). The practices and context surrounding this burial were of particular interest as all previous burials at Çatalhöyük had been under floors in houses, whereas skeleton 3368 was found in a midden. The main issue here was to explore how the treatment of his body related to the surrounding context of the burial. The questions focused on the relationship between initial posture, decay, movement and context; was he lying in his original posture, and if not, what factors had contributed to his posture and state as found on excavation?

The double burial of skeletons 2056/2058 in the South area presented a new series of problems. These two individuals were buried one on top of the other. Skeleton 2058 lay on her front and to the side with her spine upper-most and legs tucked under her chest. Skeleton 2056 lay above her on his right side. Although all elements of the long bones were present

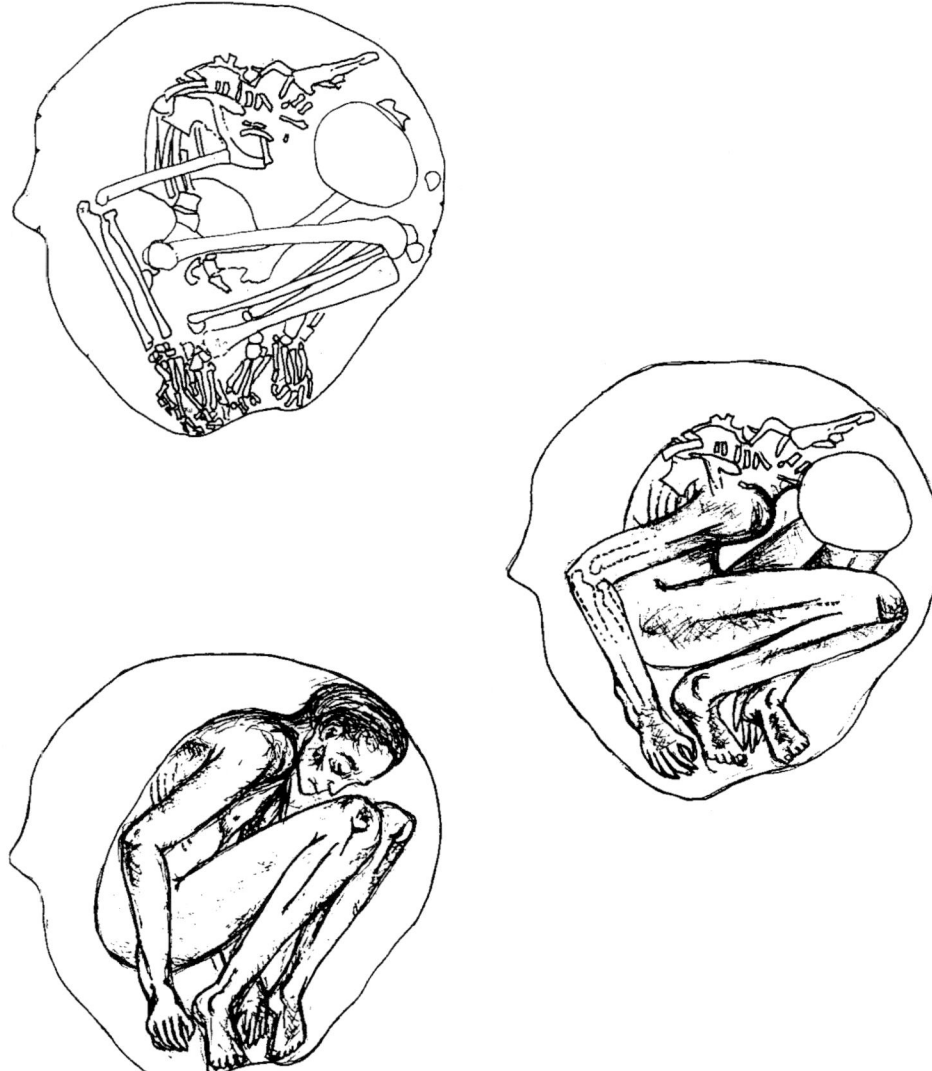

Figure 13.1. *Reconstruction of burial 3368. The series of stages illustrated demonstrates the possible relationship between posture, movement and decay.*

lematic. Three burials in this sequence were found with various parts of their skeletons in a state of entanglement and it was hotly debated which was the primary burial, and which deposition had disturbed a particular skeleton. Skeleton 2169 was a complete specimen, lying bound in a crouched position. Skeleton 1955, however, lacked articulated arms, hands or legs and her whole posture implied disturbance. There were a number of complex physical relationships between 2169 and 1955, some of which suggested that 1955 was deposited on top of 2169, and some of which indicated 1955 to be the primary burial (see Fig. 13.5). It was far from clear whether 1955 was the primary burial, removed and re-interred during the deposition of 2169, or whether they were buried together, and 1955 only later disturbed by the deposition of the infant 2125.

The next part of the chapter will describe the main aim and focus of the current work, and outline attempts to produce a coherent body of techniques to answer these questions.

in both cases, they were not all in anatomical position: skeleton 2058 had her left arm and hand lying down by her feet and skeleton 2056 had his left leg lying alongside his spine (see Figs. 13.2:1–8 & 13.3). This burial posed many questions. What was the original position of 2058? How and when had the left leg of 2056 been removed and come to lie along the spine? Was there a relationship between the postures, i.e. had 2058 been moved to fit in 2056, and had the disturbance in 2056 occurred as a result of his physical contact with 2058? What was the time interval between depositions, and the state of decay on burial?

Another multiple burial in the northwest platform of Building 1 in the North area was also prob-

Aims of reconstruction

The aim of reconstruction as defined in this chapter is not the reconstruction of the features and physique of individuals in the past (see Iscan & Helmer 1993; Prag & Neave 1997), but the exploration of the treatment of a particular body. Initially this analysis was limited to the original posture of, and spatial relationships between, bodies. However, the practice of reconstructing the body of specific skeletons has thrown light on wider aspects of how the body was treated in burial. Consequently the scope has

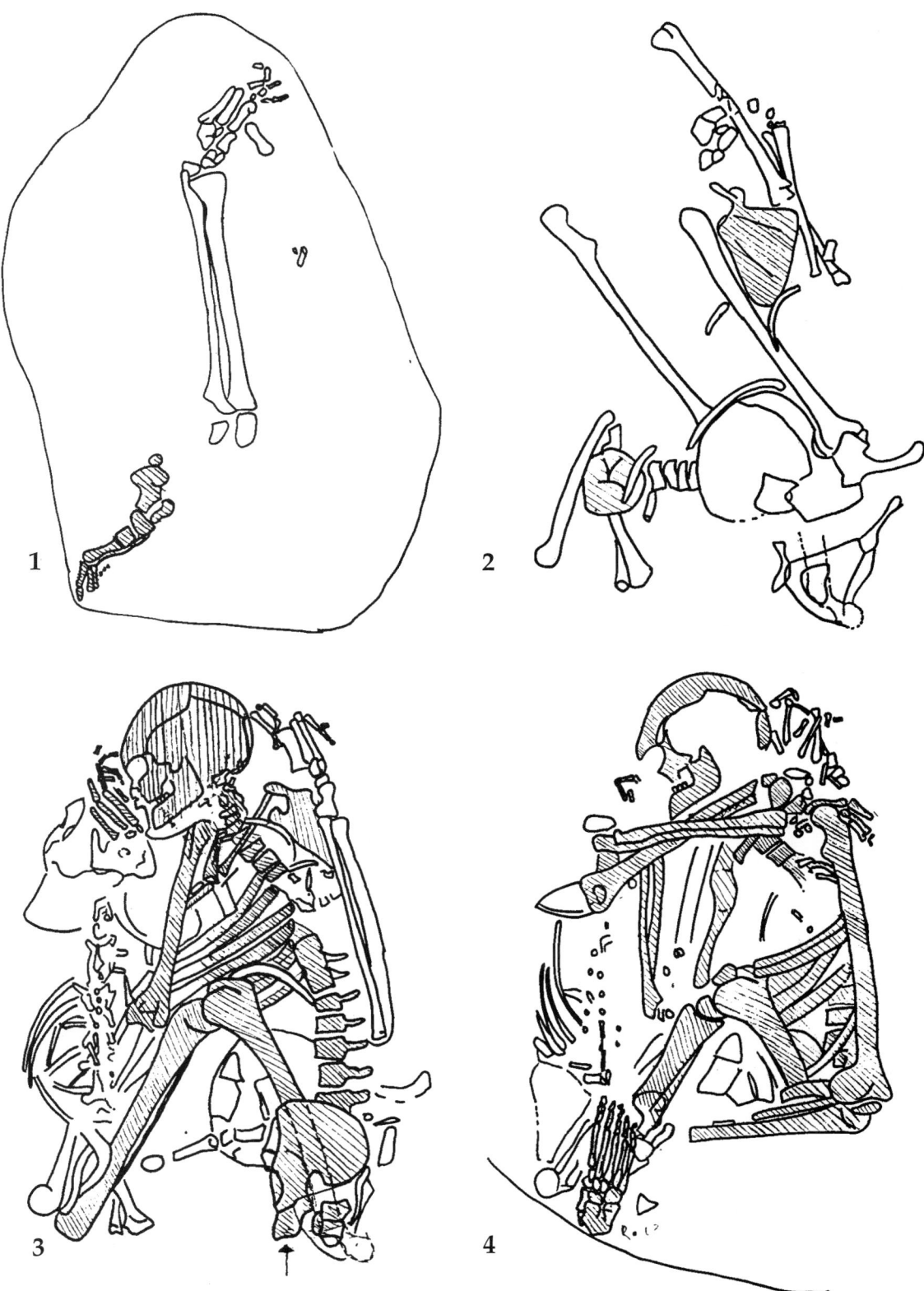

Figure 13.2. *1–5) Sequence of plans showing interrelationships between bones of individuals 2056 and 2058; 6) an impression of the final position of the body; 7) reconstructed original position of individual 2058; 8) reconstructed original position of 2056. The left leg was subsequently removed leaving the left foot in its original position. Note the position of the feet up against the edge of the cut.*

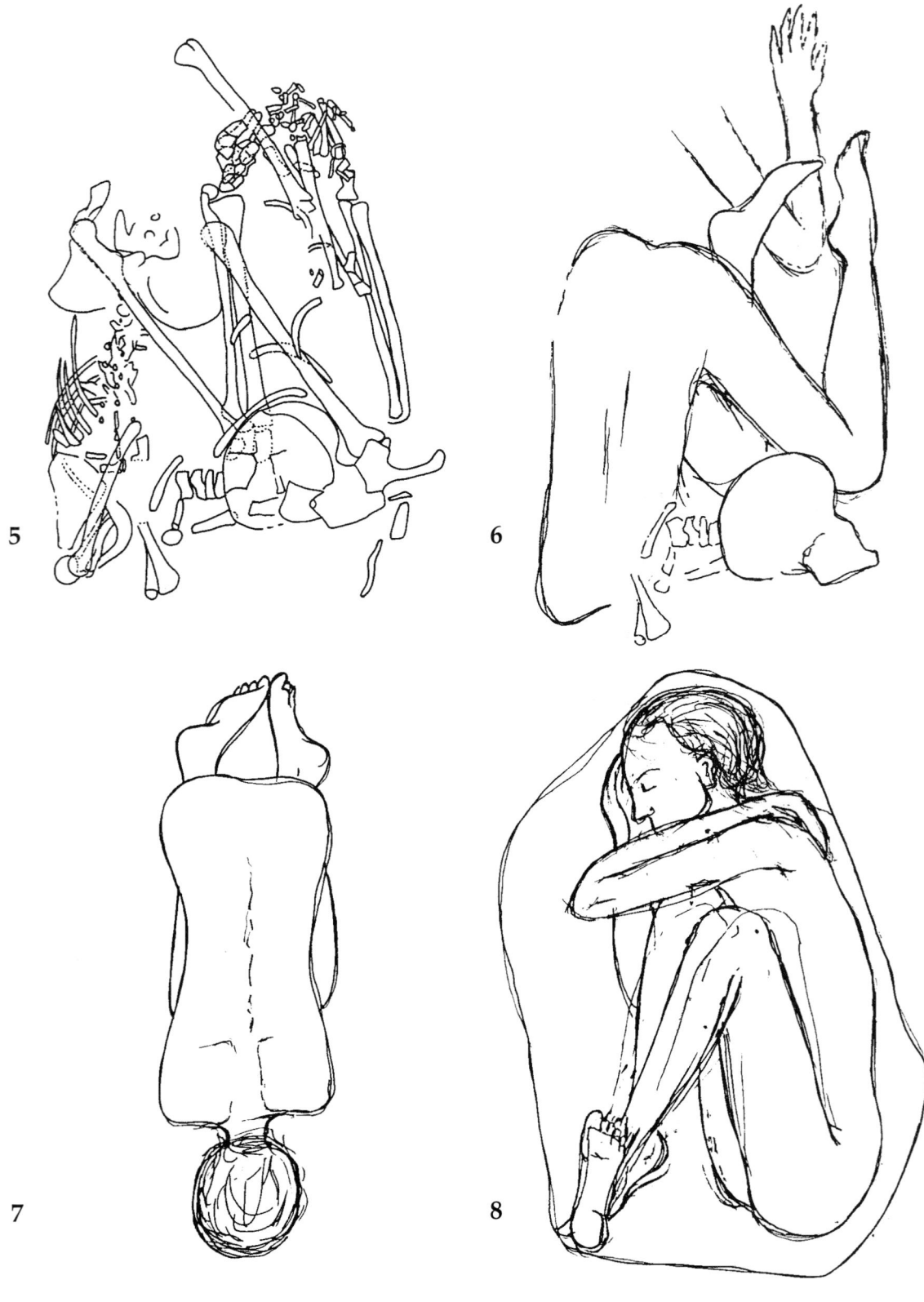

Figure 13.2. *(cont.)*

been broadened. The aim now is to recover as far as possible from the skeletal remains, all treatment and manipulation of the body prior to and during burial.

Various strands of funerary archaeology have explored the meaning of, and symbolic expression through, the body (Binford 1971; Pader 1979; Shanks & Tilley 1982; Thomas & Whittle 1986; Thomas 1991; Sofaer-Derevenski 1997). Indeed funerary ritual may be argued to involve the 'deployment of a particular range of symbolic resources which includes the corpse' (Barrett 1994, 112). Several studies focus on the negotiation of meaning through practices enacted upon or through the body (Thomas 1991). Such manipulation of the body may constitute a form of symbolic expression and negotiation. The purpose of this chapter then is to es-

Figure 13.3. *Reconstruction of the spatial relationship of 2056 and 2058.*

tablish a method with which to identify such practices of manipulation and intentional patterning of the body for further study.

Before discussing the techniques used for assessing the treatment of the body, it is necessary to outline the type of treatment upon which these techniques focus. The treatment of the body prior to deposition includes the time interval before burial and the state of the body on deposition. These aspects of burial may suggest pre-burial practices. In his study of skeletal disarticulation at Raunds, Northamptonshire, Boddington concludes that the state of decomposition and time delay prior to burial suggest transportation to the site (Boddington 1987, 41). The time interval prior to burial and the state of decay may also reveal attitudes concerning when it is appropriate to bury a body. Ucko outlines several reasons for delay in deposition, from the need to make

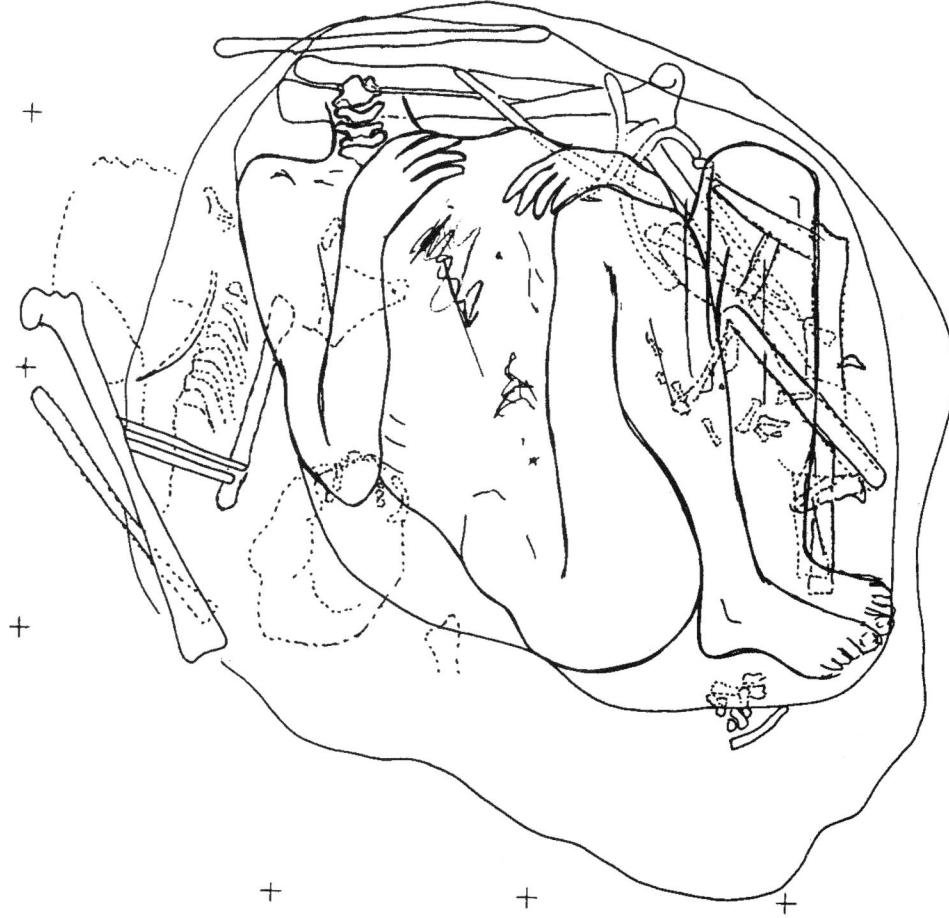

Figure 13.4. *The spatial distribution of skeletal elements of 1467 surrounding 1466 suggest that they had been disturbed by and placed in relation to the deposition of 1466.*

157

arrangements and gather funds for burial, to a 'morbid fear of premature burial' in many ethnographic cases (Ucko 1969, 269).

More direct human manipulation prior to burial includes disarticulation, binding, and burial in bags and baskets (the case studies which have been explored so far using this technique at Çatalhöyük have been of fairly complete skeletons where secondary burial is unlikely. Although this technique could in time throw light on these practices, secondary burial will not be discussed in this chapter). Such manipulation of the body may be a way of distinguishing between different types of people in the past (Barrett 1994, 112; Ucko 1969, 271). For example, at Çatalhöyük the unusual posture of skeleton 2197 suggests that it may have been buried in a bag. This unusual treatment of the body may be particularly significant as 2197 is a neonate. In many societies neonates are not considered to be full members of society and consequently receive different treatment during burial (Binford 1971, 7; Ucko 1969, 270).

Aspects of the manipulation of the body during deposition include the initial posture of the body, its spatial relationship to other bodies and its temporal relationship to other depositions. The initial posture is important for several reasons. It may suggest types of pre-burial treatment of the body such as those discussed above. Patterns of posture, orientation and direction of the head of individual skeletons have previously been studied as indicative of social difference (Binford 1971, 21; Ucko 1969, 271; O'Shea 1981, 49). Spatial relationships between bodies may indicate significant patterning (Goldstein 1981, 58). This spatial patterning between bodies may express social relations and relations of intimacy. Vertical spatial relationships may indicate a memory of previous depositions. Subsequent depositions may be placed with reference to previous ones. In the northwest platform of Building 1 in the North area at Çatalhöyük, the spatial organization of skeletons suggested this aspect of memory. The first two depositions of an old woman 2115 and child 2119 were buried together or with some recollection of the other's burial. Both lay in crouched positions, head to the west, facing north. The third burial of a young woman 1995 lay in the same crouched posture, head to the west, facing north, overlying the older woman. This deposition of 1995 over 2115 suggests an intentional act of referral back to this previous burial. A cumulative series of depositions may constitute a reworking of symbolic resources (Barrett 1991, 8). Temporal relationships between burials must be understood in order to establish whether individuals are buried together or independently.

Finally the 'treatment' of the body also includes subsequent human disturbance such as the disturbance of one burial by another. The identification of disturbance is vital in order to distinguish it from the original posture (e.g. see skeleton 3368, Fig. 13.1). Disturbance of burials in a series of depositions may reveal the importance of the integrity of the body in the past. Thomas discusses the shift in the treatment of the body from disarticulated to articulated skeletons in the Late Neolithic in southern Britain. He interprets this distinction in terms of 'concepts of personhood' expressed through the body (Thomas 1991, 40). Disturbances may also reveal intentional entangling of skeletal remains and rearranging of bones. Shanks & Tilley's work on the distribution of bones in mortuary structures in southern England and Scandinavia explores the significance of intentional rearrangement and patterning of skeletal remains (Shanks & Tilley 1982). In the northwest platform of Building 1 in the North area at Çatalhöyük there was a striking relationship between the distribution of skeletal remains in a cumulative series of burials. The scattered bones of a previous burial 1467 had been swept aside for, and laid around the perimeter of, the final deposition, skeleton 1466. They had been disturbed by and placed in relation to, this final burial (Fig. 13.4).

Techniques of investigation

The aim of this work is thus to identify the treatment and manipulation of the body prior to and during deposition. The main technique for achieving this is to 'refit' the scattered bones into a meaningful whole, to reconstruct or 'reflesh' the body. The refleshing of the body from the skeletal remains provides a conceptual tool for investigating the integrity and disintegration of the body and enables the identification of the human influences which acted upon the body from death to excavation as discussed above.

There are several strategies or techniques which have been employed so far to reconstruct the body and thus explore human manipulation. The first two techniques are not specific to this reconstruction work but play a vital role. These techniques consist of the interpretation of skeletal remains during excavation and the identification of individuals in the laboratory. The next four strategies form the core of the reconstruction work and consist of: the analysis of the skeleton plan, 're-enactment' of the three-dimensional body, the re-fleshing of the skeleton through drawing, and finally the study of the surrounding matrix. Each will now be discussed in turn.

Excavation and laboratory analysis
Interpretation, it has been said, begins at the trowel's edge (Hodder 1999, 103). Certainly, the excavation of skeletal remains involves making decisions about which bones belong to which individual, and the order of burial. These interpretations, as recorded in the field notes, are invaluable to the process of reconstructing the burials. The recording of the skeleton *in situ* constitutes the vital piece of information without which this work would not be possible.

However, whilst these insights are important, it is often not until the carefully recorded and labelled bones are examined in the laboratory that they become disentangled and separated into individuals. These two areas of interpretation in the field and in the laboratory form the backbone to the process of reconstruction. The impressions developed in these former stages feed into all further analysis.

Analysis of the skeleton plan
At present there are four main foci to the study of the skeleton plan. The first is the separation of individual skeletons and the gathering together of fragmentary parts into a whole. This is not always possible in the field. The gathering together of the individual body also involves identifying the *in situ* (as opposed to the original) posture of the skeleton. The posture of a skeleton is not always clear during excavation especially if it is excavated and planned in layers. The posture can be worked out using overlays to piece the fragmentary bones together. Such was the case with skeleton 2058 which had been planned in four stages and was partly mixed up with skeleton 2056 (see Fig. 13.2:1–5).

The second focus is a detailed study of the spatial organization of an individual skeleton. The reason for studying this is two-fold. The first is to identify pre-burial practices. A complete, integral skeleton may represent the original

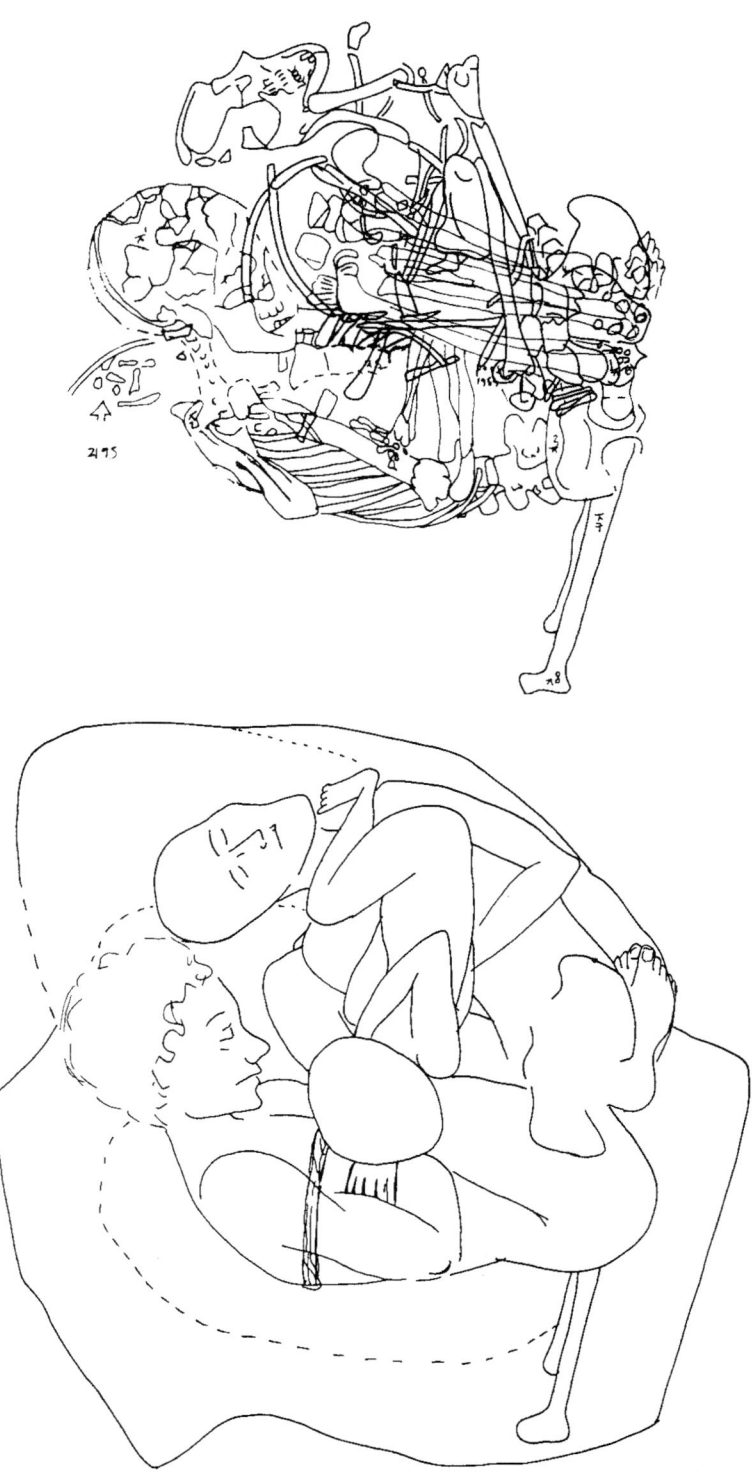

Figure 13.5. *1) Plan and 2) reconstruction of 2169, 1955 and 2125. The feet of skeleton 2169 were tucked up against the cut of skeleton 1955 suggesting that the skeletons were buried together or within a short period of time. The position of the infant 2125 correlates with an area of disturbance in the torso of 1955 and may also explain the position of 1955's head.*

159

posture and position of the body. In this case the posture can be studied to explore the impact of pre-burial practices. The posture of the skeletons at Çatalhöyük frequently suggests binding of the body. The tight flexed positions of many of the skeletons suggests this form of manipulation prior to burial, see skeleton 2169 (Fig. 13.5:2). Phytolith remains of binding were recovered on skeleton 2169 confirming this conclusion. The posture of the neonate, skeleton 2197 suggested that it was buried in a bag. It had been deposited as if sitting with its arms and legs splayed outwards and had slumped to one side. The absence of a grave cut strengthened this interpretation.

The second aspect of the spatial organization of an individual skeleton comes into play if the skeletal remains do not appear to be in their original position. In this case the relationship between the original posture and subsequent disturbance and dis-integration of the body can be explored. The posture and spatial distribution of skeletal elements in the skeleton plan may suggest disturbance and decay. Boddington uses the skeleton plans to assess tumble and decay in his study at Raunds (Boddington 1987, 28). Disturbance may occur through human manipulation during deposition or from subsequent depositions (see discussion below). If disturbance seems likely then it can be further explored through a study of a skeleton's spatial relationship to other depositions and to the surrounding context (see later discussion). The impact of disturbance on the body can be further explored and modelled through re-enactment and drawing (see below).

If there is more than one burial it is possible to expand this study of the spatial organization of remains to include a third focus — the spatial relations between skeletons. These relations are studied through the use of translucent overlays. Patterns of association and disturbance may begin to emerge. The significance of patterns of association is difficult to ascertain and has not been assessed statistically. For example, in the northwest platform in the North area there was a striking pattern in the distribution of skeletal remains. The long bones of skeleton 1955 had been separated from the body and deposited with skeleton 2169. A later burial of infant 2105 lay over these long bones. The long bones were the same length as the overlying infant and ran from its head to its feet. This spatial association was only discovered through the use of overlays during reconstruction. It suggests intentional placement of the long bones and infant. However such patterns may be accidental. Further case studies are needed to explore this area.

Patterns of disturbance are studied by identifying areas of disturbance in one individual and exploring their spatial relationship to subsequent depositions through the use of overlays (Fig. 13.3).

The fourth focus is the degree of articulation present in the skeleton plan. Study of articulation and disarticulation may allow assessment of: the degree and type of disturbance, and the state of decay and time interval prior to deposition and disturbance. This is a complex area involving many interweaving factors. Therefore the degree of articulation and disarticulation needs to be studied in the context of the former stages. It is necessary to situate disarticulation within a scenario, i.e. to relate it to a story or problem in order to make sense of it within a specific case study. Therefore a series of examples will best illustrate how this area of study may throw light on the treatment of the body.

Study of articulation may reveal the degree and type of disturbance. Human manipulation of the body (e.g. the removal of limbs prior to or during deposition) may be evident if such movement of skeletal elements cannot be explained by natural decay processes, or by other forms of disturbance. Such movement or absence of skeletal elements must be also studied in relation to the condition of the rest of the skeleton. The condition of the rest of the skeleton allows the assessment of the general degree of decay in comparison with areas of disarticulation. A similar technique was used by Thomas and Whittle in their study of skeletal remains in Neolithic monuments in southern Britain. The incompleteness of skeletal elements was compared against the presence of small bones of the hands and feet. The presence of such small parts contrasted with the incompleteness of other skeletal remains, and suggested human intervention rather than differential preservation (Thomas & Whittle 1986, 132). At Çatalhöyük, skeleton 2056 was found with its whole left leg (minus the foot) lying along its spine. However, the upper body and feet were in full articulation and no subsequent disturbance of the skeleton was indicated. Disarticulation of the legs prior to burial is unlikely as the articulated feet were still pushed up against the edge of the cut and the rest of the skeleton appeared to be in its original position (see Figs. 13.2 & 13.3 for original position). Thus the extent of movement of the left leg suggests human manipulation during or after deposition.

If the skeleton or large portions of the skeleton appear to lie in their original position, then the degree and type of decay, as well as the length of time prior to burial, can be explored. The time interval before deposition and state of decay are interrelated (Boddington 1987, 41) and must be studied together. For the purposes of this study, decay has been divided into dessication or putrefaction. Disarticulation may indicate the degree and type of decay prior to burial. In Brothwell's study of skeletal remains at Jewbury, tumbled bones in the thoracic area suggested partial decomposition prior to burial (Brothwell 1987, 26). At Çatalhöyük, the type of disarticulation of skeleton 2056 suggested that the body may have become decayed prior to deposition. The femur, patella, tibia and fibula of skeleton 2056 were present, fully articulated but not in anatomical position. They were detached at both the proximal end of the femur and the distal end of the tibia and fibula (Fig. 13.2:2–3). It appeared that they had 'snapped off' in a manner suggestive of a desiccated body (Molleson pers. comm.). The well-articulated state of the rest of the body further strengthened this interpretation. The length of time in which a body could reach this state of desiccation is difficult to assess. It does however indicate that deposition was not immediate.

Similarly the state of decay and time interval prior to disturbance can also be studied in this way. In the case of skeleton 2058, a scenario was reconstructed through re-enactment and drawing which suggested that the final posture was due to disturbance during a later deposition. Most of the skeleton was still fully articulated (except the left arm and skull, see below) suggesting that the body was fairly undecayed or desiccated on disturbance (Andrews & Molleson pers. comm.). This conclusion set limits to the time interval before and between depositions.

So, the analysis of the skeleton plan allows one to build up a picture of the manipulation, decay and disturbance of the individual body, and its relationship to other depositions. However, analysis of the skeleton plan can only take one so far. One needs to reconstruct a refleshed three-dimensional body to get a fuller picture.

Re-enactment

There are four ways in which re-enactment contributes to the interpretation of the skeleton: by translating the skeleton into a body for ease of understanding, 'testing' hypotheses, modelling movement and identifying decay and disturbance.

On one level re-enactment is simply a useful way of understanding what is going on. We are more familiar with the model of the body, than with an image of a skeleton. A skeleton is visually more difficult to comprehend than a fleshed body. This technique has proved useful on a number of occasions for coming to an understanding of the skeleton plan.

Having built up a certain level of understanding from the assessment of the skeleton plan, 're-enactment' of the posture and movement allows one to 'test' out scenarios in three-dimensions. This technique consists of imitating the posture of the skeleton with one's own body or that of a volunteer. Re-enacting the posture and movement with one's own body allows one to get a sense of how the body is likely to move and respond under pressure. This method allows one to experiment with the relationship between original posture and subsequent disturbance.

In interpreting the relationship between posture and movement in skeleton 2058 it was suggested from the study of the skeleton plan that the final position was a result of a crouched burial lying on its shins being pushed to the side owing to pressure from above. In re-enacting this scenario the body responded as hypothesized. The resulting position was strikingly similar to the final position of 2058 in the skeleton plan. However areas of disturbance were also identified that could not be explained by this simple movement. These were later accounted for as further deliberate re-arrangement in order to fit in the subsequent burial of 2056.

Re-enactment can also be used to 'translate' a skeletal position into a bodily one. Refleshing the

Figure 13.6.
Reconstruction of 2527 and 2532. The use of overlays, refleshing and extension of 2527's hands revealed a possible expression of physical intimacy in the spatial organization of the skeletal remains.

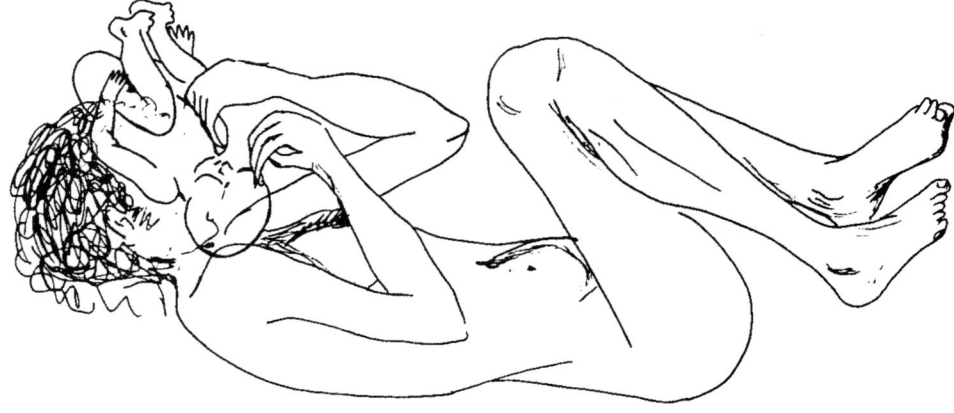

bones in this way can allow us to identify the degree of movement, decay or disturbance. Re-enactment was first used at Çatalhöyük by Molleson to interpret the posture of skeleton 3368. Immediately it became apparent that the skeleton would not translate into a body. Its posture therefore was the product of intervening manipulation, decay or disturbance. Further work suggested a combination of downward movement and disarticulation. This relationship between posture and movement was tried out using re-enactment to get the feeling of the movement of the body under pressure.

Drawing the body
Drawing the body is the main focus of the method suggested here. As with re-enactment, illustrations of the body give a clearer impression of the scenario. In this respect drawing fulfils the same function as re-enactment. However it provides more tangible and precise tools for playing with the relationship between the whole and the parts. It draws the parts back into a whole using anatomical relations and measurement of the skeleton.

Using this technique, drawing can be used to pull together and 'test' out the understanding of the burial built up in the previous stages. It may confirm or contradict these initial impressions. Study of the plan and re-enactment of skeleton 2058 had suggested a particular type of movement subsequent to deposition. This scenario was further explored through illustration. During attempts to illustrate this scenario, it was realized that this simple movement could not be used to explain the whole skeletal posture (Fig. 13.2:6–7). Explaining the position of the skull by this movement resulted in a disproportioned body. The skull had been moved downward towards the knees and rotated at an angle that could not be explained by the initial scenario. This unusual movement of the skull was later explained as disturbance or re-arrangement during the deposition of 2056. In drawing 2056 itself it was realized that the right femur was far too short in the skeleton plan as currently understood. This led to a re-interpretation of the skeleton plan.

As with re-enactment, drawing may be used to explore the relations between posture and movement. In the study of skeleton 3368 it was necessary to work out the original position (once it was realized that the body had moved). Re-enactment produced a possible scenario which then had to be translated into an accurately measured and proportioned drawing of the stages of movement and decay. To do this, it was also necessary to make a moveable

model of the skeleton, scaled to the skeleton plan, and 're-enact' the movement of the skeleton with the correct proportions. It was then possible to translate this moving model into a series of three illustrations of the stages of movement and decay (Fig. 13.1:1–3).

Drawing the body can also identify the degree of movement, disturbance and decay. It provides a focus for studying articulation and disarticulation in greater detail. In the study of 2056, it was not until a refleshed body was drawn that it was realized that there was further disarticulation at the hip.

Refleshing the bones through illustration can reveal important physical connections between individuals. A burial of a young woman (skeleton 2527) and baby (skeleton 2532), refleshed revealed that the woman's hand probably extended over the baby which lay over her head (Fig 13.5). The skeletal hand was fragmentary so this gesture was not apparent previously. Reconstruction of the body has the potential for revealing subtle aspects of body language such as this which are more easily read in a complete body than in a skeleton.

Context
In addition to building up an understanding of the body, its disintegration and disturbance, it is vital to consider the surrounding matrix. Linking the skeletal evidence with the surrounding matrix involves studying the relationship between the body, the grave cut and fill, and considering the influence of the surrounding layers on the skeletal remains. A series of examples will illustrate how such relationships are informative.

Relating the size and shape of the cut to the deposition of the burials may prove fruitful. The small size of the cut of double burial of skeletons 2056/2058 appears to have influenced the degree of disturbance of both bodies. Skeleton 2058 was pushed to one side and the skull moved upwards, and skeleton 2056 may have been disarticulated during deposition to fit it into the cut. The integrity of the body may not have taken priority over the need to fit the body into the cut.

The relationship of the body to the cut edge was of vital importance in the study of skeletons 3368 and 2056. In both cases the feet were pushed against the edge of the cut, fully articulated, suggesting that they were in their original position (Figs. 13.1 & 13.2:8). This point of stability was invaluable in understanding the nature of movement and disturbance in both cases. The final burial 1466 in the east platform of Building 1 in the North area had been found without a head. Previous work by members of the human remains team concluded that 1466 had been deposited in this state. On attempting to complete the body by adding a head, it was obvious that the close proximity to the edge of the cut made it extremely unlikely that the body was buried in a complete state (Fig. 13.4).

The relationship between cuts and depositions may also reveal insights into the order of burial. In the northwest platform of Building 1 in the North area, there were a number of complex physical relationships between skeletons 2169 and 1955. Skeleton 2169 was a complete specimen in a tight crouched position. Skeleton 1955 lacked articulated limbs and had marked disturbance in the upper body. The pelvis and sacrum lay on top of the skeletal remains of 2169. Initially it seemed as though 1955 was deposited on top of 2169, and was later disturbed by the infant 2125. However, long bones of skeleton 2169 were found under 1955 which was also found to be buried with the foot bones of 1955. The spatial organization of bones supported the theory that 1955 had been the primary burial, disturbed during the deposition of 2169 and re-interred on top of 2169. The relationship between the cuts and skeletons further supported the scenario that they had been deposited/re-interred together. Skeleton 2169 had its feet pushed up against the cut of skeleton 1955 (cut no. 2190), implying that they were deposited together or in quick succession (Fig. 13.5:1–2).

Information about the surrounding fill in the grave cut may throw light upon the way in which the skeletal remains have moved under pressure. The type and compaction of the fill is part of the context of the skeleton and influences its final position. The spatial organization of the skeletal remains of 3368 suggested that they had moved downwards from their original position (Fig. 13.1). Study of the · field notes revealed that the fill had been the same material as in the midden, and was probably quite soft and loose. The surrounding fill could have accommodated movement of the skeleton. Although this aspect of context has only been investigated in relation to this case study, it may prove useful in other studies. The type and compaction of the fill may be relevant in so far as they relate to the movement of the body within the grave cut.

Finally, the layers immediately above the skeleton may be assessed in terms of their impact on the body. This has also only been explored in the case of skeleton 3368, but may be useful in other cases. The layer above the burial had been interpreted as an 'activity surface'. This layer in the midden had had hearths built on it and bore evidence of 'puddling'

which suggested that it may have been trampled on. The underlying burial may have been subject to trampling pressure from the surface above which lay only inches above the burial. This would adequately explain the downward movement of the skeletal remains evident through study of the skeleton plan and reconstruction work outlined above.

The examination of the surrounding matrix has been found to be informative in understanding the deposition and disturbance of the body. It is therefore important not to study the skeletal remains in isolation but to link together many dimensions of evidence to produce a contextual study.

Other contextual factors

Non-human disturbance needs to be assessed in order to distinguish it from human treatment of the body. Although this is reminiscent of Schiffer's C and N transforms (Schiffer 1972; 1988), this work does not aim to quantify transforms, but rather to assess the impact of human and non-human influences on the body within the context of a specific case study. The language of transforms is not particularly relevant or useful in this context.

The separation of internal decay processes from human manipulation is also an important part of the analysis. The effects of decay processes on the body need to be modelled in order to distinguish them from human manipulation. In his discussion of taphonomy, Nawrocki warns against a simplistic reading of the posture in terms of human manipulation (Nawrocki 1995, 52), revealing how internal decay processes can result in postural changes.

It is not the aim here to give a detailed account of aspects of non-human disturbance and decay as these have been explored at length elsewhere (Andrews & Cook 1990; Boddington *et al.* 1987; Mant 1987; Mays 1998; Nawrocki 1995; Roberts *et al.* 1989).

At present, for the purposes of this chapter, it is enough to identify disturbance through the study of the spatial organization and articulation of skeletal remains (as previously outlined) and to begin to identify the nature of this disturbance. So far it has been the more striking disturbances of the body during deposition that have been identifiable as human (e.g. 1466, 2056 and 2058). Human disturbance through subsequent deposition is easier to identify and separate from non-human influences. Study of the surrounding matrix suggested indirect human influence on the skeletal remains of 3368 through overhead trampling. With the integration of taphonomic studies, the separation of human and non-human influences will become clearer.

Interpretation as dialogue

Although I have represented reconstruction as a series of stages, interpretation actually involves a constant shifting between skeleton plan, re-enactment, drawing and context, as each throws light on the others. Reconstruction is a cumulative process of understanding in which a coherent story is only gradually woven together through a process of dialogue between these different techniques.

These different techniques are actually represented by different people. The dialogue occurs between specific individuals who all contribute to, and sometimes dispute, the final interpretation. These voices comprise the excavator, whose main contribution comes through the field notes and plans, the laboratory specialists (P. Andrews and T. Molleson), and the author.

The analysis of the skeleton *in situ* and in the laboratory contributes to the understanding of the skeleton plan. Hypotheses derived from the former study feed into any drawing work. All illustration work is done in consultation with specialists, using their knowledge of decay processes and analysis of the skeletal remains. These illustrations may confirm or bring to light new insights. These then have to be evaluated in relation to the previous understanding. For example, attempts to reflesh the skeleton of 2056 forced a re-analysis of the skeleton plan. Drawing also provides new material to study, i.e. the spatial relationships between skeletons which are revealed through the use of overlays. There is thus feedback between understanding of the skeleton plan, re-enactment and drawing. This study of the body, its manipulation, disintegration and disturbance is then related back to the evidence concerning the surrounding matrix. Interpretation comes about as these different techniques and lines of evidence are woven together to form a coherent story. The interpretation is 'recursive' (Hodder 1999, 98).

An example will illustrate how the different parts of the analysis are investigated in relation to an emerging interpretation. Each stage of investigation is considered in relation to a specific scenario, but may also change this wider picture.

2058

1. Study of the skeleton plan revealed the *in situ* posture of the skeleton, and suggested a scenario in which the body is pushed to the side from an initial position on its front with the legs tucked under the chest (Fig. 13.2:6).

2. This scenario was studied in relation to the subsequent deposition of skeleton 2056 through the use of overlays. This indicated that the movement to the side may have occurred during the deposition of 2056 (Fig. 13.2:9).

3. Study of the state of articulation revealed that the skull/neck and left shoulder and arm of 2058 were disarticulated (Fig. 13.2:5). The study of this disarticulation in relation to the above scenario suggested that the skull remained in position when the body was disturbed and became disarticulated. The body must therefore have been fairly decayed in order for the skull to have become detached. However the rest of the body is fairly well articulated. This type of disarticulation could be explained if the body was desiccated.

4. Re-enactment of this scenario confirmed the possibility of movement through downward pressure. The scenario seemed feasible. However, the movement of the arm could not be explained.

5. Drawing was used to reconstruct the original position of 2058 (Fig. 13.2:7). Using measurements of the skeletal elements the parts were fitted back into a whole body. This revealed that the skull was not in the original position.

6. Using drawing, the position of the skull in relationship to the proposed movement was further modelled. Was it possible that the displacement of the skull occurred as a result of this disturbance? It was concluded that the skull had probably been moved; it had rotated and shifted toward the knees. This indicated that there were two stages to the manipulation of the body.

7. Further study of the state of articulation of the skeleton plan strengthened this interpretation of a two stage manipulation. Apart from the detachment of the head and arm, the rest of the body appeared to be fairly well articulated. This contrast in the state of articulation supported the two different types of disturbance suggested above.

8. A further analysis of the spatial relationships between the two skeletons in the light of this scenario supported the movement of the skull and arm through human manipulation. The skull of 2058 had moved to fit in to the stomach area under the ribs and under the right leg of 2056. So the skull of skeleton 2058 appeared to have been moved to fit in with the posture of 2056 (Fig. 13.2:9).

Limitations and further directions

A major drawback at present lies in the nature of the information which is recorded on excavation. Apart from the impression of the vertical spatial relationships between skeletons which emerge during excavation, this technique has so far only used two-dimensional relationships between skeletons to aid reconstruction. This failing is particularly crucial in the study of patterns of disturbance of one body by another. Through the use of overlays an impression of the patterns of disturbance can be built up. However, the three-dimensional spatial relationships need to be studied in order to confirm and 'flesh-out' these initial impressions.

This problem forces a re-examination of the techniques of recording in the field. The skeleton plan is a two-dimensional recording of the skeleton, with a few levels to provide a three-dimensional impression. However, these three-dimensional points are not sufficient for the detailed examination of the spatial relationships between skeletons required here.

There are two possible solutions to this problem. The first involves a grid system where levels are recorded at regular points on the skeleton. These grid points must be consistent so that in the case of additional burials underneath comparisons can be made. Having recorded these three-dimensional points on both skeletons, it will be possible to reconstruct a section drawing in order to examine the vertical as well as the horizontal spatial relationships between skeletons.

The second solution which should be used to compliment the first involves recording relevant three-dimensional points. The weakness of the first method is that although it gives an overall and comparable impression of the three-dimensional relationships, it may miss out crucial points of relevance to a specific case study. By suggesting that relevant vertical spatial relationships are recorded, the implication is that the interpretation of the skeleton as outlined in this chapter should begin 'at the trowel's edge'. Whilst such aspects of burial as the spatial relationships between skeletons and disturbance by subsequent depositions are no doubt considered during excavation, this is not enough. These initial impressions and interpretations must be put to use in selecting relevant three-dimensional points to be recorded to aid future reconstruction.

Conclusion

This chapter has sought to conceptualize a technique which is still in its infancy, but which through further seasons at Çatalhöyük it is hoped will reach increasing refinement. With the analysis of further case studies it is hoped that the application of these techniques at Çatalhöyük will reveal significant patterns of practice in the treatment of the body.

Acknowledgements

The interpretation of skeletal remains was also carried out by other members of the human remains team: Peter Andrews, Başak Boz, Joanna Sofaer-Derevenski, Tona Majo and Jessica Pearson. This work also benefited greatly from the plans and interpretation of burials during excavation by: Başak Boz, Adrian Chadwick, Naomi Hamilton, Jonathan Last, Gavin Lucas and Shahina Farid. I would like to thank Joanna Sofaer-Derevenski for her help and support in writing this paper. I would also like to thank Ian Hodder for his comments and encouragement.

References

Andrews, P. & J. Cook, 1990. *Owls, Caves and Fossils*. London: Natural History Museum Publications.

Barrett, J.C., 1991. Towards an archaeology of ritual, in Garwood *et al.* (eds.), 1–9.

Barrett, J.C., 1994. *Fragments from Antiquity: an Archaeology of Social Life in Britain, 2900–1200 BC*. Oxford: Blackwell.

Binford, L.R., 1971. Mortuary practices: their study and potential, in *Approaches to the Social Dimensions of Mortuary Practices*, ed. J.A. Brown. (Memoirs of the Society for American Archaeology 25.) Washington (DC): Society for American Archaeology.

Boddington, A., 1987. Chaos, disturbance and decay in an Anglo-Saxon cemetery, in Boddington *et al.* (eds.), 27–43.

Boddington, A., A.N. Garland & R.C. Janaway (eds.), 1987. *Death, Decay and Reconstruction: Approaches to Archaeology and Forensic Science*. Manchester: Manchester University Press.

Brothwell, D.R., 1987. Decay and disorder in the York Jewbury skeletons, in Boddington *et al.* (eds.), 22–7.

Chapman, R., I. Kinnes & K. Randsborg, 1981. *The Archaeology of Death*. Cambridge: Cambridge University Press.

Garwood, P., D. Jennings, R. Skeates & J. Tomes (eds.), 1991. *Sacred and Profane*. (Oxford University Committee for Archaeology Monograph 32.) Oxford: Oxford University Committee for Archaeology.

Goldstein, L., 1981. One dimensional archaeology and multidimensional spatial organisation and mortuary analysis, in Chapman *et al.*, 53–71.

Hodder, I., 1999. *The Archaeological Process: an Introduction*. Oxford: Blackwell.

Iscan, M.Y. & R.P. Helmer, 1993. *Forensic Analysis of the Skull: Craniofacial Analysis, Reconstruction and Identification*. New York (NY) & Chichester: Wiley-Liss.

Mant, A.K., 1987. Knowledge acquired from post-war exhumations, in Boddington *et al.*, 65–81.

Mays, S., 1998. *The Archaeology of Human Bones*. London:

Routledge.

Nawrocki, S.P., 1995. Taphonomic processes in historic cemeteries, in *Bodies of Evidence: Reconstructing History Through Skeletal Analysis*, ed. A.L. Grauer. New York (NY) & Chicester: Wiley-Liss, 49–69.

O'Shea, J., 1981. Spatial configurations and the archaeological study of mortuary practices: a case study, in Chapman *et al.* (eds.), 39–53.

Pader, E.J., 1979. Material symbolism and social relations in mortuary studies, in *Anglo-Saxon Cemeteries*, eds. P. Rahtz, T. Dickinson & L. Watts. (British Archaeological Reports British Series 82.) Oxford: BAR, 143–59.

Prag, A.J.N.W. & R. Neave, 1997. *Making Faces: Using Forensic and Archaeological Evidence*. London: British Museum Press.

Roberts, C.A., F. Lee & J. Bintliff (eds.), 1989. *Burial Archaeology Current Research Methods and Developments*. (British Archaeological Reports British Series 211.) Oxford: BAR.

Schiffer, M., 1972. Archaeological context and systemic context. *American Antiquity* 37, 156–64.

Schiffer, M., 1988. The structure of archaeological theory. *American Antiquity* 53, 462–79.

Shanks, M. & C. Tilley, 1982. Ideology, symbolic power and ritual communication: a reinterpretation of Neolithic mortuary practices, in *Symbolic and Structural Archaeology*, ed. I. Hodder. Cambridge: Cambridge University Press, 129–55.

Sofaer-Derevenski, J., 1997. Age and gender at the site of Tiszapolgar Basatanya, Hungary. *Antiquity* 71(274), 875–90.

Thomas, J.S., 1991. Reading the body: Beaker funerary practice in Britain, in Garwood *et al.* (eds.), 33–42.

Thomas, J.S. & A. Whittle, 1986. Anatomy of a tomb. *Oxford Journal of Archaeology* 5(2), 129–56.

Ucko, P.J., 1969. Ethnography and archaeological interpretation of funerary remains. *World Archaeology* 1, 262–80.

Chapter 14

Villagers and the Distant Past:
Three Seasons' Work at Küçükköy, Çatalhöyük[1]

David Shankland

In the first description of this research, published in *On the Surface* (Hodder 1996), I described how the project emerged from my experience of working with archaeologists at the British Institute of Archaeology at Ankara. There, I felt myself trying to devise ways that I might as a social anthropologist contribute toward the archaeological endeavour, not in the usual ethno-archaeological sense of taking an aspect of a living community and comparing it directly with the archaeological record, but more holistically by including aspects relevant to the entire society and its interaction with the past (Shankland 1996).

One of the ways that I felt this might be done is to clarify the 'voice' of the local people. Except perhaps in those exceptional cases where a community have absolutely no idea of the existence of the site, they are very likely to have developed different and perhaps complex ways of integrating those same material remains into their own conceptions of history. This is relevant not just in the post-modern sense of an alternative, and perhaps equally viable, interpretation of the past to that of the archaeologists themselves, but also pragmatically. In any multi-period site the successive communities must have had some means of accommodating the remains of the past (even if only to ignore or destroy them) and looking at the way a living community examines these issues may be potentially useful for our understanding of these earlier inhabitants.[2]

I was able to explore these ideas further during the excavations at Çatalhöyük. I also looked at the conditions of the archaeological investigation itself, and at the potential effects on the local community. This turned out to be a fruitful area. Through several decades of self-criticism, anthropologists have become sensitive to the cultural and political context of their research. This movement is said by at least one writer today to have gone too far (cf. Barret 1996) but

it has been extremely fruitful in exposing the interconnections between the researcher and the object of study.

Here, I found that there is a clear contrast between archaeology and anthropology as it is practised in Anatolia. Though often remarkably distinguished, successive decades of archaeologists have hardly remarked on the actual practice of the discipline in seminars or in their publications. Yet informal conversation reveals that there are a host of constraints on the political, national and administrative setting of the research which are extremely likely to influence and channel the academic direction of the project. Indeed, it is possible that this side of archaeological research has not yet been explored in Anatolian studies simply because of the extent of the area it opens up to questioning and doubt. Issues such as the difference between collective and individual representations of academic knowledge, the way that material data are pressed into different frameworks of meaning in excavation reports, the composition of the excavation team, the political context of the funding awarded, the international, national (and perhaps even nationalistic) motives behind permission and encouragement to excavate, the way that the knowledge is disseminated from the site: all these and more become pressingly relevant.

To take only the question of the relationship between archaeology and the local community, where I was to concentrate part of my research. It might be reasonable to suppose that the presence of a large number of foreigners may have economic, social and ideological effects within a village setting, even if only because of the money that is provided to the workmen. Contemplating the great number of other archaeological sites being researched in Anatolia, some of them large and popular, it may also be assumed that the mass tourism attracted by them has potentially a profound effect on the surrounding communities (though the actual changes may be subtle and extremely difficult to describe accurately). However, whether difficult or not, there appears to have been no systematic investigation into these intrusions into the lives of communities all over Anatolia.[3]

Turning to Çatalhöyük itself it is clear that it has had a large impact in the outside world. Ayfer Bartu, as she explains in Chapter 8 of this volume, has been studying the way that the existing and renewed popularity of the site means that images from it are refracted and interpreted within the wider world of Konya, Istanbul, Europe and even areas as far afield as America. There are also today, in 1999, a flourishing number of web-sites which discuss the site. As the new excavation grows and publicity mounts, interest groups as disparate as self-avowed radical feminists, diplomats, journalists, and besuited international businessmen have visited the site, and as they develop longer-term links their presence may influence the village, again in ways difficult to predict.

Further, it also may be noted that the site is absorbed into different layers of the Turkish state at the national, local and village level in a complex and inter-connected way. For an example of this, we might take the fact that many villagers maintained to me that they learnt about the site from the mention it gains in elementary school text books rather than from the mound itself, even though it lies in their territory. The villagers may be mistaken in this recollection, or they may be minimizing their own ideas and privileging the 'true' knowledge that is found in school text books, but even this initial, seemingly simple, enquiry indicates the complications inherent within any attempt to relate the villagers' changing world to the archaeological endeavour.

Çatalhöyük and Küçükköy

These then were some of the preoccupations in mind when my research itself first began in 1995, in the company of a government representative from the Konya Museum. The villagers kindly furnished us with a house within the village, and we were able to begin our research immediately. In sharp contrast to the enormous outside interest, it was surprising at the outset of the research to be told that the effect of the site on the local village appears to have been rather small. The villagers' most frequent comment when asked how they had been affected by it was a laconic 'Hiç yok!' (Not at all!). Even when they expanded more fully on this comment, they did not identify any specific effects.

From the economic point of view this may be comprehended. The site was closed down after four intense seasons in the 1960s. It is often stated that only 4 per cent of the mound has been dug. It was not at all developed for touristic purposes. Before the re-opening occurred in 1993, the site was no more than a fenced mound with the occasional visitor. A watchman from the village has been employed there by the local museum. He told me that he bought a little house in Konya on the strength of his regular wages. This, and fencing the site so that it could no longer be used as pasture for sheep, appeared to be the only specific financial influences that the archaeology had left behind.

Ideologically, given the way that the certain finds from the site are frequently interpreted as being representative of a female-centred 'Goddess' religion it would seem that there is potential for disruption and clashes with the Islamic religion of the villagers. Yet, this was not at all apparent. Within the village itself, most of the people who knew Mellaart, or his wife well have passed away. Those who remain were rather young at the time, and often recall only that the finds were exhibited at first in the village school house, where they were seen and admired. The villagers occasionally mentioned that they had learnt about the site from their school text books, and they were aware that it is sometimes claimed to be an early agricultural community, but, it seemed, no more than this. It is always possible to doubt one's own fieldwork, to assume that in such a short time (my total stay in the village amounts as yet to a little more than three months) nothing may be assumed, yet it seems that on this occasion the villagers' comments may be accepted, though very cautiously, as being broadly indicative of the comparatively small influence that the site has had on their lives.

The situation did not appear immediately to be greatly changed by the site's re-opening. The mound of Çatalhöyük lies about half a mile from the village itself, which consists of about a hundred households. The houses are clustered in the centre of fields which they themselves own, and most of the people in the village are engaged in intensive agricultural production. When I first began to work at Küçükköy, I was surprised to find that their agricultural production appeared to provide a degree of economic plenty far greater than in many other parts of central Anatolia. The fields are unusually fertile, a return in wheat

Konya road

Karacıhöyüğü

village boundary

100 km

Çarpık Tekke
(5)

Kartaltömeği
(4)

Tekkehöyük
(10)

Salırhöyük
(1)

□ Süttekkesi

Kızılhöyüğü

village boundary

new cemetery

Ağadamı
(7, 8)

mosque   □old cemetery

village watchman's grave

to Karkın

Kapıdalı

Byzantine/Late Roman
remains known as 'Efeköy'

Little lights, 'the souls of
those past', see between
Kapıdalı, Çatalhöyük and
Agadamı.

Güllü's grave
(3)

mound used for
water-proof earth

Çatalhöyük

to Şeytan Höyügü
(9) ⟶

Figure 14.1. *Sketch map of Küçükköy environs.*

may be as high as forty to one, whilst melons and sugar beet are grown as cash-crops. Not all families are wealthy by any means, but most have twenty or thirty *dönüm* (a *dönüm* being the amount of land traditionally ploughed by one pair of oxen in a day), and many much more. Animal husbandry is also extensively practised, for dairy produce, meat and for market. Of course, people do occasionally incur losses, particularly with delicate and risky crops such as melon, but it appears that overall many of the villagers are substantially better off than the great majority of civil servants in the town. Thus, it is certain that the money paid to the village from the

site represents only a tiny proportion of its overall economy.

There may nevertheless be some highly specific effect. The villagers who have worked for the site are often those who have the least property. Just as did the first watchman, after a number of years (particularly if more than one person from the same family works there regularly) a family may succeed in moving up the village social hierarchy by buying a house or land. The money going into the community may be important in its selective influence on the village order, but much less so in its total economy (cf. Stirling 1974; 1993, introduction).

In the future, the situation is potentially greatly different. The success of the site's re-opening is clearly attracting important people to the area. The ubiquity of tourism has made it clear to many that money can be made. Here, however, though the villagers are aware of the potential, they seem to assume that the people who will benefit from its economic development lie outside the village. They appear to be prepared, for example, to sell property which might be turned into a hotel or restaurant rather than exploit it themselves. Thus, one rather beautiful old house changed hands in 1997, bought by a person from Istanbul who was otherwise not known by the village. Though the purpose it is to be put is not yet clear, it appears at the time of writing (Summer 1998) to be purchased on behalf of a feminist organization in order to provide a base from which to study Çatalhöyük.[4]

Whilst the motives for this resigned reaction will only become clearer as the situation unfolds, it is possible to note one probable reason. The site at Çatalhöyük is actually owned by the treasury, not by one individual. Complex regulations govern the development of archaeological sites and their surrounding area. Academically, this raises questions of land tenure and archaeological heritage about which I hope to publish an account in the future. From the village point of view, however, I think that first indications are that many people do not feel powerful enough to enter into a complicated procedural battle, one which would involve both the local authorities, and various different government departments.

Further, the site lies about 10 kilometres from the local town, Çumra, which is also the sub-province centre. In contrast to the villagers, the mayor there is quite clear that Çatalhöyük is a resource to be developed for the town's greater benefit, and he is making active steps to try to ensure that this comes about. Caught between so many interested parties, the villagers simply do not at present see where they might fit into the site's developmental pattern. Unless active steps are taken to embrace their interests, the villagers themselves may become aware of the impact, both socially and economically, of the site only when they have effectively been excluded from the decision-making process which will govern its future.

The village and the remains of the past

I was at first concerned lest the site's comparative lack of importance (at least until very recently) to the villagers be reflected in their general conception of the material remains of the past. However, this does not seem the case. Indeed, my preliminary conclusion is that there is a complex but subtle and tolerant interaction between the villagers and the heritage that fills their landscape. Mounds, for example, may have a number of different roles in the life of the community. They may act variously as field boundaries, modern-day cemeteries, picnic places at festival times, repositories of waterproof earth, of buried treasure, the souls of those past, or of the devil. Other remains may play an equally complex role, so that large classical-period carved stones are often used as buffers to protect the corners of houses, or as simple decoration, but they are also often used to mark auspicious, or holy places, or the graves of holy men.

Over the course of this initial fieldwork, we concentrated on mapping some of these various aspects of the heritage within the landscape (see Fig. 14.1). The archaeological interpretation of the mounds and other sites within the village territory is progressing through a survey by Dr Douglas Baird. We concentrated therefore on the way that they are incorporated into the village cosmology.

It would be wrong to attribute any one fixed quality to any one mound, site or artefact. The process of investing the landscape with meaning is not uniform. Some objects do appear to hold a fairly constant position in the collective representations of the village: most villagers I spoke to, for example, were sure that Küçükköy was descended from the late classical remains known as 'Efeköy', near to Çatalhöyük (cf. Shankland 1996). As well as this, however, people may interpret any one mound or stone in different ways, or attribute very different qualities to it. Overall it appears that the archaeological landscape acts as a number of mnemonic points for individual and collective representations, and it is not always certain which particular mound or artefact will spark a response, nor that it will always be the same response. The map therefore is a summation of the information that we have learnt, useful for the purposes of an overview, but it does not necessarily represent any one person's conception of the world.

Nor is it part of village life to periodize the past into distinct historical and pre-historic ages. They are aware of course of the fact of the Ottoman Empire, and that various different peoples have lived on the same soil that they now inhabit, indeed their memory of the Anatolian Greek population (*Rum*), who only departed in 1923 is particularly clear. Most people do not, however, put the longer time frames into chronological or successive order, or seek even to make a very sharp distinction between the possibility that a mound may be Muslim or non-Muslim. Pragmatically, the villagers regard the mounds as being there to exploit for treasure, for grazing, or for earth unless impeded by lay of the land, the government, by the souls (*ruh*) of those who used to inhabit it and are now buried there, or other supernatural sanction.

Protecting the heritage

Once a mound is declared an archaeological site, a border is defined around it and it is then forbidden by law to plough or build on the land within that border. Nevertheless, archaeological sites are explored by treasure seekers, though at Çatalhöyük this is prevented by the presence of a guard. They may even be flattened entirely, particularly if they are not well known, by farmers who wish to turn the area into arable land, leaving behind no more than a few pot sherds in a freshly turned field. The Ministry of Culture is aware of these problems, and does its best to impede the destruction, but it is in the perennial situation of being unable to act until the damage has actually occurred.

Most mounds have within them skeletal material which becomes exposed as they are dug for soil or for treasure. Sometimes odd bones lie on the surface, mixing with the pot sherds. It is widely held that these mortal remains are guarded by their respective souls (*ruh*). The souls are usually inactive though they may on occasion haunt a particular location. Once the bones are disturbed, however, the consequences can be severe: it is said that the person responsible may suffer from trauma, misfortune, illness, or even death. In spite of this prescription, if there is a particularly important reason, any bones in the location being dug may be simply ignored. However, the particular person who disturbed them may feel perturbed later. If they do so, it is held that re-burying the remains may redress the grievance.

The following accounts, collected in 1996 and 1997, illustrate these pre-occupations. They were gleaned in conversation from people in Küçükköy, and occasionally in the surrounding villages.

Account 1
A Küçükköy man told me that he took waterproof earth for his new roof from Salırhöyük and placed it on his new house, exposing a skeleton as he did so. However, during the night he felt that the owner of the bones was strangling him. He woke up in a terrible sweat, and returned to the spot the next morning with an *imam* (mosque prayer-leader). Together, they read a burial service and he was not disturbed again.

Account 2
Two melon watchmen decided to build a little hut to shelter in whilst they watched over the melon field. As a joke, they used two skulls from the mound to support the roof of the hut. They emerged the next morning pale from fright and lack of sleep, complaining that the skulls did not let them rest for a moment. They put back the skulls, and never again returned to that place.

Account 3
In Küçükköy, there used to be a custom (common in this part of central Anatolia) known as *kadın oynatma* whereby a *danseuse* would be paid to perform a dance for a number of males. One man, who was too powerful to be opposed by the other villagers moved one of these, Güllü, to the village, where she is said to have lived separately, organizing such evenings for him. After her death, she was buried at Çatalhöyük, where her grave lies still. After some time had passed, one night two men decided to steal her gold teeth. As they were doing so, her skeleton began to rattle and terrified, they ran back to the village. The next day, they replaced those things that they had taken, and reburied her remains.

Souls are not necessarily harmful. It is sometimes said that during the night, particularly on Friday, it is possible to see little lights, moving slightly faster than walking pace, moving from one mound to another, Çatalhöyük, Ağadamı and Kapıdalı being the most frequently mentioned. Villagers variously say that these are the souls of holy men (*ermiş kişi*) who are buried in the mounds and now visiting each other. They add occasionally that only people who are themselves holy can see them. These auspicious figures can also appear during the night, or in dreams, to give aid or help. This story was told me by a local woman:

Account 4
At Kartaltömeği, my uncle was threshing grain. During this season, we used to sleep at the threshing ground. Whilst they were sleeping, a well-dressed man, as if a philosopher (*filosof*), woke up my uncle and told him that he would take him to a very good place. They began to walk. They walked until the cock began to crow, at that point they arrived at

Şeytanhöyük. As the sound of the cocks came, he disappeared. My uncle went and told his wife about his experience, very excitedly. The next night, the man came to his side again, and said because you have told another about this, you have lost your chance of riches, I would have made you wealthy.

Provisionally, then, we can say that the mounds occupy a position in the village cosmology some way between what is usually regarded as the 'folklore' of the region (that is, the activities of supernatural, mythical or archetypical beings), and the Islamic faith. Indeed, the tales and the explanations that the villagers give of their reactions to the mounds are deeply imbued with religious motifs. Thus, while evil or misfortune may embody itself in different ways, it usually does so as Şeytan (Satan), and evil cins. The villagers explain both these entities by reference to the wider cosmology of Islam as it is explained in the Koran. Şeytan is regarded as being an angel who refused to obey the word of God when instructed to bow before humanity. Thrown out of heaven, in revenge he has vowed to repay humanity for his humiliation. Şeytan has absolute powers at his disposal and should be feared at all costs. Cins (usually translated into English as 'spirits') may be either auspicious (uğurlu) or inauspicious (uğursuz). Inauspicious cin also can be extremely dangerous and to be struck by one can result in the face becoming paralyzed. The evil cins strike most frequently when a person has failed to perform a ritual cleansing, aptes.

Account 5
One day, when I was a child, the side of my face tensed and froze. I went home and showed it to my mother, who immediately locked me inside the house, saying that I had been struck by cin for not performing the aptes properly. She forbad me to look at water or a mirror, saying that the devil would get me. The next day she took me to Çarpıktekke, 100 kilometres away. There, we said prayers and rubbed a shoe on the side of my face. It got better. It is said that the shoe belonged to one of two brothers who had once gone to winnow their grain there. Both were poor. As they shared the grain out, one said, 'My brother needs the grain, he has a large family', and tried to push more on to his side. The other brother said to himself likewise, 'My brother has little enough to get by on through the winter', and tried surreptitiously to give more to his brother. As they were thus trying to help each other, they were helped by God: the pile of grain grew and grew and became ample for both families. The spot is still holy

today, and this explains its efficacy in making my face heal.

The aptes can be broken by passing wind, sexual intercourse, by suffering a cut or abrasion, by going to the toilet. It is mandatory to have performed the aptes before prayer. Usually, on encountering the devil, some protection would be afforded by called the name of God *Bismillah* but it is a sin to invoke God or to worship in an impure state unless in the direst of circumstances, as the following account shows.

Account 6
A boy rode a tractor back to the village without having performed the cleansing (aptes) needed after sexual relations. As he was returning to the village, he saw that devils rode with him in the tractor. He was unable to say 'Bismillah!' because of his impure state. However, at last, in desperation he did so. The devils vanished. When he got back to the village his face was stony white and he was quite terrified.

Between Küçükköy, and Karkın, the largest local village, there is a long flat mound known as Ağadamı. The following two accounts are said to have taken place in its vicinity. In the first, there appears to be a general warning against interfering with the land, one which is heeded by the villager concerned. In the second, the devil appears to the men concerned, placing them in a very dangerous situation.

Account 7
A family who owned a field which lies next to Ağadamı sent the youngest son out to plough. He was just about to begin on a furrow adjoining the mound when he found himself unable to move the plough, because an old man was sitting on it. Frightened, he went home saying that he was sick. He went to bed, not wanting to admit his fear. They sent out his brother, and the same thing happened. He too came home and said that he was sick, unable to confess to what he had seen. Finally the father went out to try, angry with his sons at their laziness, and the same thing happened to him. He went home, and said to his sons: 'Now I understand why you refused to work.' He drew a line around the area which had caused the trouble, and said, 'Henceforth nobody will plough here!'.

Account 8
One day, a man from Küçükköy was returning from Karkın during the night past Ağadamı. In the dark-

172

ness, he saw a woman on the path who raised her hand to stop his cart and ask for a lift. The woman was very beautiful and attractive. The man took her into the cart and continued on his journey toward the village. As he did so, he glanced behind and saw that her legs were elongated, stretching out behind the cart, impeding its progress. When the man saw this, he realized that this was Satan (Şeytan), and drove the cart immediately into a field of green shoots. The devil said. 'You recognized me for what I am straight away, and for this you will get off lightly', and floated away.

The following account is told in much of the region, here it refers to a mound just upstream from Çatalhöyük, in the territory of Karkın village, and I give it as it was recited by one local man. Two words are clumsy to translate: the first is helva: used in spoken Turkish as a generic name for a sweet dish made from a variety of ingredients. The second is bestlemesiz (adj.), literally 'without a Bismillah', a state wherein the name of God has not been intoned, in this case it refers to the food and the tray that the devils handle.

Account 9
Just below Şeytanhöyük, and man named Seyit made a *han* (inn), then about half a day's journey from the village itself. Both mounted and foot travellers used to come to the inn. One day, a man who had a caravan train of camels was arriving from his travels, and tied up his camels at the inn. It was a cold winter's day, and he sat in the corner near the fire wrapping his cloak around himself to warm up. Then, the door opened and a group of travellers entered the inn.

The whole group were devils in human shape. One of them said, 'Let each one of us take something from his bag and make a *helva* from the *bestlemesiz* goods that we have collected.'

They put together flour, sugar, oil, walnuts, hazelnuts, raisins to make a *helva*, all without a *bestleme*, that they had taken from other people's houses. One of them had taken a tray which had been put away without a *bestleme*. They made the *helva* in this tray, and put it on the table.

The camel trainer was still sitting in the corner, and one of them invited him to come the table, claiming that it is shameful that he should not be invited to share the food. They argued whether it was right for a human being to join them, but eventually they agreed that it would be possible. Then, as the camel trainer was reaching out for the food, he said 'Bismillah!'

On his doing so, the *helva* turned to buffalo dung. The devils scattered themselves into the four corners of the inn. He looked at the dog, and it began to make wild movements as if it had become possessed. He shot it, thinking that the devil had taken the dog's soul.

When he finally arrived at his house, he showed the tray to the villagers for the years to come. Because of these events, and others like it, we changed the name of the mound to Devil's Mound. When coming to plough the fields with my father, we always heard the devils talking to each other.

Those who are closer to God

The villagers maintain that all people have a soul (*ruh*) which is everlasting and life (*can*) which ceases on their mortal death. All people are subject to Allah's commandments lest through their disobedience they suffer, either in this life or the next. However, it is also widely supposed that some individuals are closer to God than others. These individuals are known variously as possessing '*keramet*', sometimes translated as 'charisma' but perhaps in the Turkish context better understood as a sign from God, usually the ability to perform miracles. Such holy figures and their teachings may also be the founding figure of a brotherhood named after them, thus the famous 'Whirling Dervishes' who had their base in Konya are known as the 'Mevlevi' after their founder, the Mevlana.

Individuals may pass this ability through their patrilineage, or it may survive them after their death and benefit those who worship at their tomb. Throughout Anatolia there is a network of tombs, often known as *tekke*, some of which are appropriate to different illnesses or worldly afflictions, such as paralysis, malaria, failure in examinations, or childlessness. Some of these are accompanied by a saintly lineage living at the town of the tomb, in which case the leading members among them may be credited with miraculous healing powers.

The people of Küçükköy, as do the other villagers in the area, attend a number of these in different locations. The tomb of the Mevlâna in Konya is perhaps the most frequently visited. Çarpıktekke, famous for curing people after struck by *cins*, has been mentioned above. There is still another, Avdan, about 130 km away in the mountains, which is famous for the power to cure mental illness. During the summer, many coachloads of people visit each day, paying their respects to the lineage which lives at the tomb, and sacrificing at the tomb of the saint buried there. I visited in 1997, and there can be no doubt as to its flourishing.

Within the immediate area of Küçükköy, there are also areas where such holy people are supposed to be buried. The most important of these two are situated at mounds. A well, known as Süttekkesi, just at the border between the village named Tekkehöyük and Küçükköy was visited by women who were unable to lactate. There used also to be a small mound there, held to be the burial place of a holy figure. It is now ploughed over, but this action is widely held to have been the source of misfortune and death to the brothers who did so. It is now rarely visited, though people remember it being so until very recently.

Just past Süttekkesi lies the large mound of Tekkehöyük itself, after which the village is named. At its foot is an enclosed cemetery and the grave of a holy figure. People still go to pray there today, some leaving little pieces of cloth in order to be cured of illness, or the clothing of those who are ill. The founding story of that tomb is known to all around the area, and is as follows:

Account 10
A man was tilling his fields, when the advance guard of the Sultan's army was passing by. They said that they were hungry. The man replied that he had enough food to feed all the troops, and placed a cauldron of rice and meat that never ended in front of them. Seeing this amazing feat, the Sultan said, 'We have need of men like you, come with us'. The man acquiesced, saying that he would do so.

Much later, when the army was returning to Istanbul they stopped again at the man's fields, and he repeated the same feat. The Sultan called him to his side and asked, 'Why were you not there?' The man replied, 'Do you recall the warrior at your side, who passed you his scarf to tie up you wounded arm at the height of the battle? That was me'. On his saying this, the Sultan realized that he was right, he had indeed been there, and recognized that he was favoured by God (*Keramet sahibi*). In recognition of this, he awarded him all the fields between the village and the Mevlâna for him and his descendants in perpetuity. When he died, he was buried at the spot where the cauldron was cooked, and people still visit there today.

Variations in belief and practice

Looking at the village from above, and plotting those parts of the landscape which may be said to play a part in the religious life of the village against the visible archaeological remains would reveal a high degree of correlation. This correlation can be traced in various ways, but one of the most important links derives from the fact that many of these remains are associated with the bones of human beings. Many villagers empathize with these bones, extending to them qualities, particularly a protective soul, whether or not they are from a Muslim culture or they lived in a distant past. This leads on occasion to attributions of sanctity and equally, recourse to Islamic means to ward off the unwished consequences when a grave is disturbed.

I do not wish to oversimplify this point. Individual villagers will have taken up different positions within this overall ideological concatenation of cultures in death. Taking the example of the *danseuse*, in account 4 above, I do not know why she was buried at Çatalhöyük: it might have been coincidence, or it might have been that her past meant that they did not wish to bury her with other Muslims. It may have been because she was thought to have been of *Rum* ancestry: some of the villagers maintain that until the founding of the Republic there were *Rum* living in this area, and they occasionally associate them with Çatalhöyük. Certainly, the villagers affirm that she was a controversial figure, and it is likely that she remained so after death.

Ideological debates surrounding the potency of people after their death is one of the single most contested areas of the Islamic faith as it moves into the modern world. Summing up a much wider debate, Gellner (1981), in his work in North Africa stressed the fact that there is a point of fission within Islam between those who accept the possibility of individual sanctity and who are comfortable with the idea of saintly influence, whether alive or dead, and those who have recourse to a different style of worship, one more based on mosque and on the requirements of the daily religious practice. He argued that these latter people tend to be against the brotherhoods, and do not approve of worshipping at tombs or religious foundations based on the supposed sanctity of a particular figure.

At one level, Turkey appears to have been exempt from the drastic consequences that such doctrinal difference can provoke (Tapper 1991 gives an overview). In particular, the brotherhoods have not gone through the process of vilification at the hands of orthodoxy that Gellner might have supposed. However, there is an emerging political Islamic movement which, at its grass-roots level, has adopted a seemingly puritanical, mosque-based worship which is strikingly similar to that which he outlines. Something of this movement can be seen in Küçükköy and the surrounding villages, where the most popular political religious party, the *Refah Partisi* (in 1998, renamed the Virtue Party, *Fazilet Partisi*) are active. Its members, often supported by the mosque *imam*, actively discourage villagers from sacrificing at tombs and are contemptuous when they leave pieces of clothing in the hope that this may aid healing. In general, it seems that such politically active Islamic villagers are more aware of the periodization of the past than the villagers are as whole, and are much more concerned as to whether an archaeological site be Islamic, Christian or from one of the pre-historical periods.

This area of Islamic practice is also relevant to gender differences. There is less research published about women's worship than about men's and to be a male foreigner in a village is far from ideal a base from which to attempt to fill in the gaps. However, it is indisputably the case that all believing Sunni men with whom I spoke regard women as being in some way qualitatively different in the eyes of God (cf. Tapper & Tapper 1987). Not necessarily formally less significant as believers, in that women too may have a place in heaven, but they were adamant that special rules apply. Among these rules are the necessity for women to wear their headscarves in public, to avoid being seen by men who are praying (and in general to avoid mixing with men during any public collective ritual, whether sacred or not), to avoid the public places of worship in the village: that is, the mosque and the cemetery, and insistence on the utter impossibility of their becoming mosque *imam*.

Perhaps because of this exclusion, women are much more prominent in just those areas of the faith which the believing politically-active men regard as being unacceptable and far from central orthodoxy. Though men visit tombs, women do so even more so (cf. Nicolas 1972). They are also more likely to practice 'alternative' healing methods. There is a term *ocak*, for example which applies to a tree, stream or stone which appears to have special healing properties. When asked, villagers usually explain this quality by assuming that there is the grave of a holy person (*yatır*) beneath. However, the term *ocak* is also used to denote a person who has the personal quality of curing people's illness. *Ocaks* cater for specific ills, just as do the *tekkes*, such as the evil eye (*nazar*), a fractious child, or illness. *Ocaks* are usually women, and they may pass their power to their daughters'-in-law as they grow older. They themselves certainly would claim that they are part of the

Islamic faith: during the healing consultation they usually use a combination of prayer and object (often a bone or a stick) held over the afflicted part, but they are not publicly approved of by the Islamic movement that I identify above.

I use the word 'publicly' advisedly, because people can take up more than one position. One man who was working very hard to try to prevent women going to alternative healers or to the tombs of saints, said to me 'It's absurd that they should go to Tekkehöyük to cure malaria, ridiculous that holy power can go through a man after he is dead'. Then he paused, and said in a hopeful manner, 'They do say, though, that the saint chucks stones at people if they pass his tomb when they are drunk!'.

In spite of any private weaknesses one small consequence of this public disapproval is already discernible. Within Anatolian Islam, there is an annual festival *Hidrellez*, which takes place in the spring. During the night before the festival, it is supposed that a holy figure, *Hızır*, sometimes referred to by folklorists as 'green man' may appear in the guise of a beggar requesting alms (cf. Walker & Uysal 1966). If his wish is granted, then it is said that the household will enjoy plenty. If ignored, they may suffer terrible misfortune. It has long been noted that the day itself is the occasion for excursions to tombs, and for picnics. At Küçükköy, I was told that Çatalhöyük used itself to be the site of such excursions, where women alone would go, taking their children and picnicking to celebrate the spring. Now Çatalhöyük is cordoned off. However, the villagers have not sought a direct replacement. Rather, those families who are not politically religious go together to a nearby municipal picnic spot, where though men and women may sit apart they are still within sight of one another, whilst other more religious families do not go. Men from these latter families are said to deplore the interaction between the sexes that might result and the potential jollity of the occasion. Thus what was once a women's preserve through exploiting an alternative 'folk' Islam within the village community as a whole has now become the object of scepticism and disapproval and led to a polarization of gender practices.

The enormous complexities of social change caution against making any generalization. However, on the basis of the research so far, I think that it is likely that this process of codification, of increasing orthodoxy will continue. The quiet, confident belief which seems characteristic of the area suggests that the religious differences will be unlikely to develop into a sharp confrontation, in spite of the split which appears to have emerged at the *Hidrellez*. Rather, it is likely that there will be gradual change whereby the unorthodox aspects of the faith will decline. Certainly they will become less obvious. As this shift occurs, there is a possibility that the mounds will become increasingly viewed as archaeological sites, with a distinct place in the past, and perhaps excluded from the incorporation into the sacred that the lack of periodization currently permits. They may then become part of an overall, national debate as to the place of prehistoric archaeology in a predominantly Islamic nation. At this point indeed, village conflicts and debates may become indistinguishable from wider issues of national policy. Both ideologically and economically, Çatalhöyük, for from being unimportant in the lives of the villagers, may then become extremely significant indeed.

Acknowledgements

This research has been funded by the British Institute of Archaeology at Ankara, by the Pantyfedwyn Fund, University of Wales, Lampeter, and by the Anthropology Unit, University of Wales, Lampeter. I am extremely grateful for their support. Permission to research was granted by the Directorate-General of Antiquities and Museums, Ankara, to whom I would also like to express my thanks. I was fortunate indeed to be helped in 1996 by Mr Lütfi Önel, and in 1996 and 1997 by Mr Nurettin Özkan. I would like to extend my deepest thanks to them both. I am grateful to Professor Ahmet Edip Uysal, himself a master of folkloric researches in Anatolia for sharing so generously the fruits of his research with me and welcoming me so splendidly in 1986, right at the beginning of my research. I am also grateful to David Barchard, Ian Hodder, Stephen Mitchell and Paul Stirling for comments on earlier drafts of this article.

Notes

1. This paper is a slightly revised version of a paper which appeared in Gazin-Schwartz, A. & C. Holtrop (eds.), 1999. *Archaeology and Folklore*. London: Routledge. Permission to reprint is gratefully acknowledged.

2. I am indebted to Douglas Baird for most helpful discussions of the issues involved in this area.
3. This is beginning to change. (See Meskell 1998.)
4. During the winter of 1998, this house was burnt to the ground for reasons which are not yet clear.

References

Barret, S., 1996. *Anthropology: a Student's Guide to Theory and Method*. Toronto: University of Toronto Press.
Gellner, E., 1981. *Muslim Society*. Cambridge: Cambridge University Press.
Hasluck, F., 1929. *Christianity and Islam among the Sultans*, 2 volumes. Oxford: Clarendon.
Hodder, I. (ed.), 1996. *On the Surface: Çatalhöyük 1993–95*. (McDonald Institute Monographs.) Cambridge: McDonald Institute for Archaeological Research; London: British Institute for Archaeology at Ankara.
Hodder, I., 1997. 'Always momentary, fluid and flexible': towards a reflexive excavation methodology. *Antiquity* 71(273), 691–700.
Meskell, L. (ed.), 1998. *Archaeology Under Fire: Nationalism, Politics and Heritage in the Eastern Mediterranean and Middle East*. London: Routledge.
Nicolas, M., 1972. *Croyances et Practiques populaires turques concernant les naissances (région de Bergama)*. Paris: Publications orientalistes de France.
Shankland, D., 1993. Diverse paths of change: Alevi and Sunni in rural Turkey, in Stirling (ed.), 46–64.
Shankland, D., 1996. The anthropology of an archaeological presence, in Hodder (ed.), 349–57.
Shankland, D., forthcoming. Absorbing the rural or Gellner and the study of Anatolia. *Middle East Studies*.
Stirling, P., 1965. *Turkish Village*. London: Weidenfeld & Nicholson.
Stirling, P., 1974. Cause, knowledge and change: Turkish village revisited', in *Choice and Change: Essays in Honour of Lucy Mair*, ed. J. David. London: Athlone, 191–229.
Stirling, P. (ed.), 1993. *Culture and the Economy: Changes in Turkish Villages*. Huntingdon: The Eothen Press.
Tapper, N. & R. Tapper, 1987. The birth of the Prophet: ritual and gender in Turkish Islam. *Man* 22, 69–92.
Tapper, R. (ed.), 1991. *Religion in Modern Turkey*. London: Taurus.
Van Bruinessan, M., 1992. *Agha, Shaikh, and State*. London: Z books.
Walker, W. & A. Uysal, 1966. *Tales Alive in Turkey*. Cambridge (MA): Harvard University Press.

Chapter 15

Ethnoarchaeology: Studies in Local Villages Aimed at Understanding Aspects of the Neolithic Site

Wendy Matthews, Christine Hastorf & Begumşen Ergenekon

with contributions from Aylan Erkal, Nurcan Yalman, Meltem Ağcabay, Banu Aydınoğlu, Ayfer Bartu, Adnan Baysal, Başak Boz, William Middleton, Julie Near, Arlene Rosen & Mirjana Stevanovic

In this chapter we consider why and how we are conducting ethnoarchaeology by providing a range of examples to illustrate how the rich knowledge of the local villagers is helping our understanding of landscape, settlement and buildings of the complex Neolithic site of Çatalhöyük.

Many of us conducting ethnoarchaeological research are archaeologists with specific sets of questions that arise in relation to issues at Çatalhöyük. Most of the methodologies applied during this research are archaeological, and include collecting observations and samples that can be compared to archaeological information. Our aim is to widen windows of interpretation and understanding of Çatalhöyük. In many ways, much of the ethnoarchaeological work is envisioned as widening the priority tours out into the villages, including discussion and interaction both with the others on the project as well as with the local villagers. We are each studying different materials, their composition, place and meaning, whilst tracing them in the landscape, within settlements as well as in and around buildings. This of course is the goal of the archaeological project and so too it is for the ethnoarchaeological research. Knowledge of a life surrounded by local materials, architecture and landscape, is enabling a much richer understanding of potential inter-connectedness between different materials and activities, as well as human experiences. Some reflexivity is generated by the interdisciplinary nature of the ethnoarchaeological research itself but we each hope to take this a step further and actively include regular interaction between the different disciplines. Study of both occupied and abandoned buildings is providing time depth and a diachronic perspective to research. Additionally, besides going out into the villages surrounding the site, the project members are also interested in bringing the site to the villagers. Chapter 8 in this volume by Ayfer Bartu discusses some of the ways in which the knowledge of the villagers are being represented in the visitor centre and is empowering their own envisioning of the past.

This chapter has been written through discussions held during the 1998 field season and by wide-ranging contributions on email by current members of the project who have been involved in ethnoarchaeological research (see Table 15.1 for the list of participants).

Why and how are we doing ethnoarchaeology?

When you travel to the site today, you pass through a series of communities and cannot help but observe the daily activities and movements of the residents. People are harvesting vegetables, herding sheep, and drying bulgar wheat. As archaeologists we begin to imagine versions of these activities at the site. How different was it 9000 years ago? Would they have tried to keep up kitchen gardens near to their congested homes on the tell at Çatalhöyük? Would kin have lived next door to each other as they often do now? Why and how often did they wash their walls with white clay? Such merging of two temporal worlds with our experiences make most participants at the site eager to move back and forth between the local villages and the excavations. This is made all the more pressing when learning of the movement of many villagers into towns and cities, and the rapid environmental changes in the Konya basin.

An important aspect to our research program is the ever-present knowledge that society and rural activities are rapidly changing. This is most keenly seen with the recent construction of an elaborate above-ground irrigation system that is allowing for a very different form of agriculture in the Konya Plain. Introduction of a range of increased drainage facilities, prior to irrigation, has resulted in a rapid and radical drop in the water table, and changing environment associated with increased desiccation (Roberts pers. comm.). The old marshes that surrounded the lake remnants are virtually gone and the resources, as well as the microclimates, of these zones are dwindling. As production links more and more into world markets, the style of life and the associated familial structures of the culture are shifting. Ethnoarchaeological research is particularly urgent given these rapid changes in lifestyle and changing knowledge and experience.

While our aims in ethnoarchaeology are in part the same as previous scholars', to gain a sense of the dynamics of the actions of the past, as well as the structuring and uses of the edifices that were built and lived in (Kent 1990; Donley 1982; Hayden & Cannon 1984; Hodder 1982), all of us have an interest in trying to get closer to some of the meanings and values of the past activities we are uncovering (Therkorn 1987; Kus 1983). These aims include understanding aspects of the physical properties of materials which would have been present in the archaeological record; possible uses and signification which may be attached to them; the participants, and motivations of individuals involved in past actions and decisions; and natural and human time-scales. Ethnoarchaeological observations and dialogue are also enabling study of discursive and non-discursive meanings, and conscious and unconscious practices.

These aims are driven both by questions arising from the site and from problems and developments within individual disciplines themselves, especially in establishing the potential nature of correlation between dynamic contexts and residual traces, whether in relation to studies of phytoliths, chemical traces on floors, or dental microwear (Table 15.2). The ethnoarchaeological research in turn is encouraging us to ask new questions of the site. So, each group of scholars is involved in its own hermeneutic spiral of knowledge as well as the amplification of each of these approaches to the past,

interacting together between the different research groups.

Equally important is our attempt to encourage an increased level of interaction that has become part of the project more generally. No-one returns to Çatalhöyük from a day outside in a village without being badgered to describe much of what was seen and experienced. Everyone must show and tell the resonances that are brought to bear to the site at the weekly ethnoarchaeology meeting. With all of this ongoing and conscious work in the present, no-one is looking for historical continuity, rather there is a sense of parallel lives in thinking simultaneously about the Neolithic and the present. We are not building new hypotheses about the past, we are trying to bring two worlds together simultaneously in our minds in order to increase knowledge relating to material remains, socio-cultural and micro-environmental context, human experience, and most important, a sense of meaning.

There are exciting new potentials for ethnoarchaeological analyses given recent holistic approaches to the study of dwellings (Carsten & Hugh-Jones 1995), and developments in the theoretical understanding of the nature of human behaviour and concepts of space (Bourdieu 1977; Horne 1994; Moore 1986; Wilson 1988) and the influence of both personal and collective experiences in interpretations of the past (Hodder 1997).

Horne suggests that, despite the fact that archaeology is expensive and time-consuming, the addition of ethnoarchaeology can assist in setting questions that are answerable and that are best answered in an archaeological context (Horne 1994, 197). For many of us, our ethnoarchaeological research is directed at accessing new research questions that will open up the project of studying the past. These new understandings of the Neolithic at the site of Çatalhöyük will also increase our understanding of human behaviour more generally, as well as address more abstract and theoretical questions and considerations.

Who is helping create this methodology?

The individuals conducting ethnoarchaeological research at Çatalhöyük are from a diverse range of sub-disciplines. As evident in the discussion below, however, there are considerable interconnections between each of our fields of study and scales of analysis, and in the implications of our observations. The current group of individuals conducting ethnoarchaeological research includes those who are study-

Table 15.1. *Researchers currently contributing to ethnoarchaeology at Çatalhöyük.*

Researcher	Institution	Research area
Begumşen Ergenekon	Middle East Technical University, Departments of Archaeometry and Modern Languages	Sociology, Social Anthropology, Ethnoarchaeology
Mirjana Stevanovic	University of California, Berkeley, Department of Anthropology Istanbul University, School of Architecture	Architecture
Frank Matero, Lindsey Falck, Ray Beauvin, Evan Kuppelsen, Kent Seversen, Kathy Myers	University of Pennsylvania, Department of Architectural Conservation, Smithsonian Institution	Architecture
Nurcan Yalman	Istanbul University, Prehistory Section	Architecture, settlement organization and development
Wendy Matthews	University of Cambridge, Department of Archaeology	Micro-stratigraphy and micromorphology
William Middleton	University of Wisconsin, Department of Anthropology	Chemical analyses, including ICP-AES
Christine Hastorf, Julie Near	University of California, Berkeley Department of Anthropology	Ethnobotany
Meltem Ağcabay	Çukurova University, Department of Biology	Ethnobotany
Arlene Rosen	University College London, Institute of Archaeology	Ethnobotany, including phytoliths
Aylan Erkal	Middle East Technical University, Department of Archaeometry	Ethnobotany
Michele Wollstonecroft, Eleni Asouti	University College London, Institute of Archaeology	Ethnobotany
Başak Boz	Çatalhöyük Research Project with The Natural History Museum, London	Tooth micro-wear
Theya Molleson	The Natural History Museum, London	Posture and movement
Louise Martin	University College London, Institute of Archaeology	Faunal remains
Banu Aydınoğlu	Istanbul University, Prehistory Section	Faunal remains
Adnan Baysal	Çatalhöyük ResearchProject	Ground stone
Sonya Suponcii	University of California, Berkeley, Department of Anthropology	Uses of clay, clay minerology, combustion
Ayfer Bartu	Koç University, Istanbul, Faculty of Sciences - Humanities and Letters	Anthropology

ing specific archaeological materials such as architecture, plant remains, animal bone and sediments, as well as those who are investigating settlement development and kinship relations. Table 15.1 presents the scholars who were interested in these aspects of research at the site in 1998.

All participants in the Çatalhöyük project however, are continually absorbing ethnoarchaeological observations, given the location of the site in the heart of the Konya Plain. These observations are being incor-

porated into interpretations on site whether consciously and unconsciously, and are being translated onto drawing boards (Nessa Leibhammer, Chapter 11, and John Swogger, Chapter 12, this volume). There should be additional ethnoarchaeological study opportunities for all members of the project.

Each member of the Çatalhöyük project tends to be engaged in specific and often time-consuming skills that have required considerable training investment. Everyone, however, is interested in the larger picture of life in and around the site during the Neolithic, and how individual studies and interpretations relate to those focused on other materials. Integration of archaeological, palaeoecological and ethnoarchaeological research is enabling study of diverse material remains in a range of contexts within settlements and landscapes. These integrated and contextual approaches are enabling study of transmutations of material forms and meanings, which can be associated with changes in contexts and natural and human agencies (see also Conolly Chapter 4, this volume).

With our new age of electronic interaction, communication between researchers will grow. The National Science Foundation even has a new grant category expressly for interactive electronic research. The methodological challenges we face are keeping up the intensity, regularity, and range of interaction and communication. From our vantage point in the 1990s, we can barely envision what archaeological communication and therefore methodology will look like in twenty years. It will surely mean more communication while people are not on site. We at Çatalhöyük are only at the beginning of this development. Will this make the past more realistic and problemitized or more distant? Such diverse, multiple and interweaving ethnoarchaeological projects hope to begin this trend but only time will tell as to their success and direction.

Where are we doing ethnoarchaeological research?

The current focus of ethnoarchaeological research is on modern local villages within the Konya basin and surrounding mountains. Villages currently being investigated include: Küçükköy (plain), and Turkmencamili (steppe environment), Hamidiye (at the edge of the old lake of Suğla), Adakale (at the edge of the old lake of Hotamış), Emirler (by Mt Karadağ), Binbirkilise (on Mt Karadağ).

Potential advantages and problems in conducting ethnoarchaeology in regions close to archaeological sites have been discussed by Ascher (1961). Although oral histories in some areas may resemble archaeological findings, as in surface survey findings at the more recent first-millennium BC site of Kerkenes Dağ in northern Turkey, and statements recorded in Şahmuratlı (Yozgat) (Ergenekon 1996; 1999; in press), we recognize that there may be little or no historical continuity between the past and the present, especially given the movement of peoples in the area and the depth of time we are dealing with

(Yalman pers. comm.).

We are also aware that the Neolithic landscape differed in a range of respects from the present, on the basis of data from palaeoecological research. The Neolithic land surface currently lies buried below 2–3 metres of alluvium in the vicinity of Çatalhöyük (Roberts *et al.* 1996). Current evidence suggests the environment may have been wetter, and that the Neolithic settlement was located next to an active branch of the Çarşamba river, surrounded by backswamp to the south.

Nevertheless, many of the features of the landscape and associated resource use that have been detected in the archaeological remains are currently present in the Konya plain and surrounding hills, including floral and faunal species, soils, obsidian and ground stone materials, for example. Even buried sediments that were present and used in the Neolithic such as Pleistocene soft lime (*ak toprak*), are currently accessible to modern villagers from the edges of deep cuts for canals, ditches or pits, and are used in the preparation of plasters (Matthews *et al.* 1996). These similarities are enabling study of ancient and modern variation in the uses and meanings of resources, behaviour and phenomenology of landscape (Hastorf & Johannessen 1991). In particular the study of plant use is moved ahead greatly by the recently completed ethnoarchaeological dissertation by Ertuğ-Yaraş in the region of the Aceramic Neolithic site of Aşıklı Höyük (1997). Local villagers close to Çatalhöyük possess a wealth of knowledge of potential uses and handling of the wild plants and their meanings (Bartu Chapter 8, this volume). We are discovering wonderful insights about some deposits, like the ubiquitous *Celtis* endocarps. We have learnt that this taxon is widely used as a sweetener in a range of foods, but that it has to be cooked to be consumed. Its placement throughout the site now makes much more sense to us. With this knowledge in mind we can go back and reinterpret the different deposits especially surrounding hearths and in middens.

A range of ethnoarchaeological studies are focusing on Küçükköy, the village next to Çatalhöyük. This village is located in an area of alluvial deposition from the Çarşamba river and has diverse sediments, some of which, as we have seen, were present in the Neolithic. The close proximity of the village to Çatalhöyük will help with the logistics of ethnoarchaeological visits, especially for those who are also closely involved with excavation and studies of archaeological materials.

Ethnoarchaeological and geological research on

ground stone source materials has been more wide-ranging, and has included a number of villages along the Çarşamba river, and the Karadağ mountain region.

Ethnoarchaeological studies will encompass other villages. These will include villages with flat-roofed houses which have entrances through the roof, and villages with houses clustered in discrete blocks or complexes, elements of which were present in Neolithic settlement at Çatalhöyük. We are considering information from settlements in other regions of the world, including those with flat-roofed houses with elaborate symbolism such as in the American Southwest.

Aspects of the methodology

Ethnoarchaeological research at Çatalhöyük, as in many earlier projects, is multidisciplinary (Aurenche *et al.* 1997; Braidwood & Howe 1960; Ertuğ-Yaraş 1997; French 1973). Many of the methodologies that are applied during ethnoarchaeological research include archaeological methods and theories of observation and similar sampling strategies. This is enabling comparison of material traits and associations, and the multiplicity and multidimensionality of material form, context and meaning in both the past and present. Whilst one class of studies aims to learn more of the physical properties of materials, the other major interest is on dynamic spatial, temporal and socio-cultural contexts and meanings associated with these materials.

We hope that our regular interdisciplinary discussions during the field season will continue to generate reflexivity. Weekly discussion meetings are held in order to discuss both the results of the previous week's research by each individual and plans for the forthcoming week on site. These meetings have a range of practical and academic benefits. They enable maximization of knowledge concerning villages and communities in the Konya basin and surrounding mountains, and of seasonal events such as the imminent construction of a new house, or gathering of wild plant foods for example, which are of interest to several members of the group. Logistics and transport arrangements are also discussed and aided by each individual, adding to a daily time-table diary of their destination and subject of study. The weekly meetings play a role similar to that of the Priority and Space tours discussed elsewhere in this volume by Hodder (Chapter 1).

Some of the methods employed in the ethnoarchaeological research projects are outlined below:

1. Dialogues are transcribed into written texts, and occasionally with permission, recorded by audio and video film. Many of those carrying out ethnoarchaeological research are Turkish, or are learning Turkish.

2. Photographs are taken at widely varying scales of analytical focus. The focus ranges from aerial photographs taken from hot air balloon in order to study organic settlement development and uses of space, to architectural details at the centimeter scale. Microscopic observations and photographs and SEM images increase analytical resolution still further. These studies include identification of phytolith and ethnobotanical remains, surface-wear on grindstones, impressions of tooth micro-wear, and micromorphology of modern floor deposits and animal stables/pens and experimental mud bricks in thin section.

3. Plans are being drawn of settlement layout, buildings, features, different surface textures, and activity residue distributions. As well as recording and sampling material remains, we are recording associated features, their artefacts and their meanings that the inhabitants relay about the activities associated with them.

4. Observations are systematically recorded of trace wear on all materials, including architectural remains and activity surfaces. In the study of activities, the biological anthropology team are curious about individual posture, movements and how individuals take part in activities.

5. Architectural and spatial studies will include measurements of the micro-environment, including light, colour, temperature, and moisture or humidity, in addition to materials used in construction.

6. Samples are being analyzed of architectural materials, deposits, plant and bone remains from abandoned houses, and where permissible and discrete in size and location, within occupied houses and compounds.

7. Habitats, collection, storage, preparation, seasonality and meanings of resources are being plotted and recorded, within landscape, settlements and buildings, as well as experiences and phenomenology of these contexts.

Analysis of diachronic change and taphonomic processes is made possible by study of both occupied and abandoned houses for which there are people who remember the household use-life.

Experimental research is a component of a range of projects, including experimental mud-brick manufacture and construction of a building at the edge of

Table 15.2. *Some of the multiscalar research aims in ethnoarchaeological studies at Çatalhöyük and current focuses.*

Analysis	Landscape	Settlement	Buildings
Architecture	Source materials	Organic development and life cycles of different buildings and areas of settlement	1) Building technology, abandonment, and renewal 2) Experimental construction 3) Uses of space within buildings and on rooftops
Microstratigraphy and micromorphology	1) Sources of architectural materials and meaning in a phenomenology of landscape 2) Impact of agriculture and field management on depositional sequences 3) Natural time-scales and interconnectedness of human activities	1) Demarcation and meaning of different spaces, and variation in nature and meaning of surface textures and accumulated deposits 2) Sociocultural, spatial and chronological relationships between households 3) Site formation processes	1) Building technology, abandonment, and renewal 2) Spatial and ideational conventions and boundaries within buildings, and variation in nature and meaning of associated surface textures and accumulated deposits 3) Interconnectedness of and changes in activities and realms of behaviour 4) Spatial ekistics, movement and micro-environment
Chemical analyses	1) Source materials 2) Characterization of natural deposits and taphonomic processes 3) Characterization of impact of activities in villages with different natural substrates	Characterizations of depositional sequences in different houses to assess effects of differences relating to variations in: 1) function/specialization 2) building materials 3) life history of building 4) sociocultural context	1) Correspondence between activities and chemical residues, and variation between specialized/non-specialized uses of space 2) Organization and uses of space 3) Impact of changes in spatial organization on formation of chemical residues
Archaeobotany	1) Resource use in the major zones of the region 2) Locations of wild species and of fields 3) Kitchen garden makeup and their relationship to the household 4) Variation of plant use between communities, linked to local microenvironments. 5) Seasonality of habitat use	1) Community access and ownership of wild resources 2) Spatial distributions of construction material 3) Variation in food procurement and use across households 4) Use of indoor and outdoor space, including extra household spaces (roofs) 5) Tools used in harvesting and processing food	1) Placement of activities that include plant use 2) Seasonality of plant use 3) Storage of wild and domestic plants 4) Food preparation, hearth use, the material remains deposited from these 5) The meanings of foods, e.g. women's vs men's foods, foods linked to certain activities, feasts 6) Midden areas and their composition

the site (Stevanovic 1997; 1999); uses of ground stone; tooth micro-wear analyses and different diets (Teaford & Lytle 1996; King 1997; Boz 1998). A project is planned to simulate taphonomy of a range of materials. One aspect will include the processing and cooking of plant taxa to learn of the taphonomic variation we are encountering on the site of both the plants themselves as well as the possible utensils. Both ethnoarchaeological and experimental observations should provide valuable resources for testing hypothesis concerning archaeological data (Tringham 1978), and thus are included as an essential part of the greater program at the site. The nuances and complexities of social life mapped onto material objects, their conditions and distributions, are unveiled through the discussions and data collection.

Multiscalar and multi-disciplinary studies

Ethnoarchaeology is enabling study of aspects of the nature, sequence and interconnectedness of activities within households, settlements and landscapes. Some of the multiscalar research elements and aims in ethnoarchaeological studies at Çatalhöyük are summarized in Table 15.2. These projects include consideration of different but interconnected spatial scales, including landscape, settlement and within buildings and other spaces, like middens, as in other ethnoarchaeological research (Watson 1979; Kramer 1982; Horne 1994). In the remaining part of this chapter we would like to mention some of the findings from initial research at each of these scales of inquiry. These findings are preliminary, as the first concerted programme of research only began in 1998.

Table 15.2. *(cont.).*

Analysis	Landscape	Settlement	Buildings
Phytoliths	1) Phytoliths in dung: are these indicative of a) regions or microenvironments where herds are grazing, and b) fodder plants 2) Effects of dry farming, irrigation, and swampland cultivation on cereal phytoliths		1) Hearth ash from different fuel types, and hearth purposes 2) Abandoned building floors: study zones of deposition from roofing material down to occupation remains 3) Courtyard floors: what is the correlation between plant use and phytolith residues on floors?
Faunal remains	1) Wild and domestic species in mountain and plain habitats 2) Socio-cultural animal management in villages in different ecological zones	1) Socio-cultural variation in animal related traditions within settlement 2) Taphonomy	1) Architecture and equipment associated with animals in modern villages 2) Depositional sequences associated with different animals and management
Dental microwear	1) Plant habitat, particularly fruits, nuts and tubers 2) Collection groups and timing	Variation in diet of households from different socio-cultural contexts	1) Food storage, preparation and cooking 2) Ingestion and impact on dental micro-wear
Ground stone	1) Source material locations and geology 2) Procurement, trade and interconnectedness with other activities	Variation in household ground stone usage	1) Food preparation: time management, calorific values, tool type and size in relation to household population 2) Gender 3) Life history of tools
Human bone	Repeated activity postures	Variation between households on repeated activity postures	Effects of different repeated activities on posture

Landscape

Palaeoecological excavation of large trenches and coring around the site is enabling multidisciplinary study of the buried Neolithic landscape surrounding Çatalhöyük and detection of traces of a range of human activities, including impact of early agriculture and the nature of land and water management (Roberts *et al.* 1996; Merrick *et al.* 1997). Many excavation and laboratory staff working on site are studying materials from this palaeoecological research (Matthews *et al.* Chapter 3, this volume). Some of these research objectives include study of buried land surfaces, human plant and animal relationships, and uses of sediments for construction and replastering.

A range of questions explored in both this palaeoecological research and the parallel ethnoarchaeological studies relate to phenomenology and meaning of landscape and resources (Bender 1993; Edmonds 1999; Thomas 1996; Tilley 1994). What do different resources such as stone, sediments and plants mean in the construction and interpretation of the landscape? In what type of natural or human habitats do these resources occur? What is the na-

ture of the physical, conceptual and social boundaries between these habitats? Are the materials wild or domesticated or conceived of in other ways? Do they belong to anyone/everyone? When and how can they be obtained, stored and used? How do people, animals and materials move through the landscape? What symbolic meanings are attached to these materials? Do these meanings change with modification or translocation of these materials to different environmental and sociocultural contexts? What are the effects of ecological and socio-cultural changes?

Archaeological and ethnoarchaeological research therefore is concentrating on identifying potential habitats of different resources or materials and the agencies and contexts of their selection, procurement, transformation, uses and meanings; potential inter-relationships of materials, people and related activities; and natural and human seasonal or socio-cultural time-scales.

Marsh micro-zones

A range of archaeobotanical and micromorphological studies are examining marsh microzones, in order to study the distribution, collecting, processing and use of tubers, reeds, and backswamp sediments, remains of which have all been identified in the Neolithic settlement. This research is particularly urgent given the current drying-up of many of the extant small lakes within the Konya Plain, owing to the falling water table. It is also enabling study of the impact of ecological change in a range of villages. Potentially similar ecological changes were taking place during the Neolithic, associated with shrinking of the once extensive Pleistocene lakes in the Konya Basin (Roberts *et al.* 1996).

Mountain micro-zones

Ethnoarchaeological research is contributing to identifications of the probable mountainous origins of a range of materials used in the Neolithic, in collaboration with archaeological and palaeoecological investigations (Roberts *et al.* 1996; Merrick *et al.* 1997; Matthews *et al.* Chapter 3, this volume). The history and memory of seasonal cycles that residents would have had for these distant microzones are particulary intriguing. Resources include autumnal fruit from the hackberry (*Celtis*), timbers and beams of juniper wood (*Juniperus* sp.), red ochre pigments, obsidian, stone, pig, and red deer. A range of very interesting information is emerging about this habitat, and the collection, preparation, and uses of resources from this distant area by the people of Çatalhöyük. Ethnoarchaeology and phytogeography are contributing to a sense of the plant ecology of these important species. It is evident that hackberry trees, for example, prefer, and currently occur on, well-drained soils in a fairly restricted environment which includes the rocky hillsides well away from and above the site, and are unlikely to have grown on the wetter, less well-drained soils around the site and therefore had to have been carried in (Hillman pers. comm.).

Juniper trees also prefer well-drained soils. Although large juniper timbers from 700 year-old trees have been found as structural members in a range of buildings at Çatalhöyük (Mellaart 1967; Newton 1996), smaller fragments of juniper wood occur only sporadically in micromorphological and charred plant remains samples from deposits throughout the settlement. This scarcity of smaller fragments of juniper suggests that juniper may have been brought to the site as finished logs, perhaps floated down on the Çarşamba river (Newton 1996; Matthews & Ergenekon 1998; Asouti pers. comm.). Ethnoarchaeological dialogues in several villages have revealed that juniper trees currently grow in the mountains to the west of the site, and traditionally used to be

transported from the Bozkır mountains at the headwaters of the Çarşamba River as trimmed timbers on the water down stream to the Konya Plain. This information confirms at least the feasibility of our archaeological hypothesis.

Ethnoarchaeological studies of ground stone have included collaborative research with Vedat Toprak and Asuman Türkemenoğlu, from the Geology Department, Middle East Technical University (METU), in search of potential sources of stones. The quantities of different stones were mapped along the course of the Çarşamba River in order to investigate the range of rocks carried down the river onto the alluvial plain. A range of researchers is also studying sources of sediment and plants used in architectural materials.

Geologists from METU are also mapping specific sources of red ochre, some of which are known to occur in the Seydişehir region (Vedat Toprak pers. comm.). Other possible mountain resources used at Çatalhöyük include red deer, bear, boar, certain herbs, and obsidian. Current ethnoarchaeological research is investigating a range of possible similar seasons and interconnectedness of past activities. Faunal analysts are keen to study the nature, habitat, and consumption patterns of wild and domestic species in different ecological zones. The phytolith analyst, Arlene Miller Rosen, plans to sample modern sheep/goat and cow dung to see if the phytoliths contained therein are indicative of the general regions or microenvironments where herds are grazing, or the fodder plants they are eating. Phytoliths from cereals growing in local fields will also be sampled for comparison to data previously collected from the Levant on irrigation (or swampland) cultivation and dry-farming indicators (Rosen & Weiner 1994). Identification of these potential sources has important implications for interpretation of archaeological remains.

Settlement

Studies of old excavation sections at the south of the site, and current excavations in a range of different areas are revealing complex sets of data on abandonment and rebuilding of structures, and settlement development (Matthews & Farid 1996; Hodder 1997; 1999).

Ethnoarchaeological research on settlement growth and organic development is identifying a range of dynamic social and physical factors that may influence settlement layout and abandonment or renewal of structures. A whole sector of one village was relocated to more raised ground owing to ground water-table problems in the mid 1970s. In this same village new buildings for married sons are preferably located within existing family compounds where tasks in the kitchen, courtyard and fields are all shared and people are economically interdependent. In other cases new buildings are located preferably in areas surrounded by large spaces, close to a road, and the mosque or school. Socio-cultural, spatial and chronological relationships between buildings and inhabitants are therefore also being recorded and tracked.

We are also studying demarcation and meaning of different spaces and areas within the settlement. Many current villagers prefer open settlement with spacious land for gardens, orchards, fields of fodder, stables/pens and large ovens within compounds, to blocks of apartment buildings in modern urban settlements which seemed almost 'prison-like'. Sitting in one of these beautiful, cool compounds in a village, the question arises why did the occupants at Çatalhöyük choose to live in blocks of buildings packed together? Did they have to for safety reasons, owing to social pressure, the need to view neighbours throughout the day, for concerns over kinship, flooding, or threats from other communities? We are also studying space within and outside compounds. Ash from domestic ovens was frequently dumped outside house compound walls onto specific dumps in open areas; is this the case in the past?

A building has a life cycle as well as an abandonment sequence. Of the recently abandoned houses within the villages being studied, one was about to be abandoned because of general degeneration in structural soundness. This included a repeatedly leaking roof, which also had heavily soot-stained timbers and reed ceiling on the underside. Another building was abandoned upon the death of the last remaining inhabitant. In both of these cases the buildings were left standing. The first was going to be left standing in honour of their father who had built it. The second, was inherited by a neighbour who had fed and looked after the last inhabitant, and was reserved for use as a guest house with some bedding still in cupboards, but was beginning to deteriorate. A range of materials from old buildings are re-used, including mud-bricks and wooden doors and window frames.

In other cases, recent buildings in many villages are being abandoned because of the recent movement of people into larger towns and cities.

Many researchers are investigating the nature of variation in socio-cultural and ecological practices

between different households, and hence interaction between households, as well as larger areas, neighbourhoods, and settlements. This research is often closely related to study of specific materials and practices including plant and animal management, diet, artefactual remains such as ground stone, and chemical and micromorphological traces of activities and spatial conventions and meanings (Table 15.2).

Houses

The house or dwelling is an exciting context for archaeological and ethnoarchaeological study for us as it is a locus in which a number of realms of human behaviour co-occur (Carsten & Hugh-Jones 1995, 4). This is especially pertinent for students of Çatalhöyük as seen in the intensity of ethnoarchaeological focus at this scale illustrated in Table 15.2. It is now widely accepted that material remains are not simply a reflection of actions and behaviour, but are also the material context and media of those actions and relationships. Further, space serves as both a mnemonic for how to proceed in social action and as the context in which social interrelationships are negotiated by individuals who are capable of independent action and interpretation. Social coherence and regularities of behaviour are the product of generative schemes which are only realized in practice (Bourdieu 1977; Hastorf 1991; Hodder 1986; Tringham 1991; Moore 1986, 78–81; Matthews 1992).

Ethnoarchaeology provides vital information on the nature of spatial ekistics, movement and microenvironment within buildings. It furnishes dynamic perspectives of the life-cycles of a house and its inhabitants and can provide examples of diversity in uses, meanings and experiences of space, as explored in anthropological studies (Bachelard 1994; Bourdieu 1978; Carsten & Hugh Jones 1995). Microstratigraphic sequences in a number of Neolithic buildings at Çatalhöyük suggest there were changes in uses and meanings of space within buildings perhaps from residential to ceremonial (Matthews et al. 1996), and towards the end-life of a building (Matthews 1998). In research in Iran, Horne observed that the uses of about 50 per cent of the houses she studied changed during the last years of the life of a building, when many living rooms became store rooms or stables (Horne 1994). Changes in uses of space observed in local houses correspond with changing socio-cultural circumstances, such as the subdivision of a kitchen during lodgment of an aging relative, as well as alterations in use and structure owing to seasonal climatic variations (heating, alternating uses of windows as covered niches according direction of sun or wind).

The architecture of Küçukköy will be recorded in detail by a joint team of architects and architectural conservators. This will not only provide an invaluable record of architectural traditions, but will provide an important documented contextual framework for other ethnoarchaeological studies of buildings. Additional ethnoarchaeological studies of architecture include analysis of materials, technology, maintenance and renewal of these houses. We have observed that the surface textures of not only floors, but walls and ceilings vary according to the nature of intended activities within these spaces and their socio-cultural signification (Matthews & Ergenekon 1998). Differences tend to include some of the characteristics listed in Table 15.3.

Within and surrounding buildings, a range of ethnoarchaeological research aims are designed to understand the nature of relationships between activities, socio-cultural context and micro-environment and associated material traces (Table 15.2).

Current specific research includes study of:

1. architecture, equipment, surface treatments and deposits associated with animals in different ecological zones throughout the Konya Plain region.
2. facilities in the houses for food preparation and storage, including pottery, tools, and storage bins and containers in order track and record material traces of activities which may help in understanding general plant, animal, and food use, deposition, and taphonomy as well as dental micro-wear.
3. courtyard floors to see if the phytolith and macro-remains plant content of the floor correlates with plant use, and what the extent is of intrusive phytolith 'noise' in a typical floor sample.
4. samples of ash from hearths in various contexts plus interview people on the use of different fuels for different purposes, to see if differences in ashes can determine the purpose of the hearth fire.
5. samples of floors from abandoned buildings to pick up zones of phytolith deposition from roofing material that has fallen down onto occupation remains;
6. samples of floors in multiple households for analysis of chemical traces of activities as well as larger traces (Middleton & Price 1996);
7. micromorphological studies of surfaces and deposits within different areas of buildings and spaces, and spatial and socio-cultural concepts, conventions, and boundaries. This research includes study of intention and meaning in selection, application and renewal of surface textures and materials, impact of different activities on surfaces and associated features, and residues linked to cleaning and discard. Ideas and motives for reapplication and renewal of plasters encompass multiple explanations and meanings within any one household, including functional (abraded or dirty), sensual (cleanliness, household routine, fresh smell), seasonal/economical/ecological (before spring work or after harvest), and ceremonial or symbolic (Holy days, when plaster was applied particularly carefully). The perception of the differences in plasters appears to be accentuated by people's descriptions of pale brown plasters as 'black' (kara) and white plasters as 'white' (ak). (Words for brown do exist in the Turkish language but are not used for plaster.)
8. Different socio-cultural realms within houses are being recorded (Donley 1982), including gender differences in uses and perceptions of domestic space.

Integrative research

Many of these multi-disciplinary studies and scales of analytical focus are closely inter-related. We can illustrate this in particular in the various studies related to food. With regard to dental micro-wear experimentation, for example, phytolith, archaeobotanical and faunal remain analyses of archaeological materials are all furnishing data on plant use and food sources present in the Neolithic. Archaeological and ethnoarchaeological research related to grindstones is helping to inform on potential food preparation techniques. Observing people harvest and process foods in different micro-environmental zones helps the team understand the labour inputs as well as the significance of those foods in a year-

Table 15.3. *House surface characteristics from modern houses.*

	Food preparation/cooking areas	Sitting/reception areas
Ceilings	rough timbers and loose reeds	fine timbers and woven mats
Walls	pale brown or white plaster	walls of white plaster with wall hangings
Floors	brown mud plaster	white plaster covered in underlay and overlying rugs

round diet. Experimental work associated with dental micro-wear studies will also link up with current ethnobotanical focus on tubers, fruits and nuts. Part of this aim is to enable close integrative research with archaeobotanists studying these plant types and thereby enhance the detailed investigation of a wide range of questions. Related questions include where are they getting their food (fruit, nut and tubers)? Are they locally grown or brought in from other places? What are the traditional techniques for cooking, preparing and storing relevant food materials? Ethnoarchaeological observations are showing surprising potential links between materials not originally thought to be food related. Some villagers mix white sediments (ak toprak) with grain during roasting. The reasons for this may be functional, associated with dispersal of heat through sediments to prevent burning during roasting. The selection of white sediments, often used to plaster walls and floors in living rooms, may have in addition other more symbolic connotations.

Conclusions

While many participants are only beginning to pursue ethnoarchaeological projects in association with the archaeological research at Çatalhöyük, the range, depth, and plan for interweaving these together should provide not only some new insights into the site but also hopefully some new methodologies. Like many other aspects of this project, it is the multiple levels of inquiry and simultaneous activities that create a continuous self-reflexive and heightened awareness of the issues that are being addressed. In this case it has an added level of sensitivity as archaeologists include the modern world in the web of analysis and interpretation.

References

Ascher, R., 1961. Analogy in archaeological interpretation. Southwestern Journal of Anthropology 17, 317–25.

Aurenche, O., M. Bazin & S. Sadler, 1997. Villages Engloutis: Enquête Ethnoarchéologique à Cafer Höyük (Vallée de l'Euphrate). Lyon: Maison de l'Orient Méditerranéen.

Bachelard, G., 1994. The Poetics of Space. Boston (MA): Beacon Press. (Translated from the French La poétique de l'espace (1958 Presses Universitaires de France) by Maria Jolas (1964 The Orion Press, Inc.), with a new foreward by John R. Stilgoe.)

Bender, B. (ed.) 1993. Landscape: Politics and Perspectives. London: Berg.

Bourdieu, P., 1977. Outline of a Theory of Practice. Cambridge: Cambridge University Press.

Bourdieu, P., 1978. The Berber house, in Rules and Meanings: the Anthropology of Everyday Knowledge, ed. M. Douglas. London: Penguin, 98–110.

Boz, B., 1998. Çatalhöyük Neolitik insanlarının dişleindeki mikroaşınma izlerine bakarak beslenme alışkanlıklarının ortaya çıkarılması. Unpublished MSc thesis, Hacettepe University.

Braidwood, R. J. & B. Howe, 1960. Prehistoric Investigations in Iraqi Kurdistan. Chicago (IL): University of Chicago Press.

Carsten, J. & S. Hugh-Jones, 1995. About the House: Levi-Strauss and Beyond. Cambridge: Cambridge University Press.

Donley, L., 1982. House power: Swahili space and symbolic markers, in Symbolic and Structural Archaeology, ed. I. Hodder. Cambridge: Cambridge University Press, 63–73.

Edmonds, M., 1999. Ancestral Geographies of the Neolithic: Landscape, Monuments and Memory. London: Routledge.

Ergenekon, B., 1996. Bir dağ efsanesinin perşinde Kerkenes Dağ [In search of the legends of a mountain]. Atlas 11, 136–44, 182.

Ergenekon, B., 1999. Ethnoarchaeology in Şahmuratlı village by Kerkenes excavations in Turkey, in Il Congreso Nacional de Arqueomteria, ed. D. M. B. Lloris. Zaragoza: Institucion 'Fernando El Catolico' (C.I.S.C.) Excama, 169–75.

Ergenekon, B., in press. An ethnoarchaeological comparison of the Kerkenes Archaeological Survey and the legend of Kerkenes city and the Keykavus Castle. Archaeolingua: Proceedings of the 31st International Symposium on Archaeometry Budapest 27 April–1 May 1998.

Ertuğ-Yaraş, F., 1997. An Ethnoarchaeological Study of Subsistence and Plant Gathering in Central Anatolia. Unpublished PhD dissertation, Department of Anthropology, Washington University.

French, D., 1973. Aşvan 1968–1972. Anatolian Studies 23, 5–307.

Gero, J. & M. Conkey (eds.), 1991. Engendering Archaeology: Women and Prehistory. Oxford: Blackwell.

Hayden, B. & A. Cannon, 1984. The Structure of Material Systems: Ethnoarchaeology in the Maya Highlands. Washington (DC): Society for American Archaeology.

Hastorf, C.A., 1991. Gender, space and food in prehistory, in Gero & Conkey (eds.), 132–59.

Hastorf, C.A. & S. Johannessen, 1991. Expanding perspectives on prehistoric people/plant relationships, in Processual and Postprocessual Archaeologies, Multiple Ways of Knowing the Past, ed. R.W. Preucel. Carbondale (IL): Southern Illinois University, Center for Archaeological Investigations, 140–55.

Hodder, I., 1982. Symbols in Action. Cambridge: Cambridge University Press.

Hodder, I., 1986. Reading the Past. Cambridge: Cambridge University Press.

Hodder, I. (ed.), 1996. On the Surface: Çatalhöyük 1993–95. (McDonald Institute Monographs.) Cambridge: McDonald Institute for Archaeological Research; London: British Institute of Archaeology at Ankara.

Hodder, I., 1997. 'Always momentary, fluid and flexible': towards a reflexive excavation methodology. *Antiquity* 71, 691–700.

Hodder, I., 1999. Renewed work at Çatalhöyük, in *Neolithic in Turkey, the Cradle of Civilization*, eds. M. Özdoğan & N. Başgelen. Istanbul: Arkeoloji ve Sanat Yayınları, 157–64.

Horne, L., 1994. *Village Spaces: Settlement and Society in Northeastern Iran*. Washington (DC): Smithsonian Institution Press.

Kent, S., 1990. *Domestic Architecture and the Use of Space*. Cambridge: Cambridge University Press.

King, T.C., 1997. Dental Microwear and Diet in *Griphopithecus alpani*. Unpublished PhD thesis, University of London.

Kramer, C., 1979. An archaeological view of a contemporary Kurdish village: domestic architecture, household size, and wealth, in *Ethnoarchaeology: Implications of Ethnography for Archaeology*, ed. C. Kramer. New York (NY): Columbia University Press, 139–63.

Kramer, C., 1982. *Village Ethnoarchaeology: Rural Iran in Archaeological Perspective*. New York (NY): Academic Press.

Kus, S., 1983. The social representation of space: dimensioning the cosmological and the quotidian, in *Archaeological Hammers and Theories*, eds. J.A. Moore & A.S. Keene. New York (NY): Academic Press, 278–99.

Matthews, W., 1992. The Micromorphology of Occupational Sequences and the Use of Space in a Sumerian city. Unpublished PhD thesis, Department of Archaeology, University of Cambridge.

Matthews, W., 1995. Micromorphological characterisation of occupation deposits and microstratigraphic sequences at Abu Salabikh, Southern Iraq, in *Archaeological Sediments and Soils: Analysis, Interpretation and Management*, eds. A.J. Barham & R.I. Macphail. London: Institute of Archaeology, University College London, 41–76.

Matthews, W., 1998. Report on sampling strategies, microstratigraphy and micromorphology of depositional sequences. *Çatalhöyük 1998 Archive Report*. http://catal.arch.cam.ac.uk/catal/Archive-rep98/matthews98.html

Matthews, W. & B. Ergenekon, 1998. Ethnoarchaeology. *Çatalhöyük 1998 Archive Report*. http://catal.arch.cam.ac.uk/catal/Archive_rep98/matthews98.html.

Matthews, W. & S. Farid, 1996. Exploring the 1960s surface: the stratigraphy of Çatalhöyük, in Hodder (ed.), 271–300.

Matthews, W., C.A.I French, T. Lawrence & D.F. Cutler, 1996. Multiple surfaces: the micromorphology, in Hodder (ed.), 301–42.

Matthews, W., C.A.I. French, T. Lawrence, D.F. Cutler & M.K. Jones, 1997. Microstratigraphic traces of site formation processes and human activities. *World Archaeology* 29, 281–308.

Mellaart, J., 1967. *Çatal Hüyük: a Neolithic Town in Anatolia*. London: Thames & Hudson.

Merrick, J., P. Boyer & N. Roberts, 1997. Archive report on work by the KOPAL team 1997. *Çatalhöyük 1997 Archive Report*. http://catal.arch.cam.ac.uk/catal/Archive_rep97/roberts97.html.

Middleton, W.D. & D.T. Price, 1996. Identification of activity areas by multi-element characterization of sediments from modern and archaeological house floors using inductively coupled plasma-atomic emission spectroscopy. *Journal of Archaeological Science* 23, 637–87.

Moore, H.L., 1986. *Space, Text and Gender: an Anthropological Study of the Marakwet of Kenya*. Cambridge: Cambridge University Press.

Newton, M., 1996. Dendrochronology at Çatal Hüyük: a 576 Tree-ring Chronology for the Early Neolithic of Anatolia. Unpublished Masters thesis, Cornell University.

Roberts, N., P. Boyer & R. Parish, 1996. Preliminary results of geoarchaeological investigations at Çatalhöyük, in Hodder (ed.), 19–41.

Rosen, A.M. & S. Weiner, 1994. Identifying ancient irrigation: a new method using opaline phytoliths from emmer wheat. *Journal of Archaeological Science* 21, 132–5.

Stevanovic, M., 1997. Report on experimental archaeology at Çatal: Manufacturing bricks for the house replica. *Çatalhöyük 1997 Archive Report*. http://catal.arch.cam.ac.uk/catal/Archive_rep97/stevano97.html.

Stevanovic, M., 1999. Report on experimental archaeology at Çatalhöyük. *Çatalhöyük 1999 Archive Report*. http://catal.arch.cam.ac.uk/catal/Archive_rep99/stevano99.html.

Teaford, M. & J.D. Lytle, 1996. Brief communication: diet induced changes in rates of human tooth microwear: a case study involving stone-ground maize. *American Journal of Physical Anthropology* 100, 143–7.

Therkorn, L., 1987. The inter-relationships of materials and meanings: some suggestions on housing concerns within Iron Age Noord-Holland, in *The Archaeology of Contextual Meanings*, ed. I. Hodder. Cambridge: Cambridge University Press, 102–10.

Thomas, J.S., 1996. *Time, Culture, and Identity: an Interpretative Archaeology*. London: Routledge.

Tilley, C., 1994. *A Phenomenology of Landscape*. Oxford: Berg.

Tringham, R., 1978. Experimentation, ethnoarchaeology, and the leapfrogs in archaeological methodology, in *Explorations in Ethnoarchaeology*, ed. R.A. Gould. Albuquerque (NM): University of New Mexico Press, 169–200.

Tringham, R., 1991. Households with faces: the challenge of gender in prehistoric architectural remains, in Gero & Conkey (eds.), 93–131.

Watson, P.J., 1979. *Archaeological Ethnography in Western Iran*. Tuscon (AZ): University of Arizona Press for the Wenner-Gren Foundation for Anthropological Research.

Wilson, P.J., 1988. *The Domestication of the Human Species*. New Haven (CT): Yale University Press.

Part C

Presenting the Sites

Part C: Presenting the Sites

By presenting Çatalhöyük to wider audiences we are also making the site 'present', translating it into a contemporary context. A problem with the processes of both 'presenting' and translating is that they need a central figure or institution — a 'presenter' or 'translator'. Such central figures can act in a variety of different ways — as paternalistic guides, as mediators, as facilitators. But always there is a responsibility to be sensitive in two directions simultaneously — towards the past (the data which inform us about the past), and towards the present (contemporary and multiple interests).

One of the potentials of the new media technologies is that they allow the central dominating role of the presenter or translator to be diminished. Of course, quite the opposite argument can be made. The dependence on high technology in order to present or translate takes the terms of the interaction out of lay hands and puts them firmly into the control of technical specialists, software writers, web managers, and so on. Certainly, villagers around Çatalhöyük are amongst those in the global community least able to find out about the site through the Internet. It is much easier to gain access to the site's data base in Minneapolis than in Küçükköy (the nearest village to Çatalhöyük).

One response to this situation being pursued by the project is to use Çatalhöyük as a catalyst to bring information technologies into the local schools in the Konya region (a scheme jointly proposed with the Turkish History Foundation — Tarih Vakfı — in Istanbul). Another response is to provide low-technology presentations, such as the community exhibit which has been prepared in collaboration with local villagers and placed on display in the on-site visitor centre (see Chapters 8 & 16). The community exhibit is participative and interactive. Other initiatives are slide shows and talks by team members in the villages (see Chapter 8).

The use of video and CD-Rom as part of the visitor centre at Çatalhöyük provides an example of the approach described by Shane and Küçük (Chapter 16) in which new multimedia and information technologies are used within easily accessible museum displays to encourage participation and interaction. While it is necessary to remain vigilant about the centralizing tendencies within the new technologies, the technologies can also be used effectively to engender participation, critique and debate from multiple interacting perspectives. The roles of the presenter and translator are transformed into those of mediator and facilitator.

In attempting to limit the role of the presenter or translator, the aim of the project has been to provide mechanisms for 'outsiders' to get as far as possible into what is normally seen as the sanctum of the 'inside'. We have wanted to erode the distinction between 'team' and 'outer world', but only in so far as professional responsibilities and proper curation of the archive are safeguarded. Thus, large parts of the data base are made available on the Web, but changing or editing the data posted on the Web is controlled by the project.

The material made available on the Web is always a selection. It has been sifted and edited for wider consumption. The editing role is a necessary one. For example, access to the Web site would be considerably slowed if a large amount of visual images were included. Thus a selection of images has been made for the Web site. A similar point is relevant to the video documentation of the excavation process. In the procedures followed by the Cambridge-based team (an alternative scheme is described by Stevanovic in Chapter 20), videos are edited into 1–2 minute clips — this is necessary for storage on the data base, and for efficient key-wording and retrieval. So here the role of the editor is strong. But the editing process can take place in a transparent and reflexive environment. For example, at Çatalhöyük it takes place on site and there are opportunities for those who have been filmed on specific clips to view, question and change the content and style of the video clips.

It can be argued that visual media are particularly effective in opening up the project and the site to a wider engagement. Again, the opposite can be argued. Because 'seeing is believing', we are easily led by visual stimuli. We are perhaps more easily misled by visual representation than by written texts and data codes. But on the other hand, there are aspects of visual data that allow or encourage critical reflexivity. For example, codified information sheets present a limited selection of data. On film there is much more peripheral information — things appear in the frame that have not been accounted for. Alternative hypotheses can be formulated on the basis of what is seen on the screen.

In future years, as researchers return to the Çatalhöyük project in order to re-evaluate the results, the video clips on the data base allow conclusions to be more fully contextualized within an on-going process. Critique and re-evaluation are enhanced.

As more multimedia recording occurs on site, within the trench (as described by Stevanovic, Chapter 20), there may be less need for the 'turning away' described in the introduction to Part A. Potentially, the use of video and audio-diary in the trench allows more of an integrated interaction with the data. On the other hand, the putting down, picking up, switching on etc. of the recording instruments may increase the sense of distance from any engagement with the excavation process. But a full recording of this type, despite the editing that is needed, allows a more immediate interaction between wider audiences and specialist archaeologists.

A greater and wider diversity of interactions with the project is also promoted by the use of non-linear systems such as hyper-text. While it is the case that the user of a hyper-textual environment can only travel down paths that have been provided, there is certainly the potential for greater critical engagement than with many linear texts. There is more opportunity to 'click' from claims made in one part of the hyper-text to check against information available in other parts. On the Çatalhöyük CD-Rom prepared by the Karlsruhe team it is possible to 'click' on virtual reconstructions of bucrania within reconstructed buildings in order to see photographs of the same bucrania as found by Mellaart. On-line it is possible for children to ask questions of project team members and to explore independent paths of enquiry.

The new media technologies are thus a mixed blessing, in archaeology as in daily *life. On the one hand, they provide all the material necessary for greater centralization, obfuscation, elitism and specialization. They allow the processes of representation of archaeological data to be controlled. On the other hand, they allow greater interactivity and openness. They facilitate the democratizing shift from hierarchy to net, allowing multiple engagements with the past.*

The role of the visual in this transformation is central. Archaeology has always placed a special importance on the visual. But it has undoubtedly given a greater emphasis to texts, which images 'illustrate'. In the general move that we see today from a text-based to an image-based archaeology, there is much potential for new forms of interaction with the past. Digital images allow new forms of interaction, in that they appear more immediate and allow more manipulation and interaction than texts. But they also require new skills and new costs. The democratization they promise can too easily be turned into a secluded elitism.

Chapter 16

Presenting Çatalhöyük

Orrin Shane & Mine Küçük

The twenty-five year long-range plan for the re-opening of Çatalhöyük envisions an integrated strategy of archaeological investigation, conservation practice, and heritage management with public presentation. One goal of this plan is to provide the Turkish Ministry of Culture with a well-planned heritage site and tourist destination, with a visitor centre, covered and protected *in situ* walls and paintings allowing year-round visitor access, and a protective constructed visitor route between displays and excavation areas. A second aim is to develop a broad range of public programmes designed to reach an international audience (Hodder 1995; 1996; 1998). Since 1993 we have collaborated with project excavators and scientific specialists, educators, exhibit designers and artists to carry this plan forward by fostering, planning and implementing a variety of reflexive, multivocal and interactive interpretive experiences about Çatalhöyük for international and multicultural audiences.

Consistent, however, with the postprocessual methodology of the excavators, our plans remain '. . . always momentary, fluid and flexible' (Hodder 1997). We are working to develop public programmes about Çatalhöyük that can accommodate new and changing information and interpretations. We are sensitive also to the changing technologies for public presentation, particularly hypermedia distributed via the Internet. One of the challenges facing public interpretation in the reflexive postprocessual environment of Çatalhöyük is working around the inherent contradiction between the crystallization of ideas in public media and the very fluid and changing nature of research.

In its broadest sense, public presentation of archaeology includes activities ranging from formal education in schools to programmes such as site tours and museum displays. It also includes popular articles, public-awareness posters and brochures, and more recently, hypermedia presentations on the World Wide Web (Jameson 1994; 1997; Tringham *et al.* Chapter 17, this volume). Programmes for public presentation of Çatalhöyük that are being implemented or are under development include the following:

- a visitor centre designed to orient local and international visitors to the site and to engage visitors in multivocal reflexive dialogue about the Çatalhöyük project;
- on-site public presentation and interpretation of mural art and sculpture in sheltered excavated buildings;
- print media brochures and site guides;
- interactive CD-ROM, computer multimedia and virtual reality reconstructions, and video presentations for small groups and for international distribution;
- inquiry-based educational hypermedia presentations for the World Wide Web;
- curriculum units, classroom demonstrations, and group programmes for elementary and secondary schools;
- a multimedia interpretive exhibition at the Science Museum of Minnesota (SMM) with object displays, interactive activity stations for archaeology, models, architectural reconstructions, and interpretive graphics;
- reconstructions of Neolithic buildings for experimental archaeology and public interpretation at the Çatalhöyük site (by Mirjana Stevanovic);
- an international travelling exhibition featuring the art and archaeology of Çatalhöyük;
- a major regional archaeological museum and research centre at Çatalhöyük maintained by the Turkish Ministry of Culture.

Thinking about public presentation

Our thinking about public presentation at Çatalhöyük has been influenced by recent research about the way the public uses museums and similar educational interpretive facilities (Csikszentmihalyi & Robinson 1990; Screven 1986; Falk & Dierking 1992; Museum Education Roundtable 1992; Hooper-Greenhill 1992; Karp *et al.* 1992), the nature of object knowledge (Csikszentmihalyi & Rochberg-Halton 1981; Csikszentmihalyi 1996; Schlereth 1992), and especially the rich and expanding literature for public presentation of archaeology (Gathercole & Lowenthal 1990; Hodder 1992; Potter 1994; 1997; Stone & Molyneaux 1994; Shanks & Hodder 1995; McManus 1996; Jameson 1994; 1997). This research shows that visitors bring to the interpretive experience their own cultural backgrounds, learning styles, and personal idiosyncrasies. Moreover, visitors tend not to engage in the interpretive experience individually, but rather in groups, e.g. a family, a school group, or a tour bus group; much research shows that learning in these settings is a socially-mediated process. Finally, an interpretive experience takes place in a physical setting, sometimes a museum gallery, but also in an historic house or out-of-doors at an archaeological excavation. Contemporary research has shown that elements of the physical setting exert significant influences on the visitor.

One framework that we have found useful in helping to understand the contextuality of the interpretive experience and as a guide for planning interpretive programmes is the Interactive Experience Model presented by Falk & Dierking (1992, 5). In *The Museum Experience* Falk & Dierking show how this model emphasizes the visitor's perspective and it has contributed much to thinking about audience research and visitor-oriented exhibit design and content in museums and science centres. As part of the design process for the Çatalhöyük visitor centre (see below), we have identified six major target audiences: foreign tourist groups, urban Turkish tourists, visitors from local communities, Turkish school groups, special interest tours (Mother Goddess and museum groups), and visiting scholars. We have identified some of the characteristics and interests of these groups, and have used these findings to inform programme development.

Foreign tour groups of 25 to 30 visitors arriving at the site by bus currently constitute the single largest audience for the Çatalhöyük site. During August and September 1997 we documented 47 such groups totalling almost 1500 visitors. A broader examination of tourism in Turkey reveals that most visitors arrive from Europe (Britain, Germany, France and Italy), the United States, and Japan, a pattern documented for Çatalhöyük as well. Therefore, we have

designed exhibits and programmes for the new Çatalhöyük visitor centre with this audience in mind. One specific example is the use of a computer projection system to project an interactive CD-ROM image on an overhead screen for group viewing while one from the group navigates through the program at the computer console. Although speakers of many languages visit the site, for practical reasons label copy for displays and for building signs is in Turkish and English. To accommodate other foreign visitors, we provide site brochures in Turkish, English, French, German, Italian and Japanese.

The Interactive Experience Model brings together recent developments in cognitive and developmental psychology, learning theory, and the psychology of perception to provide a definition of museum learning that acknowledges and takes into account the different learning styles of visitors. This approach considers that each visitor brings to the interpretive experience a unique reservoir of experience and knowledge resulting from both genetic makeup and environment. Whether related to a multiplicity of intelligences (Gardner 1983; 1993) or to different ways people perceive and process information in the brain (Kolb 1984), an appreciation that people learn in different ways has led exhibit designers to create interpretive experiences that appeal to a range of learning styles.

One of the most insightful recent studies of the museum experience is *The Art of Seeing: an Interpretation of the Aesthetic Encounter* by Mihalyi Csikszentmihalyi and Rick E. Robinson (1990). In a remarkable study that examines the aesthetic experience in the context of the public presentation of art, arguably one kind of interpretive experience, Csikszentmihalyi & Robinson use extensive interview data to define the aesthetic encounter

> . . . as an intense involvement of attention in response to a visual stimulus, for no other reason than to sustain the interaction. The experiential consequences of such a deep and autotelic involvement are an intense enjoyment characterised by feelings of personal wholeness, a sense of discovery, and a sense of human connectedness. (1990, 178)

The authors go on to explore ways of facilitating the aesthetic experience, particularly in museums and galleries.

> [These] might involve evoking art historical knowledge, exploring basic human emotions, learning about social history, or provoking the viewers' imagination. All of these entrées can be effective regardless of whether the art object in question is

contemporary, pre-modern, or a product of another culture. (1990, 139–40)

Further, they suggest that

A better strategy is for the museum to provide as many bridges as possible between the viewer and the art, drawing on all the dimensions that the work contains, from the historical-anecdotal to the starkly formal. (1990, 186)

In *The Meaning of Things: Domestic Symbols of the Self*, Csikszentmihalyi & Rochberg-Halton (1981) explore the meaning that objects have for people beyond simple function or monetary value. This study revealed a variety of ways objects take on meaning for people and the complexity of these relationships. One implication of this work is that an object can have very different meanings for its maker, its user, its discoverer, its curator, the persons preparing it for exhibition, and finally the museum visitor viewing the object in a gallery.

Based on these concepts, we are working to interpret Çatalhöyük using a range of formats and media, different presentation styles, and multiple ways of engaging visitors, all designed to provide visitors with different points of entry into the interpretive experience. Examples of our interpretive formats include object displays of artefact replicas from past and recent excavations, three-dimensional architectural models, large format interpretive panels, interpretive graphics and reconstruction drawings, interactive activity stations for archaeology, computer simulations and virtual reality, multimedia object theatre, and hypermedia presentations over the Internet.

Our own experience at the SMM, as well as a considerable body of evaluative literature, show that hands-on interactive exhibits and programmes have more visitor 'holding power' and foster more intensity of engagement than do purely didactic, flat, and impersonal presentations (Screven 1986; Falk & Dierking 1992, 67ff.). At the SMM we interpret physical science and technology using hands-on 'experiment benches', exhibits in which visitors choose which variables to control and can produce many outcomes. These exhibits engage visitors of all ages, individually and in groups (Sauber 1994).

Utilizing this expertise, we are developing a number of *interactive archaeological activity stations* that will introduce visitors to some of the scientific methods being employed at Çatalhöyük, while at the same time engaging them by challenging their problem-solving and critical-thinking skills. Activity stations are interactive exhibits that give one visitor, a family, or a small group (school group, or a group of friends from a larger tour bus group) an opportunity for hands-on engagement with real-life archaeological activity. Two examples are:

• *Sampling the Past* illustrates sampling strategies required by the constraints of time and resources that limit the amount of material that can be processed at any archaeological site, especially one the size of Çatalhöyük. Visitors to this activity station will work to solve a number of puzzles whose solutions depend on sampling strategies. One puzzle might consist of a well-known image obscured by removable pieces of another material. A visitor would try to identify the image while removing the fewest number of pieces from the overlier. This activity should be very attractive to visitors at the Çatalhöyük visitor centre, where we know visitors are curious about the small areas currently being excavated compared to the vast size of the site, and wonder about what really can be learned from such limited excavations.

• *Slices of Ancient Life* focuses on the analysis of micromorphological evidence sampled from within buildings at Çatalhöyük. Micromorphology is a powerful new scientific tool for archaeology, and Çatalhöyük is one of the international test sites for the method (see Matthews *et al.* 1996, 301–42). Visitors to this activity station will examine actual resin-impregnated thin sections of sediments taken from multiple locations within a single building. Visitors will be able to count the layers of plaster on the walls and floors, analyze differences in building materials, and identify plant and animal remains that may reflect their uses. They will also learn how the law of superposition allows archaeologists to 'read' records of stratification long after they were 'written'.

Reflexivity, the on-going and recursive critical evaluation of the assumptions underlying interpretation, is as important for public interpretation of archaeology as it is to formal academic archaeological theory. We have worked to build reflexivity into public presentation by presenting archaeological information didactically, while at the same time challenging the tyranny of the authoritative 'museum voice' by inviting and encouraging visitors to seek their own answers to questions posed by the archaeological record. One example of this approach in the new Çatalhöyük visitor centre is a full-size mural scene reproduced from a full-size transcription of an original mural in Mellaart's 'shrine' F V 1. The reproduction is in mineral pigments on a reproduced plaster, and shows costumed and naked men interacting with a variety of animals. The reproduction is positioned low on a wall, without any barrier or protective covering, so that is can be easily viewed and studied, up close and personal; visitors are encouraged to ask 'What is happening in these scenes?' and 'What do you think this means?' (Fig. 16.1). A similar inquiry-based approach that fosters contemplative reflection is incorporated throughout our educational web site, *Mysteries of Çatalhöyük* (see below).

A programme development process

To achieve our long-term goals for the presentation of Çatalhöyük we have developed an interpretive programme development process that is multivocal, interactive and reflexive. First and foremost, this process emphasizes working collaboratively and in partnership with archaeologists, exhibit designers and museologists from the Republic of Turkey, host country for the Çatalhöyük project. For programmes to be presented in Turkey, we have contracted İda Ajans, a commercial graphic design and display development firm in Ankara, to produce exhibit components manufactured .with Turkish materials purchased from Turkish vendors. İda Ajans, owned and operated by Berna Gündiler, was selected after we interviewed a number of design firms in Istanbul and Ankara. Our selection was based on the quality

of İda Ajans' design portfolio, the interest of the staff in archaeology and especially the re-opening of Çatalhöyük, and the Director's appreciation of the intellectual goals of the Çatalhöyük project. We have also brought Turkish members of the team to America to work with Science Museum exhibit developers and designers, and we have sent SMM staff to work in Turkey as well. Moreover, we have travelled extensively throughout the country, visiting archaeological sites and historic monuments, studying and researching modern tourism.

Our development process also brings exhibit and programme developers together with archaeologists and scientific specialists at Çatalhöyük, mirroring the interaction among excavators and specialists so important for the research project. It is often the case that exhibits and public programmes about archaeological sites are developed only after the excavations are completed and the final reports published. At Çatalhöyük however, exhibit designers, programme developers and educators are working side-by-side with researchers at the site, developing a deeper understanding of the process by which archaeological knowledge is constructed. This first-hand experience with the process of archaeology and archaeological interpretation then informs the exhibits and programmes being developed.

Since 1996, Timothy Ready, assistant curator for anthropology at the Science Museum and an archaeologist as well as a published ethnographic photographer, has photo-documented the archaeological process at Çatalhöyük and collected images used in various public programmes. Since 1997, Don Pohlman, head of SMM's peoples and cultures programme, Keith Braafladt, a SMM web site developer, Joshua Seaver, a web site designer, and Leslie Kratz, an educator and media consultant, have video-taped formal interviews with many teams members, travelled and worked with the regional survey and palaeoenvironmental teams, and generally documented the roles of individuals and teams within

Figure 16.1. *Ian Hodder discussing reproduced mural painting in the Çatalhöyük visitor centre.*

the archaeological process. This participation is very much more than just visiting the site to collect some photographs or videotape; as much as possible our team members live and work daily with other members of the project.

One challenge for presenting Çatalhöyük has been negotiating the special concerns and interests of project 'stakeholders', while at the same time balancing these against the needs and interests of visitors. There is a broad diversity of local and global interests in the Çatalhöyük project (Hodder 1998), from which we have identified a few individuals, groups and entities — project stakeholders — with special responsibilities and investments. Just as we consider the nature of our audience in the design process, so we also take into consideration the design implications stemming from stakeholder analysis.

In the Republic of Turkey the protection and investigation of archaeological and historical sites is taken very seriously. With the beginning of the Republic, Atatürk implemented systematic excavation of archaeological sites to establish an Anatolian heritage for the Turkish people (Lewis 1968). Initially emphasizing the archaeology of the Hittite Empire, which led to the establishment of the Hittite Museum (later the Museum of Anatolian Civilizations) to showcase Anatolian heritage, national interest has led to the creation of monumental public art in Ankara based on Hittite themes and the establishment of departments of archaeology and archaeometry in major universities. Shankland (1996) cites the refurbished and expanded exhibits about Çatalhöyük in the Museum of Anatolian Civilizations in Ankara as an indication of national recognition of the importance of the site.

The Republic of Turkey is committed to developing tourism as a major component of the national economy. According to government sources, tourism contributed over $8.3 billion to the GNP in 1998, and the Ministry of Tourism is working aggressively to increase this sector of the economy. One part of this strategy has been to support the development of Çatalhöyük as a new major tourist destination between Cappadocia in central Anatolia and Antalya on the Mediterranean coast. An implication of this stakeholder interest has been the creation of exhibits at the Çatalhöyük visitor centre that are designed to inform visitors about other nearby Neolithic sites such as Can Hasan and Pınarbaşı in Karaman, Süberde near Beyşehir, Aşıklı Höyük near Aksaray, and Kaletepe near Niğde.

The General-Directorate of Monuments and Museums is responsible for all permissions to excavate in the Republic and appoints annually one or more government representatives to represent the interests of the Directorate at Çatalhöyük. Since 1994 all of the government representatives have been museum professionals very interested in public presentation. They have reviewed and commented on prototype exhibit components displayed during the excavation season, and made very helpful editing suggestions for text copy and on important matters of presentation. The General-Directorate receives and reviews excavation reports annually, including our reports on the development of public programmes at Çatalhöyük.

The British Institute for Archaeology at Ankara (BIAA) supports a number of archaeological projects in Turkey and sponsors the research at Çatalhöyük. Project participants use the Institute's facilities in Ankara, and research reports are published in the Institute's flagship journal *Anatolian Studies*, as well as a new publication, *Anatolian Archaeology*. The BIAA has been an invaluable champion for our work, providing a residential and working base of operations in Ankara, facilitating local arrangements and governmental contacts, and providing critical technical and library services.

Konya Museum Service, as the regional archaeological museum, gives its local support to the excavation. Museum staff have assisted in the excavation, and the museum stores many of the collections from Çatalhöyük. Erdoğan Erol, Director of the Konya Museum Service, has supported the Çatalhöyük project and given permission to collect mud-brick and plaster for scientific study and for display in the visitor centre. The initial plans for the dig house, including the visitor centre, were prepared by the Konya Museum Service in consultation with us and Çatalhöyük project leaders. Minor alterations to the visitor centre design were negotiated in 1996 with the architectural department of the museum service and the Konya Heritage Commission.

The Çatalhöyük research project team includes the excavators, scientific specialists, and organizers who direct the project and who work to construct the new knowledge about Çatalhöyük that we interpret for the public. Among all stakeholders, these persons have the greatest commitment to the intellectual content of public programmes. Therefore, we have invited project participants to become advisors for specific programmes and exhibit components. For example, Wendy Matthews, who directs micromorphological research at Çatalhöyük, is also a consultant for the development of an activity station dealing with micromorphology and stratigraphy. Similarly, Ayfer Bartu, a social anthropologist interviewing local residents about their attitudes toward the work at Çatalhöyük, is a project advisor for the *Window on Çatalhöyük* project, and will provide a framework for understanding how the excavation of Çatalhöyük is being viewed in Turkey today.

The local people living in the ancient city of Konya (Pop. 1,000,000), 35 km from Çatalhöyük, the market town of Çumra (Pop. 30,000), 12 km from the site, and the villages surrounding Çatalhöyük have interests and concerns that Hodder (1998), Shankland (1996, and Chapter 14, this volume) and Bartu (Chapter 8, this volume) are working to identify. One implication of these stakeholders is the development of community exhibits for the visitor centre. The first of these, organized by Ayfer Bartu and the local women working to process flotation samples from the excavations, is *The Thinking Corner of the Working Ladies*. This exhibit is about the women's perceptions of the work at Çatalhöyük, and features their own captioned site photographs and plant specimens they have collected from the site and nearby fields for ethnobotanical study.

The Turkish Friends of Çatalhöyük is a supportive group established by Reşit Ergener and Nur Mardin to arrange lectures, publicity and fund-raising for Çatalhöyük. The Turkish Friends purchased one of the excavation shelters and provide scholarships for Turkish students working at the site. The Friends have also supported the development of public programmes for the visitor centre and have raised funds for audio-visual equipment. The American Friends of Çatalhöyük, largely from Minnesota, support the development of the visitor centre and exhibits about Çatalhöyük at the SMM. They have also provided funds for travel to Turkey and support for fieldwork.

Corporate sponsors and international funding agencies provide the financial support that makes our work possible. Visa International, Boeing and Koç Bank are major corporate sponsors of the Çatalhöyük project. The excavation is also supported by Merko (long-term sponsor), Glaxo-Wellcome, British Airways and Shell (co-sponsors). Overall, the project also receives money from different corporate sources from time to time. Major funding has also been received from the European Union, and in America from the National Science Foundation (NSF) and the National Endowment for the Humanities (NEH).

As we have developed public presentation projects, it has often been with specific funding agencies and their programme directives in mind. For example, our goal to develop an educational web site coincided nicely with the Teaching with Technology initiative at NEH, a programme intended to give applicants the opportunity to explore the use of the Internet for distance learning. Similarly, the Informal Science Education Directorate at NSF was a logical potential source for funding of projects to interpret how archaeological knowledge is being constructed at Çatalhöyük.

Our process of programme development ultimately is based on the idea that archaeologists more adequately fulfil their responsibilities to the societies in which they work by being more transparent and interactive. As the public presentation of Çatalhöyük has globalized, there is a growing need to engage a wide range of issues that both incorporate and respond to multiple voices. This plays out by our more fully considering the different kinds of visitors to whom we offer data for interpretation, as well as the many communities whose interests are represented. At the same time, our process recognizes a convergence between the aims of the public presentation of archaeology and a new perspective among museum professionals who are beginning to examine reflexively the public uses of museums.

Finally, our programme development process is designed to take advantage of the high degree of synergy among projects. Research for components designed for the Çatalhöyük visitor centre informs content for the web site, popular articles, or exhibits in America. The interactive archaeology activity stations for exhibit at the Science Museum become available for other venues as well. Furthermore, hypermedia components developed for the *Mysteries* web site can serve as updates for the CD-ROM installation at the visitor centre or be installed as additional products.

The Çatalhöyük visitor centre

When visitors arrive at Çatalhöyük their first experience of the site is the huge imposing Çatalhöyük East mound rising up from an otherwise flat landscape. The larger of the two Çatalhöyük mounds can be seen clearly from several kilometres away, standing out in stark contrast to the flat surrounding fields that stretch away towards the distant mountains. For many visitors, even those with some prior knowledge of the site, this intriguing first view raises questions about Çatalhöyük: 'How was this mound formed?', 'How old is it?', or 'How big is the mound?', this last question often asked in terms of comparison with known structures because the mound is so huge people have difficulty grasping its scale and scope. Therefore, we have designed the visitor centre to be an 'advance organizer' for the site visit, providing didactic information as well as a place for dialogue about the Çatalhöyük research project, its methods and its findings.

A 110 m² visitor centre building (Fig. 16.2), with a small shop area, a lobby and toilets was completed as a part of the dig house complex at Çatalhöyük in 1998. The centre's multimedia approach provides visitors with a variety of interpretive experiences and multiple points of engagement. Large format photomurals, interpretive panels combining text and vivid excavation images, full-size reproductions of mural paintings and sculpture, object displays, an interactive CD-ROM with virtual reality reconstructions, and a twenty-minute video presentation introduce visitors to the site and engage them in a multivocal reflexive dialogue about the Çatalhöyük project. Exhibit text is bilingual (Turkish and English) and a brochure/ site-guide is available in Turkish, English, German, French, and Japanese.

Near the entrance to the visitor centre a site orientation display welcomes visitors and provides a large format map showing the dig house ('You are here'), the Çatalhöyük East (Neolithic) and Çatalhöyük West (Chalcolithic) mounds, walking paths over the mounds, and the excavation area to be visited. Text briefly explains the age and significance of the *höyüks*, and how they were formed from the remains of mud-brick houses and trash. Highlighted text explains that nothing is to be picked up or taken away from the site, and that walking on the surface of the mounds away from designated walkways accelerates soil erosion, doing irreparable damage to the *höyüks*. A second map locates Çatalhöyük within Turkey, and in relation to other major archaeological sites and tourist attractions.

Inside the visitor centre, an introductory dis-

Figure 16.2. *The Çatalhöyük dig house complex, including the visitor centre viewed from the Çatalhöyük East mound. The visitor centre is the building on the left of the complex.*

play uses a thematic Landsat image of the western Konya Basin to provide a regional overview of the site and its geologic and geomorphic context. The interpreted satellite image shows the Çarşamba River flowing into the basin of Pleistocene Lake Konya and forming the Çarşamba alluvial fan, the vast area of fertile alluvial soils that supported farming at Çatalhöyük and is a major area of agricultural production in Turkey today. Other interpretive panels and displays treat the Mellaart era excavations and include unpublished images of the work from 1961–65, the organization, goals and objectives of the new Çatalhöyük research project, reflexive methodology and scientific methods at Çatalhöyük, new findings and discoveries from the current work.

Our visitor research of tour groups visiting the site since 1994 revealed strong interest in the wall paintings of Çatalhöyük. Many visitors came to the site specifically to see wall paintings and were disappointed to find none available for viewing or study. For this reason, we chose a dramatic hunting scene from the north and east walls of Shrine F V 1 for reproduction. Using a transcription drawn in the 1960s, a full-size mural reproduction was created by Mutlu Gündiler and installed in the visitor centre in September 1998.

To provide a place for secure display of artefact reproductions, display niches were designed for the

Figure 16.3. *Mutlu Gündiler finishing the reproduction of a hunting mural.*

Figure 16.4. *The interior of the visitor centre showing the track lighting system, object display niches in the west wall, and the central housing for lighting and the video/computer projection system. A ¹/₄ scale model of Shrine E VI 8 will be installed below the central housing.*

for display in the niches the famous seated 'Goddess' figure, two pottery vessels, and ceramic pot stands. Other artefacts reproduced as architectural adornments were two bulls heads (bucrania) and a pair of painted leopards. The leopards were installed above the west wall niches and the bull heads were placed above corner niches for audio/visual equipment. All of these reproductions are of artefacts recovered from the excavations of the 1960s. In future, we will exhibit reproductions of artefacts from the new excavations since 1993.

Two audio-visual components, an interactive CD-ROM and the twenty-minute video about the site, were developed by a team from the Staatliche Hochschule für Gestaltung-Karlsruhe. The interactive CD is a non-linear hypermedia program, currently in German and English, featuring site history, a tour of the Çatalhöyük East mound using Quick-Time virtual reality technology, and virtual tours through reconstructions of 'shrines' in two levels of Mellaart's excavation. These virtual reality tours allow visitors to see several shrines, move about a room looking at murals and sculpture, and zoom in for detailed viewing. The site video was completed in 1996, and uses interviews with project staff and on-site videography to give an overview of the goals and objectives of the new Çatalhöyük research project. These two audio-visual components are each very different between

west wall of the visitor centre (Fig. 16.4). These niches take their inspiration from the niches in the ancient rooms of Çatalhöyük. In 1998 we chose to reproduce themselves, and are distinct from other presentation media in the centre. This multimedia approach is designed explicitly to give visitors multiple points of engagement and to provide a variety of entry levels to understanding Çatalhöyük.

One of the challenges we faced in designing the visitor centre lighting system was the need for light without excessive heat and with low ultra-violet characteristics. The solution was a combination of work lighting from the ceiling and low wattage moveable track lighting around the room and from a central light housing in the middle of the room. When work illumination is required, ceiling-mounted florescent units provide ample energy-efficient light. When the centre is open for visitors, low-intensity track lighting allows directed illumination on all walls, around the room away from walls, and over the entire centre of the room. The lights are controlled in groups from a panel with rheostats controlling light power from 75 watts per lamp down to zero. Tracks and fixtures were purchased off-the shelf from a lighting store in Ankara.

From the visitor centre, guided groups are allowed to walk over the site on walkways to visit excavation areas. As a matter of cultural heritage to protect the *höyük* from erosion caused by foot traffic, visitors are restricted to these walkways when moving around the mound. At appropriate locations (near the excavations or at the mound summit) visitor overlooks have been constructed. At several excavation sites they will see the covered and protected remains of buildings with *in situ* mural paintings and sculpture. For example, Building 5, a very well-preserved domestic dwelling, has been covered by a shelter with an interior display area and a bridge allowing visitors to walk over the excavation and look inside from above. Panels along the walkway around the open building interpret living spaces, facilities (grain bins, oven, remains of the ladder to the roof) and architectural details (mud-brick wall, plasters, scars where roof support posts once stood).

Çatalhöyük on-line (*Mysteries of Çatalhöyük*)

On 30 June 1998 the Science Museum launched *Mysteries of Çatalhöyük*, a prototype educational web site (http://www.smm.org/catal) designed for American middle school and high school teachers and students (Fig. 16.5). *Mysteries* was developed from Çatalhöyük On-Line, a project funded through the Teaching with Technology programme of the National Endowment for the Humanities (Grant ED-20752-97). Using a friendly and inviting cartoon format, the web site emphasizes an inquiry-based approach and interaction with Çatalhöyük researchers to engage students in learning about Çatalhöyük. The development team created the prototype home page featuring five questions and a framework for navigation, using photographs integrated into a comic book style. The prototype also includes student activities for questions on the meaning of murals and the function of clay balls.

Mysteries was developed after extensive interview and discussion with students and their teachers, the users of this product. A major recommendation of teachers was to focus on involving students in problem-solving activities rather than just providing information. Teacher advisors tested the prototype and found the questions inviting and appreciated the diverse perspectives conveyed by the researchers within student activities and questions. We were surprised that teachers not only liked the comic book style, but also recommended its use for all of the most important text. They explained that some students do not like to read but will read texts in comic style, while others will read anything regardless of style.

Window on Çatalhöyük

On 9 November 1998 the National Science Foundation approved funding for SMM to develop *Window on Çatalhöyük: an Archaeological Work in Progress*. *Window on Çatalhöyük* will consist of four integrated public programmes on the research process at Çatalhöyük. The project will include a 4500 square foot exhibit at the SMM, a suite of archaeology interactives developed for the exhibit and other venues, a school outreach programme of related classroom activities, and an expansion of the *Mysteries of Çatalhöyük* web site for distribution over the Internet. A project team headed by Science Museum project director Don Pohlman will work with outside advisors drawn from the Çatalhöyük project, professional exhibit evaluators, and SMM staff to develop this multifaceted project.

Set in a partial reconstruction of Çatalhöyük's architecture, the exhibit will use a multimedia approach combining interactive components, models, objects displays, video programmes, computer simulations and large format photography to tell an on-going story of scientists at work. Included will be an exhibit of the geography, cultures and recent history of Turkey that will use maps, video, photographs and artefact displays to give visitors background for understanding the present-day con-

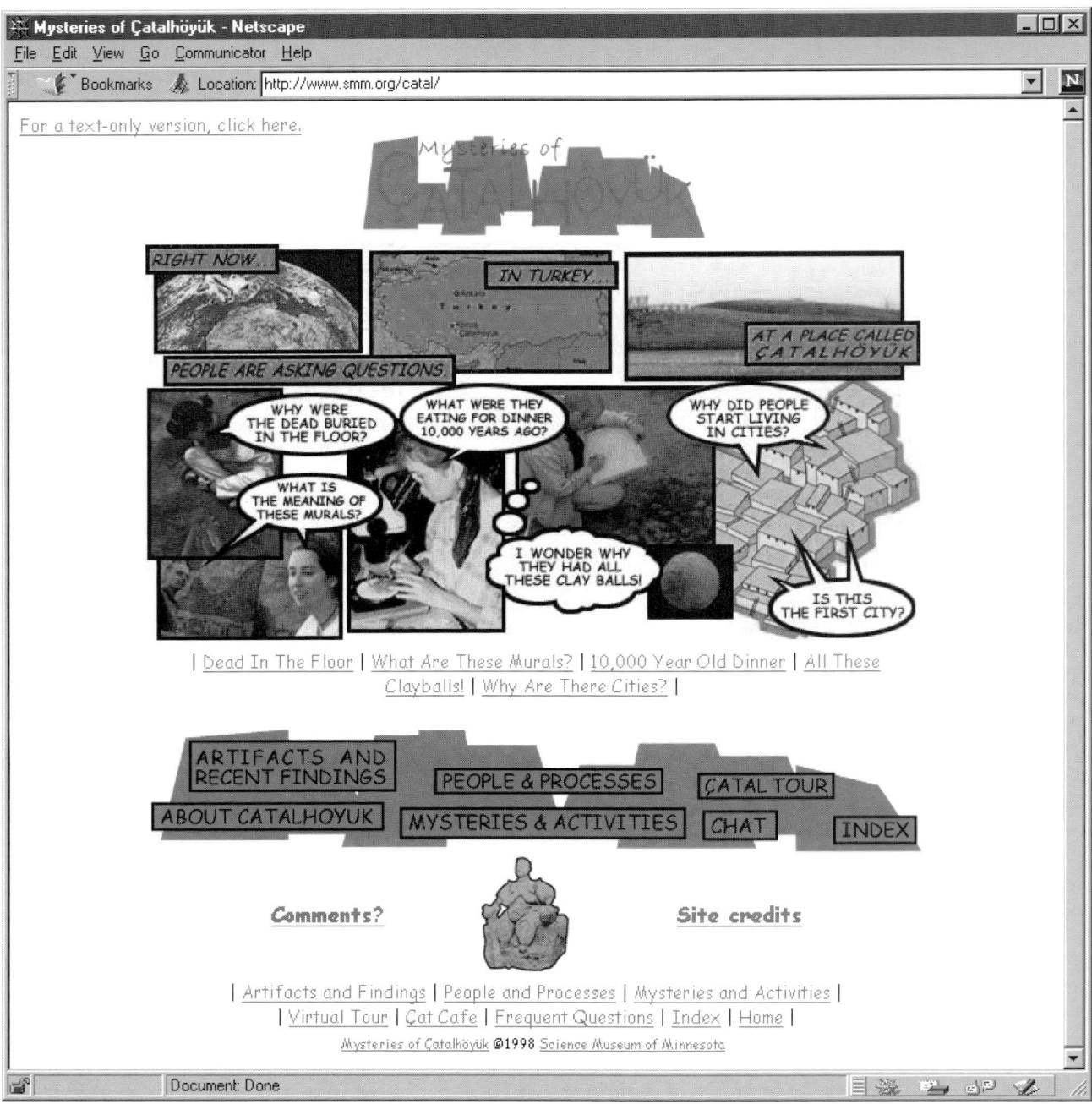

Figure 16.5. *Home page for the* Mysteries of Çatalhöyük.

text of the site and the research project.

A major component of the exhibit will be 'activity stations' that provide intensive interactive hands-on learning experiences for one or a small number of museum visitors who may spend considerable time working though activities or problems that demonstrate archaeological methods. Activity stations we will develop include micromorphology, dendrochronology, palaeoethnobotany, zooarchaeology,

surveying and mapping, and archaeological sampling.

The continuation of *Mysteries of Çatalhöyük* is also a part of the *Window* project. This will provide a vehicle for keeping the exhibit current with the ongoing research at Çatalhöyük. *Mysteries* will provide the primary means for linking the exhibition and the student investigations of the school outreach programme with researchers at Çatalhöyük in the sum-

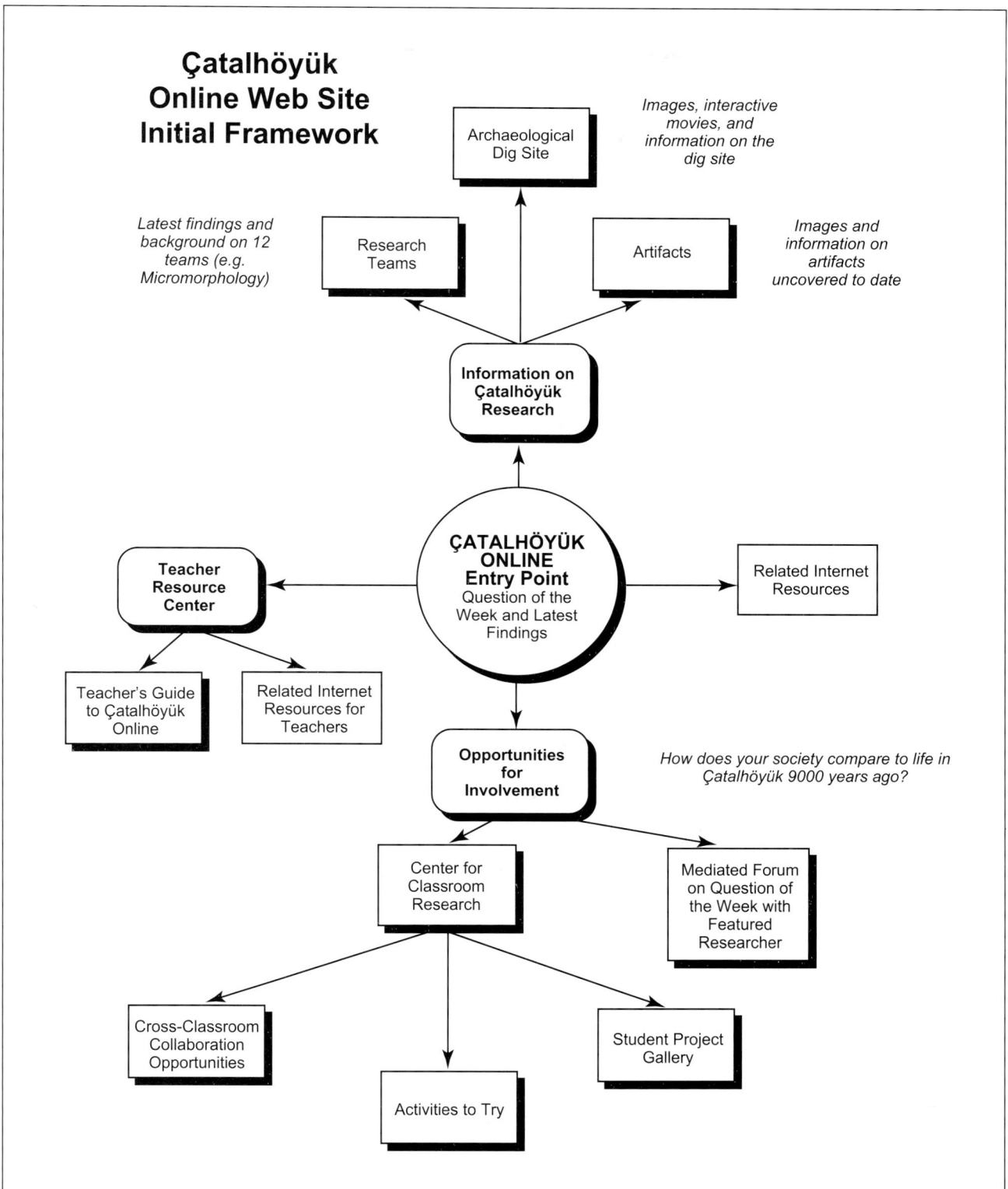

Çatalhöyük Online Web Site Initial Framework

Archaeological Dig Site

Images, interactive movies, and information on the dig site

Latest findings and background on 12 teams (e.g. Micromorphology)

Research Teams

Artifacts

Images and information on artifacts uncovered to date

Information on Çatalhöyük Research

ÇATALHÖYÜK ONLINE Entry Point Question of the Week and Latest Findings

Teacher Resource Center

Related Internet Resources

Teacher's Guide to Çatalhöyük Online

Related Internet Resources for Teachers

Opportunities for Involvement

How does your society compare to life in Çatalhöyük 9000 years ago?

Center for Classroom Research

Mediated Forum on Question of the Week with Featured Researcher

Cross-Classroom Collaboration Opportunities

Activities to Try

Student Project Gallery

Figure 16.6. *Diagram of the framework of the Web site, illustrating relationships between students, teachers, and research teams in the field. Related internet resources include other Web sites, particularly the Cambridge site, from which field data are available for student use. A very popular component is the Mediated Forum (Çat Room), featuring specific research questions or Featured Researchers.*

mer and in their laboratories and offices during the rest of the year. *Mysteries* will provide content and inspiration for users, instructions for activities, current data and resources from the Çatalhöyük excavation, and tools for recording observations and discussing interpretations.

School outreach programmes are a speciality of the Science Museum and for Çatalhöyük SMM School Services staff are planning inquiry-based activities as outreach to middle school students (ages 12–15 years) in Minnesota. The programme will be designed to include several kinds of learning experiences such as auditorium presentations for large groups, small group sessions of two- to three-hours over five days, or full-day summer camps, as well as other informal settings. Hands-on activities will combine the use of scientific tools (microscopes, maps, and mapping tools), material evidence and on-line data. For example, we envision links to the Çatalhöyük site data base at Cambridge University as one source for on-line data for these projects.

Conclusion

In this chapter we have presented a long-range plan for the public presentation of Çatalhöyük and the Çatalhöyük research project. We have also outlined a process by which public programmes are being developed and implemented. But this plan remains 'momentary, fluid and flexible,' subject to change and modification as new finds are made, inevitable new interpretations of Çatalhöyük are written and when new technologies for public presentation become available.

Acknowledgements

In this chapter we have drawn heavily from proposals and other unpublished documents prepared by ourselves, Don Pohlman, Natalie Rusk and Larry Wechsler of the Science Museum of Minnesota.

References

Csikszentmihalyi, M., 1996. *Creativity.* New York (NY): HarperCollins.

Csikszentmihalyi, M. & R.E. Robinson, 1990. *The Art of Seeing: an Interpretation of the Aesthetic Encounter.* Malibu (CA): J. Paul Getty Museum and Getty Centre for Education in the Arts.

Csikszentmihalyi, M. & E. Rochberg-Halton, 1981. *The Meaning of Things: Domestic Symbols and the Self.* New York (NY): Cambridge University Press.

Falk, J.H. & L.D. Dierking, 1992. *The Museum Experience.* Washington (DC): Whalesback Books.

Gardner, H., 1983. *Frames of Mind: the Theory of Modern Intelligences.* New York (NY): Basic Books.

Gardner, H., 1993. *Frames of Mind: the Theory of Modern Intelligences.* 2nd edition. New York (NY): Basic Books.

Gathercole, P. & D. Lowenthal (eds.), 1990. *The Politics of the Past.* London: Routledge.

Hodder, I., 1992. *Theory and Practice in Archaeology.* London & New York (NY): Routledge.

Hodder, I., 1995. Excavations at Çatalhöyük. *Anatolian Archaeology* 1, 3–5.

Hodder, I. (ed.), 1996. *On the Surface: Çatalhöyük 1993-95.* (McDonald Institute Monographs.) Cambridge: McDonald Institute of Archaeological Research; London: British Institute of Archaeology at Ankara.

Hodder, I., 1997. 'Always momentary, fluid and flexible': towards a reflexive excavation methodology. *Antiquity* 71, 691–700.

Hodder, I., 1998. The past as passion and play: Çatalhöyük as a site of conflict in the construction of multiple pasts, in Meskell (ed.), 124–39.

Hooper-Greenhill, E., 1992. *Museums and the Shaping of Knowledge.* London: Routledge.

Jameson, J.H., Jr, 1994. The importance of public outreach in archaeology. *Society of American Archaeology Bulletin* 12(3), 16–17.

Jameson, J.H., Jr (ed.), 1997. *Presenting Archaeology to the Public: Digging for Truths.* Walnut Creek (CA) & London: AltaMira Press.

Karp, I., C.M. Kreamer & S.D. Lavine (eds.), 1992. *Museums and Communities.* Washington (DC): Smithsonian Institution Press.

Kolb, D.A., 1984. *Experiential Learning: Experience as the Source of Learning and Development.* Englewood Cliffs (NJ): Prentice-Hall.

Lewis, B., 1968. *The Emergence of Modern Turkey.* 2nd edition. Oxford: Oxford University Press.

McManus, P.M. (ed.), 1996. *Archaeological Displays and the Public: Museology and Interpretation.* London: Institute of Archaeology, University College London.

Matthews, W., C. French, T. Lawrence & D. Cutler, 1996. Multiple surfaces: the micromorphology, in Hodder (ed.), 301–42.

Mellaart, J., 1967. *Catal Huyuk: a Neolithic Town in Anatolia.* London: Thames & Hudson.

Meskell, L. (ed.), 1998. *Archaeology Under Fire: Nationalism, Politics and Heritage in the Eastern Mediterranean and Middle East.* London: Routledge.

Museum Education Roundtable (eds.), 1992. *Patterns in Practice: Selections from the Journal of Museum Education.* Washington (DC): Museum Education Roundtable.

Özdoğan, M., 1998. Ideology and archaeology in Turkey, in Meskell (ed.), 111–23.

Potter, P.B., Jr, 1994. *Public Archaeology in Annapolis: a Critical Approach to History in Maryland's Ancient City.* Washington (DC): Smithsonian Institution Press.

Potter, P.B., Jr, 1997. The archaeological site as an interpretive environment, in Jameson (ed.), 35–44.

Sauber, C.M. (ed.), 1994. *Experiment Bench: a Workbook for Building Experimental Physics Exhibits.* St Paul (MN): Science Museum of Minnesota.

Schlereth, T.J., 1992. Object knowledge: every museum visitor an interpreter, in Museum Education Roundtable (eds.), 102–11.

Screven, C.G., 1986. Exhibitions and information centres: some principles and approaches. *Curator* 29(2), 109–37.

Shane, O.C., III & M. Küçük, 1998. The world's first city. *Archaeology* 51(2), 43–7.

Shankland, D.S., 1996. Çatalhöyük: the anthropology of an archaeological presence, in Hodder (ed.), 349–57.

Shanks, M. & I. Hodder, 1995. Processual, postprocessual and interpretive archaeologies, in *Interpreting Archaeology*, eds. I. Hodder, M. Shanks, A. Alexandri, V. Buchli, J. Carman, J. Last & G. Lucas. London & New York (NY): Routledge, 3–29.

Stone, P.G. & B.L. Molyneaux (eds.), 1994. *The Presented Past: Heritage, Museums and Education.* London & New York (NY): Routledge.

Yakar, J., 1991. *Prehistoric Anatolia: the Neolithic Transformation and the Early Chalcolithic Period.* Tel Aviv: Tel Aviv University.

Chapter 17

Multiple Çatalhöyüks on the World Wide Web

Anja-C. Wolle & Ruth I. Tringham

Since the 1960s, the growth of computer applications in archaeology has influenced the discipline's theoretical framework. In the 1960s the available mainframe technology had limited software and emphasis was concentrated on the number-crunching statistical abilities of these machines (for an application see for example Hodson *et al.* 1966). The requirements for data-minimal digital models fitted in with the data-minimizing theory of the New Archaeology (now known as Processual Archaeology).

In the 1980s, the move away from the reductionism and scientism that was central to processual archaeology saw the birth of postprocessualism, which in fact consists of a divergent series of theoretical approaches united in their critique of processualist methods. One theme which can be identified, and which has inevitably touched on the Çatalhöyük project, is that of context and contextualism (Hodder 1986; 1987).

As this project is explicitly theoretical and computers have played a large part in it from the start, the interrelationship between the use of computing and the theoretical approaches requires examination. Do computers play a prominent role because they fit well with the project's postprocessual paradigm, or is the paradigm itself influenced by the availability of computers? Computers are now routinely used for computerization of the archaeological record, digital imagery, publication and communication through the Internet, and desktop publication for paper or electronic (e.g. CD-ROM) media that allows the dissemination of images and texts much more cheaply and quickly than when authors are dependent on corporate professional publishing houses. The Çatalhöyük project has entered energetically into this world and has taken advantage of its potential in many different ways. For this contribution we shall focus on the aspects of computerization that could be termed multimedia productions. When work restarted at Çatalhöyük in the early 1990s, the methodological approach adopted concentrated on four main issues: increased contextual information, reflexivity, interactivity and multivocality.

At Çatalhöyük the multiplicity of voices that characterizes its research is reflected in the many faces of multimedia/hypermedia[1] expression of the site. This multiplicity is expressed in the different backgrounds and experience of the authors, their views of the purpose and audience of their multimedia productions, the physical media on which they publish (CD-ROM and/or Internet), and the intended mode of dissemination of the product (marketed or free access, for educational or commercial markets). This chapter demonstrates how several different applications of hypermedia technology have enabled us to encourage and support all of the above issues. It focuses on three multimedia/hypermedia productions directly associated with Çatalhöyük that are currently active or in preparation, since these express not only the multi-sitedness of the Çatalhöyük archaeological project itself, but also the fact that hypermedia is by no means a homogeneous monolithic mode of expression. An additional discussion of virtual reality as produced by the Hochschule für Gestaltung Karlsruhe and of approaches to alternative contextual recording, are presented in the following chapters. The *Turkish Friends of Çatalhöyük*, a friends society based in Istanbul to promote awareness of the site in Turkey, also run their own bilingual (Turkish/English) Web site at http://www.catalhoyuk.org/.

The Çatalhöyük project web site in Cambridge
(Anja-C. Wolle)
http://catal.arch.cam.ac.uk/catal/catal.html

The Web site is based in Cambridge, providing a central point of access for all teams working at Çatalhöyük, as well as a central point of access for those outside the project. Prior to the autumn of 1996, although a basic Web presence (a series of pages now designated as newsletter 1) had been published, there had been no dedicated person to work on the Web site. I joined the project at that point to expand and develop the Web site towards its full potential, whilst also managing most other computing aspects of the project. My work on the Web site represents a continuation of my interest in the practical and theoretical aspects of archaeological data dissemination and excavation report publication using the electronic medium (Wolle 1996; 1998; forthcoming; Wolle & Shennan 1996).

Archaeology is now widely recognized as being particularly suited to hypermedia, since it is multidisciplinary and uses a wide variety of data types, which all relate to each other and are rarely examined in a linear fashion (Rahtz *et al.* 1989, 21; Heyworth *et al.* 1996, 518). The use of hypermedia and electronic publishing for archaeological publications is now establishing itself as an accepted method in archaeology.[2] This section demonstrates how this method of publication has been successfully harnessed, providing access to data which is hard to publish, and is slow to be published. Since the medium of the World Wide Web is better suited for the publication of what is seen as ephemeral material which may become out of date or is regularly updated (Champion 1995, 19), it seemed ideal to use this medium for the speedy dissemination of reports on data to project members and interested parties beyond. After its initial installation in 1996, and development from the end of 1996 onwards the Çatalhöyük Web site has become an effective way of transmitting information about archaeological research at Çatalhöyük.

To allow further discussion of the Web site, its functions and achievements, a brief description is required here (see also Fig. 17.1). From the entry point of the front page, the visitor is presented with the options and material available. These again fall into two categories. Toward the top of the page the visitor is presented with recent additions to the page, which change periodically. Alongside this the newsletters can be accessed. Further down more specific or specialized information can be accessed, such as complete archive reports for past seasons, and the excavation data base. Specific materials are as follows:

- Newsletters provide readers with shortened annual season summaries, and include some photographs.
- The Archive Reports contain more detailed ac-

counts of work carried out during the excavation season. These reports are written by the subject specialists and are included on the Web site without additional editing.
- The Excavation Data Base is accessible through a series of queries which give access to excavation unit and feature data, as well as the excavators' site diaries.
- Other documents are included to open the site to voices from outside. These include a discussion with Anita Louise, a member of the Goddess community, and a prize-winning essay by Merve Tezcanly, a Turkish student, on the significance of Çatalhöyük.
- The Discussion page gives users the opportunity to take part in discussions about the site.
- A description of how to get to the site.
- A bibliography of publications, spanning from the 1960s to present.

The basic aim of the Web site is simple: to enable direct access to primary excavation and project data, thus providing increased contextual information, and to encourage dialogue, thus supporting reflexivity, and to provide previously voiceless individuals with a forum to enable multivocality.

However, the Web site can really be seen to function on two levels: first, it aims to increase awareness and distribute information about the renewed work at the site to a larger audience than can normally be reached. The audiences we reach are of course so varied it would be impossible to characterize them here. They include archaeologists, students, and Goddess groups (see below). The newsletters, written for the non-specialized audience, summarize the content of the detailed and technical archive reports. While the newsletters represent a duplication in information, they present the excavation results in a more approachable way.

Second, the Web site aims to distribute data and reports to the team as a whole, encouraging dialogue and supporting research. Of course, the specialist information such as the excavation data base is not restricted to team members, but so far has been provided primarily with this audience in mind. An important distinction is that virtually none of the material available was especially written for publication via the World Wide Web. This decision was partially dictated by minimal resources, but also represents a conscious decision to allow everyone their own voice. Despite this aim, the end result has been criticized for a lack of cohesion and overall united feel (Eiteljorg 1998).

In fact the Web site has rapidly become the

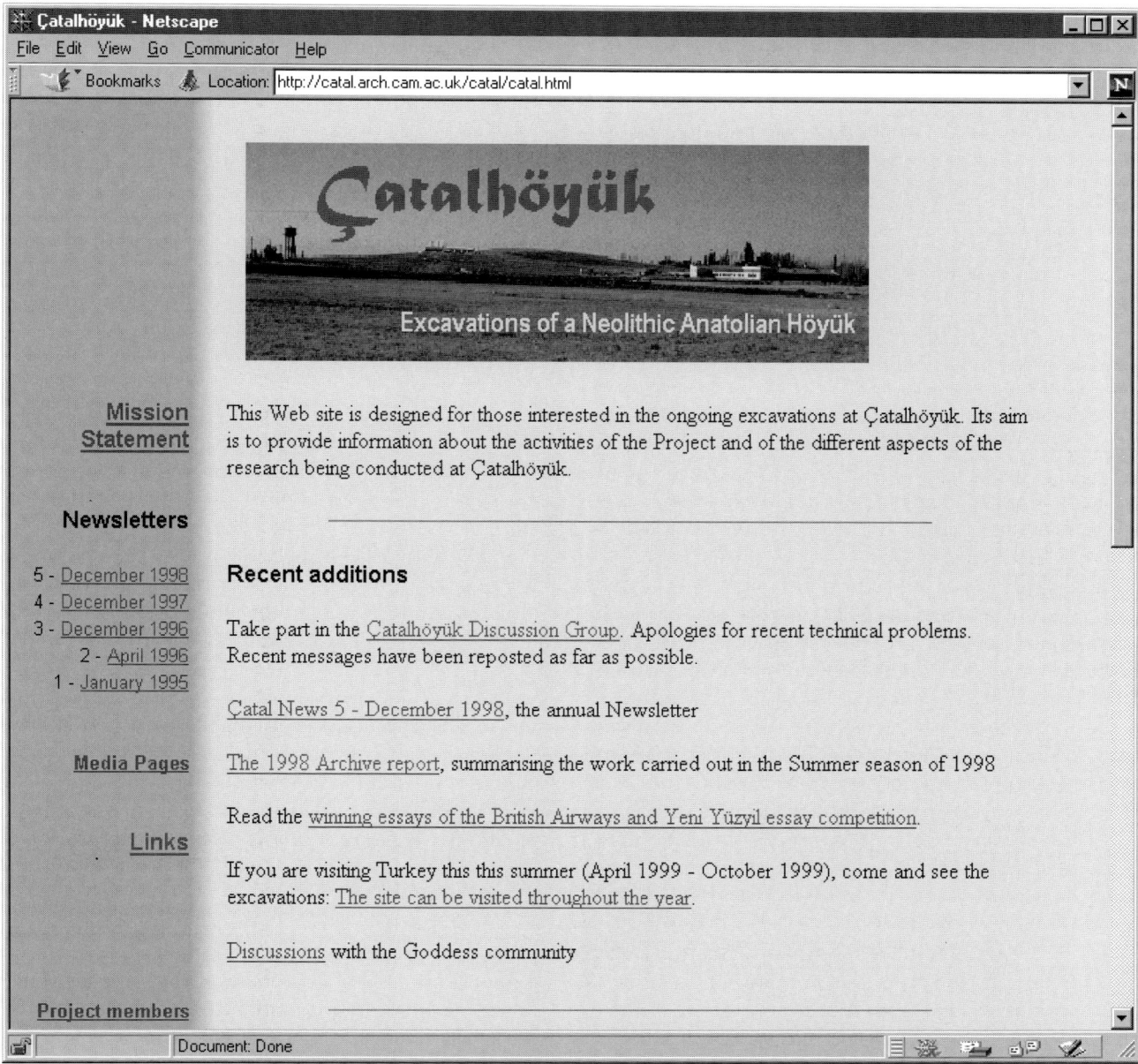

Figure 17.1. *The Çatalhöyük web site, front page (24-3-1999).*

most important way of 'publishing' the archaeological site, not only because it is widely read, but also because it is up-to-date and frequently edited and renewed. Data and reports are added as they become available. The speed of 'publication' is such that an archive report, newsletter and context and other data from the 1998 season were available on the Web site three to four months after the end of the excavation season, in fact just days or weeks after completion of the conventional paper reports. Those interested in the archaeological site are thus able to keep in touch with the most recent findings. The

speed of dissemination also encourages overall reflexivity within the team of specialists working on the data simultaneously. The Web site has enabled the Çatalhöyük project to 'break free' of conventional disciplinary format of publication as represented by the first volume in this series (Hodder 1996).

Aspects of the design of the Web site have been influenced by the aim to make it as widely accessible as possible. There is a conflict between making everything available and making it available to everyone. The solution I adopted was to keep the core materials simple to access: all basic information is accessible without the need to download specific Web browser plug-ins. Media types which do require plug-ins are made available but are not central to the information. The Web site remains accessible and useful to persons without this software. Similarly, images have been kept to a relative minimum, compared to other Web sites, to speed up access times and help people without access to cutting-edge technology. Finally, the site does not make use of frames, a popular layout tool for Web design, as there are still a number of users who cannot access Web pages that use frames.

The key aspect of the Web site is the access it provides to primary data as well as the reports derived from it. From a conventional point of view the data in archaeology can be grouped in three broad areas: the first is the primary data, which represents the information collected during the excavation and research, fields notes, plans and measurements. Secondary data is the information derived from the primary data by means of analysis and research, such as specialist reports, archive reports or reconstruction drawings for example. Finally, the published data is the body of material which is disseminated, usually by commercial means, beyond the local sphere. When considering the role primary, secondary and published data play in archaeology, it has already become apparent that improved access to and dissemination of primary and secondary data from the Çatalhöyük excavations has very much influenced the dialogue in the wider archaeological community (Hodder pers. comm.). By allowing free access to the unedited and original excavation data, the process of interpretation is made at least partially explicit and becomes more transparent. Others can now draw on the original data to offer their alternative interpretations. The inclusion of information about the original context of discovery and excavation, the conditions and the people involved, as in the diaries, reflects the methodological aims of this project. The aim is to disseminate as much contextual information as possible; the diaries and unit sheets represent aspects of the excavation process which are not normally made available to a wide audience.

With the inclusion of the excavators' diaries (discussed by Hodder Chapter 1 and Farid *et al.* Chapter 2, this volume) on the Web site, unedited and uncensored, we take the unprecedented step of revealing more about the excavation process than has become normal. Notionally adding contextual information to the excavation record, a detail frequently lacking from recent published excavation reports (Hodder 1989), the diaries also show conflict and process placing the whole of the excavation, as well as the data collected from it, into context.

The Çatalhöyük Web site opens up the site to a wider variety of people than would otherwise have been possible. Many groups have interest in the site, and we the archaeological fraternity cannot claim exclusive authority on the interpretation of the site. The Web site offers an easy way to give voices to groups outside the central archaeological research project. Examples of these 'other voices' are the discussion with a leading figure of the Goddess movement, an essay by a Turkish student reflecting on the importance of Çatalhöyük for the Turkish People, and an open unmoderated discussion forum about all aspects of the site. The inclusion of these alternative views has been commented upon favourably (Hoopes 1999), but should not be overstated. The Web as a publication medium is still not perceived as being as authoritative as a conventional paper publication. And so far the alternative voices are somewhat absent form the other published materials that the project produces (Hodder 1996), where the 'alternative' voices are those of other academics such as anthropologists. On the other hand, the Web site allows us to engage in a dialogue that does not require academic writing skills, so it is possible to open up to people outside the academic archaeological sphere, who might otherwise never read or write for a publication that comes from the Çatalhöyük research project.

Certainly the Web site plays an important role in allowing members of the project staff to get access to each other's data, especially as they are scattered across the globe. So the Web site plays a primary role in data handling by the project staff. And non-specialist non-team members too can access the data and comment on it. Interactivity, multivocality and reflexivity are encouraged. But it is also undoubtedly the case that this process excludes many people. Some people are excluded by the infrastructure required to access these pages, and not everyone has access to an internet-connected computer. While this is a criticism occasionally levelled at the Çatalhöyük Web site, I can only repeat that *with* the Web site we are able to reach a far larger audience than *without*. If we had to rely on paper publication such as the one you are holding now, possibly supplemented by the newsletter, we would only reach a considerably smaller and more restricted number of readers.

The question of unequal access is one of infrastructure but also of data structure and language: to understand someone else's data the user needs to understand the rationale for their recording, structuring and organization of that data (Huggett 1995). While the provision of site archives and site data from context forms to plans and diary entries makes the site data more accessible, this accessibility requires a user-friendly path of entry into the database. It is unlikely that outsiders could understand directly the recording mechanisms employed in the field and the details recorded. Indeed members of the research team have difficulty understanding each others' coded data. To redress this situation for the excavation data, the 'crib sheets' employed to train excavators are accessible from the Web site and are linked into the data base query pages. There is still much work to do on this for the Çatalhöyük Web site. Indeed the design requirements for open access to a codified and specialized set of data are complex, and there is much experimentation that is needed in order to provide appropriate entry systems for a wide range of different constituencies.

This Web site, with the theoretical aims that drive it and which it drives in turn, has shown that archaeology now has an opportunity to move away from being a discipline focused mainly on data collection to becoming a discipline able to concentrate on interpreting the data collected. If the archives for sites as excavated and recorded were to become more freely accessible, researchers would no longer spend the majority of their time collecting the data they require prior to interpreting it. We might have seen the last of multi-volume excavation reports or Ph.D. theses which are little more than extensive catalogues of specific materials or finds; instead archaeologists could focus on the interpretation and contextual meaning of the data. This shift of focus could have widespread effects on academic research. Instead of focusing on the general interpretation of sites based on the published data, access to primary data would empower individuals and encourage the creation of alternative narratives and interpretations.

The next Web site discussed in this chapter reflects the approach to the multivocality embraced by the project. It aims squarely at a very different audience, but draws on the same data collection.

Mysteries of Çatalhöyük
http://www.smm.org/catal/

A team from the Science Museum of Minnesota (SMM), led by Don Pohlman, has received NSF funding to produce an exhibit, entitled *Window on Çatalhöyük* which includes the following goals:

- To present the Çatalhöyük research project as a work-in-progress that reveals science as a dynamic and social process for constructing and reconstructing knowledge.
- To give audiences a deeper understanding of the tools and techniques of archaeology and how archaeologists work together to understand the past.
- To create and disseminate successful interactive exhibit components devoted to the formation processes of archaeological evidence, contemporary archaeological field and laboratory techniques, and related geological, physical and biological science.

The project consists of three major elements, a 4500 square foot exhibition, a North American Web site and a suite of related classroom activities. The Web site is the focus of this description, and is aimed at a 6th to 12th grade school audience, some of whom will be able to visit the exhibit at the Science Museum.

A prototype of the Web site entitled *Mysteries of Çatalhöyük* is already available (see Fig. 16.5) and will be re-designed extensively during exhibit development. In using the Word Wide Web to connect museum visitors and students to progress at Çatalhöyük, SMM's project reflects the research team's own extensive use of the Web to stay in touch with its far flung members and to share information with broader communities in side and outside of science. The Web site will provide the primary vehicle for linking the exhibition with the researchers at the site during the summer field seasons and their labs during the rest of the year. The Web site will also greatly extend the SMM project's audience reach and will provide opportunities for developing and evaluating ideas of the exhibit and the school programs.

This Web site offers a means to deliver the exhibition's content and many of its experiences to audiences far beyond the direct reach of the museum. For example, visitors to the Web site will be able to take a QuickTime VR tour of the mound and the excavations, or read excerpts of the excavation diary. Ultimately it is hoped to include 'live' (time difference allowing) camera feeds for the excavation, e-mail from on-site science correspondents, and digital images of recent artefact finds.

Mysteries of Çatalhöyük will feature four kinds of resources to engage its users in the continuing investigations and interpretation of Çatalhöyük:
- Context and inspiration: The entry point for the Web site is composed of images and words of several scientists from the research team offering evidence and differing opinions on actual unre-

solved questions that cut across the work of many specialists on the team. These questions will be selected for their likely appeal to young people, their power to spark student inquiry, and their capacity to illuminate the need for multiple perspectives within the investigative process.

- Instructions for investigative techniques and activities: there will be instructions that students can refer to during their investigations into the above questions, such as how to make clay balls.
- Current data and other resources from the Çatalhöyük excavation: to help answer these questions, students will be provided with access to evidence including reconstructions and models, maps and images, original data as contained on the Çatalhöyük project Web site.
- Tools for recording observations and discussing interpretations. The Web site will also provide a framework for students to record and exchange their observations, post their conclusions with supporting evidence, and discuss differences in the interpretation in an on-line forum.

This project focuses a great deal on what archaeologists do, who they are, meeting them, hearing what they say — in other words, an introduction to some of the multiple voices of Çatalhöyük, whilst encouraging the students and museum visitors to develop their own voices. Along the way these audiences gain some idea of the multiplicity of possible interpretations. Museum sites have been some of the most successful developers of multimedia for the public understanding of science and play an important role as mediators between the public and the archaeological sites and process.

Constructing multiple narratives
(Ruth Tringham)
http://www.mactia.berkeley.edu/tringham/index.html

This part of the chapter reflects a rather different route towards the use of multimedia/hypermedia from that experienced by either of the previously discussed Web sites. In this case, the construction of a hypermedia Web is seen as the ideal medium for the expression not only of archaeological research in general and its multivocal interpretation, but especially of the feminist practice of archaeology. Like postprocessual archaeology, the 'feminist archaeology' embraces a variety of practices, but for me it has come to include:

- a reflexive but intense relationship with the archaeological data in which I explore the multi-

plicity of plausible prehistories that can be written from any data base.
- writing prehistory at a multiplicity of scales, in which the regional scale of interpretation is not privileged over the individual actor scale.
- writing prehistory with multiple voices — voices of different archaeologists (directors and students), different 'readers' from popular culture (tourists, workers, bureaucrats), and different prehistoric actors (women, children, men, young, old, poor, powerful).
- critical awareness of the social and political context of my (and that of others) practice of archaeology

The presentation of such multiple strands of evidence and viewpoints and possible interpretations is hard to conceive for the archaeologist doing the presenting; it is doubly difficult for readers from within the discipline — and especially outside it — to grasp.

In the more conventional format of print on paper, I experimented with collages of texts and images in articles that juxtaposed different interpretations of the same archaeological data, the same prehistoric events viewed and voiced by prehistoric actors and modern actors (archaeologists, tourists), the same place viewed at different scales, and images of excavations juxtaposed with images of prehistoric. Such juxtaposition can bring to the reader's attention links and resonances. A reader can navigate through a collage of juxtaposed images in many different ways, coming each time to a different view of the meaning of the images. But such attempts provided a visual and textual challenge to conventional (academic) methods of reporting and presenting archaeological research. In addition even in these articles written in such an experimental format, it was still virtually impossible to avoid linearity. The surprise and effect of non-linear juxtaposition is lost, and the article becomes an editor's nightmarish complex mess of footnotes and cross-references, with the use of different fonts and formats and interjected illustrations.

It was at this point that the nature of hypertext and hypermedia — computerized texts and other media that can be juxtaposed, linked and navigated in a multitude of ways, coming to a different narrative each time — provided an obvious solution. It seemed that hypermedia productions would provide a rare medium through which the complexities of such a multiplicity of interpretations and non-linearity of their investigation and navigation can be expressed and appreciated by others beyond the confines of academic seminars, for example visitors (virtual or real) to Çatalhöyük.

The Chimera Web (Fig. 17.2a) has been my first attempt to express digitally the complex pluralities demanded by the feminist practice of archaeology. The Chimera Web is a non-linear hypermedia Web of linked texts, sounds, and images based on the field research at Neolithic sites in Southeast Europe during the last fifteen years in the former Yugoslavia, particularly at Opovo (Tringham & Krstic 1990; Tringham *et al.* 1985; 1992; in press) (see Fig. 17.2).

Using the experience of leading a team from the University of California, Berkeley, that excavates at Çatalhöyük in the BACH area, I am authoring a hypermedia production to present Çatalhöyük through the eyes of a research team. The Chimera Web provides the prototype for this hypermedia Web whose provisional title is: *Dead Women Do Tell Tales.*

The elements that already make up the Chimera Web and will be included in my hypermedia product about Çatalhöyük comprise (Fig. 17.2b):

I. THE PRIMARY ARCHAEOLOGICAL DATA:
- Selected still photographic and drawn images from the excavation: field plans, field photos, artefact photographs.
- Charts, maps and tables presenting the numerical data.
- Textual descriptions of the excavation.

II. THE ARCHAEOLOGICAL EXPERIENCE:
- Selections from archaeologists' field diaries. Digital diaries. Video diaries and clips from the excavation.
- Still photography during the excavation.

III. SELECTIONS OF THE BACKGROUND DATA
(from ethnography, material science, folklore, history and ethnohistory, personal experience) that act as the sources of the archaeologist's imagination.

IV. INTERPRETATIONS OF THE ÇATALHÖYÜK DATA:
- Conventional macro-scale constructions of prehistoric scenarios by various archaeologists
- Feminist archaeology can make a real contribution to *multiscalar* explorations of history. Archaeology has traditionally given priority to the long-term comparative view and to the regional and generational scale of analysis of social and cultural evolution. Feminist archaeology adds a focus on the *micro*-scale of the lives and intentional actions of individuals as they practise, negotiate,

and change the longer-term structures. It is essentially the prehistory of *people* — social actors who have gender, personalities, biographies. This is brought out by:
- Non-traditional interpretations in the form of narrative texts of imagined prehistoric social actors. As George Landow (Landow 1992) has pointed out, hypertext (and by extension hypermedia) is an ideal medium for expression of multivocality. We can express the viewpoints of different prehistoric actors as well as the viewpoints of archaeologists of the same landscape during and after excavation. One option in constructing these 'past realities' is to present the past as a real (or virtually real) lived-in linear past that was experienced generically and normatively by all actors. Another option — inspired by the ideas of John Berger — is to construct a past *as remembered* by these various actors, rather than trying to envision a past *as lived* (Berger 1980). If this option is followed — as it is in the Chimera Web — then the past places are presented as in a dream or remembered piecemeal, selectively, and uniquely by the different actors. In this way the prehistoric scenes and buildings and landscapes that are constructed through computer-generated imagery and other media, can be regarded as more *surreal* than virtually real.
- Animated and still computer-generated images of reconstructed landscapes and walk-through buildings form the context of these constructed memories. These images are used to construct 'views' by prehistoric actors, rather than to attempt a modern reconstruction (archaeologists' view) of the buildings and landscapes. We can fly above the site for a bird's eye view of the landscape, or enter into the most intimate heart of a building for a hearthside view.

This is visual imagery to help construct a prehistory which is essentially about people — men, women and children — in the arena of place (architecture) rather than architecture which happens to contain people. It is visual imagery that helps to construct a prehistory that is full of ambiguity and must therefore embrace comfortably a plurality of interpretations. An essential assumption here is that houses, events and places have multiple meanings and these meanings can be considered at multiple scales of social practice. Moreover, a place will be perceived differently through the eyes of the different prehistoric actors, whose differences are marked by age, gender, power, and life-history. But the challenge is how to visualize and construct images of people in

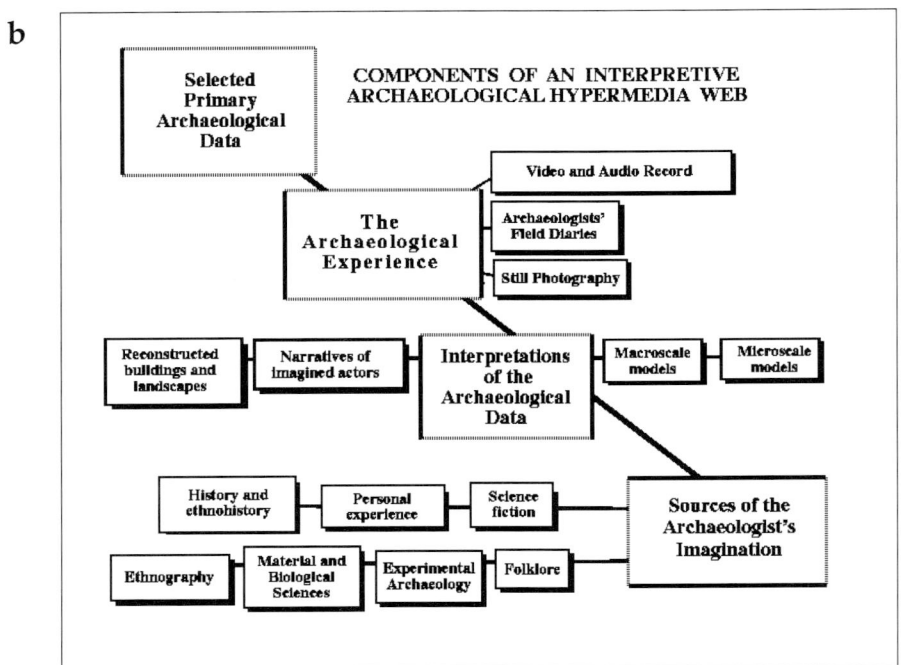

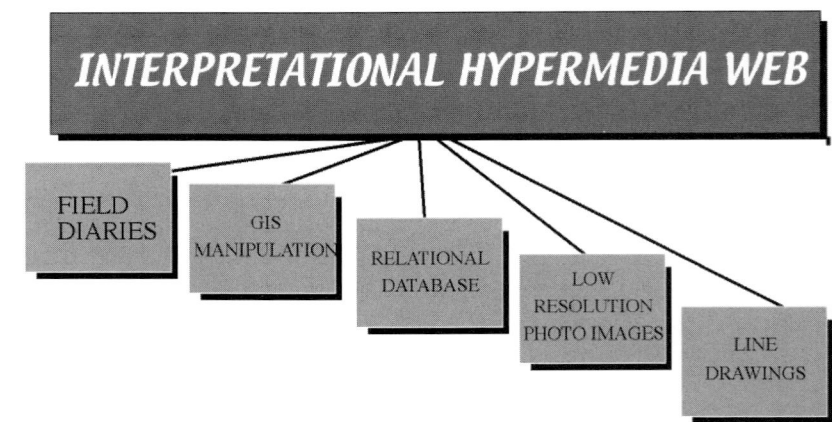

Figure 17.2. *The Chimera Web:*
a) the main navigation threshold of
the Chimera Web; b) the structure of
the Chimera Web; c) the relation of
the Chimera Web to digital
publication.

constructing a surreal prehistory which is essentially about people.

The planned hypermedia Web for Çatalhöyük — like the Chimera Web — has numerous links to the archaeological data base (Fig. 17.2c). Unlike the other hypermedia/multimedia producers at Çatalhöyük, however, *Dead Women Do Tell Tales* is produced by an archaeologist actively participating in the first line of fieldwork — excavation. This might give this production a certain sense of authority by virtue of direct experience. However, the point of my hypermedia Web is to challenge my own status as an authority who transmits knowledge and information through multimedia.

The prospective audience of the *Chimera Web* and *Dead Women Do Tell Tales* is not of any particular age. Nor does it require any particular computer or other previous knowledge about historical and geographical context. Readers can surf superficially, but they can also delve very deeply into the data and ideas and how knowledge is constructed. Prospective readers do, however, need to be willing to think for themselves, and not be seduced by any voice as the ultimate authority. The producer-archaeologist coaches how to make more rather than less plausible interpretations. The reader must be prepared to be playful, imaginative, creative — even poetic in their responses and reactions to this product and its interactivity.

As a multimedia author, I prefer to act as the mediator between the reader and the data, encouraging readers to participate seriously in the interpretation of the archaeological site. You can enter my Web and the process of interpretation of the archaeological site — Opovo or Çatalhöyük — through the medium of an intimate narrative of an imagined person or an image, or you can enter more traditionally via the archaeological data. The point is that multimedia authoring will not necessarily allow you to discover the true solutions to the mysteries of the past, but I have found in teaching through multimedia expression that it can be a quite inspirational medium for the imagination of both students and senior researchers, as well as people from a multiplicity of other backgrounds and ages. This effect is especially obvious if the reader is allowed to participate in the authoring process. I envisage *Dead Women Do Tell Tales* as being an entry point into the 'official' Çatalhöyük project Web-page in which access to the data base is provided, as described by Anja Wolle above. I also envision it as a more complex and challenging guide to the Web site than *The Mysteries of Çatalhöyük* — but one which you might want to visit/read after visiting *The Mysteries*.

The multimedia production described here differs from the Science Museum of Minnesota and Karlsruhe enterprises, not only in terms of my experience, and its orientation towards interpretation, but also in terms of who is doing the authoring. The cost of producing and writing CD-ROMs and Web pages can be very large, but can also be within the means of an archaeological unit's budget, depending on the ambition of the producer. To produce an illusion of reality in which every detail is correct, that is, to produce a virtually real Çatalhöyük can be very expensive of money and labour.

On the other hand, more modest yet creative illusions of reality (or, rather, surreality) are within the grasp of small archaeological units with access to modest technology. In many professional productions, including some of those described here, the content developer (archaeologist) is separated from the multimedia developer. The Chimera Web was started from the premise that a content developer (archaeologist) can also become multimedia author. Moreover, I have found that in teaching multimedia authoring to archaeology students and teaching archaeology through multimedia authoring, students respond with more creativity and enthusiasm in their coursework and actually learn better. This has also been the experience with younger children in the Science Museum of Minnesota. From this I can envisage a possible expansion of the multimedia presentations of Çatalhöyük in which authoring and active creativity is a participated in by visitors and the community as part of the appreciation of heritage.

Conclusions

To conclude, these three examples of some of the multimedia productions developed as part of the ongoing research at Çatalhöyük have shown how much computer technology has helped us develop and support our ideas. The theoretical stance which drives this project has of course influenced the use that was made of the available technology, but in return the availability and development of hypermedia and the World Wide Web has allowed us to develop ideas about reflexivity and multivocality in a way previously not possible.

By allowing direct access to 'raw' data, and by employing hypermedia technology we can enable individuals *within* and *without* the core team to gain their own impressions of the material, to develop their own views and ideas, less coloured by the interpretations already made by the excavator writing up the site or the material specialist interpreting a category of find.

In keeping with the multivocality of the methodology at Çatalhöyük, there are multiple hypermedia presentations or 'windows' of the site. There is overlap in terms of images, content, links to the data base and so on. They are all about Çatalhöyük, but they are very different in terms of what their window looks like. All authors are encouraged to think about how and why their product is different, and how that difference will be read by potential audiences. There is plenty of room for many different ways of telling the story of Çatalhöyük. Moreover, by the nature of their different views and access, each of these multimedia productions has a chance to contribute to the capture of the simultaneity of the multiple sites that are called Çatalhöyük.

Notes

1. There is an important (but frequently unrecognized) distinction between multimedia and hypermedia productions. Multimedia comprises essentially the enhancing of one medium, for example, text, by others, such as images, sound, motion. These productions can be quite linear in character. Such would be a simple walk-through reconstruction of a prehistoric room. Hypermedia is a term that was developed from the concept of 'hypertext'. In the latter, texts are linked in a non-linear fashion, so that a reader may navigate through them in any number of different configurations. In hypermedia, texts are supplemented by other media including sounds and images. The World Wide Web incorporates the multimedia technology of images and sounds into such linked Hypertext nodes, making it — more correctly — a Hypermedia Web.
2. See, for example, the results of a recent workshop 'The Digital Imprint' held Jan 28–30, 1999 at UCLA in which many of the potentials, practicalities and ramifications of digital publishing in archaeology were discussed [ref. http://www.sscnet.ucla.edu/ioa/labs/imprint/imprint.html].

Acknowledgements

The authors would like to thank Don Pohlman for comments on and help with the middle part of this chapter. Anja Wolle would also like to thank Craig Cessford in particular for commenting on numerous drafts of this chapter.

References

Berger, J., 1980. *About Looking*. New York (NY): Pantheon Books.

Champion, S., 1995. Archaeology and the internet. *The Field Archaeologist* 24, 18–19.

Eiteljorg II, H., 1998. Review of Çatalhöyük: excavations of a Neolithic Anatolian tell. *Bryn Mawr Electronic Resources Review*, available at http://csa.brynmawr.edu/BMERR/1998/EitelCatalAug.html (5-2-1999)

Heyworth, M., S. Ross, & J. Richards, 1996. Internet archaeology: an international electronic journal for archaeology, in Kamermans & Fennema (eds.), 517–23.

Hodder, I., 1986. *Reading the Past: Current Approaches to the Interpretation in Archaeology*. Cambridge: Cambridge University Press.

Hodder, I. (ed.), 1987. *The Archaeology of Contextual Meanings*. Cambridge: Cambridge University Press.

Hodder, I., 1989. Writing archaeology: site reports in context. *Antiquity* 63, 268–74.

Hodder, I. (ed.), 1996. *On the Surface: Çatalhöyük 1993–95*. (McDonald Institute Monographs.) Cambridge: McDonald Institute for Archaeological Research; London: British Institute of Archaeology at Ankara.

Hodson, F.R., P.H.A. Sneath, & J.E. Doran, 1966. Some experiments in the numerical analysis or archaeological data. *Biometrika* 53, 311–24.

Hoopes, J., 1999. Avoiding the driest dust that blows: Web site reports. *Society of American Archaeologists Bulletin* 17(1), 23, 26–7, 39.

Huggett, J., 1995. Democracy, data and archaeological knowledge, in Huggett & Ryan (eds.), 23–6.

Huggett, J. & N. Ryan (eds.), 1995. *Computer Applications and Quantitative Methods in Archaeology 1994*. (British Archaeological Reports International Series 600.) Oxford: BAR.

Kamermans, H. & K. Fennema (eds.), 1996. *Interfacing the Past: Computer Applications and Quantitative Methods in Archaeology, CAA95*. (Analecta Praehistorica Leidensia 28.) Leiden: University of Leiden.

Landow, G., 1992. *Hypertext: the Convergence of Contemporary Critical Theory and Technology*. Baltimore (MA): Johns Hopkins University Press.

Lock, G., 1995. Archaeological computing, archaeological theory, and moves towards contextualism, in Huggett & Ryan (eds.), 13–18.

Rahtz, S., L. Carr, & W. Hall, 1989. New designs for archaeological reports. *Science & Archaeology* 31, 20–34.

Tringham, R. & D. Krstic (eds.), 1990. *Selevac: a Prehistoric Village in Yugoslavia*. Los Angeles (CA): Institute of Archaeology Press, UCLA.

Tringham, R., B. Brukner & B. Voytek, 1985. The Opovo project: a study of socio-economic change in the Balkan Neolithic. *Journal of Field Archaeology* 12(4), 425–44.

Tringham, R., B. Brukner, T. Kaiser, K. Borojevic, N. Russell, P. Steli, M. Stevanovic & B. Voytek, 1992. The Opovo project: a study of socio-economic change in the Balkan Neolithic. 2nd preliminary report. *Journal of Field Archaeology* 19(3), 351–86.

Tringham, R., M. Stevanovic & B. Brukner (eds.), in press. *Opovo: the Construction of a Prehistoric Place in Eu-

rope. Berkeley (CA): University of California, Berkeley, Archaeological research Facility Publications.

Wolle, A.C., 1996. Multimedia methods for excavation reports and archives using Microcosm. *Archeologia e Calculatori* 7, 1167–78.

Wolle, A.C., 1998. A Tool for Multimedia Excavation Reports. Unpublished PhD Thesis, University of Southampton.

Wolle, A.C., forthcoming. Electronic publication in archaeology, in *Archaeological Computing: Theory and Practice*, eds. D. Wheatley, S. Poppy & G. Earl. London: Routledge.

Wolle, A.C., & S.J. Shennan, 1996. A tool for multimedia excavation reports — a prototype, in Kamermans & Fennema (eds.), 489–95.

Chapter 18

Virtual Spaces, Atomic Pig-bones and Miscellaneous Goddesses

Martin Emele
translated by Caroline Saltzwedel

Well. The difference between an imagined some-thing — a concept — and a real thing used to be fairly straightforward. Even the most realistic pic-ture of a house was only an image. You could *imagine* what it could be like to go inside it, but you couldn't actually go inside it. That's because it didn't fully replicate the experience of going into a real house, with all that entails. But what if you *could* make something that felt like a real thing, tasted like it, smelled like it, but wasn't that thing — wasn't a 'thing' at all, but only a symbol of a thing, like a picture? (Williams 1997, 32)

On my last flight to Turkey, I had the pleasant experience of sitting in an aeroplane where during take-off and landing I had a view not only of the visible (window) reality at 90° to the line of flight, but also — this took some getting used to — of live pictures from the nose camera relayed to the video screen above the seat in front. What made me aware that even I was not universally media-competent was the short contraction reflex in the region of my stomach when at the moment of lift-off, the image on the screen switched from the nose camera to the one at the tail. Instead of seeing the sky in front of me, I suddenly saw the runway. My brain took a whole second to deliver the message: 'We are leav-ing the ground; tail camera; you are looking for-ward, but this view is to the rear.'

In 'normal' life, we have, generally speaking, long become accustomed to the phenomenon of dou-ble or media-enhanced reality, and while we may marvel, this now only rarely shocks us. 'Real' life cannot offer us anything like such beautiful birdsong, such spectacular sunsets, such sweeping Alpine panoramas as are presented to us by the media. All of us have accepted and found our way in the new multi-media as a matter of course; we unconsciously concede that the computer-generated world, irre-spective of whether our contact with it is profes-sional or leisure-based, is cleaner, better-made and more trustworthy than the reality. Yet do we truly possess the necessary competence to work with the new image-worlds, which are to all appearances about to conquer the whole sphere of communica-tion? Have we given enough thought to the relation-ship between image, reproduction, fact and reality?

No archaeological excavation with a modicum of self-esteem can survive today without computer-aided reconstructions of its object of study: sites about which we agree that there was once something there which no longer exists or which can no longer be seen. Computers not only make history; in the fields of archaeology and palaeography, they also make history visible. And if the researchers involved are particularly ambitious, they want to use these vir-tual worlds not only as an image of visual possibili-ties, but also as a new form of data base. This is not the first point at which they find themselves in a conflict between reconstruction and imagination, knowledge and scholarship. This difficult area is one I would prefer to avoid, for reasons that will be evident. In this chapter I am solely concerned with the problematic relationship between image and 're-ality', as will be illustrated with a few concrete ex-amples from the world of New Media. 'The theme of virtuality and reconstruction is always a question of originality and authenticity; it is never about the new media alone.' (Rieche 1997, 19). I want to con-centrate here on the fine (although now by no means new) concept of 'virtual reality', which I define as our deeply-rooted belief in the factual 'reality' of images which we daily encounter. The problem it-self is an old one: the virtual computer worlds merely

Figure 18.1. *Photograph of video display from nose camera.*

the part of both the makers and the consumers) is of great importance to mass-media communication. Even today, the belief that media images must be genuine seems to have remained an inalienable principle for the consumers of the media. Horst Bredekamp once formulated a provocative counter-argument in this context: 'Nothing is wrong with manipulated images [. . .] except the disappointment that they are not representing the "truth".' (Bredekamp 1996, 44). To take one of the most famous examples: Robert Capa's photograph of the mortally wounded soldier in the Spanish Civil War was of course staged! The simple reason being that it has always been the staged images which have been most effective; one could mention for instance the couple kissing in the Paris railway station, or the Soviet soldiers on the Reichstag. Capa's staging consisted (at least) in the act of pointing the camera in a particular direction on a particular day and at a particular time. It is not the 'truth' of the image which is important but its effect. The German writer Peter Härtling expressed the idea in the following terms in his Frankfurt lectures on poetry: 'He [Capa] showed me why books are no longer any use. He epitomizes everything that injures me.' (Härtling 1984, 42).

offer an easy opportunity to reflect anew on media-generated images.

When Robert Koch, the discoverer of the tuberculosis virus, began turning micro-organisms into visually accessible realities in the 1870s and 1880s using subtle methods of coloration, the authenticity of the image was not in doubt. Yet even Koch made the plea that the viewer should 'disregard' the blurred edges, the stripes and the spots, or 'at least to take them as proof of the purely objective character of these images'. He showed especial perspicacity in his remark that 'the photographic image of an object is under certain circumstances more significant than the thing itself' (cf. Widmer 1998). Peter Krieg draws our attention to the historical dimension and to the cultural conditions surrounding image and object:

> The concept of the 'Ab-Bild' [representation, 'after-image'] as a reproduction of a 'Vor-Bild' [model, 'pre-image'] is [. . .] older than photography. The category of similarity not only exists in the debates on art but has in all likelihood always been present in the legends and creation myths of all cultures, which suggests that the question of authenticity is not a question of technical perfection but rather of temporary cultural agreements. [. . .] Belief in the capacity of images to offer proof is just as strong as the belief in the power of the relics of saints: it points to a common basic need for orientation in a complex and incomprehensible world — as well as to the myth of the power of images themselves. (Krieg 1987, 86)

Belief in the proper representation of a reality (on

Such an image is in other words supposed to transmit a higher truth, but definitely not the particular valid reality. The poet Härtling, however, wants to believe in authenticity: anything else would be destructive to his imagination. In his lecture, he cites Capa's colleague Gallagher, who wrote:

> By now people were staging downright war-games for the reporters. Men were armed and dressed in pro-Franco uniforms, and acted out a battle. The appropriate atmosphere was produced with smoke bombs. Capa later told me that he had shot a few scenes of attacking troops which a few days later were published in the papers as actual battle scenes.

'If this anecdote reflected the facts', comments Härtling, 'I might as well stop writing.'

What is clearly of greatest importance to Härtling is to preserve belief. Against history as it probably was he asserts one of wish-fulfilment: 'When they attacked for the last time, Capa held the camera over the edge of the trench and shot blind — no, blindly — into the action. That is how it may have been.' (Härtling 1984, 70f.). The camera is thus transformed into a mythic divine machine which carries out orders from above to express the good. We will encounter this spirit from the machine again, although next time it will be in a digital context.

I should like to transfer this thought — that authentic feelings can only be produced if one is certain that the subject is both sublime and genuine — onto a piece of archaeologically confirmed reality: the Trojan gold, known as the 'Treasure of Priam', which disappeared in the chaos of the Second World War. As long as the gold was lost, as long as the treasure was imaginary and its existence only suggested by a few poor black-and-white photographs, it was spectacular, a myth. Once the original treasure reappeared in Moscow, the gold lost much of its former aura. Now an expert has gone so far as to make the unheard-of suggestion, in response to the political question of its continuing location, that two identical copies should be made, parts of which should rotate secretly between the museums of Moscow, Berlin and Istanbul, without any indication to the public as to which parts were being moved. This is of course impossible, even if one disregards the legal problems such a manoeuvre would involve: all the visitors to each museum would feel cheated. The authentic aura of an object depends on the belief in its genuineness, and this applies just as much to illustrations and photographs.

Ironically, it is often the computer — a machine apparently as opinionless and neutral as the camera used to be — which is called upon to verify 'genuineness' today. The computer has become the ideal machine for a one-dimensional media world: nothing represents 'timeless', 'objective' values quite as the computer does, nothing else has an almost magical aura and yet can turn history (admittedly by presenting it in pictorial form) into natural-

Figure 18.2. *Cover of Härtling's book, showing Robert Capa's photograph of a wounded Republican soldier in the Spanish Civil War.*

Figure 18.3. *The 'Treasure of Priam'.*

221

looking, apparently concrete 'virtual reality' (cf. Emele 1998). This applies all the more, the more perfect these New Worlds become. Animations are universally smooth and pristine; they are practically interchangeable, and above all communicate the message: I am a calculated object, therefore can only be generated in a computer. I am modern and expensive (cue to viewer: applause) and what costs so much must be 'real'.

> In this way, CAD reconstructions achieve a similarly high measure of trustworthiness to constructed illustrations, only by a completely different route: these images appear to be representations of a reality, as if there were an original whose 'properness' is not in doubt. (Rieche 1997, 17)

This is taken so far that even the dream factory makes use of this topos, as was seen recently in 'the most successful film of all time'. You have all seen *Titanic* in the cinema, and if not, you should do: not for the sake of the computer animations — they are on the whole second-rate — but because of the film's claim to historical accuracy. The producers repeatedly emphasize that they have kept (with the exception of the love story) rigorously to the historical 'facts'. What then actually happens in this cold, wet narrative accompanied by music throbbing with pathos?

The end and the events which appear to have led to it are generally known. Yet despite this, the film shows us — even before the episode of the 'real' catastrophe — a computer expert demonstrating to the survivors a simulation of the sinking on a monitor. The Hollywood film finds it necessary to maintain the illusion of 'historical truth' by having it officially ratified by a computer, which 'calculates' the course of events that the film proceeds to show.

Any belief in the possibility of actually reconstructing an image of the past is of course illusory. In the future, however, one thing will be absolutely clear: this is the way, the only possible way, the Titanic sank. This film is not one in which the past has produced an image. This product of the media is not only an image of the past, but it becomes part of the past itself, in other words becomes effectually identical with it. (A similar thing happened early in film history with Eisenstein's *Battleship Potemkin*.) People listening to a story being told are far more sharply aware that imagining the past is always a form of projection. Where visual narration is concerned, this awareness is not nearly so developed.

> It should be obvious that in the case of both actual and virtual representation, the term 'reconstruction' is an unfortunate one, since it creates the impression that a process (reconstruction) is producing a result (reconstruction), as in a broken vase that has been glued together again. In fact, both forms of representation are approaches to an unknown and unattainable model. (Rieche 1997, 17)

However, I would not argue with the view that perfect digital worlds can produce exactly the opposite effect, particularly, I think, with the younger generation. Anyone who has grown up in an environment where everything can be made or visualized appears to be, at least in part, 'media-adapted'. This has been true at least since *Forrest Gump* — since apparently

Figure 18.4. *Still from film by Lumiere Bros.*

authentic and apparently manipulated images became interchangeable. When I recently found an excerpt from a film by the Lumière Brothers — most probably dated before 1900 — which showed two men on in-line skates, I was so delighted that I digitized some of the images and loaded them onto my computer as 'wallpaper'. A student later asked me how I had created the 'old' effect. When I explained, her spontaneous comment was that she would never have guessed that these could be historical images; since everything had become possible, people had forgotten how to wonder.

But let us return to the exalted educational ideals of archaeology. A young Roman team of computer reconstructionists working for the firm Altair4 has managed to resurrect Ancient Egypt in cyberspace. Has it? Of course Karnak never looked anything like this. Our Italian colleagues have simply done all that could be done within a manageable length of time: they have adapted an historical model — D.V. Denon's *Description de l'Egypte* of 1798 (Denon 1996) — to today's multimedia. If we actually were to try to approach the different levels of reality in Karnak, the new information would be produced more rapidly than the old took to be processed. Seen thus, it looks as though we multimedia makers, virtual reconstructionists and animators, grasp reality in an historically determined, blinkered manner, not in a 'full-sensory' way. At the same time we, too, consistently tend to attribute a higher quantum of reality to whatever happens to be the latest discovery.

Yet this belief in the reality of unreal computer images is only one of the problems in the use of computer animation. Where more and more is being visualized, the whole picture area has to be filled. For instance, if archaeologists have only been able to excavate one part of a lost city, the computer reconstructionists can either leave blank areas to indicate the rest or freely invent the remaining houses. Sometimes all one has to go on is only a thousandth part of the material of an early settlement. To reconstruct the complete image of a town from such fragments is like trying to restore a thousand-piece jigsaw puzzle from one piece (Hofmann 1997, 135). One has to rediscover surfaces when all that is known is the structure of a wall. Roofs are mostly freely invented or the products of speculation.

This is truer still if the visitor can move around in VR with a few degrees of freedom. In some respect the potential endlessness is a problem for the makers of multimedia worlds. For virtual reality the negative criterion described by Lev Manovich for

Figure 18.5. *Virtual reality reconstruction of Karnak.*

the 'dynamic screen' of the cinema and video world is not absolutely valid any more: 'Rather than being a neutral medium of presenting information, the screen is aggressive. It functions to filter, to screen out, to take over, rendering non-existent whatever is outside its frame.' (Manovich 1998, 28). The level of this filtering is reduced up to some point for the computer or (as Manovich called it) the 'interactive'[1] screen. For archaeological 3-D worlds one would be thankful from time to time to have more possibilities to be aggressive, to 'screen out'.

In our own project to reconstruct rooms from Çatalhöyük in the Centre for Art and Media Technology (http://www.zkm.de/), the College of Design (http://www.hfg-karlsruhe.de/) and the University of Karlsruhe (http://goethe.ira.uka.de/), we based our plans on James Mellaart's drawings. Naturally we encountered various contradictions and queries in our attempt to give individual discoveries a 'virtually concrete' form; but these problems mostly had to do with the state of documentation. Questions of architectural structure were more straightforward; this can be seen for instance in Mellaart's well-known view of a two-storey high room. My colleague Burkhard Detzler, who is trained as an architect, correctly pointed out the structural impossibility of this sort of roof design. Nevertheless, we realized the roof according to the drawn model. Drawings on paper and virtual spaces have, after all, one invaluable advantage in common: they cannot collapse and bury the whole construct beneath them.

This does not speak fundamentally against the idea of organizing large quantities of data to produce a spatial representation of object-related three-

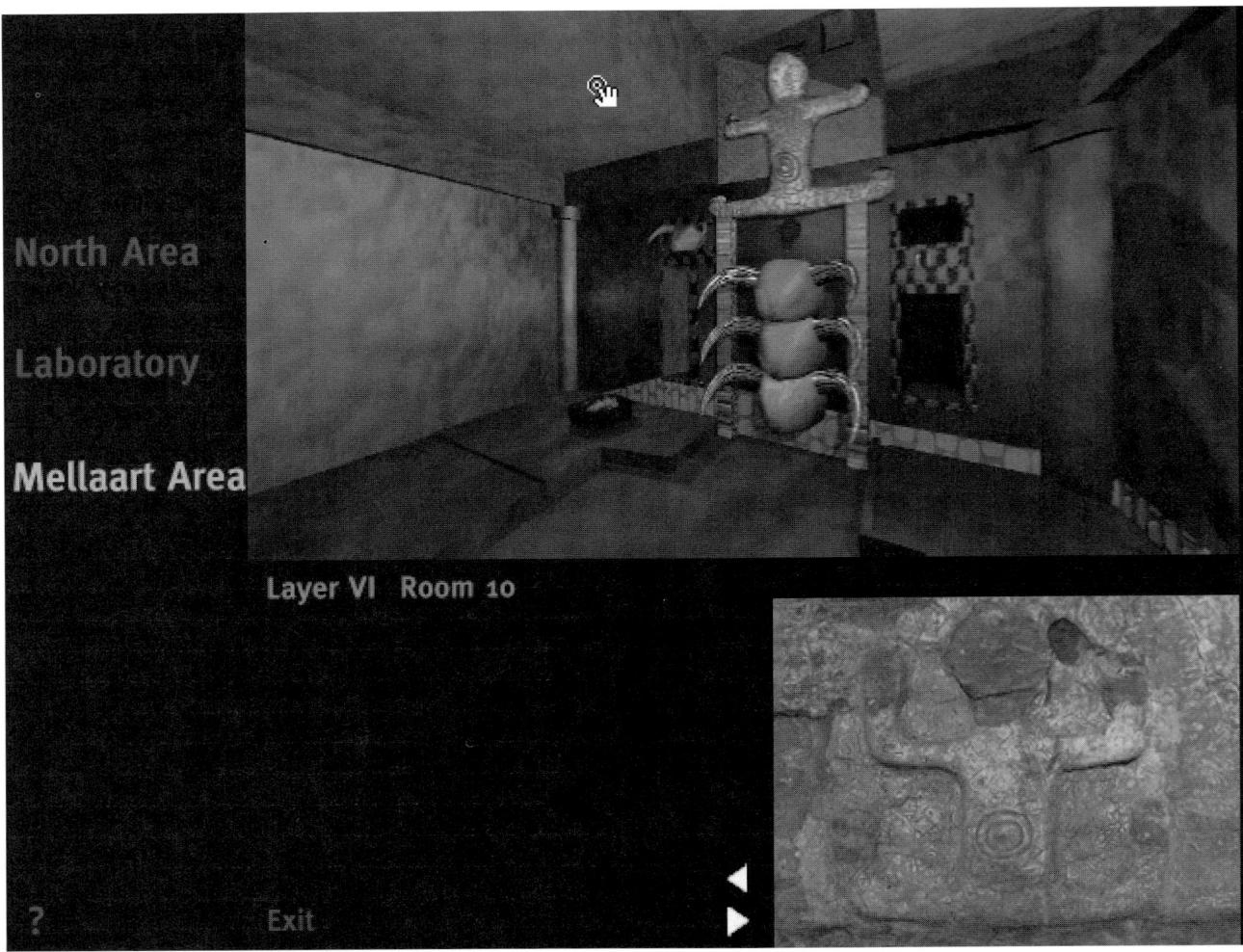

Figure 18.6. *Virtual reality reconstruction by University of Karlsruhe of two-storey room excavated by Mellaart.*

or four-dimensional environments in the multimedia reality of a Virtual Museum. The only question is how many dimensions we can comprehend at once. In Çatalhöyük we face the problem that not only do we want to reconstruct the three-dimensional space, but also, firstly, the transformation of that space through time, and secondly, possible or probable variations in the building at any one time. Furthermore, the areas of actually excavated building substance should be optically distinct from the scientifically projected or structurally necessary parts. If we were to offer variations alongside our reconstructions of the rooms, or allow for variations to be viewed (is for instance the two-storey room really two storeys high, or were there two rooms from different periods, one above the other?), we would find ourselves as it were in a five-dimensional documentation. This sort of space is practically impenetrable.

However, in the reality of virtual reality we are

often driven by quite different, more mundane problems. The leader of the excavations, Ian Hodder, wanted virtual rooms that were less sacred, less sterile, more animated. He wanted pigs running around in them. Technically, this no longer poses a problem. The size and weight of these animals could be calculated and adequately reconstructed on the basis of found, that is, 'real' pig bones, consisting of atoms: we could in other words call them 'atomic' bones. But the animation ran into a problem when it came to choosing the colour of the animals. Should it be piglet pink or wild boar black? We knew neither the colour nor the degree of hairiness, and did not want to predetermine the viewers' imagination. Where the world seen on the monitor becomes too concrete, the view of the possible is distorted. It is well known that a correspondence exists between the images which remain unseen and those which the brain then produces. Digital visualization forces an on-screen situation where an off-screen element might be far more effective. This has always been an important part of the traditional interpretation of paintings: the aspect an image does not show explicitly, its atmosphere.

Such 'spatializing' always has the effect of cementing the viewer's image of the past, even if the cement is only virtual. Virtual reality, says Hodder, has already proved invaluable in the case of Çatalhöyük, in providing a deeper understanding of what it could have been like to move around within and between the buildings at the site (Hodder 1997). Yet there is also the danger that virtual reality will merely reinforce our own preconceived ideas about the world as it was then. One or two archaeologists have meanwhile complained that the computer reconstruction has become so lodged in their minds that they no longer actually see what is in front of them when excavating at the site. Computer animation, if permanently in use, leads to the disappearance of historical time and space. The sensation proper to archaeology, the historical dimension, atrophies. These days a more or less complete stage set flickers on our screens, or in our heads, and the past can be called up with a mouse-click. It is concrete and actual, no longer bound by time or space — in other words, by history. This is, in a nutshell, an assault by the computer-generated world on the rest of time.[2] I can see no fundamental change of the media by the new technologies, but a dramatic change of the world. Not only with the absolute availability and storage capacity of moving image can one notice the disappearance of the historical dimension. Today, actions do not happen once and are over. We no longer have to go to a football stadium at a special time to see the game. And if we are there, we are missing the reality of slow-motion and close-up.

There is no shortage of theorists who see these pictographic worlds as indicating the dawn of a dominance of the now, of the moment. These worlds are of course not primarily verbal — not analytical — but rather mythic; they are frequently placed in the category of the concrete, the illogical or the irrational. In my view, however, we should consider that an order within space and time has its own logic, even if this is not necessarily a verbal one. An internal, idiosyncratic logic is after all found in all kinds of mythic narrative. Burghart Schmidt, for instance, sees the only difference between 'mythic thinking' and modern rationalism as being the way myth aligns concrete and complex things causally, or otherwise creates a relation between them. (Schmidt 1985, 278) It is as it were the thinking itself that changes direction: instead of scientific analysis, of dissection into elements, we have a juxtaposition

according to similarities of character and quality.[3] Put another way, according to this view mythical thinking is on the whole a generalizing, commonplace way of thinking, while the order above this would be that of three-dimensional space and its development in time.

Where analytical thought distinguishes between the causal origins of different 'fast-moving objects', say an animal and an automobile, mythic thinking would seize on the concept 'fast-moving' and establish a link between all the fast-moving things in the world, which would produce the logic of a sentence like 'Ferrari racing cars exist because cheetahs exist'. Such statements seem at first absurd, yet on closer observation are not unlike the 'image-related thought' which does in fact determine the way certain apparently similar characteristics, such as colours and movements, become associated with one another.[4] It is not until thought becomes dominated by the written word, say some written-word-dominated thinkers, that it becomes linear, allows for sequentiality and thus provide for complex methods of narrative. I have no definite verdict on this question. I would, however, point out that the new pictorial worlds also open up new spaces: not linear, but penetrable, multidimensional and certainly complex. Perhaps they are for this reason 'graspable' in a new way, and can no longer be comprehended using traditional logic.

It is noticeable that there has been an accelerating tendency to a multi-sensory representation of reality in the realm of the 'Ab-bild' or representation in the last 100 years. (Every step in this direction also caused kultural-pessimistic angst in the socially empowered sections of society). VR brings not only a new dimension to media, but also a new *reality* where it becomes the non-atomic 'Vor-bild' or model instead of merely being the 'Ab-bild' or representation. In the end, one of the fundamental questions is whether we are (or will become) competent enough in the media ever to come to possess these brave new media-worlds. This is not least a question of the social and socio-demographic balance of power. On this topic, I was deeply impressed by a sentence by John Barlow:

> At the very beginning there is a sense of pure fear: you feel like an immigrant in a country where your children immediately make themselves at home — yet where you are always lagging behind, since others are developing their technology faster than you can learn it. I describe this as the learning curve of Sisyphus. Here the only people to succeed are those who are not fazed by confusion or complexity. (John Barlow)

Belief in the 'truth' of images is the real reason for the fear of their manipulation by digital technology. Unlike analogue methods, of which photomontage is the most prevalent, the digital media, which can transform an image leaving no trace of manipulation, have in the view of today's cultural pessimists suddenly rendered the concept of 'original illustration' obsolete. The belief that illustrations can possibly be 'true' is however to my mind generally a wrong one. In a documentary context, images have at most a representative function. It is in the end irrelevant that the transformation of the original into a digital copy means that the new image cannot be cited, because it no longer is a copy in the strict sense. The new technologies have achieved one thing in particular: they have created a fluid passage between digital and real manipulation, between analogue images of the world and the digital world. The world is changing, yet its relation to the medium will not necessarily change. As Härtling said in the lecture on the photographer cited above, 'they attempt to grasp truths, yet only entangle themselves in countless realities' (Härtling 1984, 67).

We must ceaselessly undergo a 'training of the eye', submit ourselves to a 'school of iconization', in order to understand the multiple interconnections of the multimedia world (Bredekamp 1996, 45). The real world and the media world mix and penetrate one another on various different levels:[5] 'Neither the old-fashioned picture of the real or really build reality nor the virtual reality makes us unhappy, it's the obviously unbounded mixture between them.' (Seesslen 1998, 107). I can give one example here: In the Museum of Anatolian Civizations in Ankara, we placed a 'mother goddess', in other words a 'real', 'atomic' artefact, on a rotating stand and photographed it. The 'real' shots were used by my colleague Burkhard Detzler to produce a three-dimensional vector model. Finally, this projection is used as a base onto which to 'stick' the surface of the photograph. The finished object in the data base represents all the information possible, yet it can also be retrieved in a classical film sequence in any position, movement and lighting. If we pan with a camera between the glass cases in 'real life', only to find when we look in the editing computer that this particular case with the 'mother goddess' shows up an ugly reflection, then we can substitute the real photograph with a perfectly positioned computer copy. This 'mixed' mother goddess represents a new reality of its own. Does she, the 'goddess', then for this reason already harbour an expression of the relationship between 'real' and 'imaginary', and does

this automatically enrol her in the 'school of iconization'? Or will we find our tendency to forget how to wonder intensifying?

To cite Horst Bredekamp again:

> Cyberspace should be understood as a new version of the Kantian challenge to see the world as a projection of our own consciousness: a metaphor not just of the represented world but also of the criteria we use to distinguish between the different layers of reality, which communicate themselves through the senses in various and variously complete ways. (Bredekamp 1996, 45)

Virtual reality is in this sense not a new media reality, but rather a new chance to understand the medium. In the words of Jean-Luc Godard, we should 'no longer say 'This is a correct image', but rather 'This is correctly speaking an image'; instead of saying 'This is an officer of the Northern States on a horse', we would now say 'This is a PICTURE of a horse bearing an officer.' (cf. Bourdieu 1998, 12).

Notes

1. I would prefer 'active' screen.
2. A reference to the film by Alexander Kluge, *The Attack of Contemporary Reality on the Rest of Time*.
3. Myth is also seen as a form of juxtaposition (though far less categorically) in other situations, such as in 'historical myth-making'. 'This does not mean that the historical reports were false and the events invented; it has rather to do with the way facts are analysed and linked together and their consequences are interpreted, in other words, with a mythic reading of reality.' — Ramer 1987, 83; cf. also Graevenitz 1987.
4. Cf. for instance the television commercial in which the shadow of a new model of automobile alternates between that of a Mustang, an eagle and a tiger. The result is that the information society ends up with its own hybrid: Michael Schumacher, the cheetah. Where the most important aspects are the effect and the possible application, it is in the end immaterial whether this causality shift is seen as a phenomenon of physiological development, a stage of human development, a fundamental form of human expression, the 'primacy of expressive intelligence', or a basic human need. On physiological development, Mikunda points to a change in the brain's physiology which could be relevant here: 'Since the struggle for survival in modern society demands faculties other than the physical ability to hunt or fight, certain areas of so-called leisure activity have developed to take their place. Sport and certain art media, such as film, can communicate powerful physical feelings. One is more aware of the physical nature of one's own existence.' (Mikunda 1986, 125.) 'Other authors see analogies to other senses: 'Truth is not narrated in myth but rather breathed,

made palpable' (Hant 1992, 133). On the question of human development cf. *inter alia* Christian Gottlieb Heyne's terms '*infantia generis humana*' and '*sermo mythicus seu symbolicus*'; see Horstmann 1972, 60ff. On forms of human expression: 'Jung's most important insight is that humankind is just as dependent on old and traditional forms of expression as it has ever been.' (Kirk 1987, 75). On basic human need: the possibility of holistic mythical thought is explored by Grassi 1990, 81ff.; 'the longing for an irrational, unitarian and harmonious world view', Ramer 1987, 151. Ramer understands myth as 'the iconographic solidification of a society's world view' (Ramer 1987, 283). In the context of communication, what is important is the rational use of images, however they were acquired.

5. Cf: 'Mit den digitalen Technologien sind die Grenzen fließender denn je geworden, die Grenzaufhebung zwischen abgefilmten, abfilmbaren und synthetisch generierten Ereignissen ist vielleicht sogar vollendet.' (Gehr 1998, 17).

References

Barlow, J., 1998. Cited at http://www.kulturprozent.ch/brainstorming/.

Bourdieu, P., 1998. *Über das Fernsehen*. Frankfurt am Main: Suhrkamp.

Bredekamp, H., 1996. Politische Theorien des Cyberspace, in *Die Frage nach dem Kunstwerk unter den heutigen Bildern*, eds. H. Belting & S. Gohr. Stuttgart: Cantz, 31–50.

Denon, D.V., 1996. *La description de l'Egypte, ou Recueil des observations et des recherches qui ont été faites en Egypte pendant l'Expédition de l'armée française publié sous les ordres de Napoléon Bonaparte*. Tours. (Originally published in 24 vols., 1809–1813.)

Elsaesser, T. & K. Hoffmann, 1998. *Cinema Futures: Cain, Able or Cable?: the Screen Arts in the Digital Age*. Amsterdam: Amsterdam University Press.

Emele, M., 1998. The assault of computer-generated worlds on the rest of time, in Elsaesser & Hoffmann (eds.), 251–66.

Gehr, H., 1998. Neuer Wein in alten Schläuchen?, in *Film & Computer — Digital Media Visions*. Frankfurt am Main: Deutsches Filmmuseum, 12–31.

Graevenitz, G. von, 1987. *Mythos — Zur Geschichte einer Denkgewohnheit*. Stuttgart: Metzler.

Grassi, E., 1990. *Kunst und Mythos*. Revised edition. Frankfurt am Main: Suhrkamp.

Hant, P., 1992. *Das Drehbuch; Praktische Filmdramaturgie*, Waldeck.

Härtling, P., 1984. *Der spanische Soldat, oder Finden und Erfinden: Frankfurter Poetik-Vorlesungen*. Darmstadt: Hermann Luchterhand Verlag.

Hodder, I., 1997. 'Always momentary, fluid and flexible': towards a reflexive excavation methodology. *Antiquity* 71, 691–700.

Hofmann, K., 1997. Funde im Netz. Archäologie zum Anklicken — eine multimediale Spurensuche. *Antike Welt* 2, 135–9.

Horstmann, E.-A., 1972. Mythologie und Altertumswissenschaft. Der Mythologie-Begriff bei Christian Gottlieb Heyne. *Archäologische Begriffsgeschichte* 16.

Kirk, G.S., 1987. *Griechische Mythen. Ihre Formen und ihre Bedeutung*. Hamburg: Rowohlt.

Krieg, P., 1987. Die Inszenierung des Authentischen, in *Trau — Schau — Wem: Digitalisierung und dokumentarische Form*, ed. K. Hoffmann. Konstanz: UVK Medien, 85–96.

Manovich, L., 1998. Towards an archaeology of the computer screen, in Elsaesser & Hoffmann (eds.), 27–43.

Mikunda, C., 1986. *Kino spüren: Strategien der emotionalen Filmgestaltung*. Munich: Filmland Presse.

Ramer, U., 1987. *Mythos und Kommunikation*. Frankfurt am Main: Fischer Verlag.

Rieche, A., 1997. Materiell und Virtuell — Die Rekonstruktion der Colonia Ulpia Traiana. *Inform! Museen im Rheinland* 2, 16–19.

Schmidt, B., 1985. Kunst: Fluchtlinie zum Mythos? — Retten des Mythos?, in *Faszination des Mythos: Studien zu modernen und antiken Interpretationen*, ed. R. Schlesier. Basel & Frankfurt am Main: Stroemfeld/Roter Stern, 275–94.

Seesslen, G., 1998. Schöne neue Bilder-Welt, in *Film & Computer — Digital Media Visions*. Frankfurt am Main: Deutches Filmmuseum, 92–115.

Widmer, R., 1998. Grosser Effekt? null Erkenntnis, in *Weltwoche* 26; http://www.weltwoche.ch/2698/.

Williams, T., 1997. *Otherland — City of Golden Shadow*. New York (NY): DAW Books.

Chapter 19

Video-recording as Part of the Critical Archaeological Process[1]

Dorothée Brill

The following contribution is a report on a project which has been carried out at Çatalhöyük since the summer of 1995. Since the first year of digging, video-documentation was performed for the duration of the whole season. It was based on the idea of recording, via an additional medium, the daily evolution of the dig as well as the accompanying processes of interpretation and decision-making. The basis of archaeological decision-making and interpretation is captured and integrated as another type of archaeological data, which can then be examined to reveal the variable and dialectic process between data recording and data interpretation.

The main body of this chapter presents a report of the project developed over the last four years, the different ways of its realization, the technical context, aims and difficulties in the processing of the material, its storage and accessibility, the status and function of the film work in the wider context of the excavation and the response of the team. First, though, some preliminary thoughts about the role of mixed-media documentation in current archaeology are worth raising.

The changing demands of documentation

> Epistemologie ist die Wissenschaft davon, wie wir Dinge wissen. Epistemologie wird mehr und mehr zur Wissenschaft davon, wie Medien die Realität der Dinge, die wir wissen, konstruieren. (de Kerckhove 1997, 194)[2]

The changing views about the construction of knowledge and the formation of meaning which have grown in the background of interpretive archaeological theory, have also raised questions about appropriate ways of archiving knowledge. What media are suitable for meeting the archival demands of scientific work?

The impossibility of an archaeologist proceeding neutrally and objectively in the process of collecting and processing archaeological data (Hodder 1992), the inevitable conditioning and formation as a child of one's time (Shanks & Tilley 1992), and the loss of a recognizable or discernible 'genuine past' (Shanks & Tilley 1992, 95), reveal parallels to the process of disillusionment in our relationship with text and image media. Just as archaeology cannot provide an abstract system in which the reality of the past becomes fixed once and for all as a self-sufficient reconstruction (Shanks & Tilley 1992), so it is not merely epistemology itself, but also the possibilities of its mediation that are recognized as being integral to an 'entire set of culturally encoded beliefs' (Tilley 1993, 12). In understanding archaeological knowledge as 'a result of (specifiable) discursive practices operative in a culture at a time and in a place' (Tilley 1993, 12) and in the emphasis on 'polysemy and material culture as a multivocal code' (Tilley 1993, 4), concepts are being expressed that also concern and question the documentation process.

The linguistic turn which Tilley (1993) describes in theoretical archaeology supports the idea of archaeology's media-based limitation. As any other science, archaeology is formed to a certain extent by the characteristics of the tools of media, and by those of language. The second determination is found in its subject-specific context, i.e. in the tradition of archaeological writing in which any further statement is inevitably posed, and in which certain linguistic styles are traditionally charged with a certain impact. The inherent element of language, the narration, is rediscovered to emphasize the narrative just as part of the processual character of the excavation itself and the evolution of ideas (e.g. Hodder 1992, 272).

The site-report could be written as a complex

interweaving of sequences of events in the past (what happened on the site) and sequences of events in the present (what happened on the excavation) . . . The disagreement should spill over into the text so that the reader can insert herself into a process of argument rather than having to consume pre-packed, supposedly neutral fare. (Hodder 1992, 272–3)

In these suggestions there are aims expressed that call on language, but they can also be read as demands for cinematic and digital forms of mediation. A bilinear linguistic structure, for example, can be extended not only into its cinematic equivalent but into a multilinear way of communicating with a freedom to interact through combinations of several different media, enabling different constructions of the past. It thus helps to reveal alternative interpretations or understandings of the past. The following section outlines the possibilities of using video as part of a multimedia documentation in this way.

The advantages of video-recording in the critical archaeological process

The suitability of the medium of video — in view of the demands by interpretative archaeology — rests in the motion of the image. A moving image is the simplest expression of a process; in their basic character, moving images are narratives. By means of film duration, flexible camera viewpoint and the combination of images via montage, the basis for a narration via images is provided. In the use of video documentation at Çatalhöyük the advantages seem to be the immediate combination of image and text and more so the level of spontaneity and the strengthened individual expression in spoken, over written, language. Spoken language appears to be less dominated by handed-down scientific codes. In this sense the filmed interview is continuing an approach which has already started in the different styles of site-reports, diaries, and personal narratives. Awareness of the complexity of the narrative in the interpretative evaluation of material culture forms the basis of the video documentation at Çatalhöyük.

The work process
Over the last four years there have been, at any one time, one or two students from the Karlsruhe Hochschule für Gestaltung based at Çatalhöyük for the duration of the whole season, organized in shifts of two to four weeks. The video documentation was connected to a wider project of a slightly different interest, called CHAMP (The Cultural Heritage and Archaeology Multimedia Project).[3] In CHAMP, digital image-processing, image-generating and animation techniques were applied in the field of archaeological research and communication. One aim was the production of a CD-ROM about the Çatalhöyük excavation, published in 1997, in which different types of image media, such as video footage, computer reconstructions, panoramic pictures etc., were combined with texts to provide a wide range of information connected by a hypertextual structure. Its target-group was the general public. It is important to point out that differences between the interests of the Karlsruhe and Çatalhöyük teams — i.e. between the multimedia interest of CHAMP, and the approach based on archaeological motivation — were not fully reconciled. This became obvious in those elements of the filming which were needed for archaeological documentation, and not for public consumption. These difficulties and their results on the project will be discussed at a later point.

Video documentation for the data base did not start before 1996. The technical equipment and the objectives were slightly different before that. In 1995, the work had been done with a simple Hi-8 camcorder and an appropriate editing unit. Already by then, the film team was out on site every day, filming everyday events. However, because of the technical situation, the video material was processed into three succeeding documentaries of about 20 to 30 minutes each. They were conceived of as a sort of video-diary, and were a commission for the Science Museum of Minnesota. Although simple editing and processing facilities were already at site, the major part of the post-production process had to be undertaken in the far better technical surroundings of Karlsruhe university. The 1996 season can be seen as the proper starting point of the 'video data base' project. It was then that the on-site technical equipment eventually improved in some crucial aspects. These consisted, for example, of a terminal with a greater memory capacity dedicated to digital video processing, and a CD-writer. The video footage was shot with a high-quality digital video camera and was (ideally) edited in the computer the same day. In reality, however, some of the processing of the material still had to be finished after the season, in Karlsruhe.

As well as the cheaper materials and the absence of any developing costs, the key advantage of video in comparison with film is its immediate availability. The video image is an instant image, visible immediately after the moment of its recording. In the context of our documentation there are two advantages to this. On the one hand it enables the team, at least theoretically, to work with topical material *on site*. As such, it can serve immediately as an exchange of information. With a team of 50 to 80 archaeologists spread over five excavation areas and several laboratories, it can be difficult not to lose track of the respective stages of development in other areas of the excavation. In particular, daily changes to the shape and character of the excavations are naturally difficult to mediate in words. Thus, the video material provides the possibility to follow the course of events retrospectively. This complements the site tours undertaken by the laboratory specialists every other day, the weekly walk by the complete team, and — above all — the personal interactions between team members.

The easily-handled equipment enables a fairly spontaneous recording of on-site events that is essential to the success of the project. After the video material has been downloaded into the computer it is edited into video clips, each of a few minutes length, according to thematic entities. As such, short video clips about an artefact, a feature, an interpretation, a laboratory analysis etc., can form part of the data base. The necessary brevity of the clips is currently technically determined, as computers find the task of handling the enormous data-rates of moving images (in an accessible form) considerable.

The decision to digitize footage and to store and present it via a computer has a consequence on working method — as well as on the topics filmed — that should not be underestimated. The major constraint is the film length, as this has implications for data storage, accessibility and quality. Thus, the possibility of filming talks, interviews etc., in their original length is in opposition to the need of keeping film-time to a limit in order to produce a reasonable result in terms of disk space and play-back quality. Short clips can be integrated in the data base. Longer films, which can thus be no longer stored digitally, but would need to remain on videotapes, therefore would loose the status of 'data' and instead turn into stand-alone products. Spontaneous links between texts, figures, tables on one hand, and spoken language and moving image on the other, would be hardly possible with sequences on longer film. A further advantage of the computer-based administration of the footage is that there are much better possibilities for it being archived and being made accessible to other users for their research-oriented purposes. This is aided by the digital video clips being separated into thematic units, that can be found by searching for special subjects with the help of keywords. A comparable, but still time-consuming, archival system for tapes is conceivable. However, the main advantage in digital video is its accessibility independent of place; in contrast to a 'video-library', the digital video-clips are designed to be accessible in the future through the World Wide Web, easily copied CD-ROMs, or digital transfer like ftp.

It is worth considering the effects of the time limits on the process of filming, and the effect on the film content. Owing to the technologically demanded brevity, some things are limited, or entirely excluded, from video documentation at Çatalhöyük. Interviews with team members, for example, cannot exceed a duration of three to four minutes. Thus the information has to be cut down to some basic elements and a selection of the subjects talked about needs to take place. Group discussions are entirely excluded, as are all discussions which develop in an extended form. These are especially important during the process of constructing meaning and knowledge, and their exclusion is problematic. On the other hand, it is right to question to what extent should image documentation be relevant to the archiving of linguistic processes. A pure audio documentation (with far fewer data implications), or its written transcription, are possibilities too.

Information and mediation

The issues concerning the practical limits to the means of digital image data storage and access have already been referred to. At this point, however, sensible archival administration of potential 'information overload' needs to be considered. Where can we possibly impose a reasonable limit to documentation in an area that extends between the poles of presentation of final results, and permanent surveillance? Some hindrance to research can be caused by sparse data and a lack of accompanying information. The alternative — the recording and preservation of all information — has its own difficulties as differentiation between the significant and the insignificant is fundamentally hindered.

Here again, there is an aspect that refers us towards multimedia and multilinear documentation systems. The archiving of information in different layers and densities could turn out to be useful, insofar as prevailing research interests would be satisfied. Different media are well known to deliver information about the same facts in differing codes. Differing elements become either emphasized or disguised. The combination of different media in a database, and their connection via hyperlinks leaves it up to the user to knit their information net with a tight or loose mesh.

One can consider the specific conditions of video as a medium for documentation against the ideas being expressed by Shanks (1997) concerning photography. The issues raised by Shanks are, in my opinion, also applicable to video documentation in their fundamental aspects. As a visual medium, the moving image profits just as much from a historically formed ocular-centrism, in which visual sensory perception seems to be granted a heightened value of authenticity (Shanks 1997, 73–4, 80–82). This unconscious trust remains, in spite of the continued omnipresent suspicion about the conversion of visible reality into a visible image. The conversion is inevitably a translation. On this point, Shanks' distinction between naturalistic and realistic images might be helpful: 'a realistic representation is not only or necessarily naturalistic' (Shanks 1997, 78) as it is already a construction of the characteristic, and the conception of reality is itself a historical convention. Furthermore, 'a photograph may be considered realistic because it conforms to the canon of realism laid down by discourse, rather than because it has some special and objective relationship with reality' (Shanks 1997, 80). Such a canon has been built up just as much for scientific text, as for factual photography, or the aesthetic image.

Text, photographs, and film images are influenced in production and reception by conventions of representation, which suggest reality and — as a subsumable concept — 'scientific-ness'. What appears through the representation of reality in media, are finally 'products of discourse' (Shanks 1997, 81). The moving image is showing in itself a unified concept of reality. To reveal media-intrinsic tendencies and to make them visible as the rhetoric of a certain medium it might be a help to give information about the same topic in a variety of different media. The supposed innocence of a medium with regard to the communication of its contents has been repeatedly questioned (e.g. McLuhan 1964). However, the mere presence of a recording medium is also far from innocent, in the sense that the sheer fact of its being part of a situation has an unavoidable altering effect on the situation as recorded. The intensity with which this happens is a function of the clarity of its presence. In the case of the video documentation at Çatalhöyük, this side-effect is significant as it contradicts the purpose of documentation. The reason why a camera influences our behaviour is at the same time a drawback in using video at Çatalhöyük: the direct connection of image and word,

and the immediate recording of language. Thus the speaker is focused, the 'I' of the narration is obvious. Video documentation seems to be capable of counteracting the commonly used de-personification of texts as a proof for scientific objectivity (Hodder 1992, 263–74). But it is precisely this immediacy between an action and its recording which has an inhibiting effect on the people in front of the camera. Everybody knows this from his or her own experience; the presence of a camera inevitably changes behaviour, in so far as its presence is not 'normal'.

But the experiences at Çatalhöyük showed that the transition from an exceptional towards a normal situation happened fairly quickly. The transition began during the course of the first season, and the presence of a video camera eventually became the norm during subsequent years, particularly for those on the team who had direct contact with this tool of documentation. This growing familiarity was supported by the growing confidence and trust between the archaeologists and the film team and by an increasing knowledge on the part of the film team about the site with its ongoing excavation processes. Trust and knowledge had to develop as new members of the film crew arrived during the season. On reflection it would therefore be an advantage to have a single permanent film team at the site.

Owing to their different context the members of the film team brought hardly any archaeological knowledge with them. Their background was basically determined by an interest in documentary film and film aesthetic. This was originally seen to be an advantage, as the 'camera-view' was therefore an archaeologically arbitrary one. If it was still not neutral, it was at least naïve. On the part of the film team there was no selective choice guided by scientific motives or convictions. Instead, much was influenced by aesthetic criteria. Their 'archaeological greenness' might really have had — to a certain extent — the advantage of 'objectivity', but the reverse was actually seen through their lack of capability in making decisions or better yet, in making decisions based on contextual criteria (Farid Chapter 2, this volume).

The selection of topics and people being filmed
There is necessarily a process of selection of the things and topics being filmed. This selection is inevitably a result of the interpretation of something as either being significant and important, or not. As this selective choice is essential, it turned out to be done by just a few people, e.g. the field director, the area supervisors, professional excavators, and laboratory staff. This, however, was not forced by any hierar-

chically-motivated decision, but rather developed through time. Everybody was theoretically welcome to get in touch with the film team and to suggest current topics for documentation. As there were rarely suggestions coming from the laboratory staff, the people being interviewed formed a fairly small and constant group, whose members became the most familiar with speaking in front of the camera and were thus over time more willing to be filmed than others. The reluctance of the others was in part caused by the idea of having their individual thoughts and opinions filmed at a stage when conclusions remain uncertain (Farid Chapter 2, this volume). This was particularly so with students or other newcomers.

Conclusion

The irrelevance of the principles of 'film aesthetics' in shooting and editing the footage for the video data base, and the lack of *visually*-striking subject matter conflicts with the fundamental *raison d'être* of filming. On the other hand, the film team may have lacked the ability to distinguish details of archaeological interest. Long-term plans suggest that it will be necessary to re-evaluate the advantages and disadvantages of having people filming with no real background in the subject. The technical equipment and the digital-editing facilities are now at a level which makes the filming and editing easy to continue. In terms of the archaeological value of the video documentation, it is therefore reasonable to hand it over to someone more closely connected to the archaeological process, and with a long-term interest in its function and use as a research tool.[4]

As a member of the film team, I find it fairly difficult to judge substantively on the long-term use of a video data base for this kind for archaeological research. This decision will have to be made by those who are using the tool for their work, as well as by those who do not use it as a result of a conscious decision. A definitive judgement might not yet be possible though, as the video data base is still in its infancy even after three years of work. A certain quantity of available video clips is necessary to make them work as a proper research facility, and to let them lose their status of a secondary and incomplete illustration. At present, the limited supply seems to furthermore create the demand, instead of having a situation where any demand can be satisfied by the existing supply. To reach the latter, a certain number of available video clips is necessary.

As a final point, the core users of the data base are archaeologists who are themselves working at Çatalhöyük and are thus more or less familiar with the site and its recent developments. Thus, they naturally depend considerable less on a media record, as they have the essential steps of the excavation — and its differing interpretations — in mind. It is perhaps only in the future that the video material might prove its value. I remember the answer I received after once having expressed some doubts about the benefit of the video data base in practice: 'Imagine we had such a detailed visual record from Mellaart's work in the sixties . . .'.

Notes

1. Translated from German with James Conolly.
2. 'Epistemology is the science of the way we know things. Epistemology is turning more and more into the science about the way media construct the reality of the things we know' (author's translation).
3. CHAMP is a project by the film-department at the Hochschule für Gestaltung Karlsruhe (HfG) in Germany. Partners are the ZKM (Zentrum für Kunst und Medientechnologie) Karlsruhe, the European Institute of Cinema EIKK Karlsruhe, the Universität Karlsruhe (Inst. für Rechnerentwurf und Fehlertoleranz), the Fachhochschule Karlsruhe (dep. of Geoinformationswesen) and the University of Tübingen (Archaeological Institute), Zabern-publishing Mainz (together with Thames and Hudson, London), the University of Cambridge, UK and the Multimedia-developer Altair4/ Rome, Italy. The project was encouraged by the European Commission within the programme INFO2000. For further information www.catal.arch.cam.ac.uk/ catal/catal.html or www.goethe.ira.uka.de/catal.
4. This change took place in the 1999 season, when it was decided to shift to a single archaeologists trained specifically in video and editing. However, the reasons for this change are mainly pragmatic, due to an extended digging season of six months.

References

de Kerckhove, D., 1997. Brauchen wir, in einer Realität wie der unseren, noch Fiktion?, in *Medien-Welten Wirklichkeiten*, eds. G. Vattima & W. Welsch. München & Paderborn: Wilhelm Fink Verlag, 187–200.

Hodder, I., 1992. *Theory and Practice in Archaeology*. London: Routledge.

McLuhan, M., 1964. *Understanding Media: the Extensions of Man*. London: Routledge & Kegan Paul.

Shanks, M., 1997. Photography and archaeology, in *The Cultural Life of Images*, ed. B.L. Molyneaux. London: Routledge, 73–107.

Shanks, M. & C. Tilley, 1992. *Reconstructing Archaeology*. Cambridge: Cambridge University Press.

Tilley, C., 1993. Introduction: interpretation and a poetics of the past, in *Interpretative Archaeology*, ed. C. Tilley. Oxford: Berg Publishers, 1–13.

Chapter 20

Visualizing and Vocalizing the Archaeological *Archival* Record: Narrative vs Image

Mirjana Stevanovic

Both narrative and image are fundamental to archaeology. They constitute the formal archaeological record and are necessary elements in the presentation of archaeology to the public. It is clear to archaeologists that a narrative alone is insufficient for describing the past, and drafting, drawing and photography continue to be basic tools for visualizing the archaeological record. Recently, with the application of computers and multimedia to the manipulation and interpretation of archaeological data, the relationship between the narrative and the image is being further refined. It seems that computers and multimedia (3-D, QuickTime virtual reality (QTVR) animation and other forms) offer a dynamic view of the archaeological record whereas narrative remains static. As this chapter suggests, there is more room for exploring the relationship between text and image through the use of multimedia in constructing the archival archaeological record.

Computer and multimedia technology is involved in innovative ways in the Çatalhöyük project. Computers are used by the archaeologists on the team as repositories of compiled data and are active in the field during the excavation, as well as throughout the rest of the year. Film teams from Karlsruhe and Minnesota are part of the field team that meets at Çatalhöyük annually. The aim of the two film teams is to follow the work of archaeologists at Çatalhöyük and to capture on film different aspects of archaeological practice at the site. Their work is coordinated with the work of the other members of the project, but what gets recorded on film is to a degree dictated by the presentation of the archeological process at Çatalhöyük to the public. In my view, these film crews are involved to a much lesser degree in the compilation and production of the *archaeological* archival record at Çatalhöyük.

This chapter will suggest that computers and

multimedia tools can be fundamental to archival recording and that they can be operated by the archaeologists themselves. The production of the archival archaeological record in this case requires not only a knowledge of how to combine audio, video, animation, and virtual reality imagery with text and traditional imagery, but also requires that archaeologists design effective day-to-day recording strategies incorporating each of the media. And to make it useful, it requires cross-referencing and linking of textual, visual, and audio information in a user-friendly data base.

To bring the variety of media at Çatalhöyük closer to the excavation trench in the BACH area we have designed a multimedia recording method which we call the *BACH Integrative Archival Diary*. As part of our excavation strategy, we are investigating the possibility of fuller and more diverse systematic recording of recovered material culture. Recording the fragile and momentary nature (archaeology is by definition destructive) of archaeological materials can, in our view, be attempted only by utilizing the full variety of available recording methods.

Video recording at Çatalhöyük

An aspect of the innovative methodology of the new Çatalhöyük project is the continuous presence of video cameras on site and regular video recording. The presence of cameras at Çatalhöyük is informed by theoretical concepts in archaeology different from those used for standard public presentation of archaeology to the public. The popular video recordings produced by National Geographic (e.g. the Nova series) are the major film forums through which the general public visualizes archaeology as a scientific discipline. Archaeology videos made by National Geographic and similar groups record some selected events during an excavation which are considered to be the most exciting for the general public as well as extraordinary finds. Excavation is sometimes repeated after the fact in order to record it on the film. They also produce thematic videos that have a time-period or regional perspective.

These traditional video presentations are popular, but can be criticized from several points of view. In particular, their cost, in terms of expertise, time and equipment, is enormous. Consequently, decisions on what will be featured and how it is presented are matters for business experts, and re-evaluation of those decisions by the archaeological community is sometimes lacking. These circumstances make the popular video series on archaeology informative, but only on a selected subject matter or about selected 'actors'.

As several chapters in this volume show, video filming at Çatalhöyük is aimed at documenting the process of archaeology at this site as completely as possible and from as many angles as possible. The video filming comprises:

i.   the constant presence of video-teams;
ii. the systematic recording of selected moments on the site, such as the recovery of a flint dagger, bear claw, or certain burials;
iii. recording of the regular site-tours by laboratory staff and their moderated discussion with the field staff;
iv. recording tours by some visitors and by the workers employed on the site;
v.   the systematic filming of the summary remarks on developments at the site given by the field staff in each excavation area, and by the laboratory staff;
vi. filming in a range of situations related to the site, but which take place away from the site, for instance ethnoarchaeological tours and visits to the nearby villages, local fairs etc.

The video records of Çatalhöyük produced by the Karlsruhe and Minnesota teams provide the public with a taste of archeological practice as a complex and dynamic enterprise. Moreover, many of the recorded video clips are included in the main Çatalhöyük data base and they enrich the pool of information for the team members and other interested parties. Despite this however, the role of video and other media has limited relevance to the recording of an archive.

The practice of video recording of selected moments, situations, and finds could, in the long run, prove to contribute to creating an uneven, fragmented and incomplete archaeological record at Çatalhöyük.

By selecting some events and finds to film we are keeping the unfilmed ones out of the same context. For example, 'small' or 'special' finds, which are in traditional archaeological methodology recorded separately from the bulk of other finds and valued for their museum display qualities, have haunted archaeologists who have been trying to treat and record all finds contextually. Selective filming does nothing to address this problem.

BACH Integrative Archival Diary

In order to employ the whole variety of media in fuller and less selective archaeological recording, data accumulation and storage, we are introducing the BACH Integrative Archival Diary.

In our reexamination of how much we actually record and how much of our daily routine as we excavate and document is lost, we saw great gaps in what we do and what we could do. It is difficult enough during the excavation to define what we see at the edge of the trowel but it is even more difficult to record it in precise and explicit ways, to accommodate current interpretations and leave room for the future, and possibly different interpretations.

To produce a more diverse archival record, the BACH Integrative Archival Diary currently works towards combining textual records with traditional photography, digital photography, and video and audio diaries of the excavation.

Photography
The BACH Project has been developing a method for the standardization of the photographic record. This method involves systematically taking more photographs in the field (i.e. not just when there is a prepared picture), and linking those still images into the integrative data base. This is aided by the fact that the BACH photographs are processed into digital images on PhotoCDs, as well as slides. As PhotoCDs the slides are much easier to catalogue (using specialized software to integrate them into the main data base), to reproduce, and to include in a presentation.

In addition, the still images are taken at certain points in the excavation (arriving on a house floor, or at the beginning or end of a sequence of deposits) and are used to produce QTVR short films. QTVR short films combine still images and computer-generated sequences to produce a dynamic image. Such images capture quite realistically the situation in the excavation trench at the time the still images were taken. This is a very helpful visual tool in reviewing the record in order to relationships of the excavated surfaces and features, and can be applied in further computer-generated modelling.

Furthermore, QTVR is used systematically for recording a number of finds. This takes place in the photography laboratory. The objects are photographed/filmed from all sides in a continuous process. This kind of record provides more insight about the appearance of the object than two or three side views drawn as part of a standard record.

Digital diary

This is produced daily and each day cross-referenced with the standard, textual diary. We use a digital camera during the excavation which at the end of each day equips us with numerous still images of the BACH area, accompanied with short textual or audio messages (a feature of digital cameras). Digital camera images to some extent overlap with the still photography. However, the still and digital images are of different quality and are manipulated and used in different ways. They are both used for daily documentation of new developments in the trench as well as for a series of 'synthesizing shoots' of the trench that are taken at the end of each day. Unlike still photographs, digital camera images are instantaneous, and they are daily uploaded in the computer and linked with the standard textual diary. In this way, they provide the illustrations for the textual diary. Digital cameras are very easy to use in the field and offer an unlimited quantity of images that can be used instantaneously. Thus, the textual diary can be equipped with a number of digital illustrations which are more efficient than drawings or sketches as part of the textual diary. Also, digital images can be computer manipulated and incorporated into computer-generated reconstructions. Traditional still photography, on the other hand, takes longer processing to produce an image and is not so flexible (e.g. it cannot be processed on site, and is more costly). The final photographic images are, however, of higher quality and more suitable for publication purposes then digital ones.

Video-recording

Our strategy is to maintain systematic video recording of the archaeological deposits within the excavation trench. Special attention is given to the locations with unclear, and very complex, features and stratigraphic relationships. In these video clips the excavators operate the camera to record the deposits and simultaneously voice-guide through the problems that are being recorded. Video recordings are structured in a diary format. They are taken at regular intervals during the excavation but are more intensive when and where there is need for more thorough coverage. Until now video recording of deposits has been used for illustrating the vertical and horizontal relationships of different infill layers inside the building under excavation, and to show the relationships between various features within the excavation area. Video records more thoroughly, and often more precisely than other visual media, the continuous and complex nature of the material culture.

Video clips produced in this way can later be manipulated and used in a variety of ways. On the computer screen the video film can be captured as a series of still images and visually analyzed, i.e. re-evaluated, as well as being turned into slides, prints, drawings etc. One example from our experience is the combination of drawn elevations of the baulks with their video-records. We have drawn and filmed the stratigraphy-control baulks which run through the infilled deposits of the Building 3. In the course of house excavation, the baulks have been removed in vertical and horizontal segments and in the same locations later continued. It is of considerable value to us to be able to consult both the video record of the baulk sections and their architectural drawings in our reconstruction of horizons in Building 3.

Audio-diary

Daily audio recording comprises:

i. general and synthesizing observations in the trench;
ii. detailed description of the complex issues that come up during the excavation which cannot be resolved in a single day and need to be followed carefully;
iii. discussions in the trench during the excavation;
iv. impressions and feelings that an excavator goes through daily, which range from professional dilemmas and doubts to personal feelings and their state of mind. This is informal part of the archive audio record.

The archaeological archive presently relies almost exclusively on the textual and the visual that complement it (drawings and still photography). The vocal record is present only to the extent that it follows the video recordings. Vocalizing the archaeological record is necessary to develop fuller recording. At Çatalhöyük, archival audio recording is achieved by using suitable tape-recorders that are easy to operate in the field, but in the future computerized audio recording methods will be applied.

The final goal will be to minimize the writing of the textual documents, such as unit sheets, during the excavation but rather to audio-record them. This will be achieved by using computer software, which is fast developing, that provides a computerized 'reader' for audio documents and turns sound into text (such as Dragon Naturally Speaking). The audio entry of the unit sheets will most likely be organized on a key-word principle. In other words, our vision of the twenty-first-century archaeologist is a person with a trowel in a back pocket, cordless earphones and a microphone on the head and a computer station with video next to the excavation trench.

Discussion

There is no reason why archaeological archival documentation should not be fuller than it is at present. It can be made fuller if the multimedia tools at our disposal are integrated more thoroughly into archaeological excavation and the construction of the archival record. There are quite a few challenges to be met in this endeavour.

The first set of challenges is related to the application of the multimedia archival record. For instance, how to achieve the best results without wasting expensive materials, such as our time, film and audio tapes? How are we not to be left with recorded tapes of material that is never used?

It is relatively easy to apply multimedia tools and make digital, video and audio recordings during the excavation, but more difficult to devise ways in which the record can be used afterwards. According to the project director Ian Hodder, this is why the Cambridge-based team has gone down a more selective route, with less recording and more editing, and retention of only edited clips in the data base. The Cambridge-based team believes that recording will remain selective, and that accessibility to large amount of unedited stored audio and video material will remain limited, at least with existing technologies.

The most important task from the beginning of BACH recording has been to have it in a structured form which will allow the data to be used with ease. On the most general level the recorded input is divided between the formal presentation of the subject that is filmed and described, and the free flow of ideas and impressions that revolve around it and relate to it. The film and audio records as well as the photographic record are catalogued into segments by date. They are linked to the textual diary and site-plans to form the integrative archival diary. Integrating these data with the main data base and also using them for other forms of multimedia-generated reconstructions are the primary goals.

The second challenge is on a more conceptual level. The multimedia archival record allows for the recording and storing of information for both short-term use (to aid our own interpretations and the publication of data), and long-term use (for future reconsideration of the material culture, and the methods of excavation and explanation). The question arises that if one believes that the archaeological data are never 'raw', how are multimedia archival records going to be of value for future professionals with a different theoretical stance?

Video, digital and audio recording during excavation does not just add more of the same textual description of the material culture that is recorded in different media. It is as much part of a process for formulating an explanation as the textual description that gets recorded in a traditional diary. Each recording medium (text, digital and still photography, video and audio) forces an archaeologist to take a different angle from which to observe and discuss the subject, so that at the end of each day a problem has been viewed from a variety of angles and perspectives. Video and audio recording of discussions in the trench, which often happen spontaneously, are an invaluable source of ideas and information. Video recording of the material culture, accompanied by the excavator's voice, can be conducted in a more relaxed atmosphere than 'staged' filming recorded by the official film crew, and therefore contributes further to a more thorough record of the event and the situation. Multimedia recording as we seek to practise it facilitates better, and more complete, observation and consequently more complete explanation.

Acknowledgements

The 1998 season was funded by a senior research grant from the National Science Foundation (SBR-9805755).